Decoding Religion in the Bible
Learning to Recognize the Diversity of Biblical Texts

S. Daniel Breslauer
University of Kansas

2007
SLOAN PUBLISHING
Cornwall-on-Hudson, NY 12520

Library of Congress Control Number: 2006929848

Breslauer, S. Daniel
   Decoding Religion in the Bible: Learning to Recognize Diversity of Biblical Texts / S. Daniel Breslauer
     p.   cm.
   Includes bibliographic references and index.
   ISBN 1-59738-001-6

Cover designer: Amy Rosen
Cover image: Erich Lessing / Art Resource, NY Musée Condé, Chantily France

© 2007
Sloan Publishing, LLC
220 Maple Road
Cornwall-on-Hudson, NY 12520

All rights reserved. No part of this book may be reproduced, in any form or by any means, without permission in writing from the publisher.

Printed in Canada
10 9 8 7 6 5 4 3 2 1

ISBN 1-59738-001-6

Table of Contents

Preface — xi

1 Introduction to the Jewish Bible — 1
  Introduction   1
  Academic Studies of the Bible   3
  Religions in the Bible   5
  The Religions of the Bible in Ecclesiaticus   8
  Organizing the Jewish Canon   11
  Summary Questions   17

2 Religion in the Jewish Bible — 20
  Introduction   20
  The Development of the Jewish Canon: Views of the Divine and Ethics   22
  Ritual in the Canon   26
  Alternative Canons   28
  Summary Questions   30

3 Introduction to Christian Scriptures — 33
  Introduction   34
  History and the Two Tiered Christian Bible   35
  Three Parts to the New Testament: Three Views of Ethics   39
  New Testament as a Ritual Enactment   48
  Summary Questions   50

4 Religions of the Torah — 52
Introduction 52
The Composition of the Torah 53
Israel's History and Its Implications 59
Views of History, Ritual, the Supernatural, and Ethics 62
History and Ritual: The Stories of Abraham 64
Covenant and Ethics in the Pentateuch 65
Myth in the Bible and the Ancient Near East 70
Summary Questions 76

5 Religions and Israel's History — 79
Introduction 80
History in the Hebrew Bible 81
History, Ethics, and Ritual in Israel's Settlement in its Land 85
Historical Presentations of Israel's Period of Kingship 89
Historical Views of the Babylonian Exile and its Aftermath 97
Three Examples of Transformed Consciousness: David, Passover, Satan 101
Summary Questions 106

6 Religions of the Prophets — 109
Introduction 109
What Are the Prophets? 112
Concerns of the Deuteronomic Prophets 115
The Writing Prophets in the Deuteronomic Style 120
Religious Approaches in the Writing Prophets 123
Ethics, History, and Belief in Hosea and Haggai 124
Ritual in Prophetic Perspective 126
Summary Questions 129

7 Religions of the Writings — 132
Introduction 133
What Are the Writings? 134
History and Divinity in the Psalms and Wisdom Literature 143
Divinity and Ethics in the Wisdom Literature of the Writings 148
History and Ethics in the Narratives of the Writings 150
Ritual and Divinity in the Narratives of the Writings 155
Summary Questions 158

Table of Contents   vii

8 Religions of Hellenistic Writings   **160**
Introduction   160
Apocrypha and Pseudepigrapha   162
History and the Apocrypha   163
Hellenism and Religious Views in Ben Sirah   174
Hellenism and Religious Views in Maccabees   178
Hellenistic Philosophy, Philo of Alexandria, and the Wisdom of Solomon   183
Religious Perspectives in Additions to Jeremiah, Esther, Daniel   186
The Religious Perspectives of Tobit and Judith   187
Summary Questions   189

9 Introduction to the Gospels   **191**
Introduction   191
Sectarian Groups in Roman Judaism   193
Jesus in the Jewish Context   198
The Gospels of the New Testament Canon   203
Summary Questions   209

10 Religions of the Gospels   **211**
Introduction   211
Beliefs About History and the Opening Chapters of the Gospels   213
Beliefs about the Supernatural and the Endings of the Gospels   216
Miracle Stories and Ethics in the Gospels   218
Ethics and Ritual in the Gospel of Matthew and the Gospel of Luke   228
Ritual and Ethical Alternatives in Mark and John   232
Summary Questions   235

11 Religions Associated with the Apostle Paul   **237**
Introduction   238
Paul of Tarsus and the Growth of Christianity   240
The Paul of Acts and the Paul of the Letters   244
Paul's Religion: The Book of Acts   249
Pauline Religion: Genuine and Disputed Letters   252
Summary Questions   257

12 Religions of the Later Writings   **260**
Introduction   261
The Historical Context of the Later Letters   262
The Development of Views of the Devil   265

viii   Table of Contents

    Religion in the Pastoral Letters and Ephesians   270
    Religious Perspectives in the Johannine Letters   273
    Religious Perspectives in James 1, 2, Peter, and Jude   274
    Religious Perspectives in the Book of Hebrews   276
    Summary Questions   279

13 Apocalyptic Religions   282

    Introduction   283
    Understanding Apocalyptic Visions   285
    Apocalypticism in the Hebrew Bible and Later Jewish Writings   288
    Apocalypticism in Mark 13, Matthew 24, and Luke 21   291
    The Apocalypse of John Introduced   293
    Further Reflections on the Revelation of John   294
    Summary Questions   297

14 Review Summary   300

    Introduction   300
    Continuity in History   302
    Discontinuity in History   304
    Immanent Views of the Supernatural   305
    Transcendent Views of the Supernatural   307
    Types of Ethical Exclusivism   308
    Inclusive Types of Ethics   310
    Transformative Types of Ritual   310
    Types of Symbolic Ritual   311
    Exercises in Biblical Interpretation   313

Glossary   313

Index   337

Photo Credits   343

Preface

WHY I WROTE THIS BOOK

I have been fortunate in having, from the beginning of my teaching career over thirty years ago, taught courses that spanned not only the Hebrew Bible but also the Apocrypha and New Testament. My teaching has never been restricted to "Jewish Studies" narrowly defined, but to the entire range of "religious studies." Investigation of "the Bible" could only mean a study of the texts that certain communities consider "canon" and not of any "essential" texts of revelation. When presenting biblical studies to students, I have sought neither to reinforce any particular conception of the Bible and its "message" nor to reduce the book to a purely literary exercise and ignore its role in human religious activity.

Students often approach the Bible with expectations grounded in their own faith tradition or in the general culture of which they are a part. Teaching them to stand back and look at the texts they study as data from which to deduce how humanity in general expresses its religiousness tends to be an arduous task. Over the course of my career, I have concluded that one way to free students from their preconceptions is to provide them with a clearly arbitrary and artificial apparatus of analysis. They can then use this formal device as an intellectual exercise. It need not challenge their own beliefs or values. This liberation allows them room for a creative and imaginative play with the passages they read.

This book supplies readers with this apparatus in hopes that they will discover the same type of freedom I try to give my students. I supply my own analysis of texts not because I think they are definitive, but because I think they are challenging and can lead students to question whether any single interpretation of a text is entirely persuasive. My effort to bring texts under the rubric of religious studies is meant to encourage students to experiment with this type of thinking.

No single textbook provides the perfect means by which students can master the facts that scholars have debated regarding the history, text, and meaning of various biblical canons. Books offer several types of introductions to the Bible, ranging from detailed summaries of the contents of the Bible, to scholarly discussion about the formation and canonization of the Bible, to interpretations of the "religion" of the Bible, to political, social, and anthropological visions of it, or to some combination of these approaches. Some of the best introductory books offer so much material, so many pictures, maps, and supplementary materials, that they overwhelm students. This book seeks to supplement such an encyclopedic work by a simpler approach that seeks to stimulate thought even while reinforcing lessons students may have acquired from other sources.

This book explains basic concepts in religious studies and applies them to biblical examples. It covers material from the Hebrew Bible, the Apocrypha, and the New Testament, supplemented with references to works outside of these canonical texts. It emphasizes basic thinking, applying general categories to specific cases, and teaches elementary essay writing. The rationale for such a book is to provide a guide to students who may feel overwhelmed by the information given by a general introduction and who need guidance in structuring essay answers to questions.

Instructors using this book may want to use it as a stand-alone textbook. The glossary, maps, and boxed information will facilitate such usage. In this case, supplementary pictures, charts, and other types of learning aids from outside the book can be useful. They are readily available in other textbooks covering the Bible and biblical history, atlases of the Bible, companions to biblical studies, and collections of texts and artifacts from the Ancient Near East.

This book is unusual insofar as it seeks to show how both the Hebrew Bible and the New Testament fit the same general categories and that, as anthologies, both contain conflicting models of religiousness within them. The point is to help students see that there is no single "biblical religion," and no singular "religion of the Old Testament" that could be placed beside, or in contrast, to the "religion of the New Testament." Instead, students are introduced to four general categories—views of the divine, views of history, views of ritual, and views of ethics—each of which is subdivided into two types. This dichotomization is done for pedagogical purposes. All human activities are more complex than a simple two-fold division can suggest; nevertheless, for the sake of learning basic techniques of analysis, this introductory text looks at two types of religiousness in each of these categories. This textbook uses the Bible as a casebook for the study of these eight forms of religious expression.

The book begins with three introductory chapters focusing on the process and significance of canonization. Chapter One explains the approach used in this book and begins discussing the Jewish canon. Chapter Two continues that focus on the Jewish canon, and Chapter Three concentrates on various Christian canons. Each subsequent chapter looks at a different section of the biblical corpus to show how that section contains a variety of religious perspectives. While each chapter presents this evidence in a narrative form, students are also expected to exercise their own thinking and ingenuity. The chapters end with sample essay questions, one of which I work out for them.

Each chapter begins with a set of Learning Objectives that specifies the content in the chapter in relationship to the four types of religiousness used in the book. After a brief introduction sketching the outline of the chapter, each chapter lists important terms in boldface type. Students should refer to the glossary at the back of the book and the contex of the chapter itself to find explanations for these terms. Names of books of the Bible discussed in the chapter are not included in the glossary. Instructors may want to review these terms with students before they read the chapter.

Each chapter concludes by posing five summary questions that challenge students to review the facts and ideas of the chapter. A list of books for Further Reading is appended to each chapter except the last. These bibliographies do not seek to be comprehensive but rather suggestive. They include general introductions to the subject matter of the chapter, as well as other works that may stimulate further thought.

Chapter One includes a short introduction to the writing of essay answers. This introduction is *not* repeated in subsequent lessons, so students should be told to review it frequently. After that introduction, the chapter continues with four essay questions arising from discussions in the chapter and an exercise based on an answer to one of those questions. Subsequent chapters of the book include four such questions, followed by an exercise designed to sharpen students' skills in composing essays. Students may use the other three questions to write original essays of their own.

My influences on the method and content of this book have come from several sources. I have learned much from colleagues in several different universities. My students, both in classes on campus and through distance learning, have helped me discern the difficulties of studying the Bible in an academic setting and some of the ways those difficulties might be addressed. Celia Sinclair of the University of North Carolina at Charlotte and Kang Na of Westminster College served as reviewers and provided helpful comments and suggestions as the manuscript was being prepared.

My wife, Frances, and her mother, Esther Gurian, my children, and granddaughters were a source of strength and inspiration while working on this book. As I wrote, I kept in mind future generations who might find this book useful, as well as past generations from whom I have gained insight. My children and their spouses, Don Breslauer and Irene Royzman, Tamar Breslauer and Anindya Banerjee, certainly provided an impetus for my work. Of these, Tamar Breslauer became an unofficial editor whose sharp reading and insightful suggestions have improved this book immeasurably. My granddaughters, Rohini Yalta Banerjee, Moitreyi Nira Banerjee, and Sophie Royzman Breslauer, kept me mindful of future generations of readers.

Sophie Breslauer, born November 1, 2002, bears the same name as a great aunt of mine, Sophie Loeb Breslauer (1882–1963), whom I remember as the great matriarch of the Breslauer family. My granddaughter Sophie represents the challenge and promise of what lies ahead, as do my children and other granddaughters. My great aunt represents a heritage that includes the influence of my deceased parents, Daniel Joseph Breslauer and Lynette Myrle Breslauer, and my father-in-law, Louis Gurian. The two Sophies stand for the dialectic between generations past and future that a study of the Bible such as this one represents, and I dedicate the book in honor of the first named and in memory of the latter.

1

Introduction to the Jewish Bible

READING ASSIGNMENT

Psalm 137
Ecclesiasticus (Prologue) 51

LEARNING OBJECTIVES

By the end of this lesson, you will be able to:
- Describe the ways the modern academic study of the Bible analyzes biblical passages.
- Describe two ways of viewing history, two ways of understanding the supernatural, two ways of construing ethics, and two ways of using rituals.
- Apply these ways of understanding to the original teachings of Ben Sirah and to his grandson's revision of them.
- Apply the categories of history to the canonical order used in the Jewish Bible.

INTRODUCTION

This book introduces you to ways of reading the **Bible** from the perspective of the academic study of religion. This chapter begins with an introduction to the academic study of the Bible—an approach that differs from the religious study of the Bible with which you might be familiar. It continues by defining "religion" as used in this tbook and noting the variety of religious possibilities found in the Bible. Each chapter supplies you with an "Interpretive Matrix" to guide your analysis of "religion" in various biblical texts. The chapter introduces the

Interpretive Matrix for Chapter One

View of the Divine: How people interact with God and the supernatural; how God interacts with the world.	View of History: How past, present and future are related; who controls the shape of events.	View of Ethics: How people behave toward other people; how they behave toward people like themselves and to those who are different.	View of Ritual: How people behave toward the divine; how they perform religious actions.
The Divine as Transcendent: God does not interfere with human events.	*History as Continuous:* A traditional language is used.	*Inclusive Ethics:* Ideas and behavior are modified to fit the general society.	*Ritual as Transforming:* Ritual makes normal time sacred. Ritual needs to be practiced by an expert class.
The Divine as Immanent: God intervenes into history to influence human events.	*History as Discontinuous:* Translations and modifications of ancient texts are made. Dramatic changes mean that the present is very different from the past. Chronology shows sharp transitions from one age to another.	*Exclusive Ethics:* Religion can be practiced only in a certain land and by a certain ethinic group.	*Ritual as Symbolic:* Ritual can be practiced by anyone. Ritual teaches ideas.

Jewish canon, using the Wisdom of Ben Sirah as a guide, and defines each of the three parts of that canon. The chapter concludes by studying the historical perspective revealed in the organization of the Jewish canon.

Some Important Terms

The following terms are important in this chapter. They are also listed in the Glossary at the end of the textbook.

Adam	Ecclesiasticus (Ben Sirah)	Hebrews
Alexander the Great	Egypt	Hellenism
Apocrypha	Esther	High Priest
Babylonian Exile	Exodus from Egypt	Historical Criticism
Bible	Eve	Israel, Israelites
Canon	Ezra	Jamnia (Yavneh)
Chronicles	Former Prophets	Jerusalem
Diaspora	Habiru	Jerusalem Temple

Jews	Merneptah	Rabbi
Judah	Moses	Samaria
Judea	Necho	Septuagint
Judeans	Nehemiah	Song of Songs
Ketuvim	Neviim	Torah
Latter Prophets	Pentateuch	Wisdom Literature
Liturgy	Ptolemies	Writings
Maccabees	Prophets	

ACADEMIC STUDIES OF THE BIBLE

An introduction to any subject necessarily reduces the complexity of that subject. Introducing the **Bible** is even more difficult, since it plays such an important role in the history and present lives of so many people. The approach used in this book is that of **Historical Criticism** and has developed from the seventeenth century through today. It also uses other modern ways of looking at the Bible (see Box 1–1).

These approaches are different from that used within communities of faith. This textbook does not ask you to give up your beliefs, but rather to suspend them as you learn academic techniques. The academic approach does not tell you everything "true" about the Bible. Instead, it provides an exercise in using your skills at analysis and your imagination in thinking as applied to a particular text. This approach reads the Bible as a document written by human beings in particular historical settings. It seeks to determine the context in which particular biblical passages originated, the way in which those passages developed, changed, and were transmitted, and their relationship to the intellectual and religious conditions of their times.

This approach may be surprising because you may have learned to think of the Bible as a completed whole, as a single and undivided entity. Students often come to the Bible with preconceptions about what it "must" say. They "know" their Bible. The academic study of the Bible, however, looks at the Bible not as a repository of truth or as the statement of any particular religious group. From the academic standpoint, the Bible is an anthology of literary works (in fact, the word *Biblia* from which Bible derives is plural, implying a collection of little books) originally written for separate purposes and eventually put together over a long period of time by leaders of later groups.

That anthology exhibits many interesting features. It can be studied as literature, as examples of how people develop rituals, as examples of how people think about the divine, about how people create rules and regulations for themselves and society, about how people construct an identity for themselves. To help you begin this study, this book provides exercises in this type of thinking. The various chapters look at examples from the Bible to see how they show different ways of approaching what you read there. Remember that these are just exercises. Try to develop your own interpretations of the examples. There are more passages

> **BOX 1.1** PRIMARY ACADEMIC APPROACHES TO THE BIBLE
>
> ***Textual Criticism***   This study of the biblical text recognizes that the present biblical manuscripts may have been corrupted in transmission. It seeks to establish an "original" text through comparing ancient manuscripts, translations, and variant traditions. It often suggests *emendations*—corrections to the biblical text based on the assumption that the present textual data may be inaccurate.
>
> ***Historical Criticism***   Begun in the nineteenth century, Historical Criticism examines the biblical documents to determine when they were written, the background behind their composition, and the relation of their historical claims to evidence from such sources as archeology and independent historical records.
>
> ***Literary Criticism***   This approach, also begun in the nineteenth century, studies the Bible as a literary creation. Originally this meant dividing the text into its component parts and recognizing the variety of stylistic characteristics of different sections of the Bible. More recently it has included investigation of the literary purpose behind the repetitive patterns, character development, and plot lines of the Bible, as well as intertextual references, assumptions, and techniques.
>
> ***Form Criticism***   Developed in the early twentieth century, this approach to the Bible looks at both the oral and documentary sources of biblical passages. It determines the stylistic patterns used, the types of literary genre used, and the variety of purposes behind the different types of expression in the Bible.
>
> ***Redaction Criticism***   A more recent development, this approach focuses on the editor who compiled the biblical texts and the manner in which earlier material was put together to create the final shape of the Bible.

to read and discuss than the ones analyzed here. Use your imagination. Do not let the limitations of this method restrict the way you think and respond to texts from the Bible.

Never underestimate the value of review. Reading facts you already know in a different context helps you retain that information. This book, therefore, will sketch facts that you have probably already encountered either in a lecture or in other readings. This book uses those facts as a basis for understanding the Bible as an anthology of diverse religious expressions, using categories employed in the academic study of religion. The modern study of religious data takes several forms. These different approaches, however, share a single concern: decoding what believers affirm in humanistic terms. *Humanistic*, as used here, means the implications for human living. Whatever the origins of the biblical text or its status as a divine revelation, biblical texts do exercise an influence on how human beings live, act, and respond. This book investigates that influence.

Rather than taking the statements of faith at face value, the academic study of religion analyzes them as expressions of human beings in particular social, psychological, and historical situations. Using this book should help you understand the difference between examining the Bible from an academic perspective and reading it from the perspective of faith. The believer who reads the Bible as an act of faith considers it a guide to right belief, a textbook for ethics and morality, a unique statement of God's word, and a standard of truth. Academic scholars approach the Bible from a comparative perspective. They compare the significance of the Bible for its believers to the significance of other religious texts for their believers. They compare one type of religious life to another. They also compare one section of the Bible to another. Not every biblical passage calls for the same type of religious response from its readers. Academic scholars take those differences seriously without trying to develop a univocal "message" or uniform purpose to the entire Bible.

RELIGIONS IN THE BIBLE

This textbook uses the term "religion" to refer to ways of looking at reality and ways of acting in relationship to that reality (see Box 1–2). Religion in this case does not mean an organized and institutionalized system. Instead, it refers to different ways the Bible approaches *history*, the *divine*, *ethics*, and *ritual*. Scholars in religious studies analyze many different types of texts and have evolved complex theories about beliefs and actions. This introductory text simplifies this complexity.

Each of the italicized terms listed above has many meanings. *History*, in this textbook, means stories and ideas about events that have taken place in the past, are taking place now, or will take place in the future. While some writers may think of history as only about the past, this book looks at all events as history. The term *divine* means anything taken as supernatural. Words such as "God" or "gods" or "divinity" are used interchangeably to refer to this general idea. Students of religions argue at length over the differences between ethics, morality, and custom. This book accepts any behavioral standard as *ethics*. A view of ethics, accordingly, means any statement about how people should act. *Ritual* is also a term used in many ways. Brushing one's teeth could be a ritual, just as well as saying one's prayers. In this book, ritual refers to actions taken in relationship to some divine being. Whether that ritual is spoken as prayer or acted out, the crucial point is that it is oriented toward the divine.

For sake of this study, you will act as if there are only two types of beliefs about history, two types of beliefs about the supernatural, two types of ethics, and two types of rituals. They are discussed later in this chapter. Note that this set of eight dichotomies vastly reduces the variety of distinctions made by scholars in religious studies. This oversimplification will, however, help you achieve the major task of this study: gaining practice in the methods of study used in the academic discipline of religious studies.

The Bible, understood as a collection of "little books," is an anthology and contains a diversity of material. For the sake of simplicity, in this introductory study, you can divide the

6 Chapter 1

BOX 1–2   WHAT IS BIBLICAL RELIGION?

As used in this textbook the term "religion" refers to ways in which the Bible looks at aspects of the world or ways it instructs people to behave. The following definitions can guide you as you read through the chapter.

Definition

Approaches to the meaning of human life, the cosmos, and divinity as expressed in a set of texts canonized by Jews and/or Christians.

Expressions of Religion

View of History:

> History is understood as a set of events interconnected and continuous to each other
> *or*
> disconnected and discontinuous with each other

View of Divinity:

> Divinity is understood as a power greater than humanity transcendent to and beyond the reach of human beings
> *or*
> immanent in and concerned with human activities

View of Ethics:

> Ethics consist of actions directed toward behavior intended to include members of outside groups
> *or*
> intended to exclude members of outside groups

View of Rituals:

> Rituals consist of actions directed to the divinity seeking substantive change or alteration in aspects of reality
> *or*
> celebrating and drawing attention to aspects of reality in the past or present

---

material into four types: *views of history, views of the divine, ethics,* and *ritual laws*. Each of these four types can be subdivided again. The first two types of material are narrative and evocative; they describe events or things, and they arouse a response to that which they describe. The second two types are prescriptive; they demand actions and establish rules. In this book the word *ethics* refers to actions that people perform toward one another; the word *ritual* refers to actions that they perform toward the deity.

History, in this book, refers to interpretations of events. History is not just a retelling of the past. It explains the relation of the past to the future. Descriptions of history convey a group's self-understanding. By reviewing their past, people evoke a sense of identity. This identity can take one of two forms. In one form, a group affirms a particular past, claiming continuity with groups that preceded it. In the other form, a group retells its history to show its discontinuity with the past. In this case, the group claims to represent a new departure, an interruption that breaks the chain of transmission from the past in order to introduce an innovation.

Descriptions of supernatural beings also reflect a group's view of reality. Sometimes the supernatural appears to ensure continuity and order. Divine beings act so that humanity can live in a predictable world. Predictability depends on the divine remaining aloof from the world. God intervenes only to keep the system working. At other times, however, divine beings are presented as unpredictable, as a source of disruptive power that thwarts human expectations. This latter description of divinity expresses human frustrations, and the inability of humanity to understand its world. In this case, God is understood as intimately involved in all events. God intervenes and thus manipulates the forces of history. This textbook calls the first view that of *transcendence* and the second that of *immanence*.

Ethical prescriptions derive from a particular cultural setting and reflect that setting. In this book, you will focus on that aspect of ethics. One type of ethics reinforces the particular culture of an ethnic group, stressing the difference between that group and all other groups. This ethics of *exclusivism* prescribes actions that affirm the distinctive identity of members of the group. Another type of ethics emphasizes assimilation, *inclusiveness*, and the acceptance of the morality and customs of other groups.

Ritual involves many types of action—personal and private, public and official. This book focuses on two alternative views of ritual. According to one view, ritual celebrates the way things are; it makes people conscious of the world in which they live and the experiences that they undergo. Another view, however, emphasizes that ritual effects substantial changes in the world, and that how ritual is carried out makes the world different. The first view can be called *symbolic*; it symbolizes some aspect of reality. The second view can be called *transformative*; it changes the individuals participating in it, the world around them, or objects within the ritual. A transformative ritual succeeds when the changes it instigates actually occur.

With these categories in mind, we can turn to our first subject for investigation, the Hebrew Bible. As we look at its organization, development, and content, we will analyze the religious perspectives it expresses. The Apocryphal book of Ben Sirah includes one of the earliest references to the three-fold division of the Jewish Bible. As such, it provides a good example of how an organization of the Bible expresses religious ideas. Ecclesiasticus is even more useful since it is really *two* books—an original, written in Hebrew, that reflects

Jewish life in the land of Israel, and a translation of that original into Greek, with a new introduction by the grandson of the original author. The religious ideas expressed by the grandfather and the grandson differ.

THE RELIGIONS OF THE BIBLE IN ECCLESIASTICUS

The book **Ecclesiasticus**, or The Wisdom of Ben Sirah, is part of what has been called the **Apocrypha**. These are works found in the **Septuagint**, the Greek translation of the Bible, and accepted as part of the authoritative Old Testament by Roman Catholics. They are, however, not included in the Jewish Bible and are relegated to a separate section of the Protestant Bible. Ecclesiasticus, then, unlike the book of Ecclesiastes found in the Jewish Scriptures, is accepted by some traditions as part of the Bible but not by others. Understanding this unusual work means placing it in its historical context. A religious work becomes an authoritative standard of beliefs and actions, a **canon,** only through a historical process. The Bible, as used by religious communities today, developed over centuries and took shape only slowly. Ecclesiasticus presents a rather late version of the Jewish canon, one that became the standard one. That version developed gradually, and usually a crisis stimulated a new effort at canonization (see Timeline 1–1). What was the crisis behind the canon of Ben Sirah?

The book was apparently written in Hebrew by a Jewish sage around the year 180 B.C.E., but is now found primarily in a Greek translation made by his grandson around the year 132 B.C.E.. The book itself tends to emphasize a priestly view of Jewish religion. Priests inform Jews of the "law" and have the primary responsibility for administering it. Ben Sirah claims that wisdom comes when a person listens to inspired teachers, and particularly to inspired priests. Ben Sirah's grandson, however, not only translated the book into Greek, but also added a prologue to the book. In that prologue, he claimed that his grandfather's wisdom came from studying the holy books of the Jewish people—books he enumerated as "**Torah, Prophets**, and Other **Writings**" (Ecclesiasticus, prologue). Between 180 B.C.E. and 132 B.C.E. something dramatic had taken place. A set of books had replaced the priestly authority as the basis for Jewish wisdom and learning. Is this change a dramatic alteration of biblical religion? Is it continuous with that religion? Ben Sirah seemed to respond to the changes that occurred after **Alexander the Great** (356–323 B.C.E.) conquered the ancient world, and his generals, carrying on his work, transmitted Greek culture to the native peoples. One place influenced by this new culture was the territory of **Judea**. Judea was the southern part of a land that claimed to have once been a united kingdom, the kingdom of **Israel**. By the time of Alexander, the northern part had become independent and called itself **Samaria**. The southern part claimed to continue the "true" traditions of the **Israelites**, and its inhabitants, at first called **Judeans**, came in the period after Alexander to be known as Jews.

The capital city of Judea was Jerusalem, a place in which a priestly hierarchy ruled and in which the Jerusalem Temple provided a focus for religious life. The central authority was held by the High Priest, a position implied but not directly described in the first five books of

Introduction to the Jewish Bible 9

TIMELINE 1-1 HISTORY OF CANONIZATION OF THE JEWISH BIBLE

Canonization often occurs during a time of crisis. This list notes the date of the canonization, the part of the Bible canonized, and the crisis associated with it.

621 B.C.E.	Josiah's Reformation; the book of Deuteronomy; with the two empires of Egypt and Assyria weakened, Josiah saw an opportunity for Judean expansion.
587 B.C.E.	Collection of traditions about early histories and laws of the Israelites and Judeans; composition of documents writing down these traditions; exile of Judeans from the land of Israel to Babylonia.
450–400 B.C..E.	Creation of the "Torah of Moses"; established by Ezra; Jews return to Israel after exile to Babylonia in 587
450–323 B.C.E.	Composition of histories, prophetic collections, wisdom collections; the development of Jewish communities both in Israel and in the Diaspora.
323–160 B.C.E.	Composition of Esther, Ruth, Job, Ecclesiastes, Song of Songs, Daniel; Hellenization and the growth of Greek culture among Jews.
250–180 B.C.E.	Septuagint translation of the Bible into Greek; the rise of Alexandrian Jewry as a major center of Jewish culture and learning.

---

the Bible. This position represents a view of the divine as transcendent. Those who seek God must use the priests as intermediaries for communication. God is not accessible to everyone. Only the specially chosen leader, the person anointed with oil to serve as priest—the Hebrew word for this is "mashiah," transliterated as "Messiah"—can enter God's presence. Access to the supernatural takes place only when priests perform their functions.

This ritual importance of the priest—the priest can transform normal time into sacred time, can move from everyday space into holy space—was later augmented with political importance. After the time of Alexander the Great, this position became increasingly important in the political life of the Jerusalem community. Some priests in Jerusalem embraced this new influence, **Hellenism** as it came to be called, while others rejected it. Ben Sirah tried to find a way of responding to this new challenge of Hellenistic cultural influence by reiterating the traditional wisdom of the Jewish people. He opposed Greek thought with the aphorisms and history passed down from the Jewish past, which represents a continuity with what has come before. The learning of previous generations has an application in the present. His grandson, perhaps stimulated by the changes created by the flourishing Alexandrian Jewish community and the Maccabean revolution in the land of Israel, introduced discontinuity. By translating a Hebrew work into Greek, he accepted the very Hellenization that his grandfather had rejected. He portrayed his grandfather in terms of an interpretive tradition very different from the priestly approach that Ben Sirah himself considered fundamental.

Such a rendition of the past represents a break from continuity and the view that history requires innovation and change.

The three-fold division in the prologue to Ben Sirah echoes the three-fold division of the Hebrew Bible discussed later in this chapter. Here we should note that this division not only says something about the view of history held, but also the view of divinity. Making books rather than people the central authority of a tradition involves a major religious change. God, in this view, does not change; the divine concerns for humanity remain so constant that they can be enshrined in an unalterable text. This means God is accessible to everyone. A person does not need special authorization to know God's will. The divine commandment is open to all who wish to read it. An emphasis on the need for priests—particularly a High Priest—contrasts with that view. A priestly perspective claims that God's desires are changing and must be communicated through the immediacy of people who have direct access to them.

Many dramatic historical events intervened between Ben Sirah's Hebrew text and his grandson's Greek translation. Canonization often occurs at periods of crisis in a community's history. These situations cause a community to debate who actually belongs to them and who should be excluded. One major consideration for Jews at the time of both Ben Sirah and his grandson was the existence of Jewish communities outside the land of Israel. Those communities were considered in "exile," or **Diaspora**—the dispersion of Judeans from their homeland to various other countries. How could Jews live in exile, in a Diaspora? Psalm 137 expresses distress at living outside of the holy land and the impossibility of worship on foreign soil: "How can we sing the Lord's song in a foreign land?" (Psalm 137: 4). While members of the Diaspora community considered themselves fully Jewish, often the concessions they made to the general culture rendered them suspect to other Jews. Other biblical works as well as Ben Sirah debate this issue. The biblical book of Esther seems to approve of such concessions; the book of Daniel seems to disapprove of them. In the prologue to his Greek translation, Ben Sirah's grandson states "those who read the scriptures must not only themselves understand them, but must also as lovers of learning be able through the spoken and written word to help the outsiders" (Ben Sirah, Prologue).

Ethical reflections on how canonization forms communal identity suggest the importance of the selection and authorization of books for religious life. This act of canonization has profound influence on a community. The term *canon*, meaning "standard" or "measuring rod," is used to describe such a set of books. They provide a set of authoritative texts by which a community governs itself. Through using a certain book, a community comes to accept it as instruction or as a guide for living. Nevertheless, establishing a set number of selected works and rejecting others does represent an official act, often perceived as a dramatic change in communal self-understanding. When a community sees its integrity threatened, either by an internal or external force, it reinforces its sense of identity by setting up a canon as a test of loyalty. Only those who affirm the canon are considered part of the community. In addition to the history of the canon, then, the effect of the canon on ethics is important.

Finally, Ben Sirah's original writing accentuates the rituals performed by the priests, and in particular the High Priest in Jerusalem. His grandson lived in Hellenistic **Egypt**. Egypt plays an important role throughout the Bible. It served as the cradle of Israelite nationhood; the slaves who escaped from there were said to have been the basis for the later Israelite nations. Pharaohs of Egypt from **Merneptah** (1224–1211 B.C.E.) to **Necho** (610–594 B.C.E.) influenced the political life of Israel. In Hellenistic times, the **Ptolemies**, a ruling class descended from Ptolemy I, a general in the army of Alexander the Great, made Egypt into a center of Greek culture. The Jews living there, of which Ben Sirah's grandson was one, created very different rituals and understood their meaning differently from the Jerusalem community.

Two very different views of ritual dominate the end of Ben Sirah. Ben Sirah 51:1–12 claims that God intervenes to change reality. Vv. 13–30 (excluding some material that the original Hebrew preserves but that the Greek omits) emphasizes how learning and wisdom provide the true rewards. Living by wisdom, "I shall never be disappointed" (51:18). Laboring only in study, one finds serenity (51:25). A ritual incantation of wisdom does not change reality, but it does remind people of the basis of that reality. Ritual *teaches* rather than transforms.

ORGANIZING THE JEWISH CANON

Ben Sirah's grandson's division of Jewish scriptures into Torah, Prophets (Hebrew **Neviim**), and other Writings (Hebrew **Ketuvim**) represents one strand of canonization in early Judaism. The Greek translation of the Hebrew Bible chose a different approach. The tri-partite division became the official organization of the Jewish Bible when, after the destruction of the Jerusalem Temple (70 C.E.), a group of Jewish leaders bearing the title **Rabbi**, decided on the authoritative books for the Jewish people (see Box 1–3 for the canonized texts of the Jewish Bible). Tradition claims that this occurred in the city of **Jamnia** (known in Hebrew as Yavneh), although modern scholars think that the process took a longer period and probably did not reach completion until much later. The exact dating of this canonization is unclear, but the ideology involved is more evident.

The canon of the Jewish Bible tells the story of "Torah"—that is God's revealed word—in its origins, its application to history, and its general implications. That story embodies a single pattern in human events—exile and return—that is used to begin and end the canonical text. Look at a list of the Jewish canon (found in Box 1–3 and often in annotated editions of the Bible). The first part, called the Torah, consists of five books attributed to the leader **Moses** (thus these books are called the "Mosaic Torah" or the Torah of Moses), a hero said to have lead the Israelites from Egypt to the edge of their promised land, Israel. It supplies the basic ideas, stories, and laws of Jewish life. The term **Pentateuch** (meaning "five books") is often used to describe this part of the Bible. While the Jewish and Christian canons differ in their organization, both begin with the Pentateuch. The second part, called the Prophets, emphasizes how the elements in the Torah are lived out in history. The final section, the Writings, provides material for general education, for liturgical and ritual use, and for

> **BOX 1–3   THE JEWISH CANON**
>
> The list that follows shows the Jewish canon. It should be compared to the organization of the Christian Old Testament described in the next chapter.
>
> **The Pentateuch (Torah)**
>   Genesis (Bereshit)
>   Exodus (Shemot)
>   Leviticus (Vayikra)
>   Numbers (Bamidbar)
>   Deuteronomy (Devarim)
>
> **The Prophets (Neviim)**
>   **Former Prophets:**
>   Joshua (Jehoshua)
>   Judges (Shoftim)
>   1 and 2 Samuel (Shmuel)
>   1 and 2 Kings (Melakhim)
>   **Latter Prophets:**
>   Isaiah (Yeshiyahu)
>   Jeremiah (Yermiyahu)
>   Ezekiel (Yekhezkil)
>   Hosea (Hoshea)
>   Joel (Yoel)
>   Amos (Ahmos)
>   Obediah (Ovadya)
>   Jonah (Yonah)
>   Micah (Meecah)
>   Nahum (Nahum)
>   Habakkuk (Habakkuk)
>   Zephaniah(Tzefanya)
>   Haggai (Haggai)
>   Zechariah (Zekharya)
>   Malachi (Malachi)
>
> **The Writings (Ketuvim):**
>   Psalms (Tehillim)
>   Proverbs (Mishlei)
>   Job (Iyov)
>   Song of Songs (Shir HaShirim)
>   Ruth (Rut)
>   Lamentations (Eichah)
>   Ecclesiastes (Qohelet)
>   Esther (Ester)
>   Daniel (Daniyyel)
>   Ezra (Ezra)
>   Nehemiah (Nekhemya)
>   1 and 2 Chronicles (Divrei HaYammim)

meditation. The Mosaic Torah sets the stage for everything that follows; the prophetic books show how the ideals of the Mosaic Torah take shape in reality; the Writings reflect on the basic teachings in terms of philosophical and universal principles.

This organization, then, is cumulative: it goes from the foundation, to its application, to specific spiritual exercises useful in any time or place. From this perspective, *prophecy* refers to interpretations of history. The Jewish Bible considers as prophetic writing the entire history of the Jewish people, as told in the books from Joshua through II Kings. See Timeline

1–2, and notice that the Former Prophets exclude any mention of life during the Jewish exile to Babylonia and its aftermath, as well as Ruth, **Chronicles**, **Ezra**, **Nehemiah**, and **Esther**, considered as history in the Christian Bible, and Esdras, Tobit, and **Maccabees**, from the Greek additions accepted by the Roman Catholics. These books precede a section composed of books of individually named prophets, some of which do include experiences during the **Babylonian Exile**, but it excludes Daniel, which Christian Bibles include as part of the Prophets, and Lamentations, which Christian Bibles attached to Jeremiah. The first set is called the **Former Prophets** and the next the **Latter Prophets**. Those designations refer to the position of these books in the canon. Parts of the Former Prophets narrate history that occurs after the history of parts of the Latter Prophets. The combining of these two compilations as a set of former and latter prophets suggests the irrelevance of chronology for the program intended by the editors of this canon.

The Jewish canon includes these particular texts as prophecy because it understands the prophetic task in a peculiar way. The term *Neviim* does not mean people who predict the future; it means people who speak out about history. Hebrew words for prophet—*roeh* (seer); *hoseh* (vi-

---

TIMELINE 1–2 HISTORICAL EVENTS RELATED TO THE JEWISH BIBLE

These events provide a backdrop against which to understand the process by which the Jewish Bible developed.

2000–1750 B.C.E.	Age of Abraham, Isaac, Jacob
1750—1250 B.C.E.	Age of Moses and Settlement in the Land
1000 B.C.E.	Founding of Davidic Dynasty, United Kingdom of Israel
950 B.C.E.	Construction of King Solomon's Temple in Jerusalem
922 B.C.E.	Division into Kingdoms of Israel and Judah
721 B.C.E.	Assyria Conquers Israel, besieges Judah
587 B.C.E.	Nebuchadnezzar conquers Judah and deports Jews to Babylonia; destroys Temple
538 B.C.E.	Cyrus the Great, conqueror of Babylonia, allows Jews to return to Israel
530–515 B.C.E.	Rebuilding the Jerusalem Temple
425–400 B.C.E.	Ezra and Nehemiah
331 B.C.E.	Alexander the Great conquers the Near East
323 B.C.E.	Babylonia claimed for Seleucid Empire
301 B.C.E.	Land of Israel under Ptolemaic rule
300 B.C.E.	Hellenization of Jews in Alexandria begins
201 B.C.E.	Syrian Seleucids establish rule over Land of Israel
168–165 B.C.E	Maccabean Revolution in Land of Israel
63 B.C.E.	The Romans take over Judea
66 C.E.–73 C.E.	Judea's war against Rome; destruction of Jerusalem Temple

sionary); and *navi* (mouthpiece)—indicate heightened insight, being able to perceive the meaning and significance of history. Prophetic works claim to disclose the relevance of historical events for religious life. From the perspective of the Hebrew Bible, stories about the early heroes of Israel, no less than the writings of individual prophets, are expositions of Torah (this word is prominent in the book of Joshua, the first book of the Prophets).

The third section of the Hebrew Bible begins with a collection of liturgical poems—songs recited during public and private prayer—the Psalms. The first Psalm contrasts the wicked person with the righteous, concluding that the latter studies Torah day and night. Poetry makes up a major portion of this section of the Bible, often taking as its theme human knowledge and understanding. Such works are called **Wisdom Literature** because they investigate both divine wisdom and the ability of human beings to gain wisdom for themselves; books such as Psalms, Proverbs, Ecclesiastes, and Job represent this type of writing. Some poetry included seems odd in a religious setting. One book in particular seems out of place—the **Song of Songs** (although this biblical book is also known as "Song of Solomon," this textbook refers to it by its Hebrew name). This poetic work celebrates erotic love without indicating any official religious aspects to it. The Writings also include prose material, narrative tales that either expound the value of wisdom (such as Daniel), teach general pietistic lessons (such as Ruth), or rewrite earlier history (such as 1 and 2 Chronicles). These narrative works also include liturgical material; prayers recited by both Jews and non-Jews make up much of the book of Daniel. Jewish **liturgy** draws many elements from the prayers cited in 1 Chronicles through Nehemiah. Although the historical narratives of the exilic period found in Esther, in Ezra, and in Nehemiah augment the history presented in the second part of the Jewish Bible, their inclusion in the Writings suggests that their purpose is more than merely the recounting of past events.

What do these works have in common? Why are they placed together? One answer, to be discussed below, is that they are liturgical; they include prayers and rituals performed by the Jewish community. Another commonality is the inclusiveness they express. The lessons taught in the wisdom literature are applicable to all people in all times and places. They are not restricted to Jews or to any historical period. The erotic poetry in Song of Songs expresses universal themes. The heroes in the stories tend to interact with important non-Jewish leaders; they appear in the courts of Babylonian and Persian rulers. The point seems to be that Torah should not be restricted to Jews or to Jewish history. Torah has a wider, more universal application and appeal than either the first five books or the prophetic writings suggest.

CONTINUITY OF HISTORY AND THE JEWISH CANON

Everything about this organization emphasizes continuity rather than discontinuity. The theme of Torah as the single unifying principle of history emerges in the first five books—books that collectively are called the Torah—and then is reiterated in the first chapter of the Prophets and the first chapter of the Writings. The pattern of exile and return is described in the opening chapters of the Pentateuch, telling of the first human beings (**Adam** and **Eve**), settled in the Garden of Eden, expelled from the garden, and then seeking reconciliation with God. That pattern recurs in the story of the Jewish people, who are given a covenant with God, disobey God, are sent into exile, and then are allowed to return from that exile.

The tale of the Jewish people told in the Torah focuses on one particular event, the **Exodus from Egypt**. Most of the Pentateuch retells that narrative (Exodus, Leviticus, Numbers, and Deuteronomy). According to the text, the Jewish people are enslaved in Egypt. Under the leadership of a man named Moses, they escape from that slavery. Moses brings them to God's mountain to receive divine revelation. Rather than follow the laws of that revelation, however, the people continually rebel against it. Moses predicts dire consequences of this action—one of which is exile (Deuteronomy 28–31). Exile seems to be the final word in the Torah, just as it seems to be the human condition visited upon Adam and Eve.

The second section of the Bible, the Prophets, offers a more hopeful vision. Exile will be followed by a return—a second Exodus, a second kingdom, a perfected social and political life. The prophetic section of the Hebrew Bible opens with the story of the rise and fall of the Israelite kingdoms and their eventual exile (Joshua–2 Kings). It continues with prophetic books like Isaiah 1–39, Jeremiah, and Amos, which predict exile and disaster. It ends, however, with promises for restoration and renewal (Isaiah 40–66, Zechariah, Haggai, Malachi). The books of Ezra and Nehemiah tell about that period of return and renewal and paint a realistic picture unlike that imagined by the prophets. To make the pattern of exile and promise of return more explicit, the Jewish Bible reverses the historical order and places 1 and 2 Chronicles as its final two books; 2 Chronicles ends with a proclamation allowing Jews to return to their homeland, Israel. The Writings, then, like the Prophets, ends with the reality of exile and the hope of a return from the exile. This reversal emphasizes the pattern that was established in the Eden story. After all, the story does *not* tell of Adam and Eve *returning* to Eden, only a promised reconciliation with God).

The canon as finalized presents a view of history as continuous, as the manifestation of a single theme—Torah—and exemplifying a single pattern of exile and return. The need to reverse the historical order of the final four books of the canon, however, suggests a tension between the organization of the Jewish canon and the content in that canon. The organization of the canon assumes that the story told is the story of a single people—the Jewish people. The content, however, makes it clear that the peoples involved were **Hebrews**, Israelites, Judeans, and **Jews**—not always identical with one another (see Timeline 1–3).

The term *Hebrews* refers to a social status comparable to that of an ethnically diverse class of "outsiders" known generally as Apiru, or **Habiru**. The Israelites were citizens of a nation-state that lasted from about 1000–721 B.C.E. and was often in conflict with its more southern constituent, centered around Jerusalem. This southern group eventually became an independent kingdom, **Judah**, whose inhabitants were called Judeans. That kingdom lasted from about 922 B.C.E. to about 587 B.C.E. Some portion of these Judeans were taken into ex-

> **TIMELINE 1–3   NAMES FOR THE "JEWISH" PEOPLE**
>
> **Before the Common Era**
> 1735   Amarna Letters mention Hapiru
> 1222   Mernephta Stele mentions destroying Israel
> 860   Moabite Stone mentions throwing off Israel's domination
> 721   Sargon II boasts of conquering Israel
> 701   Sennacherib boasts of besieging Judah
> 612–581   Judah mentioned in Assyrian Chronicles
> 525–400   Judeans mentioned in Elephantine Letters
> 455–400   Judean names in Murashu Tablets
> 400–165   "Jew" (*yehudi*) used as a religious designation in the biblical book of Esther
> 285   Egyptian papyri refer to *Ioudaioi* (Jews)
>
> **Common Era**
> 100   Jewish and Christian texts identify "Jew," "Hebrew," and "Israel"
> 1948   The modern State of Israel creates the term Israelia

ile in Babylonia, from which a few returned in 538 B.C.E. That new group, together with those it saw as compatriots in places such as Persia, Egypt, and Rome, took on the name of Jews (*ioudious*). The editors of the Hebrew Bible collapsed these different groups into a single unit, but the history suggests that dramatic and transformative events shaped each of the three differently.

SUMMARY QUESTIONS

1. What is the meaning of the term *Bible*, and what are some ways scholars of religious studies look at that book?

2. How do Ben Sirah and his grandson differ in their response to the challenge of Hellenism created by Alexander the Great and his successors?

3. What are the three parts of the Jewish canon, and how do they emphasize continuity of history?

4. What is the meaning of the term *Diaspora*, and what are some different ways of looking at the importance of it?

5. How does Ben Sirah's view of the priesthood illustrate a transforming view of ritual rather than a view of ritual as symbolic?

ESSAY EXERCISE

These exercises are meant to develop your skills in writing a cohesive short essay. Every essay must have the following parts:

1. An introduction of one paragraph that sets out the relevant concepts and their definitions; nothing in the essay that follows it should be unrelated to the introduction.

2. At least two paragraphs developing the ideas in the introduction in relationship to the examples specified in the question.

3. A one-paragraph conclusion that draws together the ideas discussed in each of the previous two paragraphs.

Every paragraph must have at least three sentences: a topic sentence, followed by at least two sentences developing the ideas it has raised.

As you develop your essays try to do the following:

1. Start in the middle by thinking about the two examples that you will use. See the ways in which they contrast with each other. Try to isolate two primary ideas on which they differ.

2. Think about these two ideas and develop an introductory essay with a topic sentence stating the basic concept and at least two sentences for each of two ways in which that concept can be understood.

3. As you write the main body of the essay, always refer back to your introduction. Ask yourself which part of the introduction each sentence of the main body illustrates.

4. As you write your conclusion, be sure that you show how the specific examples you have used illustrate the introductory ideas you have set up.

5. Unacknowledged use of any source material is *plagiarism* and should be avoided. In these essay exercises, however, you may use the *facts* provided in this text (dates, names, events) without needing to cite your source.

6. When illustrating your essays with examples from the Bible be sure to put the source in parentheses; for example (see Ecclesiasticus 51:16–22). Do not expect your reader to know the source of our example.

7. Use exact quotations only when a paraphrase is inadequate. For example, you want to claim that Ben Sirah's grandson was more conscious of the needs of the Diaspora than his grandfather (Ben Sirah, Prologue). You might cite the prologue to Ecclesiasticus that urges "lovers of learning" to "be able through the spoken and written word to help the outsiders." Your essay would then show how the terms "lovers of learning" (philosophers) and "outsiders" show a concern for Diaspora communities.

FOUR SUGGESTED ESSAY QUESTIONS FOR CHAPTER ONE

1. Explain two ways in which a tradition may view history. Apply one of them to Psalm 137:4 and the other to the theme of exile as found in the Jewish canon.

2. Explain two ways in which a tradition may view the supernatural. Apply one of them to Ben Sirah's enshrining God's will in a set of books and the other to Ben Sirah's emphasis on the High Priest in Jerusalem.

3. Explain two ways in which a tradition may view ethics. Apply one of them to Ben Sirah's use of Hebrew to communicate Jewish Wisdom and the other to his grandson's decision to translate that wisdom into Greek.

4. Explain two ways in which a tradition may view ritual. Apply one of them to the idea of reciting wisdom as a ritual that teaches success and the other to the reliance on the rituals of the High Priest expressed by Ben Sirah.

Exercise

Read the following introduction for an essay answering the first question:

> Religious views of history sometimes claim that past events require a change in human living and sometimes claim that events in the past, present, and future merely exhibit an eternal pattern that never changes. When religions view historical changes as dramatic alterations of reality, they often expect people to alter their behavior. That alteration often takes the form of reminders of how different the present is from the remembered past. When religions imagine certain eternal patterns in history, they often overlook changes that, in fact, have occurred. They may alter the retelling of past events to make the enduring patterns they see even more evident. Such a view means that no changes in human action are required or even possible.

Now answer the following five questions:

1. Which sentences develop the first idea in the topic sentence?

2. Which sentences develop the second idea in the topic sentence?

3. Which sentences seem to fit the view expressed in Psalm 137:4?

4. Which sentences seem to fit the view of history expressed by the organization of the Jewish Bible?

5. Would you want to use an exact quotation from Psalm 137:4 to illustrate one idea of history developed in this introductory paragraph, or would a paraphrase be sufficient? Why or why not?

FOR FURTHER READING

The books listed below should be a point of departure for your future study. Each includes a bibliography that will guide you beyond its basic information. The books listed for this chapter focus on ways of studying the Jewish Bible.

1. Knight, Douglas A. and Gene M. Tucker, *The Hebrew Bible and Its Modern Interpreters* (Philadelphia, PA and Chico, CA: Scholars Press, 1985).

2. Preminger, Alex and Edward L. Greenstein, eds. and compilers, *The Hebrew Bible in Literary Criticism* (New York: Ungar, 1986).

3. Soggin, J. Albert, *Introduction to the Old Testament From Its Origins to the Closing of the Alexandrian Canon* (Valley Forge, PA: Trinity Press International, 1993).

4. Wenham, Gordon J., *Story As Torah: Reading the Old Testament Ethically* (Edinburgh: T&T Clark, 2000).

5. Scholz, Susanne, ed., *Biblical Studies Alternatively: An Introductory Reader* (Upper Saddle River, NJ: Prentice-Hall, 2003).

2

Religion in the Jewish Bible

READING ASSIGNMENT

Joshua 1; 24
2 Kings 22–23
Ezra 7
1 Maccabees 4:46–48
2 Maccabees 2:13–14

LEARNING OBJECTIVES

By the end of this lesson, you will be able to:
- Describe two ways of understanding history and apply them to the organization of the Jewish Bible.
- Describe two ways of viewing the supernatural and apply them to the process of canonization of the Hebrew Bible.
- Describe two ways of understanding ethics and apply them to the process by which the Jewish Bible developed.
- Describe two ways of construing ritual and apply them to the use of the Writings in the Jewish Bible.

INTRODUCTION

The previous chapter introduced you to the Jewish Bible and its history. In general the content of that Bible is the same as that found in the Christian Old Testament. The historical de-

Interpretive Matrix for Chapter Two

View of the Divine: How people interact with God and the supernatural; how God interacts with the world.	View of History: How past, present, and future are related; who controls the shape of events.	View of Ethics: How people behave toward other people; how they behave toward people like themselves and to those who are different.	View of Ritual: How people behave toward the Divine; how they perform religious actions.
The Divine as Transcendent: God does not change over time.	*History as Continuous:* The same patterns permeate all history so chronology does not really matter. God's revelation is relevant in all places at all times.	*Inclusive Ethics:* Several alternative ethical codes are equally acceptable. Anyone who adopts certain practices can join the religious group.	*Ritual as Transforming:* Ritual practice influences how God interacts with an individual or a nation.
The Divine as Immanent: God intervenes into history to influence human events. God intervenes in history to reveal new commandments.	*History as Discontinuous:* New discoveries lead to new types of religious actions. Dramatic changes mean that the present is very different from the past. God provides new revelations for new communities.	*Exclusive Ethics:* Religious identity depends on belonging to a specially chosen group.	*Ritual as Symbolic:* Ritual practices separate one group from another. Ritual reminds people of shared values. Rituals reflect seasonal changes.

velopment of the Jewish Bible offers an example not only of views of history, but also of differing approaches to the supernatural. That development also illuminates different ways of using a canon either to include a diverse group or to exclude some people from membership in a group. Each stage also manifests a distinctive approach to ritual. The chapter ends with a short description of alternative canons to that of the Jewish Bible.

SOME IMPORTANT TERMS

The following terms are important in this chapter. They are also listed in the Glossary at the end of the textbook.

Booths	Chronicles	Deuteronomy
Calendar	Day of Atonement	Dietary Laws
Canon	Dead Sea Scrolls	Josiah

Judges	Necho	Pentecost
Nebuchadnezzar	Passover	Samuel

THE DEVELOPMENT OF THE JEWISH CANON: VIEWS OF THE DIVINE AND ETHICS

The canon described in Chapter 1 does more than intimate a view of history. If a single theme, pattern, and history pervade the message, this suggests that God provides an unchanging plan and purpose. Understanding the pattern of exile and return, according to this view, enables an accurate prediction of historical events. God does not arbitrarily change the basic forces of life; they are embedded in the cosmos. This means that God does not take a hand in day-to-day history. God does not intervene to change events or reality. The divine stands transcendently over the whole of creation without needing to get involved in everyday events.

The perspective of the finalized canon suggests an ethics as well as a view of the divine. By incorporating the wisdom literature that appeals to all human beings, that canon reaches out beyond the ethnic community of Judaism. It offers lessons for *all* people and a wisdom accessible beyond the confines of any particular group. The Bible teaches truths that embrace all reality. Jewish religion, from this perspective, is not exclusively Jewish. The values and teachings of the Bible belong to the world at large. Jews may have had a foundational revelation and have experimented in history with putting that revelation into practice. The ultimate Jewish task, however, involves interaction with non-Jews and outreach to the general human community.

Although in its final incarnation the Jewish canon articulates a view of God as transcendent and unchanging and an inclusive ethics, such was not always the case. The Jewish canon took shape slowly over many hundreds of years. Examining that process of canonization shows how different groups stressed God's changing and dynamic nature, while others stressed God's unchanging ideals and commandments. Some stages of canonization emphasize how a book will bind diverse individuals together; other stages seek to exclude certain individuals or groups from the community. Studying these stages of canonization also helps discover the views of the divine and the views of ethics involved.

Although the figure of Moses is not introduced until the second of the first five books of the Bible (Exodus), the five together are usually referred to as the Torah of Moses, or the Five Books of Moses. This suggests that the Jewish people, from the time of Moses onwards, had a basic text, a central set of books that guided their life. Such a view reflects the editorial conviction that God has a single unchanging plan that continually illustrates the variety of concerns expressed in the Torah.

Readers of the first five books, then, might well expect all subsequent books to refer to a book called the Torah. The book of Joshua, the book that follows the Pentateuch, does indeed begin with a reference to "torah" (Joshua 1:8), but it quickly suggests that the word of their leader, rather than a book, will be their more authoritative guide (Joshua 1:16–18). The ending of the book of Joshua is also ambiguous. The review of history given there does not mention revelation or a covenant with Moses. Instead, Joshua makes a covenant and writes its particulars in "the book of the Torah of God" (Joshua 24:26). That description suggests that, instead of a Mosaic Torah (the Torah of Moses), the community developed a different Torah depending upon their current leader to guide them. Such a perspective implies that God's will changes depending on the historical situation. New situations require new responses. God makes new demands to suit new conditions. God, in this account, intervenes in the world and plays an immanent role in human affairs. Unlike the canonized Bible, the perspective in Joshua seems to be that God has not set an unchanging plan in motion and remains transcendent to history, but that the divine reacts to human behavior.

The situation gets even more curious. The books from **Judges** (the book that follows Joshua) through 2 Kings 23–24 make no mention of any Torah. After Joshua, it would seem, no one remembered Moses' Torah for several hundred years. The story in 2 Kings 22–23 is certainly intriguing. One of the last rulers of a kingdom called Judah (in the southern part of the land that was once said to have been ruled by King David and King Solomon), King *Josiah* in 621 B.C.E. began a transformation of the religious life of his country. As part of his reformation of Jewish religion, he instituted what most scholars think was the book of **Deuteronomy** as the center of faith. Josiah introduced this book during a time of political and social change. His reform originally entailed improving the conditions of the priestly Temple in Jerusalem. During that process of repair, however, the leading priest, the High Priest Hilkiah, reported: "I have found the Book of the Law in the house of the Lord" (2 Kings 22:8). The king's reaction was one of surprise. He seems to have doubted its authenticity and called upon the prophet Hulda to verify its authority. The contents needed to be read aloud since no one else seemed to know about it either. The book prescribed a new centralization of ritual and a new legitimization for leaders, and it advanced descriptively a new theory of Judean identity and history. From that time on, Judaism became a book religion. The idea of an authoritative canon seems to have been imposed on the word *torah* rather late in its development.

Josiah's reformation introduced a new view of the divinity. God's will does not change from situation to situation. God has created a single set of guidelines that all people should follow at all times and in all places. Josiah's Book of the Law or the Book of Moses supersedes what prophets or priests may claim to be divine revelation. Only revelations that add nothing new, that do not challenge the established norms of the book, can be accepted. God's transcendence leaves no room for direct communication with human beings.

By making prophecy and priestly inspiration a secondary authority, this reformation does more than state God's unchanging nature. It also demands that previously rival leadership groups work together. Not only the priest and prophet, of course, but also the king and the other secular leaders, the elders, must accept the will of the book. Josiah has introduced an inclusive ethics. While some biblical texts claim that only prophets speak with God's voice and others favor priestly power, Josiah's compromise incorporates *both* within a wider framework. This is an inclusive ethics that creates new coalitions among previously opposing groups.

Scholars debate the exact content of Josiah's canon, of the Book of the Law that he put into place. The next stage of canonical development is less controversial. The Bible tells how King Artaxerxes of Persia authorized Ezra, "a scribe skilled in the law of Moses," to introduce that law as the official legal code for the Jews who had left Babylonia to make a home in the land of Israel (Ezra 7). Ezra comes to this rebuilt community with "the law of Moses" in his hand and the king of Persia's army at his back to give weight to his authority. Most scholars agree that Ezra brought with him what we now call the Pentateuch. Thus, the first five books of the Hebrew Bible were finally set as a canon at about 400 B.C.E.

The crisis stimulating this canon was the exile of the Jewish people from their land into Babylonia. This Babylonian Exile engendered changes in biblical religiousness. During that exile, the leaders collected the traditions of the people, edited them, and shaped the canon of the Torah. When Ezra the scribe returned from Babylonia to oversee the rebuilding of the Jewish community, he instituted this canon as the constitution of the new settlement. This canon preserves a variety of laws and views of reality. Since the Jewish community under Ezra had little independent political power, the Torah does not legitimize any single political leadership class. Instead, it focuses on the rituals and practices that distinguish Jews from non-Jews and descriptively suggests a variety of world views.

Two distinctive traits characterize that work. First, it emphasizes the exclusive ethnic nature of Jewish identity. It tells the story of God's choice of Abraham and his family and their subsequent formation into a cohesive group called the Israelites. It stops before the formation of the nation of Israel because it focuses on familial and ethnic identity, rather than political or national identity. Second, the exact legal teachings of the Pentateuch are ambiguous. It includes not one but several different law codes; several different retellings of what appear to be the same event; conflicting reports of such important matters as the creation of the world, the development of human culture, and the affairs of early family leaders.

One way to understand the canonization of the Pentateuch is to see it against its environmental background (see Timeline 1–2). Ezra needed to affirm the unity of the Jewish people despite its being scattered in Persia, the land of Israel, and in other places such as Egypt. At the same time, Ezra needed to reassure the Persians that the Jews had no political aspirations for independence. The Torah solves these problems by offering an exclusive ethics of Jewish identity that depends on ethnic origins. Even marriage into the group is forbidden, and non-Jewish partners must be divorced. At the same time, the Torah allows for different traditions, laws, and practices by including them all within a single text. What binds Jews together is not political aspiration, which would alarm the Persians, or a single legal or folk tradition, which might exclude Jews living in different places who have developed or preserved distinctive stories and laws. Like Josiah, Ezra's Torah affirms a transcendent God whose will is both unchanging and enshrined in a book. Unlike Josiah, however, he has an exclusive ethics regarding non-ethnic Jews, but an inclusive ethics for all those who share the same ethnic heritage.

While both Josiah's canon and Ezra's view the divine as transcendent, the canonization that introduced the prophetic writings interrupts this progression. The canonization of the second part of the Hebrew Bible, the Prophets, occurred sometime after the rise of a priestly leadership group among the restored community that Ezra had founded. These works reintroduced a political emphasis in Jewish life, descriptively identifying the nation as the center of Jewish identity. Prescriptively, the prophetic books introduce flexibility into legal decision making, suggesting that God sends new messages to each new leadership group. Adding the Prophets to the canon provides a mechanism for choosing between competing prescriptions; thus, unlike the Torah, the prophetic books give guidance in making definitive legal decisions.

The books of 1 and 2 Maccabees (part of the Apocrypha; see Box 2–1) illustrate how this new development occurred. The "Law of Moses" as established by Ezra had become an indispensable part of Jewish identity by this time. When the Maccabees led a revolt against Syrian influence in their country, they could not reject that law. Nevertheless, they made provisions for cases either unmentioned by Mosaic legislation or left ambiguous in that law. When, for example, the Maccabees, after their successful revolution, dismantle the polluted Temple and build another, they do not know how to proceed. They therefore resolve to "wait until a prophet should come to tell them what to do" (1 Maccabees 4:46). This procedure had precedents in narratives and sayings reported of earlier prophetic leaders. Those writings were gathered together and became institutionalized as sacred texts. 2 Maccabees 2:13 describes the founding of a library to include the stories of the earlier kings from David onward. This description suggests that the prophetic canon was becoming authoritative.

The obvious implication of this reliance on prophecy is that of divine immanence. God's will changes in response to changing human situations. God enters into history—at least to communicate new commandments to special messengers. The stories in the prophetic section of the Bible show divine immanence in more dramatic ways as well—God intervenes in human affairs to win victories for the Jewish people. That concept of an active divinity fit the experience of a revolutionary army whose triumph over its enemies seemed to defy ordinary odds.

A second aspect of the prophetic canon moves beyond ethnic identity to political allegiance as the basis for self-understanding. Being a member of the Jewish community came to mean accepting the authority of the Jerusalem government and its leaders. Being a Jew entailed following certain laws and practices that characterized Jewish life. This aspect of the prophetic canon identifies members of a group and emphasizes communal solidarity, not on the basis of ethnicity, but on the basis of obedience to certain ideas and ideals. The **dietary laws** of the Hebrew Bible provide such a ritual unity. The Book of 2 Maccabees describes Jews who are willing to die bearing witness to their loyalty to this ritual tradition. These Jews refuse to eat forbidden food (pork in this case, 2 Maccabees 7) as a symbol of who they are. The ritual prohibitions on food provide an external sign of identity unifying all those who share this taboo on certain foods.

This prophetic canon moves away from religious exclusiveness based on ethnicity to a universal ethics welcoming anyone who will accept the values and practices of the community. The finalized canon neutralized the emphasis on divine immanence by placing the prophets in the center of the Bible, making the period of such divine involvement safely located in the past. That final canon, however, continued and augmented the incipient universalism of the prophetic writings.

RITUAL IN THE CANON

Each stage of canonization included an emphasis upon ritual and its performance. Josiah's canonization was authenticated by a **Passover** celebration in which the commandments for a centralized and unified cult were put into practice. The story suggests that Josiah hoped that this ritual would placate an angry deity. Such expectations of ritual observance seek substantial changes in outward reality. Josiah thought that a successful ritual performance would lead his nation to military victory and his kingship to success. Historical events seemed to prove otherwise. Josiah died while fighting the Egyptian Pharaoh Necho. More than that, the country suffered a great defeat at the hands of the Babylonians, and the elite were led off to Babylonia. The Babylonian king **Nebuchadnezzar** ended the hopes that the Judeans may have had that the ritual changes instituted by Josiah would lead to a reversal of their fortunes.

The prophets had long contended that ritual could not perform the type of salvation that Josiah expected. The prophetic writings as a whole consider ritual a supplement to ethical and moral commitment. When in 1 Samuel 15 the Israelite King **Saul** uses cattle captured in battle to offer a sacrifice, he is reprimanded by the prophet **Samuel** who tells him: "Has the Lord as great a delight in offerings and sacrifices as in obedience to the Lord's commands? Indeed, obedience is better than sacrifice" (1 Samuel 15:22). That theme continues in both the individual prophetic books and in the types of rituals established by the Maccabees. Ritual does not create substantive changes in the world. Instead, ritual serves to symbolize ideas and ideals. It celebrates—that is, draws attention to—certain realities that teach important lessons. Ritual acts as a reminder to people not to transform the world.

This celebratory approach is both congenial to and antagonistic toward the view of rituals found in the Torah as established by Ezra. Several passages in the Torah indicate that holidays such as Passover, **Booths**, **Pentecost**, and the **Day of Atonement** show how ritual transforms reality. The three holidays of Passover, Booths, and Pentecost are understood as part of the rules the observance of which maintain God's favor and bring divine guardianship over Israel (see Exodus 23:12–22). The Day of Atonement is meant to transform individuals so that they and the priestly service can win forgiveness before God and be atoned for their sins (Leviticus 16–17). Obedience to various ritual regulations will gain favor with God so that he will "look down your holy habitation, from heaven, and bless your people Israel and the ground that you have given us" (Deuteronomy 26:15). In these cases, the ritual transforms reality.

At the same time, these festivals are clearly celebratory. Passover reminds Jews of the Exodus from Egypt. Booths recalls the wandering in the wilderness. Pentecost expresses gratitude for having reached the land promised to Abraham in the Torah. Ezra's Torah also intertwines different types of biblical **calendar**. One type focuses on the movement of the sun; it establishes holidays based upon the seasons. Exodus 23, for example, makes the festival of Passover occur in the Aviv, or springtime; the festival of in-gathering occurs "at the end of the year;" and between them falls the festival of the harvest (23:14–16). Leviticus 23, however, introduces a calendar based on the moon, a lunar calendar with holidays listed according to the months in which they occur. The Levitical calendar, like that of Numbers 28–29 introduces holidays not found in Exodus, in particular the Day of Atonement and the day of the blowing of the ram's horn. These different calendars coexist because they are all considered symbolic rather than substantive. They commemorate important events or ideas.

For the Maccabees, who established the prophetic canon, ritual served a public function: it reminded people of their heroic past. The rabbinic organization of the Bible neutralizes this aspect of these holidays by associating each festival with a specific biblical book. Five works, placed together in the Jewish Bible but separately in the Christian Bible, illustrate this point. The so-called five festival scrolls—Song of Songs, Ruth, Lamentations, Ecclesiastes, and Esther—are read at the Jewish festivals of Passover, Pentecost, the Fast of Av, Booths, and Purim (considering Passover as the beginning of the year and progressing through Purim at the close of the year). The order of these books in the Jewish canon follows the calendar of holidays. While some early manuscripts suggest a different placement of these works, their association with Jewish liturgy finally determined where they would go in the canon.

Many scholars date the composition of some of these books to the Hellenistic age. Even the older works, however, take on new meaning by being associated with national holidays. By adding the private recitation of these books to the public ceremonies of the festivals, the rabbis acknowledged the individualistic and personalist attitude of Hellenistic culture. Reading Ruth at Pentecost associated that harvest festival with the idea of accepting the "yoke of the Torah" and affirmed that religious commitment is a matter of personal choice, not just national destiny. The holiday becomes less a time to ask for blessings on the harvest than a time to remember one's commitment to the tradition. Reciting Song of Songs at the festival of Israel's national freedom implies that personal liberty and self-expression are as important as political independence. The story of the Passover tells how the nation became free. Song of Songs celebrates personal freedom. Passover symbolizes God's love of the Jewish people. Song of Songs augments this by celebrating erotic love. Acknowledging the pessimistic skepticism of Ecclesiastes during the holiday of Booths, commemorating Israel's wandering in the wilderness, suggests that the ritual teaches an existential lesson about human nature, rather than appealing for divine intervention in atmospheric conditions. In a similar move, the holiday of Yom Kippur, the Day of Atonement, was associated with the prophetic book of Jonah, suggesting that the point of the celebration was personal self-reflection, rather than divine intervention into human affairs. The holidays that once sought changes in outer reality now become symbols of the emotional dynamics at work within every individual. When the rabbis at Jamnia decided to end the Jewish canon with the Writings, they shaped the entire ritual process into an expressive rather than transformative performance.

ALTERNATIVE CANONS

The Jewish organization of the books of the Bible follows what was, apparently, a fairly ancient tradition. Other traditions, equally ancient, organized them differently. You may be aware of the discovery of several ancient biblical manuscripts in caves near the Dead Sea, at a place called Qumran. Collectively, these works are known as the **Dead Sea Scrolls**. These scrolls include fragments from most of the books in the Jewish Bible, as well as some books that have survived intact only in Greek and some books unknown before. The authoritative canon used by those who wrote the scrolls can only be surmised, since no listing of "official" and "rejected" books or an ordering of them has been found. Nevertheless, it is clear that the canon of the **Jewish Bible** differed from that of the community in Qumran.

Another alternative canon was that of the Greek translation of the **Hebrew Bible** upon which the later Jewish Bible was based (see Box 2–1). That translation, called the Septuagint (abbreviated LXX), became an authoritative work of its own. It reflects the urban culture of Hellenistic Jews. Sometimes a change is small and insignificant; thus, a reference to flax and wool (as in Hosea 2:9) becomes a reference to manufactured cloth such as linen that was more familiar to an urban audience. Other changes reflect an ideological difference. Numbers 24:17 in the Hebrew Bible reads: "A star shall go forth out of Jacob, a scepter shall rise out of Israel." The Septuagint, taking this phrase as a messianic prediction, reads: "A star shall go forth out of Jacob, a man shall arise out of Israel." These changes that translators—presumably Jewish—introduced into the Greek Septuagint had a profound effect on Christianity. The Septuagint alters the meaning of many psalms and prophets. Since this Greek translation influenced early Christians, particularly the Apostle Paul, its differences from the Hebrew Bible are particularly important.

The religious significance of the Septuagint cannot be overestimated. It conveyed a sense of history, the divine, ethics, and ritual of its own. That translation, presumably made by Jews for other Jews, claimed a miraculous origin. An ancient tale relates that the Hellenistic ruler Ptolemy I (he was a general under Alexander the Great and governed in Egypt from 323 to 285 B.C.E.) sought to gather all the important books of the civilized world together in a library in Egypt. Among those books was the Jewish Bible. To ensure that he would get a valid translation of that work, he summoned elders from Judea: six from each of the twelve

> **BOX 2–1 DEUTEROCANONICAL WORKS**
>
> Several writings were included in the Greek Septuagint but rejected from the Jewish canon. These are considered "Apocrypha" or "hidden books" by Protestants but most are included as canon in the present Roman Catholic Bible. The books marked by an asterisk are not found in the present Roman Catholic canon.
>
> Additions to Esther
> Susanna
> Bel and the Dragon
> Prayer of Asariah
> Baruch (appended to Jeremiah)
> Letter of Jeremiah
> Tobit
> Judith
> 1 Maccabees
> 2 Maccabees
> 3 Maccabees*
> 4 Maccabees*
> Ecclesiasticus (Ben Sirah)
> Wisdom of Solomon
> 1 Esdras*
> 2 Esdras*
> Prayer of Manasseh*

Israelite tribes, making up seventy-two in all. He locked each of them in an isolated room and ordered them to translate the Hebrew Bible into Greek. Miraculously, each translation was identical to every other one. This miracle proved that God had intended a revelation in Greek no less than in Hebrew.

This story implies that history changes. The creation of the Septuagint occasions a break with the past, a discontinuity with the rural, Hebraic originating tradition. God has decided to do something new and unexpected. Thus, not only is history discontinuous, but also God is immanent and active in human affairs. The choice of language and the revision of expression found in the Septuagint indicates an even broader universalism and inclusiveness than the ethics in the Jewish Bible. The message of the Bible must be transformed to meet the wider needs of the general culture. Finally, the Jews of Alexandria, Egypt, turned the anniversary of the translation into a holiday and celebration. Ritual, as performed on that occasion, celebrates God's intervention in the world but does not create any new reality itself.

This view of the Septuagint's divine approval did not go unopposed. While the religious ideas involved seem similar to those of the Jewish canon, the organization of the books, the reshaping of the message, and the introduction of new rituals dismayed Jewish leaders in Judea. These leaders claimed that the day this translation was made was as unfortunate for the Jewish people as was the day on which Israel worshiped the Golden Calf (Exodus 32)—the symbol of Israel's early sinfulness. The primary response was to make the inclusive ethics of the Jewish Bible a little less inclusive. The Jewish Bible emphasizes the priority of the Hebrew language and Hebraic culture. That Bible excluded works found only in the Greek translation. Whereas the Septuagint worked to include a wider audience in the divine revelation, those who insisted on the authenticity and primacy of the Hebrew original narrowed the community addressed by God's words.

SUMMARY QUESTIONS

1. What evidence in the Hebrew Bible supports the idea of a single Torah written by Moses, and what evidence suggests this idea was a later development?
2. Why might both Josiah's Torah and Ezra's be said to illustrate an idea of God as transcendent?
3. What view of ethics and ritual illuminates why the Maccabees canonized the Neviim?
4. How are the ethics and ritual of the rabbis of Jamnia related to the canonization of the Ketuvim?
5. What implications does the creation and structure of the Septuagint have for views of the divine and of ethics?

Four Suggested Essay Questions

1. Explain two ways in which a tradition may view history. Apply one of them to the Maccabean addition of the Prophets to the canon and one to the use of the terms Hebrews, Israelites, Judeans, and Jews as referring to an unchanging community.
2. Explain two ways in which a tradition may view the supernatural. Apply one of them to the story of the miraculous creation of the Septuagint and one to the view suggested by the arrangement of the Prophets in the Jewish canon.
3. Explain two ways in which a tradition may view ethics. Apply one of them to Ezra's use of a canon in Ezra 7 to unify the exilic community and the other to the rabbinic decision to canonize the writings as the conclusion of the Jewish canon.
4. Explain two ways in which a tradition may view ritual. Apply one of them to the rabbinic choice of the book of Ruth as an appropriate reading for Pentecost and the other to Josiah's expectation that his Passover observance might lead to favor in God's eyes.

Exercise

Read the following paragraph from an essay answering the second question:

The Jewish canon, unlike the Septuagint canon, places both the Former and Latter Prophets between the Torah and the Writings. This placement suggests that prophets, while acting as intermediaries for God, do not communicate new information; they reiterate the teachings of the Torah and anticipate the teachings of the Writings. The Former Prophets interpret the history of Israel in a narrative leading from Joshua through 2 Kings. The Latter Prophets use that history to inform Israel of how God's unchanging will is active in their lives. Although the prophets described in both sets of writings all claim immediate inspiration from the divine, they are each responding to different historical challenges. They are all placed together to show that they express a single idea. God uses the prophets to reiterate a pre-existing plan and pattern that never changes. To make this point even clearer, these books were placed between the Torah and the Writings, suggesting that they are all merely repeating the main ideas found elsewhere in the Bible. This reiteration suggests that God does not need to intervene in history with new messages, but rather raises up leaders who will reassert the same primal concerns. Humanity needs to listen anew to the eternal lessons concerning God's desires.

Now answer the following five questions:

1. Based on the first sentence of this paragraph, what are the two ideas that will be developed?
2. Which sentences show that the prophetic section of the Jewish canon illustrates the first idea?
3. Which sentences show that the prophetic section of the Jewish canon illustrates the second idea?
4. Why do you think the answer describes both the Former and Latter Prophets?
5. Why do you think the answer mentions the Septuagint?

FOR FURTHER READING

The books listed below should be a point of departure for your future study. Each includes a bibliography that will guide you beyond its basic information.

1. Collins, John J., "Before the Canon: Scriptures in Second Temple Judaism" in *Old Testament Interpretation: Past, Present, and Future, Essays in Honor of Gene M. Tucker*, James Luther et al., eds. (Nashville: Abingdon Press, 1995), 225–241.

2. Halbertal, Moshe, *People of the Book: Canon, Meaning, and Authority* (Cambridge: Harvard University Press, 1997).

3. Sanders, James A., *From Sacred Story to Sacred Text: Canon As Paradigm* (Philadelphia: Fortress, 1987).

4. Smith, Morton, *Palestinian Parties and Politics That Shaped the Old Testament* (New York: Columbia University Press, 1971).

3

Introduction to Christian Scriptures

READING ASSIGNMENT

    Matthew 5:17–20
    Luke 22:14–20
    Luke 24:28–49
    2 Peter 3:14–16
    Revelation 22:18–19

LEARNING OBJECTIVES

By the end of this lesson, you will be able to:
- Describe two ways of understanding history and apply them to the two-tiered nature of the Christian Scriptures.
- Describe two ways of viewing the supernatural and apply them to the organization of the Christian Scriptures.
- Describe two ways of understanding ethics and apply them to the canonization of the Gospels, letters, and apocalypse as Christian Scriptures.
- Describe two ways of construing ritual and apply them to the original meaning of the term "New Covenant" and to the application of that term to the Christian Bible.

Introduction to Christian Scriptures 33

Interpretive Matrix for Chapter Three			
View of the Divine: How people interact with God and the supernatural; how God interacts with the world.	*View of History:* How past, present, and future are related; who controls the shape of events.	*View of Ethics:* How people behave toward other people; how they behave toward people like themselves and to those who are different.	*View of Ritual:* How people behave toward the Divine; how they perform religious actions.
The Divine as Transcendent: God maintains a consistent and predictable pattern in human events. God is approachable only through special intermediaries.	*History as Continuous:* Covenant provides a continual basis for the divine-human relationship. Texts from earlier traditions are included with later texts. Using an ancient language for worship even when using a different language in daily speech.	*Inclusive Ethics:* All people can understand the teachings of a tradition. The group is open to all genders and classes of people.	*Ritual as Transforming:* Ritual transforms participants so they become one with the divinity.
The Divine as Immanent: God enters history to change the future of human events.	*History as Discontinuous:* Covenant introduces a change in the relationship between the divine and the human. Texts from earlier traditions are excluded from later texts.	*Exclusive Ethics:* Practices associated with other traditions are forbidden to members of a group. One message is given to the masses and another to a select elite.	*Ritual as Symbolic:* Ritual use of scriptures unites members of a group.

INTRODUCTION

This chapter continues the introduction to the biblical corpus begun in the previous chapter, focusing on the Christian canon rather than the Jewish canon. The chapter begins by looking at how the Christian canon understands itself as the continuation and completion of the Jewish Bible. The terms Old Testament and New Testament suggest both continuity with the past and a transformation that goes beyond it. The chapter then reviews the general organization of the Christian Bible and examines the view of divinity involved. Different versions of the Christian Old Testament reveal distinctive views of the divine. Turning to the New Testament, the chapter looks at the intention behind its particular organization (see Box 3–2). Decisions concerning the presentation of the material, which books to canonize, and the ordering of those books express a variety of ethical perspectives in the early church. Finally, the use of the Bible as a liturgical tool combined with the original ways of thinking about the term *New Covenant* or *New Testament* highlight distinctive approaches to ritual.

Before reading this chapter, you might want to study lists comparing different Christian Bibles, in particular those of Protestants and Roman Catholics (see Box 3–1). Become familiar with the sequence of events leading to the final canonization of the Christian canon (see Timeline 3–1) and correlate that sequence with the development of the canon as a whole (see Timeline 3–2).

SOME IMPORTANT TERMS

The following terms are important in this chapter. They are also found in the Glossary.

Acts of the Apostles	Didache	Muratorian Canon
Acts of Paul	Elijah	Nag Hammadi
Apocalypse of Peter	Eucharist	Parousia
Aramic	Gospel	Paul of Tarsus
Athanasius	Gospel of Thomas	Pseudepigrapha
Christ	Gnosticism	Resurrection
Christian Apocrypha	Holy Spirit	Revelation
Codex	Jesus of Nazareth	Shepherd of Hermas
Sinaiticus	Justin Martyr	Testament
Constantine	Marcion	
Covenant	Messiah	

HISTORY AND THE TWO TIERED CHRISTIAN BIBLE

Christians call their scriptures the New Testament and the Jewish Bible the Old Testament. The word **testament** is a Latin rendering for what, in English, we would call a **covenant**, or agreement. The term comes from a Greek translation for the Hebrew word *brith* or "covenant." Covenant is a term meaning agreement or contract. Used theologically, the term suggests that the divine has entered into a contract with human beings.

The Hebrew Bible portrays several covenants at different junctures in human history. An early example of such an action occurs after God sends a great flood to destroy the world (Genesis 6–9). One human family survives and, with it, the rest of creation—the family of Noah. At the conclusion of this event, God makes a covenant with Noah. That agreement encompasses all human beings. Certain types of behavior are expected of all people, primarily the prohibition against shedding blood. In exchange, the divine promises not to destroy the world by flood. There are two elements here: an expectation by God of how humanity will behave, and an expectation by human beings of how God will behave.

From this perspective, a change in covenant implies either a change in the divine or a change in the human. The Hebrew Bible describes several covenants that suggest God makes agreements with different leaders (see Genesis 12 and 2 Samuel 7). Early leaders such as Abraham and David are represented as enjoying a covenant with God. Such covenants suggest that historical changes, especially political ones, require God to make a new covenant. Another type of change is more radical. The Hebrew Bible portrays a covenant made with the entire Jewish people: the covenant made by Moses at Mount Sinai (see Exodus 19–24). In this case, God alters the nature of covenant-making entirely. God no longer makes covenants with individuals, but with a nation as a whole. In this act of radical discontinuity, God's covenants embrace neither an individual nor all humanity, but a special "chosen group"—Israel.

Christianity understands itself as standing under a new covenant, one established by the first coming of the Jewish redeemer, the **Christ**. This title (literally meaning someone anointed for leadership) became used as a name for **Jesus of Nazareth**, around whom the new covenant was created. From that title, which they took as a name, Christians derived their own name. By placing its own covenant as part of an ongoing series, Christianity emphasizes its continuity with Jewish religiousness.

During its earliest history, the Christian community used the Jewish canon as its primary scriptures. The New Testament opens with the **Gospels**, narratives describing the life and teachings of Jesus of Nazareth. The Gospels suggest continuity with Judaism by having Jesus refer to the Jewish Bible. In Matthew 5:17–20 Jesus tells his followers to fulfill all that is written in the Torah and Prophets; in Luke 24: 28–49 Jesus points to passages in the "Torah, Prophets, and Psalms" that predict the trajectory of his career. Perhaps the authors of these two passages in these Gospels were using different Jewish canons, one of which included the writings and another of which did not. In addition to these narratives about Jesus, the New Testament contains letters ascribed to **Paul of Tarsus**. The Apostle Paul continually makes use of the Jewish Bible, usually employing the Greek translation, the Septuagint, as proof for Christian claims. Later parts of the New Testament affirm continuity by referring to Paul's letters themselves as scriptures (see 2 Peter 3:14–16), and an even later text applies scriptural authority to itself (Revelation 22:18–19). Eventually, Christianity maintained continuity with Judaism by creating a two-tiered scripture, the lower tier being taken up by the Old Testament, the Jewish Bible, and the upper tier consisting of the New Testament, including four Gospels, a narrative, several letters, and an apocalyptic book imagining the final days of history (see Box 3–2).

Nevertheless, the decision to include the Jewish scriptures within the Christian canon did not come easily. A second-century Roman Christian who was later declared a heretic, **Marcion**, responding to the common tendencies of the time, sorted through the various traditions at his disposal to create his version of Christian Scriptures (see Timeline 3–2). He selected only those stories and sayings that agreed with his view of Christianity. He created an edited version of Jesus' life and teachings that he claimed represented the "true" doctrine of

Christianity. Perhaps the most extraordinary aspect of Marcion's work lay in his claim that Jesus had not been a Jew and that the devil had composed the Old Testament. He believed that Christians should reject anything from that source. Later teachers rejected Marcion, but he represents a common pattern—that of creating one's own view of what Jesus really said and meant, and writing it down as the true story of Christian religion.

The rejection of Marcion entails a view of history as continuous. Christianity links events of the past to those of the present and the future. Including the books of the Old Testament within their own canon meant that Christians could use history to justify their own claims, to prove the validity of their perspectives, and to gain acceptance in the wider community. Since Jews were members of a legal community, Christians could acquire legitimacy though an association with Judaism (see Timeline 3–1). Many elements in the Christian message stressed the Judaic aspects of the religion. Jesus of Nazareth, the central messianic figure of Christianity, lived and died as a Jew, as evidenced by his "last supper," almost certainly a Passover meal that became the basis for the central Christian ritual, the **Eucharist**, or thanksgiving ceremony. Jesus apparently preached to Jews and sought to reform Jewish practice and theology. The implication of texts such as those in Matthew 5 and Luke 24 is that Christianity represents the historical consequences of the plan begun and developed in the Jewish Bible.

Calling that Bible an "old" testament, however, contrasts it to a "new" one; that contrast introduces an idea of discontinuity and innovation. The new covenant that Christianity envisioned was a similarly radical act of discontinuity. Not only does it revert from the Jews to a "New Israel," but it entails a new act of the divine: being incarnated in and suffering through physical existence. Those who affirm this new covenant and accept the divine act of self-sacrifice become part of the New Israel that enjoys the benefits of this covenant.

To qualify for membership in Christianity, two sets of expectations must be met. First, an initiate must accept the beliefs and practices of the Christian community. Second, an initiate must recognize in these beliefs and practices an extension of the "Christ event"—the teachings, life, suffering, death, and **resurrection** of Jesus of Nazareth. That final event, the resurrection, creates a new reality. Death has been defeated; humanity been given the gift of life. In this way the "new" covenant is seen as an extension of the "old" one. In the first case, the Jewish covenant's laws and beliefs are brought to their ultimate conclusion in the teachings of Jesus. In the second, the stories and narratives of the Jewish covenant find their true meaning in the story of Jesus' life, death, and resurrection.

An example of these two ways of looking at covenant or testament (remember these are translations of the same word) occurs in two passages in the New Testament. According to Matthew 5:17–22, Jesus tells his disciples that he has not come to abolish earlier scriptures (the Law and the Prophets), but to fulfill them. He then urges his followers to "fulfill" the scriptures just as he does. He gives several examples of such fulfillment: if the scripture says one should not murder another person, then Jesus says that it means do not even be angry at anyone. Jesus teaches that "fulfilling" the scriptures means acting according to the law even more rigorously than had been previously thought.

According to Luke 24:44–49, Jesus, after his death, appears to his followers and explains that everything that has happened to him has been "to fulfill" earlier scriptures (Law, Prophets, and Psalms). He then teaches them how all these scriptures were really predicting events in his life and tells them to teach this interpretation of the Bible to others. In Matthew 5, the "old" testament refers to an old way of understanding the laws one should obey and the "new" to a new and stricter way of obeying the laws. In Luke 24, the "old" testament refers to an old way of understanding the events to which the scriptures refer and the "new" to a new event now understood as their true meaning.

One aspect of the new consciousness evinced by Christianity was its choice of language. Jews insisted on using the Hebrew Bible. While individual Jews would speak the vernacular of the lands in which they lived—**Aramaic** in the Near East, Latin or Greek in the Hellenized world—they prayed and studied their scriptures in the original language. Christians decided to use Greek as their means of communication. Greek, however, has more than one dialect. Literary Greek—the Greek of Homer or Plato—is a sophisticated language and demands intense training and study. Rather than choose such a language, the early Christians framed their works in everyday speech, in the business vernacular of the time, Koine Greek. This was the language used by merchants, workers, and ordinary people. Such a choice represents the inclusiveness of the new religious movement.

The transition from Aramaic to Greek as the medium of expression has particular relevance for understanding the New Testament. Jesus and his earliest disciples, as presented in the Christian Gospels, spoke Aramaic. The entire New Testament, however, is written in the popular form of Koine Greek, derived from the fusion of classical Greek with the commercial vernacular of Near Eastern peoples. Use of this language has implications beyond identifying Christian religion as Hellenistic. Translating Aramaic traditions into Koine Greek transformed the meaning of Christian ideas since any translation alters the content of the original.

The Christian tradition, then, affirms continuity with the Jewish canon through its inclusion of its content within its own canon, its acceptance of the validity of the claim that God made a covenant with Israel in the past, and its use of that covenant to prove the legitimacy of its own beliefs. It rejects continuity and argues for a radical discontinuity through its choice of the Greek language, its insistence that God has changed the terms of the agreement both for the divine and for the human, and in the community it considers "true Israel." Naturally, a group seeks to define itself in distinction from its closest rivals. In Christianity this meant showing that its covenant differed significantly from that of Judaism. At the same time, Christianity needed to claim continuity with Judaism so it could enjoy the rights and privileges given Jews in the Roman empire. This ambivalence found expression in the creation of a two-tiered canon that included an Old Testament for continuity and a New Testament for discontinuity.

THE ORGANIZATION OF THE CHRISTIAN BIBLE AND VIEWS OF THE DIVINITY

Although the Christian Old Testament retains most of the content of the Jewish Bible, its organization, following that of the Septuagint, represents a distinctive view of divinity. While the Jewish canon divides into three sections, the Christian Old Testament divides into four: the first five books, books of history (including what the Jewish canon considers the Former Prophets but adding others that that canon puts among the Writings; see Box 3–1). The order follows a clear chronological pattern, progressing from Israel's entrance into its own land, its creation of an independent kingdom, the collapse of that kingdom, its exile to other lands, and its return to that land. The Former Prophets, with their historical narratives, serve for Christians as a bridge from Old Israel to the New Church.

Since that bridge must extend from earliest history to the final stages of biblical history both in Israel and the Diaspora, both Protestants and Catholics include in this section books excluded from "prophecy" by the Jewish canon. These books (1 and 2 Chronicles, Ezra, Nehemiah, Esther, and Ruth) advance Israel's story through its exile. Putting that history together in a coherent tale prepares readers for its culmination and fulfillment in the New Testament story of the growth of the Christian church. The Catholic canon includes even later works, considering Judith and Maccabees as important links in the chain of history. The Protestant canon, however, no less than the Roman Catholic, ends with Israel's return from exile in Babylonia and the flourishing of Jewish life in the Diaspora. Once the Christian canon creates this bridge to the present, it moves into wisdom writings. It concludes with the Latter Prophets, writings understood as predictions of the future rather than as interpretations of past events.

This organization moves from preliminary considerations to history, to literature, and finally to prophecy. As the ultimate statement of the Old Testament, prophecy points beyond itself to a predicted future. This difference represents a major break with Jewish tradition. Malachi, the final prophetic book, proclaims the coming of **Elijah** to announce the "Great Day" of God (Malachi 4:5). While Elijah is one of the central figures in the book of 1 Kings, he became a symbolic hero in later Jewish thought. Exiled from their country and dependent on foreign powers, Jews imagined a triumphant reversal of their fortunes. Many stories claimed that Elijah the Prophet would return at that time to announce the coming reversal.

Christians make this imminent change a personal testimony referring to the coming of Jesus, declaring that they have become the fulfillment of that prophecy. The Christian story as told in the Gospel of Mark begins with just that proclamation (Mark 1:2). For the Christian, a prophet does not merely expand the meaning of the Torah; a prophet prepares the way for a new Torah: the Torah of Jesus. The prophetic works, from this perspective, predict a religious revolution. While the Jewish canon emphasizes prophetic continuity, the Christian canon emphasizes discontinuity as an anticipation of an entirely new situation.

BOX 3–1 THE OLD TESTAMENT CANON OF PROTESTANTS AND ROMAN CATHOLICS

All Christian canons of the Old Testament begin with the Pentateuch, the first five books of the Hebrew Bible. Substantial differences exist among the next sections of the canon for several Christian groups. For the sake of the discussion in this chapter, only the Roman Catholic and Protestant canons are listed. Books found only in the Roman Catholic Canon are in parenthesis; differences in terminology are not included.

The Pentateuch
 Genesis
 Exodus
 Leviticus
 Numbers
 Deuteronomy

The Historical Books
 Joshua
 Judges
 Ruth
 1–2 Samuel
 1–2 Kings
 1–2 Chronicles
 Ezra
 Nehemiah
 (Tobit)
 (Judith)
 Esther
 (additions to Esther)
 (1–2 Maccabees)

Poetry and Wisdom
 Job
 Psalms
 Proverbs
 Ecclesiastes
 Song of Solomon
 (Ecclesiasticus—Wisdom of Jesus Ben Sirah)

Prophetic Books
 Isaiah
 Jeremiah
 Lamentations
 (Baruch)
 Ezekiel
 Daniel
 (Prayer of Azariah, Susanna,
  Bel and the Dragon)
 Hosea
 Joel
 Amos
 Obediah
 Jonah
 Micah
 Nahum
 Habakkuk
 Zephaniah
 Haggai
 Zechariah
 Malachi

Such a view explains why the Christian canon includes the book of Daniel as a prophetic work. That book combines folk tales lauding loyalty to Torah rules with visions about the future. From the perspective of the Hebrew Bible, Daniel is not prophetic literature, but rather a book of education; both the folktales and the visions serve to strengthen loyalty to the Jewish people. The Christian canon, however, perceives Daniel's visions of the end of time as essential predictions of the events realized in Christian history. Reality, in this case, consists of unexpected events that overtake humanity despite itself. Prophecy warns people not to rely on the expected, the predictable, or the logical. By including Daniel among the prophets, Christians testify to a world in which "anything is possible to God" and in which people should expect change and surprise.

When divine transcendence entails the view of the predictability of God's plan, such a picture of unpredictability points to divine immanence. The organization of the Christian New Testament reinforces this view (see Box 3–2). Notice that the dates of composition of the New Testament books differ from their placement in the canon (see Timeline 3–2 on page 45). The Gospels have been placed first, despite the fact that the letters of Paul were written first. Within the Gospels, Matthew's Gospel, which begins with a genealogy tracing Jesus back to Abraham, links the New Testament to the Hebrew tradition.

BOX 3–2   THE NEW TESTAMENT CANON OF PROTESTANTS AND ROMAN CATHOLICS

This list looks only at the canons of contemporary Protestants and Roman Catholics. Since these share a single canonical tradition, only one listing is given. You should compare the order of the books in this canon to the order of their composition as found in Timeline 3–2.

The Gospels
  Matthew
  Mark
  Luke
  John

The Historical Book
  The Book of Acts

The Letters of Apostles
  Roman
  1, 2 Corinthians
  Galatians
  Ephesians
  Philippians
  Colossians
  1–2 Thessalonians
  1, 2 Timothy
  Titus
  Philemon
  Hebrews
  1, 2 Peter
  1, 2, 3, John
  Jude

Apocalyptic Book
  Revelation of John of Patmos

After the Gospels, the New Testament introduces a narrative history, **Acts of the Apostles**. That history describes how the church developed, beginning with the earliest disciples such as Peter and culminating in the story of the apostleship of Paul of Tarsus. The use of Acts to introduce Paul means that his genuine letters will be colored by the later reflections in the Book of Acts. The addition of letters written in Paul's name but clearly later than Paul also ensures that readers will temper their understanding of the authentically Pauline works by how later writers reconceived them.

The New Testament concludes with a book of prophetic visions—the book of **Revelation of John**. After reviewing the shortcomings of many Christian churches, the book envisions a cataclysmic conflict between good and evil that will end cosmic history. At the end of that conflict, the wicked receive unexpected punishment and the faithful unexpected blessing. The transformation anticipated for the end of time emphasizes the temporary nature of this historical period and creates a future orientation for the entire biblical corpus. In one way, this organization of the Christian canon emphasizes continuity: the four parts of the New Testament mirror the four parts of the Old Testament. In another way, it reiterates the view of divine immanence: God's hand is always at work in history, so one should always expect the unexpected. Immanence entails more than just the unexpected: it imagines divine involvement in the world. God's immanence implies an interest, concern, and activity within history. God takes a hand in what occurs in human life.

Such a way of understanding immanence suggests that views requiring intermediaries between individuals and the divine have introduced transcendence into the picture. When a book portrays God as interacting with nations and leaders rather than with ordinary individuals, then it emphasizes transcendence rather than immanence. Compare, for example, the difference between the Roman Catholic biblical canon and that of the Protestants. The Roman Catholic Bible extends the history recorded in the Jewish canon. It adds certain Jewish books written in the period after the return from the exile. Several of these books were apparently originally written in Hebrew but are now extant only in Greek. The Jews who created the Hebrew Bible rejected these books because they did not fit into the historical period that they considered determinative. These works, however, are found in an early Greek translation of the Bible, the Septuagint. Technically, these books are called Apocrypha—a word that means "hidden," because not only the Jews but also Protestants refused to acknowledge these texts as part of their official authoritative Bible. The books were sometimes considered "inspired scriptures" but often were excluded from canonical authority. Other works, both those accepted by the Septuagint and those accepted by some Christians but later rejected by the church, fall into another category. Because the majority of them are written by later writers using the names of earlier authors (a practice called pseudonymous authorship), the works, collectively, are called **pseudepigrapha**.

By including such works as the books of Maccabees and Ecclesiasticus, the Roman Catholic canon extends the biblical story into the period of Israel's second period of kingship. After the fall of the first kingdoms and exile from their land, the Jews did create a

"Second Jewish Commonwealth" that lasted nearly one hundred years, from 165 B.C.E. to 66 B.C.E.. In addition, and most obviously, the Roman Catholic canon extends the biblical story from the period of Judaism into the period of Christianity, with Israel's history culminating in the history of the Christian church. From this perspective, God's interest focuses on communities, on the institutional expressions of covenant. God's concern involves the Israelite nation, the Second Commonwealth, and the New Israel of Christendom. God interacts with heroes and leaders, kings, princes, and empires. This emphasis on kingdoms, on the politically powerful, and on leadership places the divine at a distance from ordinary individuals.

The Protestant canon, by contrast, focuses on divine interaction with individuals, on the intimacy of the divine with the human. This canon, like the Jewish one, rejects the Apocrypha, but, like the Roman Catholic canon, it sees the history of Christianity as the completion of Israel's story. The history ends, for example, with Esther, not with the Maccabees. While Esther was a queen, the story focuses on her importance as an individual. The wisdom and poetry section ends with the Song of Songs. While sometimes interpreted as a dialogue of love between God and the church, the more plausible interpretation of the poem understands it as an evocation of individuals under an erotic spell. These two choices emphasize divine interest in persons rather than in kingdoms, in individuals rather than communities. This interest shows divine activity occurring in the intimate sphere of a person's life rather than in just the public sphere of group destinies. In this way, the Protestant canon suggests a greater degree of immanence than does the Roman Catholic.

THREE PARTS TO THE NEW TESTAMENT: THREE VIEWS OF ETHICS

While the Old Testament of the Protestant and Roman Catholic canons differ, their New Testaments remain identical (see Box 3–2). They begin with four Gospels—retellings of the career of Jesus of Nazareth. Those retellings differ in substantial detail from one another, the specifics of which are discussed later in Chapter Seven. They continue with a historical narrative about the early church: Acts of the Apostles, a continuation of the Gospel of Luke; they include several letters attributed to early followers (apostles) of Jesus, and conclude with a single apocalyptic vision. This uniformity contrasts with the variety and diversity of materials that early Christians considered canon (see Timeline 3–2, and note the variety of canons persisting through the fifth century).

The decision to include four Gospels within the canon suggests a willingness to accept variations among Christian communities. Early Christians had circulated several stories about the life and teachings of Jesus of Nazareth. Books of sayings appeared in Greek purporting to be exact quotations from the Christ, authored by people whose identity was often hidden under an assumed name. Competition among the disciples exacerbated the confusion that existed in the various reports about Jesus' life, teachings, and sayings. Some Christian leaders felt uncomfortable with the diversity that reigned. To remedy it, officials such as

TIMELINE 3–1 HISTORICAL EVENTS RELATED TO THE CHRISTIAN BIBLE

This list of events provides background against which to understand the development of the Christian Bible. All events are C.E.—referring to the Common Era.

27–30	Career of Jesus of Nazareth
30	First Christian communities are formed
35–62	Career of Paul of Tarsus
54–68	Nero is Emperor of Rome; persecution of Christians
140–320	Various dissenting groups such as Marcionites and Montanists flourish and are condemned
176	Persecution of Christians by Marcus Aurelius
202	Persecution of Christians by Septimus Severus
211–217	Persecution of Christians by Caracalla
212	Roman citizenship granted to the Jews
250–259	Persecution of Christians by Emperors Decius and Valerian
303	Persecution of Christians by Diocletion
313	Emperor Constantine makes Christianity a legal religion in the Roman Empire
325	Council of Nicea

Justin Martyr, a second-century Christian teacher, called upon the Gospels as authorities. To answer Jewish critics, Christians felt they needed historical documents to prove their argument. They collected and edited the stories about Jesus, composing coherent narratives about him. As different teachers composed their different versions of these stories, divergent gospels or narratives, including tales and sayings of Jesus, evolved. Each of these various gospels claimed to tell the one truth about Jesus.

Many Christians felt uneasy with the diversity implied by the proliferation of Christian writings. Marcion, in the second century, for example, sorted through the various traditions at his disposal to create his version of Christian Scriptures. He selected only those stories and sayings that agreed with his view of Christianity. He created an edited version of Jesus' life and teachings that he claimed represented the "true" doctrine of Christianity. Marcion's approach had the advantage of simplicity: he created one seamless narrative unmarred by differences of opinion. The disadvantage of his approach lay in its exclusiveness. By shaping one, and only one, legitimate telling of the Jesus story, he relegated all diversity to heresy. That approach to the Gospels was eventually rejected.

Diversity abounded not only in the traditions surrounding Jesus' teaching. Several works once held as canonical, but eventually rejected from the official Christian Bible, offered varied perspectives on Christian life. These suppressed books making up the Christian, or New Testament—apocrypha as opposed to apocryphal works associated with the Old Testament—

testify to the complexity of Christian culture in its earliest phrases. Some of these consist of manuals for Christian practice.

One important work, the **Didache** (the Teaching of the Twelve Apostles), tries to impose an official order on Christian life and ritual. It gives detailed instruction on church behavior, on moral life, and on the importance of learning a craft. Among its details is a prohibition on being an astrologer. Another, **The Shepherd of Hermas**, which often occurs among early lists of accepted canons, reveals secrets thought to be reserved for the elite. Still another work, the **Acts of Paul**, includes women among the leaders of early Christian churches. Many of these works were suppressed by authorities and remained unknown until rediscovered in modern times. Among texts recently found in 1947 at **Nag Hammadi**, Egypt, **The Gospel of Thomas**, an ancient apocryphal work, seems to come from a community of Gnostics, a group of people claiming that Jesus taught a secret message that only the elite could understand. This book portrays Jesus as preaching one message for the masses and another for the special disciples. The church fathers ultimately rejected the canonical status of these books.

The development of Christianity until the fourth century took place under the threat of persecution (see Timeline 3–1). Survival rather than centralization was the major concern of Christians during this time. Only when free from the distraction of such persecution could Christian leaders attempt to enforce a single perspective on all believers. Under Emperor **Constantine** of Rome, Christianity became the official religion. Seeking to unify a divided empire, Constantine used Christianity as an ideology to bind his realm together. To achieve this end, he and the Christian priests he appointed sought to create a uniform Christian faith through a council of leaders. These councils, such as the one held in Nicea in 325 C.E. authorized and rejected religious beliefs and doctrines. Church councils selected which books and ideas would receive official approbation. Their new power enabled these leaders to determine the final shape of the literature that had been developing over centuries.

During this period, lists of sacred works began to appear. The second-century **Muratorian Canon** from Rome listed a basic canonical consensus: four Gospels, Acts, thirteen letters of Paul, some of the non-Pauline letters, the Wisdom of Solomon, and the **Apocalypse of Peter**. Although official Christianity never accepted some of these works, the pattern established by that canon became authoritative. The New Testament as presently canonized dates from the fourth century, as the letter of **Athanasius** shows, although even later codices suggest that a great variety of works were included as canonical. Much that is today considered **Christian Apocrypha** and stands outside the official canon is found in fifth-century manuscripts, such as the so-called Codex Vaticanus, Codex Alexandriunus, and the **Codex Sinaiticus**. While the present canon has clearly "shrunk" in size from those early versions, it still retains great variety and diversity (see Timeline 3–2).

Note that the canonized New Testament includes four Gospels. This legitimates an inclusive ethics. Four variant traditions achieve authorized status. This acceptance of difference allows members of different communities to affirm their perspectives on the life and meaning of Jesus of Nazareth without being rejected from the community as a whole. Insofar as

TIMELINE 3–2 THE CANONIZATION OF THE CHRISTIAN BIBLE

This list of events suggests the composition and canonization of the New Testament canon. All events are c.e.—referring to the Common Era.

50–62	Writing of the Pauline Letters in response to needs of various communities
66–70	Composition of the Gospel of Mark in response to the variety of versions of Jesus' career and in the aftermath of the Jewish revolt against Rome
80–90	The Gospels of Matthew and Luke and the Book of Acts are composed with a growing concern for the life and culture outside the land of Israel
85–95	Letters of Hebrews, 1 Peter, Ephesians, and James reflect growing Christian self-understanding; Gospel of John takes shape
95–150	Letters of John, 1 and 2 Timothy, Titus, Jude, and 2 Peter are composed; The Book of Revelation is written
100–168	Justin Martyr whose writings suggest the letters of Paul have become canon
140	The Church leader Marcion is expelled from Rome and his canon labeled heretical
170	Muratorian Canon is presumed to have been compiled
367	Letter of Athanasius suggesting the shape of the eventually finalized canon
400–450	Codices such as Sinaiticus, Alexandrinus, and Vaticanus show the variety of materials still included in fifth century Christian canons

Head of a colossal statue of Constantine from the apse of Basilica of Maxentius. Rome, Conservator's Palace, inner court.

Jesus provides both a model for Christians to follow and an image of the ideal Christian person, the inclusion of four Gospels offers a range of Christian possibilities, rather than limiting Christian living to a single paradigm.

That the New Testament ends with a single apocalyptic book suggests an exclusive ethics, an ethics that focuses on being part of the "good" community that will be saved, in contrast to the "evil" community that will be annihilated. In this case, traditions about Jesus' life in the past have been replaced by another sort of story—projections about Jesus' triumphant return to earth. Early Christians expected that Jesus would soon reappear to initiate a new kingdom, the kingdom of God. Although Christians did not always agree about what the new kingdom would be, many were disappointed as time passed and the hoped-for appearance did not occur. The word for appearance, **Parousia**, took on a technical meaning; it referred to Jesus' return to earth to inaugurate the final days of history. Throughout this period, writings emerged that predicted the end of the world, the second coming of the **Messiah**—or Christ—and the transformation of the world order. As with the Gospel traditions, these visions were not always in agreement. A plethora of stories and projected scenarios flooded the Christian communities. One such work, the **Revelation of John**, did indeed eventually win the support of most Christian communities and become part of the official canon. The fate of this book, however, was not certain, and some Christian churches even in modern times resist including it in their canon. Other apocalyptic works were eventually suppressed and have only been unearthed recently.

The Revelation of John introduces the idea of an immutable canon. It concludes by declaring "I warn everyone who hears the words of the prophecy of this book: if anyone adds to them, God will add to that person the plagues described in this book; if anyone takes away from the words of the book of this prophecy, God will take away that person's share in the tree of life and in the holy city which are described in this book" (Revelation 22: 18–19). This statement echoes a warning found in Deuteronomy 4:2 and 12:32. Just as Deuteronomy ended the Pentateuch, so the Revelation of John ends the Christian canon. In both cases a warning not to add or subtract from the content of the book makes that work authoritative. Membership in the religious community depends on accepting the authority of the canon. Acceptance of the selections made in the canon determines correct behavior. Insiders to the community differ from outsiders by what they consider the "true" revelation to be. Bishop Athanasius alluded to a definitive list of canonical books in 367. By concluding that Bible with Revelation, Athanasius made Christian authenticity dependent upon the affirmation of a fixed canon. Henceforth no "true" Christian was allowed to add any new revelation to the canon; Christians were also forbidden to reject any of the books found in the authoritative list.

While the Gospels represent an inclusive and flexible ethics, and the book of Revelation a fixed and immutable exclusive ethics, the variety of apostolic letters that form the center of the New Testament show an ethics mediating between these extremes. The letters are attributed to various early Christian leaders: Paul of Tarsus, Peter, John, and even an anonymous author in the case of Hebrews. They express concerns about Christian behavior and offer guidelines to direct that behavior. They provide instructions for private actions, interpersonal relationships, and liturgical forms. In this way, the letters do offer an exclusive ethics. They suggest criteria by which to recognize "authentic" Christian behavior and to reject people who prove to be "inauthentic."

At the same time, these letters are written to different communities facing distinctive problems and issues. The letters present differences in instruction (for example on the behavior of women in church) that reflect the occasions and audiences for which they were composed. This aspect of the letters recognizes diversity and allows for the inclusion of diverse actions depending on different situations. This approach uses the authority of past leaders to legitimate decisions in the present. Yet the use of such authority takes several forms. Any scriptures can be given a variety of interpretations. The letters, therefore, offer both instruction and the opportunity to derive new possibilities from that instruction. The author of 2 Peter, for example, bolsters the argument being made by stating, "So also our beloved brother Paul wrote to you according to the wisdom given him, speaking of this as he does in all his letters." The danger of such an appeal, however, leads the author to continue with this warning: "There are some things in them hard to understand which the ignorant and unstable twist to their own destruction, as they do the other scriptures" (2 Peter 3:15–16). This ethics suggests that even those who accept certain scriptures may not be part of the "true" community if they misinterpret those texts. This ethics allows certain variations and differences, but rejects others.

NEW TESTAMENT AS A RITUAL ENACTMENT

2 Peter 3:15–16 indicates one use of scriptures among early Christians: justification of ethical injunctions. A second use was liturgical: including texts during worship. When churches incorporated writings in their prayers, those texts took on special meaning and sanctity. By such liturgical usage, these texts verified their holiness and vouched for their place in the canon. The formation of the canon reflects the challenges faced by the church fathers, the name given leading figures in Christianity in the first several centuries C.E. These leaders decided on definitive criteria for canonicity. The books included must be from eyewitnesses to the Jesus event; in that way, the church fathers maintained continuity with the past and could limit the influence and undermine the authority of contemporary claimants to power such as Marcion. Second, the works must be popular within church rituals; liturgical practice can be as powerful as a pedigree reaching back to Jesus in authorizing books.

This liturgical practice helps explain why the Christians called their Bible the New Testament. Use of the phrase *New Testament* or *New Covenant* to describe what eventually became the Christian Scriptures represents an extension of meaning from a ritual confirming a contractual event to the book in which that ritual appears. The origin of the term *New Testament* is Jesus' action at the Last Supper (see Matthew 26:27–28 and Luke 22:14–20), an event memorialized thereafter in the Christian celebration called the Eucharist. The text describes Jesus sharing wine and declaring it his blood, sharing bread and declaring it his body. Whatever may have occurred at that time, later thinkers divide over their interpretation of what that ritual means when performed by Christians in imitation of Christ. The meaning and purpose of the ritual is ambiguous. Some versions of the text refer to this as a New Covenant (Luke 22:20). A new relationship between humanity and the divine has been created by Jesus' self-sacrifice. Other versions only refer to "my blood of the covenant which is poured out for the forgiveness of many" (Matthew 26:28). Even more significantly, some texts instruct the disciples to follow this ritual "in remembrance of me" (Luke 22:19), whereas others do not use this phrase. These differences lead to different views about the ritual of the New Covenant. Was it an act done once, and only once, that transformed reality on that one occasion, but that thereafter was only a symbol and a reminder celebrating what had happened in the past? Or was the New Covenant always being recreated, always being reenacted and reestablished, whenever Christians perform this ritual?

Some claim that every time the ritual occurs, the wine and bread actually become the blood and body of Christ. Through this reenactment of a primal event, the salvific effects of that event recur. Note that two sorts of transformation occur in this understanding of the ritual. In the first, the actual elements used in the ritual change. Physical properties of wine and bread become transformed. In the second, the relationship between the divine and the human is altered; divine mercy and forgiveness reach out and touch the participants of the ritual. Those who perform the ceremony are different after it than they were before; they are linked to the divine in a new way. They are also now part of an extended community, literally, the body of Christ.

A second view of the Christian ritual of sharing bread and wine is that it merely reminds worshipers of an event that occurred in history. Through enacting this ceremony, believers affirm that a new covenant has already been established, that God at a certain time entered into a new agreement with humanity. The various parts of the ritual become tangible symbols, bringing both the historical event of God's actions and the ontological nature of humanity in the world as a consequence of that event. Here again, two elements are present in the ritual. The first consists of the symbolic nature of the performance; the performance does not change reality but rather draws attention to it. The second arises from the use of material that has significance to believers, either as historical reminders or in conjunction with their daily life and experience. This aspect of ritual identifies members of a group and emphasizes communal solidarity.

The ritual significance of reading the Christian scriptures divides into the same two forms. The Bible, in one account, presents a New Covenant because it tells the story of how that covenant took shape. Reciting the narrative reaffirms the historical transformation that Christians associate with the career (birth, life, death, resurrection) of Jesus. Using the scriptures in this way functions as a reminder of the beliefs of the community. This ritual recitation celebrates ideas the community already holds and recommits the individual to belief in those ideas. From another perspective, however, the reading of the Bible not only reminds people of what occurred in the past, but it also revitalizes the power and experience of that past. God's presence (sometimes called the **Holy Spirit**) is understood to pervade the text. When thus engaged with the words of the Bible, Christians undergo an immediate change: they are reconnected to the divine in a direct way.

Why is liturgical usage a basis for canonization of a biblical text? First, such usage creates a common community. It establishes the beliefs and history that form the identity of membership in the group. Second, however, such usage provides a framework within which common experience takes place. It provides the opportunity for the creation of communal history. As a substantive ritual, such exposure to the Bible stimulates those changes by which outsiders become insiders.

SUMMARY QUESTIONS

1. What do the terms *testament* and *covenant* mean, and how does the idea of an "old" and "new" covenant indicate both continuity and discontinuity with the past?

2. What was the background of Jesus of Nazareth, and what is the significance of identifying him as "Christ" and the different ways he might be said to "fulfill" the Jewish Bible?

3. How does the Old Testament of the Protestants contrast with that of the Roman Catholics?

4. Why did early Christianity decide to canonize some books and reject others?

5. How is the term New Covenant used in the New Testament, and what ritual is associated with that New Covenant?

Four Suggested Essay Questions

1. Explain two ways in which a tradition may view history. Apply one of them to Jesus' relationship to the Hebrew Bible as expressed in Matthew 5:17–20 and the other to that expressed in Luke 24:28–49.

2. Explain two ways in which a tradition may view the supernatural. Apply one of them to the placement of the prophets in the Christian canon and the other to the view suggested by the Roman Catholic inclusion of the Apocrypha in its canon.

3. Explain two ways in which a tradition may view ethics. Apply one of them to the decision to include four Gospels in the Christian canon and the other to the view expressed in Revelation 22:18–19.

4. Explain two ways in which a tradition may view ritual. Apply one of them to the view that Jesus' Last Supper was a ritual of transformation that is repeated whenever Chris-

tians imitate it and one to the view that Christian performance of this ritual is merely in "remembrance" of what Jesus did.

Exercise

Read the following paragraph from an essay answering the third question:

> When the Church Fathers rejected Marcion's idea of a single Gospel in favor of including four different Gospels in their final New Testament canon, they expressed an inclusive ethics both for communities and individuals. One reason for including all four Gospels was because different churches were already using them in their liturgy. This expresses a willingness to allow variation in worship. Each of the four Gospels offers a different portrayal of Jesus. Matthew 5:17–23 imagines Jesus as a model who obeys every Jewish law. Luke 24:28–49 imagines Jesus as a model disclosing the hidden meaning of biblical texts. Including each of them legitimizes both models of Jesus as a religious ideal. Offering these different models indicates an ethics that accepts different and distinctive modes of religious living.

Now answer the following five questions:

1. How does the topic sentence prepare for the two parts of the paragraph that follow?
2. What general idea does the first reason for including all four Gospels illustrate?
3. What general idea does the second reason for including all four Gospels illustrate?
4. Why do you think the topic sentence mentions Marcion, even though he is not central to the entire paragraph? Would an exact quotation from Luke 24 or Matthew 5 be more useful than the paraphrase given here?

FOR FURTHER READING

The books listed below should be a point of departure for your future study. Each includes a bibliography that will guide you beyond its basic information.

1. Brown, Raymond Edward, *An Introduction to the New Testament* (New York: Doubleday, 1997).
2. Mack, Burton L., *Who Wrote the New Testament?: The Making of the Christian Myth* (San Francisco, CA: HarperSanFrancisco, 1995).
3. Metzger, Bruce Manning, *The Canon of the New Testament: Its Origin, Development, and Significance* (Oxford: Clarendon Press, 1987).
4. Theissen, Gerd, *Fortress Introduction to the New Testament* (Minneapolis, MN: Fortress, 2003).
5. Van de Sandt, Huub, *Didache: Its Jewish Source and Its Place in Early Judaism and Christianity* (Minneapolis, MN: Ausburg Fortress, 2002).

6. Wall, Robert W. and Eugene E. Lemcio, eds., *The New Testament As Canon: A Reader in Canonical Criticism* (Sheffield: JSOT Press, 1992).

4

Religions of the Torah

READING ASSIGNMENT

Genesis 1–11
Genesis 12, 15, 17, 20, 21
Exodus 20–23, Leviticus, 18–24; Deuteronomy, 4–6, 15–26

LEARNING OBJECTIVES

By the end of this lesson, you will be able to:
- Describe the different types of content found in the Pentateuch.
- Describe the different views of history found in the Pentateuch.
- Describe the different views of divinity found in the Pentateuch.
- Describe the different views of ethics and law found in the Pentateuch.
- Describe the different views of ritual found in the Pentateuch.

INTRODUCTION

This chapter examines the first five books of the Bible, the Pentateuch. The term *Torah* is broad and ambiguous. The first section of this chapter examines what it means in the context of the Pentateuch. Much of the Torah consists of historical narratives. The next sections take up these materials. The historical narratives often portray life differently from the facts as determined by archeology. Comparisons with other ancient Near Eastern materials illuminate what is distinctive about the writings of the Torah.

Interpretive Matrix for Chapter Four

View of the Divine: How people interact with God and the supernatural; how God interacts with the world.	View of History: How past, present, and future are related; who controls the shape of events.	View of Ethics: How people behave toward other people; how they behave toward people like themselves and to those who are different.	View of Ritual: How people behave toward the Divine; how they perform religious actions.
The Divine as Transcendent: God interacts with people only through a covenant made with leaders. God creates a stable and ordered world according to an unfolding divine plan.	*History as Continuous:* Events in the present grow out of promises from the past.	*Inclusive Ethics:* All members of society are responsible for the weakest members such as women, orphans, and the landless. Law enacts pragmatic rules appropriate for all people. The law applies to men, women, and all classes of people.	*Ritual as Transforming:* Ritual ensures personal or national prosperity. Ritual creates a covenant between a person and the divine.
The Divine as Immanent: God provides immediate answers to human prayers. God responds to human actions by either rewarding or punishing them. God creates by responding to the changing needs of the world.	*History as Discontinuous:* Events in the past dramatically changed the course of human experience.	*Exclusive Ethics:* God favors one group over all others. God makes special demands on a chosen people. Men and women and different classes of people are treated differently.	*Ritual as Symbolic:* Ritual gives thanks for prosperity already received. Ritual symbolizes an individual's relationship with God.

    Historical reviews often come embedded in ritual performances. Deuteronomy 26 offers an example of such a review and the ways in which history interacts with views of the divine, of ritual, and of ethics. The legal elements in the Torah require study by themselves. They may occur in narratives or as lists of regulations. Once again, understanding these rules depends on placing them in their context—in relationship to each other and to other ancient legal texts. Narration need not always take as its purpose the reporting of exact facts. Sometimes stories serve to communicate general ideas, approaches to reality, or social and cultural ideals. These types of tales are called "myth," not because they are untrue, but because they have a function over and beyond transmission of facts. The myths of the Torah stand in dialogue with those of other ancient Near Eastern cultures and can be read together with those other myths. Some anthropologists argue that ancient Near Eastern myths are

54   Chapter 4

closely linked to the rituals people followed. The same linkage may occur between the myths and rituals of the Torah.

SOME IMPORTANT TERMS

The following terms are important for this chapter. Some of them have been listed in previous chapters; in those cases the term is not **bold** in the main body of this chapter. The terms are also found in the Glossary.

Aaron	Hagar	Moses
Abel	Ham	Myth
Abraham	Hammurabi	Noah
Adah	Hyksos	Priest
Akhenaton	Inanna	Rachel
Akkadian	Isaac	Ras Shamra Tablets
Amarna Letters	Ishmael	Rebecca
Ammon	Ishtar	Sabbath
Apiru	Israel	Sarah
Assyria	Jacob	Semites
Baal	Jafet	Seth
Babel	Joseph	Shem
Babylonia	Lamech	Sinai
Cain	Leah	Sodom
Canaan	Levite	Syria
Circumcision	Lex Taliones	Tamar
Documentary Hypothesis	Lot	Utnapishtim
Exodus from Egypt	Marduk	YHWH
Egypt	Merneptah	Ziggurat
Enki	Mesha	Zillah
Enuma Elish	Mesopotamia	
Gilgamesh	Moab	

THE COMPOSITION OF THE TORAH

That the first five books of the Bible, called the Pentateuch, contain several "religions" may not come as a surprise. The "plot" of the narrative in those books (see Box 4–1) moves from the primal history of humanity (Genesis 1–11) through the experience of Abraham and his family (Genesis 12–50), culminating in the creation of an Israelite "people" (Exodus through Deuteronomy). Certainly each of these three stages might express a religious perspective of its own. The textual evidence, however, is more complicated. These three parts

> **BOX 4–1   THE CONTENT OF THE PENTATEUCH**
>
> This chart outlines the contents of the first five books of the Bible. It summarizes the narrative and legal contents book by book.
>
> *Genesis 1–11*   These chapters focus on primal history, describing the creation of the world and the beginnings of human civilization. The sources include material from a northern Israelite document (E), from a southern Judean document (J), and from a priestly document (P).
>
> *Genesis 12–50*   These chapter narrate the history of the founders of the people of Israel. It includes stories about important men such as Abraham, Isaac, Jacob, Judah, and Joseph as well as those about women whose actions were crucial in the developing of the Israelite ethnic group—Sarah, Rebecca, Rachel, Leah, Tamar. The latter is important since her story (Genesis 38) interrupts the narrative about Joseph (Genesis 37–50) and draws special attention to Judah and his descendants.
>
> *Exodus–Numbers*   As a narrative this section of the Pentateuch tells how the Israelites were enslaved in Egypt, how under the leadership of Moses they escaped that slavery and, after wandering in the wilderness, were brought to the edge of the land promised the early founders. As a collection of laws this section includes some striking legal codes that do not always agree with one another (see box 3–4 for an example of this).
>
> *Deuteronomy*   This final book of the Pentateuch narrates the death of Moses and reiterates both the histories and laws that have gone before. Biblical scholarship suggests that this section of the Pentateuch is the earliest document that became a code in ancient Israel.

of the Pentateuch are themselves composite works; they give evidence of several authors, of divergent viewpoints, of conflicting approaches.

Most scholars follow some variation of what has been called the **Documentary Hypothesis.** This theory, propounded in the nineteenth century by Julius Wellhausen, contends that the Pentateuch came into being when the people who finally called themselves "Jews," and related themselves to former traditions of groups called Israelites and Judeans, combined several different traditions—many of them already in written form—into a composite whole. Wellhausen's central claim, followed in this chapter, was that Deuteronomy came first. He associated Deuteronomy with Josiah's reformation in 621 B.C.E. (see Timeline 1.1). He concluded that other parts of the Pentateuch had been compiled from documents originating among the prophets in northern Israel, or Ephraim; he called those documents "E." Some other documents had been created in southern Israel or Judah; he called those documents "J." Still later documents had been produced by Israelite priests; he called those documents "P." Each of the documents possesses distinctive vocabularies, styles, and uses of God's name (see Box 4–2).

56 Chapter 4

> **BOX 4–2   THE DOCUMENTARY HYPOTHESIS**
>
> This chart summarizes the basic characteristics that the documentary hypothesis associates with the sources in the Pentateuch. While biblical scholarship has questioned and modified many details in that hypothesis, this analysis of the characteristics of the sources remains persuasive.
>
> *J (The Yahwist)*   This source is dated to about 950 B.C.E. and uses the name YHWH for God from the very beginning of human civilization. It portrays the divine as anthropomorphic. The story of the Garden of Eden comes from that source as does the motif of a promised land of great prosperity.
>
> *E (The Elohist)*   This source is associated with the northern part of Israel and uses the name Elohim for God until Exodus 3. It emphasizes divine transcendence—making prophetic intercession necessary. The source stresses ethics and principled laws.
>
> *D (The Deuteronomist)*   This source is associated first with Josiah and then with later Judean authors reflecting on the exile to Babylonia. It is identified with the book of Deuteronomy. It emphasizes Moses and Mosaic law, expressing an inclusive and humanitarian ethics. It alone demands centralized worship in Jerusalem.
>
> *P (The Priestly)*   The documentary hypothesis dates this source at the Babylonian exile, but many contemporary biblical scholars doubt that dating. This source sometimes uses the name "YHWH Elohim" in the early parts of Genesis, but more usually stresses just Elohim and introduces the name YHWH only in Exodus 6. It is characterized by an interest in genealogies, priestly ritual, and laws of purity and holiness. Aaron becomes a major figure in this source, sometimes even overshadowing Moses.

    The Hebrew name for the first five books is the Torah of Moses, or more simply, the Torah. That word translates as "teaching" or "guidance." Several verses in the Pentateuch refer to "Torah": the Torah of the priests, for example, refers to teachings specifically addressed to the Israelite sacrificial system (see Leviticus 6). Nevertheless, the first five books as a whole are thought to have a single "Torah"—a Torah associated with Moses the Lawgiver, the hero said to have led the Israelites out of Egypt and to the edge of their promised land. Tradition claims the Torah was written by Moses. Most contemporary scholars, however, consider it a composite work built out of oral traditions, ancient documents, and editorial additions. A clever saying suggests that these stories are not Mosaic (written by Moses) but are rather a mosaic (a composite of separate pieces). You need not trace each of these pieces back to its origins; nevertheless, scholars of religious studies do divide the text into many different documentary sources. Remember this as you encounter the vastly divergent stories within the book.

    The discipline of religious studies uses the supposition of documentary sources and comparison with the styles and concerns found among several different Ancient Near Eastern cultures to decode the meaning of the Pentateuch (see Box 4–3). One genre focuses on stories of ancient leaders. The history of these leaders does more than recall great people from the past; the tales evoke the nature of the group itself. How these narratives construe history

---

BOX 4–3   THE PENTATEUCH AND ANCIENT NEAR EASTERN CULTURES

This chart focuses on commonalities shared by the Pentateuch and other ancient Near Eastern documents. The document is named and its commonality described.

Merneptah Stele   This Egyptian victory stone erected about 1220 B.C.E., mentions Israel as an unsettled group of nomads. This view of the earliest Israelites reinforces some of the portraits given of figures such as Abraham, Isaac, or Jacob. The Hebrew Bible, however, makes no mention of a defeat by Mernephta.

Hymn to the Aton   This Egyptian hymn from the Pharaoh Amenhotep IV—otherwise known as Akhenhenaton (1375–1358 B.C.E.) expresses a transcendent view of the divine creator echoed in various biblical Psalms, Psalm 104 in particular.

Enuma Elish   This Akkadian myth, probably recited during a New Year ritual, exists only in texts of the first millennium B.C.E., nevertheless most scholars date its creation to the second millennium. It features a conflict between the gods that leads to the creation of humanity out of the blood of a rebel divinity and the building of a Ziggurat called BabEl as means of serving the divine. Many elements in Genesis share commonalities with this Mesopotamian myth of creation.

Epic of Gilgamesh   This legendary poem about a king of Uruk in Mesopotamia exists in many, often fragmentary, versions from as early as 3000 B.C.E.. It includes stories that resemble the Eden narrative and the biblical flood story.

Code of Hammurabi   This stone monument written in Akkadian was erected by Hammurabi, a king of Babylonia's First Dynasty (1728–1686 B.C.E.). It contains many laws similar to those found in the Hebrew Bible, including the so-called *Lex Taliones*. The context of those laws, however, often suggests a class system rejected by the Hebrew Bible.

Ras Shamra Tablets   These tablets from about 1600–1400 B.C.E. are written in Ugaritic—the ancient Canaanite language that eventually became the Hebrew language. The topics in these tablets include various references to the divine. Many titles given to Israel's God YHWH are anticipated in these tablets. Beyond that the idea of covenant—an agreement between the divine and the human—occurs in some of the writing.

Moabite Stone   This stele erected by Mesh of Moab (849–820 B.C.E.) reflects a theology very similar to that expressed by several biblical passages—national failure occurs when the nation's divinity has been angered; national prosperity occurs when the divinity acts favorably toward the people.

reflects how the authors understood the qualities of their present-day constituency. Sometimes these narratives include references to rituals and ethics. They do more, however, than justify or legitimate current practices. They introduce a view of continuity or discontinuity between the early history of the group and its current status.

Another genre is that of *covenant*—a combination of narrative and legal regulations found throughout the Ancient Near East, but associated especially with the peoples of Ugarit (ancient Canaan or Palestine). The Ugaritic material is drawn from the **Ras Shamra Tablets**. The Pentateuch contains several examples of covenant and covenant law, not all of them consistent with one another. Tracing the variations between these examples displays the distinctive religious approaches in the material composing the Pentateuch.

A third genre explores the category of **myth** as understood in religious studies. Many people misunderstand when scholars in religious studies label a story as a myth. Colloquially people use the term *myth* to refer to an untrue story, a false view of an event, or an inaccurate perception of reality. In the technical sense used by scholars in religious studies, however, the term *myth* lacks the pejorative overtones of common usage. In the discipline of religious studies, myth is defined as a narrative using literal and concrete language to convey abstract ideas about the world and human nature. The truth or falsity in a myth lies not in its literal meaning, but in the abstract idea it communicates.

The myths of the Bible often appear as stories explaining the origin of some cultural or religious phenomenon, such as the institution of marriage, various human handicrafts, and cultic shrines. Such tales (technically called etiologies) seem to demand a literal interpretation. Further reflection, however, raises questions about the intended meaning. One way to emphasize the continuing importance and enduring significance of an element in human experience is to trace its origin to antiquity. If a cultural practice has a pedigree reaching back to creation itself, then it must be a valuable and important part of human life. Biblical etiologies may intend to convey beliefs about the value of certain aspects of life, rather than to record factual events.

This book looks at biblical tales as examples of how people communicate ideas about the world, rather than as descriptions of how the empirical world operates. Scholars of religious studies consider the stories people tell about the creation of the world, about the history of humanity, and about their own origins extremely important. They see these stories as ways people express their views about the nature of human life, the values that should govern that life, and the patterns that govern history and nature. Determining whether those stories are factually accurate is less important than determining the ideas they are meant to convey.

Some people today argue whether the biblical descriptions of creation, of ancient history, or of the natural world are historically correct. While this may well be an important exercise, it is not one with which this book deals. This book looks at such biblical material and seeks to determine how that material communicates particular approaches to reality. Calling the Torah a book of myths means that it contains stories we will study as expressions of ideas, rather than as claims about empirical reality.

Finally, the Torah contains several law codes. Look carefully at the leadership groups involved. The type of leader called a **priest** is prominent in many of the codes. How priests act and who can act as a priest are important ritual questions. Other laws speak of "judges," or "elders," or "kings." You will note that these codes do not always agree with each other, particularly because they have different views of leadership and authority. No single code contains all the laws that Jews today consider binding. The law codes in the Torah resemble the codes of other ancient Near Eastern cultures, and that resemblance helps in understanding the meaning of the biblical texts.

ISRAEL'S HISTORY AND ITS IMPLICATIONS

The stories about Israel's early leaders indicate its relationship to other ancient Near Eastern cultures. The following sketch of Israel's descriptive history demonstrates its self-image. The nation considered itself a foreign unit in **Canaan**, its promised land, the land now thought of as the Land of Israel. The Israelites, however, were a conglomerate group composed of elements influenced by the other ancient Near Eastern cultures. Its identity had evolved through combining the history of many groups into a story about a single sociopolitical entity.

The earliest narratives about Israel in the Bible are represented by stories found in the Torah, from Genesis 12 through the end of Deuteronomy (see Box 4–1). These stories draw on folk memories. Generation after generation passed down traditions about the ancestors as part of the nation's cultural legacy. By the final stage, the stories about primal times served to authenticate later institutions. Association with Israelite leaders justified ancient shrines that, according to modern archeologists, come from a pre-Israelite period. Stories about such early figures as **Abraham**, **Sarah**, **Isaac**, **Rebecca**, **Jacob**, **Rachel**, **Leah**, **Tamar**, **Joseph**, Moses, and **Aaron** reflect tribal memories that have been given the shape of historical narratives. Abraham is the key figure in expressing these memories.

The early stories focus on a figure called at first Abram and then Abraham. No external evidence testifies to his existence, so his status as founder of the Hebrew people must be considered putative—assumed but unproven. According to the tale, he came from **Mesopotamia**, stayed in **Syria**, wandered into Egypt, and settled in Canaan (see Genesis 12). Abraham married Sarah, said to be his close relative. When she seemed barren, he took her Egyptian handmaid, **Hagar** as a wife. With her he had a son, **Ishmael** who is said to be the progenitor of the Arabs. In this way, the Israelites see themselves connected to Egypt and the Ishmaelites.

The story also suggests that Hagar and Ishmael were eventually alienated from Abraham (Genesis 16 and 21). Another set of stories link Abraham with **Lot,** said to be his nephew. The two travel together from Mesopotamia to Aram, and from there to Canaan. While Abraham settles in Canaan, Lot goes to **Sodom** to live. When Sodom is eventually destroyed, Lot flees to a cave, and his daughters commit incest with him in order to propagate

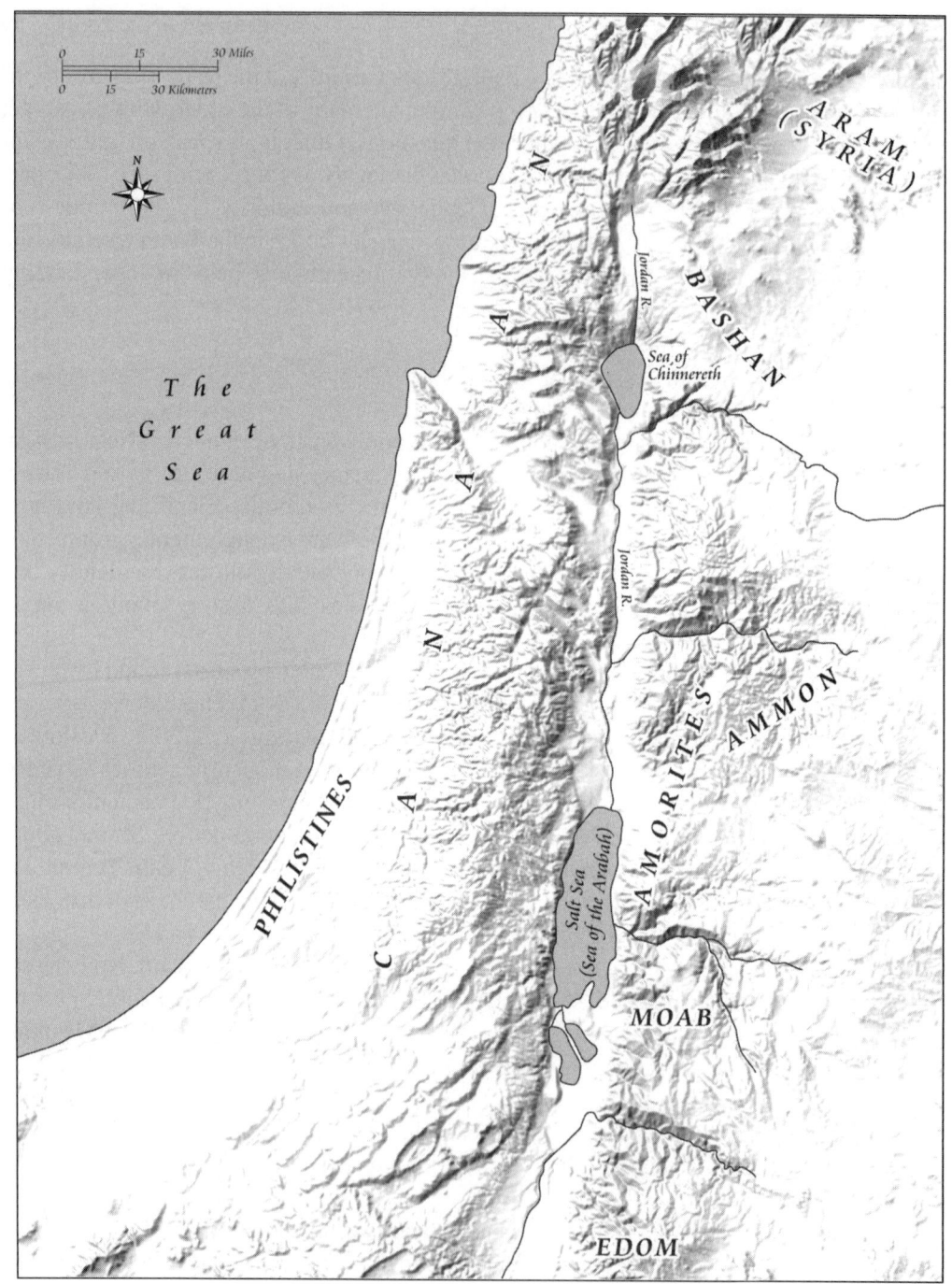

Map 4–1　The land of Canaan

their lineage. From this incestuous relationship came **Moab** and **Ammon**—two rival nations with whom the Israelites continually struggled. While these legendary stories may be creations of later authors, they do show that the biblical writers connected Israelite culture with the major centers of civilization in the ancient Near East. As noted in the previous chapter, these stories tend to reflect an ancient Near Eastern milieu. Some of these leaders founded cultic sites; others are associated with tribal leadership; still others are described because they teach lessons about human nature or human behavior.

Not only Abraham's itinerary but also his designation "Hebrew" may reflect that ancient culture. The term may well derive from the word **Apiru**, which describes a certain type of landless social group often employed by the Egyptians for military maneuvers. This connection with Egypt plays an important role in the biblical story of Moses. According to this story, the Israelites rose to power in Egypt, were enslaved, and finally escaped under their leader Moses. This Exodus from Egypt shares many narrative details with the experience of a wave of Semitic invaders, the **Hyksos**. It is impossible to identify the ancient Israelites with the historical Hyksos, just as a simple identification of Hebrews and Apiru is unlikely.

The Bible uses the term Israel in several ways. The name refers to a religious group, a political nation, and one segment of a divided nation. This multiple usage recognizes the composite nature of ancient Israel and the way the Bible created a single history by combining once-separate stories. Originally, the name *Israel* apparently developed independently of the national group that eventually composed the Hebrew Bible. The Egyptian ruler Pharaoh Merneptah wrote in 1220 B.C.E. that he had conquered that group. Hundreds of years pass before the archeological record sees that name again.

In this inscription, Mernephtah claims to have destroyed Israel in 1200 B.C.E.—and the name does not reappear in ancient texts for hundreds of years.

When it surfaces again, it is associated with a specific kingdom in the north of what once was called Canaan. The term is used in writings from Moab, **Assyria**, and Babylonia in ways that show it cannot be identified with the group that Merneptah defeated. The Hebrew Bible invents a genealogy for the name not substantiated by archeological data. It associates the name with a particular founder of later Israelite culture. That leader receives the name Jacob in most early texts. Only late in the story does the hero win the name Israel, interpreted as "one who struggles with God," although most interpreters today think it originally meant something like "God is my ruler" (see Genesis 32:28). Many scholars believe that the change of name reflects the combination of several stories into a single tradition. These stories convey Israel's belief that it had an evolving, changing, and developing identity. It testifies to a will for continuity combined with a recognition of change

VIEWS OF HISTORY, RITUAL, THE SUPERNATURAL, AND ETHICS

Deuteronomy 26 offers a singular example of the composite nature of the Pentateuch, its complex blend of different religious perspectives, and its views of history. Wellhausen astutely looked to Deuteronomy first when establishing his documentary hypothesis. Certainly Deuteronomy illustrates how originally separate strands of narrative were woven into a complex whole. Analyzing Deuteronomy 26 and its distinctive sections shows both the composite nature of the Torah and the way a religious studies approach might seek to understand it. This analysis will take the biblical narrative itself as a clue about when to investigate views of history, of the divine, of ethics, or of ritual.

vv. 1–4: These introductory verses focus on the ritual of offering some of the first fruits of the harvest to God as a way of acknowledging that God has promised the ancestors entrance into a promised land. This suggests a history of continuity that leads into verses 12–15.

vv. 5–11: These verses apparently sketch a second ritual proclamation. Most scholars think that they come from an *alternative* ritual proclamation to that in the opening verses. Notice that while in v. 4 the priest has already set down the basket, here in v. 10 the basket is once again "set down before the Lord." In this proclamation, discontinuity rather than continuity is stressed. This story stresses the unexpectedness of having descendants of a wandering Aramean (this is clearly *not* Abraham) and a group of slaves inherit a land flowing with milk and honey. While the God of the ancestors is mentioned, no promise to the ancestors is mentioned. The story suggests that the Israelites did not see themselves as having an ancient claim to the land of Israel; it therefore emphasizes discontinuity. God is identified as "the deity of the ancestors" who provides agricultural prosperity and who pities the oppressed. This belief suggests that people experience success as an unexpected gift; they see the world as unpredictable.

Two rituals occur here. First, there is an offering of produce, which an individual makes in a local shrine as a sign of gratitude and is presided over by a local priest. (You need not worry about the names given to the priests; the **Levites** are a type of priests who are scattered around the country and have no landholdings of their own.) Second, there is a public recitation of national history, which, written in the first person plural, declares the individual's self-identification with the entire people of Israel. Both are celebratory rituals. These verses include no specific ethical regulations, but do imply that Israel's history and practice are distinctive, thus suggesting an exclusivist ethics.

vv. 12–15: These verses include only one "story" reference—that God promised the "ancestors" a land flowing with milk and honey—which emphasizes a sense of continuity with the past. What is interesting here is that the promise does not appear to be unconditional. The verses include a prayer testifying that since this worshiper has kept his part of the bargain, God should do likewise. The story sets up the preconditions for this ritual but does not assure its success. Here God's personality becomes more a focus than in the earlier verses. God's blessings are not arbitrary, but are based on what an individual does. Even so, the individual cannot be sure of what will happen. The world, in these verses, appears as slightly unpredictable; events usually display a predictable pattern of reward and punishment, but that pattern is not always clearly evident.

Whereas the rituals in vv. 1–11 expressed gratitude for blessings already received, the rituals in this section are performed *to attain future blessings*. Two sorts of rituals are prescribed. First, the individual must observe both positive and negative rules for remaining in a state of "purity." Such purity does not refer to keeping free from germs or microbes; it refers to practicing personal ritual actions. Second, the verses include a public prayer focused on the welfare of the nation. Not only must the individual perform certain personal functions, but must also recite a petition on behalf of the nation as a whole. These rituals appear substantive rather than merely celebratory.

The individual's obligations extend beyond offerings to the divine to include supporting other people. The Levites, widows, orphans, and strangers have one thing in common: they all possess no land. In ancient Israel, all land was held by family inheritance; theoretically, there was no unencumbered land. Men inherit land from their fathers. Women are supported either by their parents or, after marriage, by their husbands. Children are supported by their father. Widows and orphans, then, have no source of sustenance. Levites, as mentioned before, are unlanded priests. Strangers who come from other places have no inherited land in their new settlements. A person living in an agrarian society cannot subsist without land. The ethics involved here requires supporting those people who have no ordinary means of providing for themselves. By mentioning the stranger, this ethics broadens its involvement to become inclusive.

vv. 16–19: The story in these verses is that of covenant-making. The story begins "on this day" and refers to the commandments that define Israel as a "holy" people. These laws are, technically, the details of a covenant, an agreement by which two parties are related to each other. In this case, the two parties are God and the people of Israel. As a legend, this story justifies the discontinuity between Israel's political laws and those that had governed the people previously. Unlike vv. 1–11, the legend claims that Israel became a nation because it accepted a divine law code, not because it came out of slavery in Egypt. God in this section, unlike in the previous verses, does not seem to have had a historical relationship with Israel. God becomes the national deity only through the event of covenant making. This suggests that reality depends upon social or political construction.

Unlike the previous verses, this section includes no specific rules for ritual behavior but rather a broad injunction to follow *all* the regulations implied by the event of God's making a covenant with the people. The laws, however, can be construed as a substantive ritualism, which, by creating a common national character, strengthens the bonds of community throughout the nation.

As in the case of ritual, here too no specific rules are included, since the broad category of covenantal obedience covers actions toward other people no less than actions toward God. This is an exclusivist ethic that emphasizes Israel's peculiar national character.

HISTORY AND RITUAL: THE STORIES OF ABRAHAM

The story of Abraham offers a paradigm case of how historical narratives create a composite figure. In some stories (Genesis 12, 14, 16, 21, for example), Abraham is a tribal patriarch, leading his family through difficult times and even acting as the military leader of an armed unit that defends Sodom. In other stories (Genesis 18–20, for example), Abraham acts more like a prophetic seer who intercedes on behalf of the needy, who argues with the divinity, and who has a particular concern for ethics. Still other stories (Genesis 15, 17, 22, for example) portray Abraham as a priestly figure who inaugurates sacrificial rituals and performs special priestly tasks.

The rituals involved are particularly important for our discussion. Genesis 15 is transformative. Abraham undergoes a visionary experience, after which God enters into covenant with him. Analysis of the stories about Abraham show how the same figure sometimes exhibits ritual celebration—affirming an already existing reality—and sometimes ritual transformation—seeking to change the nature of reality.

Genesis 17 traces the ritual of **circumcision** back to Abraham. This ritual consists of removing the male foreskin as an initiatory rite; Genesis 17 commands it to be done when a male infant is eight days old. As Genesis 17 describes it, the ritual is celebratory. Abraham's covenant with God and his change of name occur *before* any ritual takes place. Its performance is a *sign* of the covenant between God and Abraham. The ritual act does not *create* the agreement, but merely symbolizes it. The ritual of circumcision here contrasts to its portrayal in either Exodus 4 or Joshua 5. In Exodus 4, God attacks Moses as he returns to his people because he (or his son) is not circumcised. The mark indicates that a person has become a member of the covenanted community and is thereby protected by the divinity. The ritual is transformative both because it initiates a person into the group and because it protects a person

Religions of the Torah 65

from divine attack. Although a physical change takes place—the actual body of the person undergoing the ritual is altered—the central aspect of the ritual is less physical than relational; the person now has a new relationship to God and to the Israelite people. In Joshua 5, the people are instructed that only circumcised males may partake of the Passover celebration. In order to be transformed and made worthy to celebrate that ritual, all the men undergo a mass act of circumcision. Genesis 17 differs from Exodus 4 and Joshua 5 because, while it points to the covenant, it neither initiates it, as in Exodus, nor is a condition for it, as in Joshua.

Finally, the ritual in Genesis 22 is particularly extraordinary. It looks as if it were transformative. God is testing Abraham to see if the ritual will be carried out correctly. In fact, eventually Abraham learns that ritual is irrelevant, that God demands only loyalty, not actual ritual actions. In these stories, Abraham also exemplifies alternative ethical approaches. On the one hand, he often separates himself from those around him and from his environment; this represents an ethics of exclusivism. On the other hand, he enters into agreements with his neighbors and acts in defense of his friends and allies, exemplifying an ethics of involvement.

COVENANT AND ETHICS IN THE PENTATEUCH

The Abraham stories illustrate how much of the Pentateuch orients its narratives and concerns to the welfare of the nation. Perhaps the most important ethical concept defining both the distinctiveness of the nation and its relationship to others is that of covenant. The terms refer to an agreement, a negotiated contract, most often among human beings, but frequently also including a divinity either to enforce the agreement or as a partner to it. Both the idea of covenant and the ethical theory and moral rules flowing from it are not unique to the Bible. (Throughout this section of the chapter you may want to refer to Box 4–3 on page 57 to note the dates and content of the ancient Near Eastern texts discussed.)

One such text, the Moabite stone, erected by King **Mesha** of Moab, Israel's neighbor, shows the similarity between biblical thought and that of other nations of the Ancient Near East. That stone expresses Mesha's faith in Chemosh, the God of Moab, and is very similar to the Israelite faith in **YHWH**. These letters represent the "ineffable" divine name—that is, the name used in the Hebrew Bible for God, but which later Jews considered too sacred to pronounce. The monument describes how Chemosh, being angry with Moab, delivered the nation into the hands of its rival Israel and how, when pacified, restored his people to independence. Several biblical passages interpret Israel's national history as reflecting the changing will of YHWH, the nation's deity. When good things occur, it is because God is pleased. When bad things occur, it is because God is angry. The typical ancient Near Eastern theology projects the idea of a comprehensible historical order. The Bible often applies this theology to its understanding of events in Israel's history.

Several biblical stories emphasize in prescriptive and descriptive ways the importance of obedience to covenantal regulations. Genesis 6–9, for example, describes a great

This inscription by King Mesha of Moab in the ninth century before the Common Era describes the Moabite God Chemosh with the same attributes that Deuteronomy ascribes to Israel's God YHWH.

flood—its causes, its survivors, and its aftermath. According to the tale, the deity becomes angry at the evil humanity causes in the world. In response, God determines to destroy all creation except for one family, that of **Noah.** Noah not only survives, but also enables the rest of creation to survive as well. The story culminates in the offering of a sacrifice; Noah and his children praise God by slaughtering animals and burning them on an altar. God heeds the sacrifice and makes an agreement, a covenant, with humanity. The rainbow appears in the sky as the sign of that covenant. God will never again destroy the world because of human evil; humanity, on its part, must establish courts of law. As God governs the world through covenant, so humanity must imitate the divine and establish covenants among itself.

The various elements in that story go back to ancient Near Eastern sources. The Mesopotamian tale of **Gilgamesh** presents the exploits of a great semi-divine being. This hero battles giants and tames a savage man by sending him a prostitute and teaching him to eat cooked meat. The epic's rendition of the flood narrative takes as its context rivalry among the gods. The gods become annoyed because humanity is making too much noise and they cannot sleep. The god **Enki**, however, likes humanity and by subterfuge warns one human being of the impending disaster. After the flood, the gods become hungry and lament the loss of the sacrifices that humanity had given them. At that point, **Utnapishtim** (the name of the survivor of the flood) offers a sacrifice. The gods "hover like flies around the sweet scent of the offering." In gratitude, **Innanna** (or, in a Babylonian version, **Ishtar**), a beautiful and merciful goddess, thrusts her lapis lazuli necklace into the sky, creating the blue expanse as a sign of recognition that the gods need and depend upon their human servants despite their contentiousness.

In terms of ritual, ethics, and belief about the world, this story presents some interesting parallels to the biblical flood narrative. Both stories picture divine beings who interfere with human life. The world appears filled with conflict and unpredictable events. Both stories portray ritual actions that bind the human and the divine: the ritual of sacrifice occurs in both tales, as does the heavenly sign of reconciliation. Nevertheless, there are significant differences. The biblical story emphasizes ethical and moral behavior as the basis for divine anger and uses covenant as an ethical contract that humanity must emulate. Covenant, a theory not found in Babylonian materials, derives from a nearer tradition to the Israelites, that of the Canaanites, known from their chief city Ugarit. Adapting the idea of covenant shows how the Israelites pursued an ethics that emphasizes assimilation to many different cultural traditions.

Ugaritic mythology focuses on the development of civilization, agriculture, and politics. The stories told in Canaan emphasize how the gods warred to control the world, in particular their heroic deity **Baal** (the word means Master). In one story, Baal seeks to build a Temple but must first appeal to the assembly of the gods. The god **Marduk** gives him permission to construct the palace, but an argument ensues about whether to build a window in this palace. The building of the window brings catastrophes. Those who quibble about details, who overlook the tenuous nature of their social contract, and who seek legal loopholes bring tragedy not only to themselves, but also to society as a whole. This story seems to parallel the cultural life of little Canaan, where conquering peoples and imperial neighbors dominate the natives. The Canaanites protect themselves by making legal contracts (covenants) and agreements with these neighbors. The covenantal theme in the Bible reflects the Ugaritic myths of covenants made among the gods and between gods and people.

Biblical stories about human rivalries and about the development of civilization seem to echo these myths. This type of myth emphasizes both ritual and ethics and focuses on the specific deeds that humanity can perform to bring order and meaning to a chaotic world. The Noahide covenant exemplifies such an attempt to give meaning to the world. A more pessimistic view, still influenced by ancient Near Eastern stories, occurs in the tale of the Tower of Babel in Genesis 11. There the Mesopotamian symbol of the link between the divine and the human, the circular tower or **Ziggurat**, becomes the symbol of human failure to abide by covenantal ethics.

Such symbolism is ironic, because Mesopotamian models for law and ethics underlie much of the biblical material. The stories of covenants with early heroes such as Noah, Abraham, and Moses move into specific legal codes that reflect the influence of earlier similar codes. Ancient Near Eastern literature commonly justifies national regulations as divine

This relief from the eighteenth century B.C.E. shows Hammurabi, Babylonia's king, receiving his law code from Shamash, the solar deity.

revelation. Archeologists have unearthed law codes such as those of **Hammurabi** (1728–1686 B.C.E.) or customary laws such as those in the **Amarna letters** (1300–1200 B.C.E.) that root social legislation in a divine revelation. The law code of Hammurabi, for example, bears considerable resemblance to the codes found in the Bible. One of the most striking parallels occurs between Hammurabi's code and the Mosaic law. Both are said to have been delivered to a human being through the divine. Moses ascended Mount **Sinai** (sometimes called Horeb) to receive God's law. While there he experiences a theophany—a divine appearance. At God's instructions, he takes the laws "written by the finger of God" (Exodus 24:12, 31:18, 32:15–16) given at Sinai. Hammurabi also legitimates his law code by claiming to have received it from the god of justice, the sun deity Shamash. This divine origin of the law and the need for a human intermediary justifies Hammurabi's role as lawgiver.

Hammurabi, like the biblical Moses, was a leader seeking to organize a diverse society. Moses, like Hammurabi, seeks to establish evenhanded justice through the lex talionis, the law of exact recompense (an eye for an eye). Both codes claim that their laws are given by a supernatural being for the good of a particular nation. The ethics here is pragmatic: what works is what is good. The moral nation follows the rules given by its deity and thereby succeeds; the immoral nation disobeys these rules and thereby fails. Scholars also think that both Hammurabi's code and the biblical laws were ideal models, rather than representatives of the actual legal practices of their times. While the Bible includes several different examples of covenants (which will be analyzed below), they share the general structure and intention of Hammurabi's code. This shows that the biblical covenant codes accept the general ethics of their time. They assimilate the basic features of the morality practiced in the ancient

Near East. Here the covenantal form represents an inclusive ethics, one that affirms the general approaches of the context in which the Bible takes shape.

Together with the covenant form, the Bible includes the legal formulations that usually accompanied ancient Near Eastern covenant treaties. What is extraordinary in the biblical corpus, however, is the presentation of more than one set of laws. The Bible includes several variations in the law codes it presents. Three important examples (Exodus 21–24, Deuteronomy 15–24, and Leviticus 17–23) illustrate the ethical implications of that difference. Contrasting the laws of slavery in Exodus 21 to those in Deuteronomy 15 reveals one sort of difference in ethics. Exodus 21 seeks to maintain the social order and its hierarchic structure. Female slaves are treated differently from male slaves. Gender distinctions are considered essential and shape the laws governing behavior. Slaves when freed are expected to fend for themselves; they do not change their social status, only their indentured obligations. Deuteronomy 15 provides a more egalitarian approach. In that text, male and female slaves are freed in exactly the same way; there is no gender distinction in the law. Also, Deuteronomic law provides for the needs of the freed slave. Everything needed to start afresh and become an equal member of society is given with manumission. The laws in Exodus represent an ethics of exclusion—through social status and through gender. The laws of Deuteronomy represent an ethics of inclusion—bringing together different genders and social classes into a single category of law.

Another set of differences becomes evident when comparing the Lex Taliones in each of the law codes. Exodus 21:22–25 brings up this maxim only in connection with injury to a pregnant woman. The situation described involves a pregnant woman who suffers harm to her fetus when caught up in a fight between two others. The text suggests that while injury to the woman herself should require compensation—eye for eye, tooth for tooth, limb for limb—injury to a fetus only requires that compensation be given to the father. The point seems to be, once again, that of making distinctions between classes, in this case between a "human being"—the mother—and that of an unborn child who is not considered a human being yet.

Deuteronomy 19:16–21 uses this maxim for a different purpose. Those verses apply it only to the case of someone who gives false witness. Such malicious testimony is to be punished by like for like; what the lying parties sought to be done to their victim should be done to them. Here, as in the earlier case, the emphasis seems to be on a broad universalism, an inclusive ethics. No matter what the status, gender, or concerns of the false witnesses, they should suffer the penalty they had attempted to perpetrate on others.

Leviticus 24:18–22 employs this maxim to make two points. The first is that the Lex Taliones should be applied only to cases in which humans have been injured; injury to animals requires a different sort of compensation. The second is that this law applies equally to citizens and to non-citizens. That evenhandedness also appears in Leviticus 19 in a set of verses that are often incorrectly separated from each other. Leviticus 19:18 declares: "You shall love your neighbor as yourself," and Leviticus 19:34 adds: "You shall love the stranger

> **BOX 4–4   VERSIONS OF THE *LEX TALIONES***
>
> This chart shows different versions of the law of "limb for limb." It begins with the version of that law found in Hammurabi's code and then turns to the different versions in the Hebrew Bible.
>
> ***Code of Hammurabi 196–201***   If a lord has destroyed the eye of another member of the aristocracy, they shall destroy his eye. If he has broken another lord's bone, they shall break his bone. If he has destroyed the eye of a commoner or broken the bone of a commoner, he shall pay one mina of silver. If he has destroyed the eye of a lord's slave or broken the bone of a lord's slave, he shall pay one-half his value.
>
> ***Exodus 21:22–25***   When people who are fighting injure a pregnant woman so that there is a miscarriage and yet no further harm follows, the one responsible shall be fined what the woman's husband demands as the judges determine. If any harm follows, then you shall give life for life, eye for eye, tooth for tooth, hand for hand, foot for foot, burn for burn, wound for wound, stripe for stripe.
>
> ***Deuteronomy 19:16–21***   If a false witness comes forward to accuse someone of wrongdoing, then both parties shall appear before the Lord, before the priests and judges then in office, and the judges shall make a thorough inquiry. If the witness is a false witness, having testified falsely against another, then you shall do to the false witness just as the false witness had meant to do to the other. So you shall purge the evil from your midst. The rest shall hear and be afraid, and a crime such as this shall never be committed among you. Show no pity: life for life, eye for eye, tooth for tooth, hand for hand, foot for foot.
>
> ***Leviticus 24:17–21***   Anyone who kills a human being shall be put to death. Anyone who kills an animal shall make restitution for it, life for life. Anyone who maims another shall suffer the same injury in return: fracture for fracture, eye for eye, tooth for tooth; the injury inflicted is the injury to be suffered. One who kills an animal shall make restitution for it; but one who kills a human being shall be put to death.

as yourself." This equality arises from the all-encompassing humanism of the Levitical code. Not only are animals and humans treated differently from each other; the different treatment of humanity applies not only to citizens, to neighbors, to those who are like you, but also to strangers, to all human beings. The three different law codes examined here, then, imply different views of the inclusive or exclusive nature of society.

MYTH IN THE BIBLE AND THE ANCIENT NEAR EAST

The Bible shares its mythology as well as its law codes with much of the ancient Near East. Ancient Near Eastern mythology presents a complex and ambivalent picture of nature and human relationships and of the meaning of ritual. Egyptian creation stories suggest order, the power of the word, predictability, and cosmic peace. Perhaps the most famous example of such a view is that attributed to the Pharaoh **Akhenaton**, who reformed worship in Egypt under a single deity, Aton-Re, God of the Sun (for his dates, see Box 4–2). This monotheistic religion emphasized the unity of all things and the order of nature by tracing creation back to a single deity. The Pharaoh made the worship of that deity the central ritual of his religion.

An associated ritual, the hymn to the sun god, reveals the ideas of this religion (see Box 4–5). The hymn pictures the sun god as the source of all life, the nurturing deity of all creatures, above the entire creation. This god, however, seeks a place to stand, a footstool, and therefore establishes the primal mountain. Priests at that mountain perform rituals exalting the sun god and promulgate the eternal laws the deity gave at the beginning of creation. This story evokes a world unchanged and unchanging since primal times. Order and predictability mark the deity's actions, the priestly order, and the pattern of natural and social life.

While the world view of the Egyptians emphasizes order and predictability, Mesopotamian myths portray conflict among the gods, among human beings, between the sexes, and within the various trades and national interests of civilization. Mesopotamian tales of fratricide, of female trickery, and of the tragedy of human mortality spring from this source. The **Enuma Elish**, an **Akkadian** hymn of creation, describes creation as part of a

---

BOX 4–5 VERSIONS OF A CREATION HYMN

This chart shows the similarities between the monotheism of Akhenaton's monotheistic revolution in Egypt and Psalm 104 in the Hebrew Bible. While some of the language is strikingly similar, the common theology is even more evident. Both texts think of a single divinity as responsible for all life on earth and see that divinity as immanent in the world maintaining and sustaining it.

Hymn to the Aton (Akhenaton—Amenhotep IV, 1375–1358 B.C.E.) Creator ...who givest breath to sustain all that he has made. When the child descends from the womb to breathe, on the day when he is born, thou openest his mouth completely, thou suppliest his necessities. When the chick in the egg speaks within the shell, thou givest him breath within it to maintain him... How manifold it is what thou hast made... Thou didst create the world according to thy desire, whilst thou were alone: all men, cattle, and wild beasts...

Psalm 104:24, 27–30   O Lord, how manifold are your works. In wisdom you have made them all; the earth is full of your creatures... These all look to you to give them their food in due season; when you give it to them, they gather it up; when you open your hand, they are filled with good things. When you hide your face, they are dismayed; when you take away their breath, they die and return to their dust. When you send forth your spirit, they are created, and you renew the face of the ground.

great war between the gods. After the mother goddess Tiamat creates the world and takes as her consort the God Kingu, the other gods grow restless. They resent the power of the mother goddess and rebel against her, choosing as their champion the God Marduk. Marduk wages a successful battle against the goddess and slays her, creating the world out of her body. He then decides that the gods need a Temple and worshipers. Out of the blood of the rebel god Kingu, he creates "savage man" to be the servant of the gods. As a token of their servitude, the human beings are to bring sacrifices before the gods at the great tower that links heaven and earth—the tower at **Babel**. The very name suggests its religious function (Bab = gate; El = God) as the gateway to the divine, the means by which rebellious humanity discovers its true purpose—obedience to divine beings. The shape of this tower, called a ziggurat, served as a basic ritual symbol throughout the ancient Near East.

MYTH IN GENESIS

Genesis 1–11 includes elements from each of these traditions. One set of materials seems to reflect the Egyptian motif of order and meaning. Genesis 1:1–2:4a (the first part of verse 4) portrays everything as created according to a clear divine plan. As the plan unfolds, the deity punctuates the process of creation with a pronouncement on its goodness. The creation of humanity, no less than of the rest of the world, displays order, goodness, and value. God takes the initiative and creates humanity—male and female at the same time. Humanity is to the world what God is to all creation: the rule or guide organizing natural life.

The development of the mythic narrative goes from the simpler to the more complex. The story begins with a simple dualism: light and dark. Creative act after creative act unfolds greater complexity, introducing one set of polarities after another (land and sea, sky and earth, flying and creeping things). Creatures of the sky seem to alternate with creatures of the earth. Eventually, an intricate pattern of creatures emerges as the perfected ideal of divine intention.

Humans are among the last creatures developed. The narrative portrays humanity as a complex creation that mirrors in itself everything else. God is reported as saying, "Let us make humanity in our image, according to our likeness; and let them be a ruler for the fish of the sea and over the birds of the air and over the cattle and over all the wild animals of the earth, and over every creeping thing that creeps upon earth" (Genesis 1:26). Both men and women are to serve this purpose. Later genealogies in Genesis 5 and 10 refer to this "image of God" and its presence in all human beings.

What point does this author make by emphasizing the joint rulership that males and females have over the world? The term *rule* ("mashal" in Hebrew) in this verse has been taken to mean governance and power. Other contexts in which it is used suggest different meanings. Sometimes the word indicates the standard or model against which everything else is evaluated. If that meaning is attributed to the word in this verse, then human beings are said to "rule" the rest of creation in the sense in which a yardstick rules or measures everything. The idea seems similar to that attributed to the Greek philosopher Protagoras: "Man is the measure of all things." The purpose and value of every created thing depends upon its relationship to humanity.

If creation is measured by humanity, then how is humanity measured? The creation myth culminates with God blessing the seventh day, a day on which God ceases labor. On the seventh day, everything works as it should, and God enjoys a rest. God stops, but the world goes on. This implies that the Sabbath is the measure of humanity. If the world works perfectly, if everything within creation flows naturally and harmoniously, then humanity has "measured up" to God's intentions.

The story in Genesis 1:1–2:4 envisions life as ordered, meaningful, and predictable. By conveying belief in a deity controlling all things according to a beneficent plan, this story evokes a positive attitude toward existence. This optimistic approach to life finds expression in other parts of Genesis as well. The divine image, for example, continues through several generations, as the genealogies in Genesis 5 and 10 imply. These genealogies portray a constant transmission of the "image of God" through human generations. The reiteration of the divine intention for human life culminates in the selection of Abraham (Genesis 11).

Beginning in Genesis 2:4b (the second half of verse 4), however, a contrasting tale of the beginnings of the world and humanity unfolds. This creation story begins with an unproductive garden, since agriculture apparently depends on human work. God then experimentally creates a male human being (the Hebrew word is Adam). Because that human being seems lonely, God experiments to find him a partner. One after another, God creates the animals and brings them to the man. The man names each of them but does not consider any a fit partner. Finally, God puts the man to sleep and, from his rib, makes a female. The man names her "woman." The text comments that, since woman was taken from man, a man leaves his parents, following his woman and cleaving to her. The process described shows how the sexual drive, here taken as a drive to discover one's original mate, impels men to abandon their ancestral families to chase after females.

The story does not end happily here. Instead, tragedy occurs. God instructs the man that he could eat from all the trees in the garden except two: the tree of the knowledge of good and evil and the tree of life. He would die the very day that he ate the forbidden fruit, according to the divine warning (Genesis 2:17). Oddly, the tale mentions man's obligations towards agriculture but leaves his relationship with animals unexplained. That relationship eventually leads to disaster.

The author introduces a new character, the snake (called "arum" in Hebrew, a word with the basic meaning of "naked" and an extended meaning of "clever"). The snake is both most exposed and most subtle. This character works to destroy human happiness. The story gives no motivation for his act, but it describes how the snake persuades the woman to eat of the forbidden fruit, and she then feeds the food to the man. After eating, the two become aware "of their nakedness" (note the artistic pun—they are now aware that they resemble the snake!). Although they do not in fact die from the fruit, they suffer punishment. The man must labor hard in agriculture, and the woman must labor hard in childbirth. The woman, however, gets the better deal. At the end of the story, she has received a real name, Eve, and declares, "I have got me a son from the Lord!" (Notice that the man is left out of this!)

This entire Eden story combines various motifs from Mesopotamian, Egyptian, and Ugaritic lore. Taken as a whole, however, the story traces the divine creation of men, the experimental creation of women, the insidious interaction of human and animal life, and the conflict-laden aspect of interpersonal relationships. The story encapsulates human disillusionment with the world in a creation myth locating disenchantment at the beginning of time.

The author of the Eden story tends to focus on conflict and tragedy. The Eden story is followed by a tale of fratricide—Cain murders his brother Abel (Genesis 4:1–16). As the story continues, Cain establishes a city and his descendant Lamech takes two wives, Adah and Zillah, who beget the founders of tent-dwelling shepherds, musicians, tool makers, and finally a woman, named "Naamah" (in Hebrew this name means "attractive" and some scholars claim that she founded "the oldest profession"). Thus civilization begins (4:17–23).

Does civilization lead to peace and tranquility? Not at all! In regard to Cain's children's contributions to civilization, Lamech boasts: "I have killed a man for wounding me, a young man for striking me" (Genesis 4:24). Lamech expresses glee in murder. His forebearer Cain was at least confused and upset, if not penitent. Lamech has no qualms or guilt. Where does civilization lead? To increased violence and murder.

This second narrative strand, stretching from Genesis 2:5 through the end of Genesis 4, contrasts markedly with the views expressed in Genesis 1:1–2:4. Humanity is no longer the "measure" of creation. Creation no longer works smoothly in accordance with divine intention. Unpredictability rather than ordered unfolding characterizes the events of creation. God responds to the surprises of history. Human life encounters dramatic shifts in purpose, moving from being gardeners to laborers in several senses. Human activities become increasingly complex, but also increasingly dangerous. The world imagined in this story differs significantly from that intended in Genesis 1:1–2:4.

Most biblical scholars today recognize these two tales as having been created independently of one another. Originally, each one claimed to offer a true perspective on human existence. A final editor put these stories together and thereby created a third story: the story of a "Fall." At first, according to the stories as they now stand, humanity lived in a perfect world. This is Genesis 1:1–2:4 with its view of an ordered unfolding of a divine plan. Without transition, however, and without mention of the word "sin," the editors appended a second story that, taken by itself, envisions a world as unpredictable and imperfect before the eating of the forbidden fruit as afterward. The editors, by combining the texts, create a new myth: humanity, by the destiny of its creation, yearns for a perfect world that is no longer attainable. The ideal vision of the first story becomes an ironic commentary on the reality described in the second story, reminding people of the less than perfect world to which fate condemns them. Perhaps the editor who combined the tales intended this new story as motivation for human striving. By covenantal living, this editor implied, human beings can restore order and meaning to an unpredictable world. The final mythic portrait in Genesis, then, is complex. It joins optimism and pessimism, an affirmation of enduring order and a recognition of danger and of change. The same complex pattern also appears in the ethical and ritual dimensions of these stories.

Perhaps the most dramatic ethical issue concerns gender. Genesis 1:1–2:4 imagines an ideal world of gender equality. Both male and female human beings receive the same instruction: to rule the creatures (Genesis 1:26–28). Gender entails no distinctive role. This is an ethics that projects an ideal on reality and expects humanity to change its ways to live up to that ideal. Genesis 2:5–4:1, however, accepts the gender distinctions commonly found in the ancient Near East. Men are given priority. Their role consists in agricultural labor. Without them humanity could not exist. Women have a secondary, but equally essential, role. They labor in giving birth to children. Without them, humanity could not persist.

The combining of these two accounts, however, adds a new element—that of negotiation. Instead of an ideal ethics or an ethics of separate tasks, the final version, the *redacted* version, emphasizes the give and take between the sexes. Men and women work together to make a less than perfect world more bearable. In the final version, the ideal of sharing the same task is surrendered to the more practical situation in which men and women cooperate but pursue distinctive, gender-related occupations. This ethics of compromise allows the ideal to exist, but tempers it with recognition of the actual situation within which people live.

The story of Noah also reflects a similar variety of ethics. Noah is descended from Adam's son **Seth**—the only son who actualizes the "image of God" in which his father was created. In this way Noah represents a perfected humanity. The covenant God makes with Noah extends to all human beings. Such an inclusive view of the flood and its survivor emphasizes the unity of humanity. After the flood, however, the world splits into diverse social, political, and ethnic groups.

These are symbolized by Noah's three sons: **Shem**, **Ham**, and **Jafet** (see Genesis 9:20–27 and Genesis 10:1–32). Shem is considered progenitor of the *Semites*—a group that includes the Hebrews, the Syrians, Moabites, and others that the Bible sees related to the Israelites. This group is particularly blessed. Ham, on the other hand, was said to have dishonored his father (probably by having sexual relations with his mother) and, therefore, Canaan, the offspring of this forbidden union, was cursed and made a slave of the Israelite Semites (Genesis 9:26). Some sort of compromise existed between the Semitic group of Israelites and the "Sea Peoples" said to be descended from Jafet. The Bible claims that Noah gave the descendants of Jafet a claim to live in "the tents of Shem" (Genesis 9:27). These anecdotal reports suggest the way the Israelites understood themselves in relationship to their neighbors. Telling this story suggests an exclusive ethics, with the Semites clearly favored and other nations being given some sort of subordinate position.

In the matter of ritual, the texts also reveal several strands. Genesis 1:1–2:4 culminates in a ritual event: the creation of the **Sabbath**. Observance of the seventh day as a day of rest commemorates the story of creation. Ritual, apparently although not explicitly, celebrates a reality: that of the sacredness of the seventh day that has already been established by God. The celebration of that day does not make it holy, but calls attention to a pre-existing holiness inherent in the day. In contrast, Genesis 8 describes Noah's punctilious following of divine directives and his offering of sacrifice only on the deity's demand. Ritual performances win favor from the deity and enable people to draw closer to the divine. God responds favorably and gives assurances of a stable future: "And when the Lord smelled the pleasing odor, the Lord said to himself, 'I will never again curse the ground because of humanity and the inclination of the human heart which is evil from youth; nor will I ever again destroy every living creature as I have done'" (Genesis 8:21).

Genesis 4, however, provides a strikingly different view. There Cain and Abel offer sacrifices for no apparent reason. The seasonal cycle comes around and so, without being told, they bring their ritual offerings. The result is disastrous. Genesis 11 offers a similar caution when recounting the disaster that follows when humanity attempts to build a "Gate to God" (the literal meaning of the term Bab-El, as noted earlier). Ritual, according to Genesis 11, derives from human imaginings. It celebrates a human view of themselves and the world. The builders of the tower reportedly declared, "Come let us build ourselves a city and a tower with its top in the heavens and let us make a name for ourselves; otherwise we shall be scattered abroad upon the face of the whole earth" (Genesis 11:4). God becomes angry, not at the ritual itself, but rather because of the audacity that inspired it. The builders are scattered because "this is only the beginning of what they will do; nothing that they propose to do will now be impossible for them" (Genesis 11:7). Ritual that leads to reckless actions is rejected.

Between the positive view of ritual in the first set of texts and the negative in the second lies a middle ground: that of ritual as covenant, as the means of affirming a relationship between the divine and the human. Some parts of the Noah story emphasize this aspect of ritual. Genesis 9 records a reciprocal covenant between humanity and the divine. Humanity is permitted to eat living creatures but must ritually remove the blood "Only you shall not eat flesh with its life, that is its blood" (Genesis 9:4). Humanity performs this ritual to maintain a relationship that God has initiated, but that human beings, through disobedience, can destroy. In this case, ritual is symbolic of a relationship between the divine and the human; it celebrates a pre-existing reality. God's establishing of the rainbow as his covenantal sign, of course, does not admit to disconfirmation. God will not violate the covenant.

SUMMARY QUESTIONS

1. How does Deuteronomy 26 reveal the composite nature of the Torah as a "mosaic" rather than as Mosaic (written by Moses)?
2. How do the early stories of Israel's heroes convey later relationships between different social and political groups?
3. How do the myths in Genesis 1:1–11:32 compare to myths from Egypt, Mesopotamia, or Ugarit?
4. How does intention of the Lex Taliones differ in Exodus 21:22–25, Deuteronomy 19:16–21, and Leviticus 24:18–22?

Religions of the Torah 77

5. How do the ritual covenants in Genesis 8, 15, 17, and 22 differ from the rituals portrayed in Genesis 4 and 11?

Four Suggested Essay Questions

1. Explain two ways in which a tradition may view history. Show how Genesis 22 reflects one view and Deuteronomy 26 the other.
2. Explain two ways in which a tradition may view the supernatural. Apply one of them to the narrative in Genesis 1:1–2:4a and the other to the narrative in Genesis 2:4b–4:1.
3. Explain two ways in which a tradition may view ethics. Apply one to the Lex Taliones as found in Exodus and the other to the law of retaliation as found in Leviticus. Be sure to consult Box 4-4.
4. Explain two ways in which a tradition may view ritual. Apply one of them to the view of the Tower Bab-El in Mesopotamian tradition and the other to the Tower of Babel as described in Genesis 11.

Exercise

Answer the following questions based on Question 1:

1. What does the promise in Genesis 22:17–18 suggest about the predictability of the future?
2. What does the history in Deuteronomy 16:5–9 suggest about the predictability of the future? Note that only Deuteronomy 26:15 mentions a divine promise; verses 5–9 do not.
3. What does Genesis 22:17–18 seem to take as the basis on which Abraham's descendants will become victorious and successful?
4. What does Deuteronomy 26:16–17 suggest as the basis on which the Israelites will become a successful nation?
5. Formulate a general principle to express how Genesis 22:17–18 and Deuteronomy 26:5–9 differ about the predictability of the future and another principle to express how Genesis 22:17–18 and Deuteronomy 26:16–17 differ on how actions in the past influence the future.

FOR FURTHER READING

The books listed below should be a point of departure for your future study. Each includes a bibliography that will guide you beyond its basic information.

1. Alter, Robert, *The Five Books of Moses: A Translation with Commentary* (New York: W.W. Norton and Company, 2004).

2. Blenkinsopp, Joseph, *The Pentateuch: An Introduction to the First Five Books of the Bible* (New York: Doubleday, 1992).

3. Brenner, Athalya, ed., *A Feminist Companion to Exodus to Deuteronomy* (Sheffield, England: Sheffield Academic Press, 1994).

4. ———, *A Feminist Companion to Genesis* (Sheffield, England: Sheffield Academic Press, 1993).

5. Fox, Everett., *Five Books of Moses: Genesis, Exodus, Leviticus, Numbers, Deuteronomy: A New Translation With Introductions* (New York: Schocken, 1995).

6. Friedman, Richard Elliot, *Commentary on the Torah With a New English Translation* (San Francisco, CA: HarperSanFrancisco, 2001).

5

Religions and Israel's History

READING ASSIGNMENT

Joshua 23–24
Judges 7–16
1 Samuel 12, 24
2 Samuel 7, 23
2 Kings 22:1–23:27
1 Chronicles 21
2 Chronicles 34:1–35:27

LEARNING OBJECTIVES

By the end of this lesson, you will be able to:
- Describe different versions of Israelite history found in the Hebrew Scriptures.
- Describe the ethical and ritual views associated with the Israelite settlement in the land of Israel.
- Describe the different leadership groups as presented in different histories of Israelite kingship and their views of the divine, ritual, ethics, and history.
- Describe the influence of these differences on the ritual of Passover.
- Describe how views of Satan develop in historical writings of the Hebrew Bible.

Interpretive Matrix for Chapter Five

View of the Divine: How people interact with God and the supernatural; how God interacts with the world.	View of History: How past, present, and future are related; who controls the shape of events.	View of Ethics: How people behave toward other people; how they behave toward people like themselves and to those who are different.	View of Ritual: How people behave toward the Divine; how they perform religious actions.
The Divine as Transcendent: A royal or priestly intermediary must intercede with God for the sake of the group. God does not create evil but assigns that task to angels.	*History as Continuous:* Events occur gradually without creating major changes. Covenantal principles ensure continuity of events.	*Inclusive Ethics:* Ideas and behavior from outside groups are integrated into a group's own tradition. Women play as prominent a role as men.	*Ritual as Transforming:* Ritual enables success in military endeavors. Ritual procedure demands a special class of ritual experts.
The Divine as Immanent: National events reflect God's attitude toward the nation. God is directly responsible for evil.	*History as Discontinuous:* Crucial events introduce radical changes into human history. The unexpected intrudes on human events.	*Exclusive Ethics:* Members of one group should not follow the practices of another group. Women are seen as dangerous and separate from men.	*Ritual as Symbolic:* Ritual can symbolize a group's difference from other groups. Ritual obedience shows loyalty to the divine.

INTRODUCTION

The Hebrew Bible includes two major reviews of Israel's history: the books from Joshua through 2 Kings and the so-called "Chronicler's history" (comprising 1and 2 Chronicles, Ezra, and Nehemiah). This chapter traces this biblical history as given in these different versions. The differences often reflect changing political, cultural, and geographical realities. Maps will help give you a perspective on the contexts in which the narratives discussed in this chapter developed. We look first at views of Israelite history as expressed in the books of Joshua and Judges. The next section focuses on the rise of kingship and the ethics associated with it (the readings from 1 Samuel, 2 Kings, and 2 Chronicles are crucial in that discussion). Examining different views of the holiday of Passover (described in 2 Kings 22 and 2 Chronicles 34, as well as Ezekiel 45–46) illuminates approaches to ritual. Finally, the development of the idea of Satan, occurring only in later biblical books, provides insight into ways of understanding divinity.

This chapter opens with a brief introduction to the biblical history—that is, the history presented in the Hebrew Bible. It includes a timeline of biblical events and boxes summariz-

Religions and Israel's History   81

ing the books of the Former Prophets (Joshua through 2 Kings). Each following section opens with a map showing the cultural and political contours of a particular period in Israelite history. Familiarize yourself with these basic facts.

SOME IMPORTANT TERMS

The following terms are important in this chapter. Some of them have been listed in previous chapters; in those cases the term is not in **bold** in the main body of this chapter. Where names of books are also the names of individuals (such as Joshua), the name does not appear in the Glossary.

Abimelech	Exilarch	Passover
Amalekites	Gibeonites	Philistines
Ammonites	Gideon	Post-Exilic
Angel	Hezikiah	Samaria
Babylonian Exile	Jepthah	Samaritans
Barak	Jericho	Samson
Cyrus Cylinder	Jerusalem Temple	Sargon the Great
Cyrus the Great	Joshua	Samuel
David	Holy Ark	Satan
Deborah	Nathan	Saul
Deuteronomic History	Nazirite	Sennacherib
Diaspora	Nebuchadnezzar	Solomon
Eli	Omri	

HISTORY IN THE HEBREW BIBLE

The history of the Israelites given in the Hebrew Bible describes several stages that seem to have distinctive leaders, rituals, and ethics. It moves from a period of settlement in the land, to a united kingdom over all Canaan, to a divided kingdom with two independent entities: Israel in the north and Judah in the south. That northern kingdom is often called Samaria after the name of the capital city built there by **Omri** (1 Kings 16:24). To avoid confusion with a later group, the **Samaritans**, this textbook will used the term *Israel* to refer to the northern kingdom.

The Former Prophets ends by describing the destruction of Israel, the continuation of the kingdom of Judah, and the deportation of the Judeans to Babylonia. As presented in the biblical text, each distinct period had its own unique culture, but most scholars think that this impression represents a later adaptation of earlier material. This narrative occurs in what we called the Former Prophets in the first chapter. Another name for that stretch of biblical writings has been the **Deuteronomic History**. That name suggests an underlying theological agenda behind the entire narrative related to the ideas found in the book of Deuteronomy.

Deuteronomy, associated with the reform begun by Josiah in 621 B.C.E., suggests that the misfortunes of the nation occur because of an infraction of God's law. Moses predicts the destruction of the Israelite nations as a result of idolatry and apostasy from YHWH. The Deuteronomic History begins with the conquest of the promised land after the death of Moses and continues through the exile of the Judeans to Babylonia. The entire tale reinforces the claim that when a nation follows the Torah of Moses as Josiah understood it, the nation will succeed; when the nation disobeys that Torah, it will fail (Judges 2:11–15 summarizes this theology). Despite the apparently distinctive types of leaders and rituals passing through this history, the single theological point is that of God's involvement in the world. That theology changes only after the Babylonian exile, a change that needs to be understood in relationship to the experiences following the fall of Judah to the Babylonians.

The previous chapter examined what could be called the "prehistory," ranging from the creation of the world to the establishment of a sociopolitical group calling itself Israel. The history of the nation as a whole begins with its putative settlement in the Land of Canaan (later to be called the Land of Israel) and continues through the destruction of the two kingdoms—Israel and Judah—that developed in that territory (see Timeline 5–1).

The Bible portrays the first period, that of settlement in the land, as a time of diversity and disorganization in which "people did what was right in their own eyes" without a unified culture (Judges 17:6; 21:25). Both Joshua and Judges suggest a social and political organization in which neither a book nor a leader united the people (see Box 5–1). These two books, however, seem strangely opposed in other ways. The first portrays a swift and triumphant conquest of the land. The latter implies a slow assimilation into the cultures of Canaan, accompanied by periods of renewed adherence to the religion that preceded entrance into the land. It may be impossible to decide whether these models—or others that modern scholars have reconstructed—are accurate, but it is possible to discern why the biblical authors may have composed their stories in this way.

The narrative that follows these tales traces the rise and fall of the kingship in the land of Israel (see both Timeline 5–1 and Box 5–2). The story begins by relating the disenchantment with priestly leadership, first through the family of **Eli**, the priest at Shiloh, and then with Samuel, educated by Eli, whose children also show a tendency toward waywardness.

The narrative continues by portraying a united Israel under the kings **Saul**, **David**, and **Solomon.** That "Golden Age" is followed by a divided kingdom, with Israel in the north governed by several successive dynasties, and Judah in the south governed by the Davidic dynasty. The final period described portrays Judah alone surviving after Israel had been destroyed by the Assyrians. Judah's disastrous history culminates in its conquest by the Babylonians, after which its leading citizens are carried into exile into Babylonia. Echoes of this narrative occur in the stories told by the chronicler and by several prophetic writers that will be important to consider when looking at the biblical record about this period in greater detail.

TIMELINE 5–1 HISTORY OF THE ISRAELITE KINGDOMS

This list begins with the biblical events associated with the Israelite entrance into Canaan and continues through the destruction of the northern kingdom, Israel, and the southern kingdom Judah. For the sake of completeness the return from the exile is also included.

2000–1400	Various ruins of places said to have been destroyed by Joshua such as Ai and Jericho date from within this period. They were probably already decimated before the time of Joshua.
1220–1000	Merneptah's Stele suggests that some entity called "Israel" was in the area around Canaan sometime around 1220. The settlement of the Israelites may well have occurred at that time. The so-called "judges" governed during this period.
1069	Samuel begins to minister
1043	Saul becomes king
1011	Saul and Jonathan slain; David become king of Judah
1004	David becomes king over all Israel
971	Solomon ascends the throne
966	Solomon begins to build the Temple in Jerusalem
931	Rehoboam becomes king of Israel and Judah
931	Jeroboam rebels; sets up a rival kingdom in the north thus creating two rival kingdoms—Judah and Israel
880	Omri becomes king of Israel
874	Ahab becomes king of Israel; Elijah and Elisha are prophets in the northern kingdom.
841	Elisha helps Jehu become king of Israel through a coup against Ahab
841	Athaliah seizes the throne of Judah so that both kingdoms have an Omride ruler
734–733	Israel seeks to engage Judah in a coalition with Syria against the Assyrians in the so-called Syro-Ephraimite war
722	Shalmaneser IV of Assyria invades Israel, exiles its inhabitants, and replaces them with a new population
715	Hezekiah becomes king of Judah and begins a religious reform
701	Judah invaded by the Assyrians but escapes conquest
640	Josiah becomes king of Judah
621	Josiah's reform in Judah
609	Josiah dies in battle against Necho II of Egypt
605	The Babylonians invade Judah
586	The Babylonians destroy Jerusalem and the Temple and send its inhabitants into exile
538	Cyrus the Great, conqueror of Babylonia, allows Jews to return to Israel
530–515	Rebuilding the Jerusalem Temple under Joshua and Zerubabel

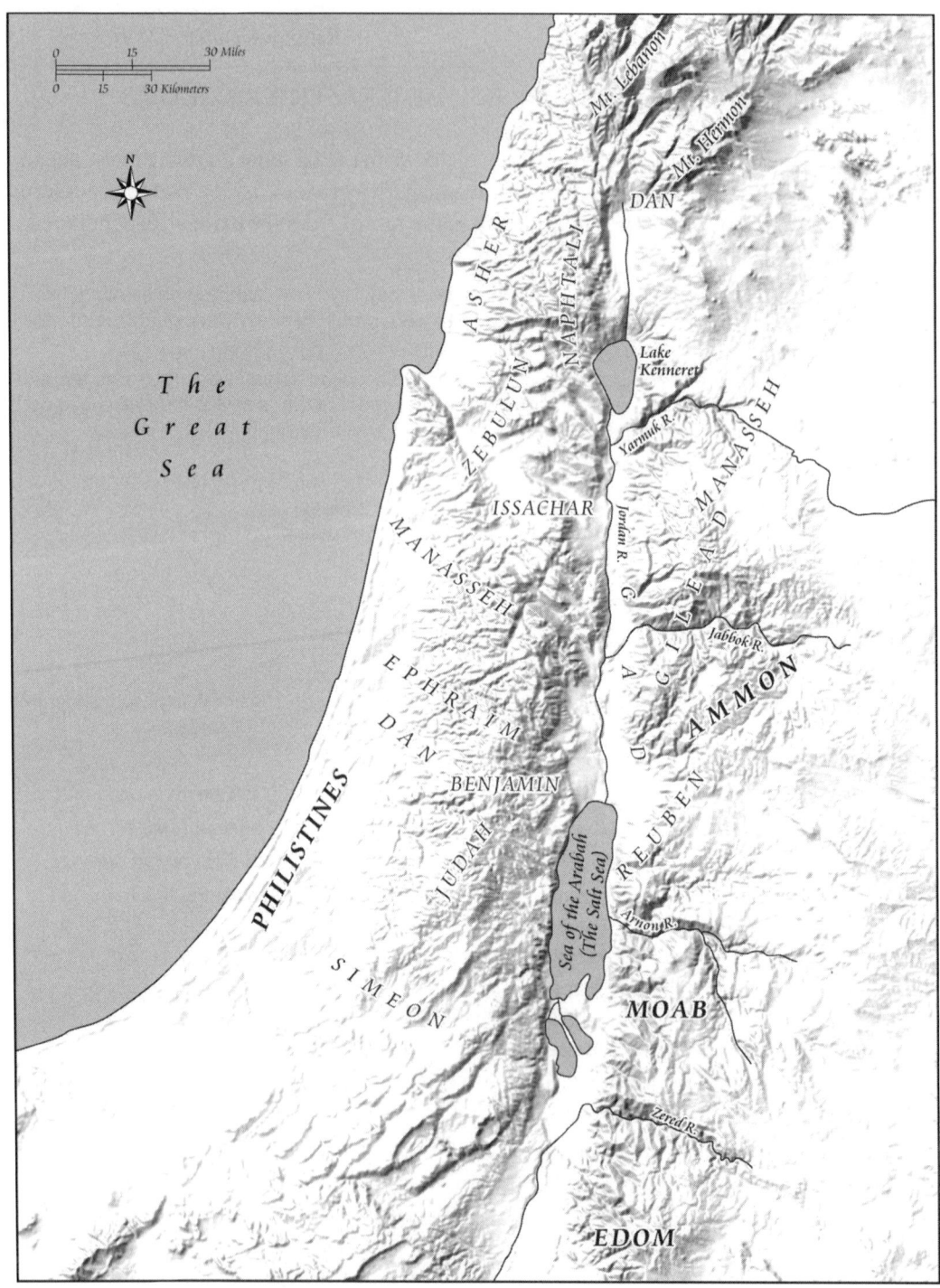

Map 5–1   Israel in Canaan

HISTORY, ETHICS, AND RITUAL IN ISRAEL'S SETTLEMENT IN ITS LAND

During its earliest period, the Israelites entered the land of Canaan and took possession of the territory there. By the end of the period of the judges (perhaps more accurately "tribal leaders"), Israelite communities dot the entire landscape of Canaan. The tendentious nature of biblical history appears in the ambiguous reports given about Israel's settling in the land of Canaan. At times, it appears as if Israel comes to the land as an external invader. This is an exclusivist ethics, an ethics that rejects the environment in which a community lives. Another strand within the stories of this period, however, emphasizes assimilation. Here, the Israelites emerge from within a pre-existing Canaanite population. This ethics of involvement with others stands beside the ethics of exclusivity. Both views are tendentious, not historical. The first view also stresses a history of continuity. From that perspective the legitimacy of Israelite government and leadership lies in its ties to the past, its continuation of a plan already unfolding. The second view stresses discontinuity. God intervenes in Israelite history and determines its result. This ensures that the "righteous" prevail and the "unrighteous" fail.

An example of the tension in these stories occurs in the often contradictory legends clustered around the figure of Joshua and how he brought **Jericho** under Israelite control. The Bible claims that **Joshua** destroyed the city of Jericho. The stories told about this destruction, however, differ. Joshua 6 describes a miraculous victory occasioned by the performance of a ritual involving the **Holy Ark** of the Covenant and the sounding of rams' horns. An alternative approach evident in Joshua 2 and Joshua 6:17, 22–25, however, hints at infiltration into Jericho and the use of insiders in the city as allies in taking the town. Neither of these views have any corroboration from historical data. Archaeologists, exploring the ruins of Jericho, have discovered evidence of its destruction centuries before Joshua.

The story, as found in Joshua 6, concludes with a strange curse: the city will be rebuilt only at the cost of child sacrifice (v. 26). 1 Kings 16:34 seems to verify this curse. However, it may well be the case that child sacrifice as a means of securing the foundation of a city occurred first. The idea of this as a "curse" from the time of Joshua could be an editorial comment meant to explain what, to that editor, seemed an inexplicable action.

As historical narratives, then, these stories must be regarded with suspicion, but they are exemplary theological tales. The ritual emphasis found in most of Joshua 6 emphasizes the cultic distinctiveness of the Israelites. Their peculiar theology and practice win them victory in the land. This portrays an ethics of difference and separation from other cultures. The narrative in Joshua 2 that is also echoed in parts of Joshua 6 suggests that some type of integration with the native population was not only possible but also desirable. In that strand, an ethics of accommodation and inclusion prevails.

The same difference occurs in other parts of Joshua. Joshua 5 focuses on the ritual of circumcision. The Israelites circumcise themselves as a sign distinguishing them from others in Canaan. Immediately upon this act, Joshua encounters an **angel** of God and prostrates

> **BOX 5–1 THE BOOKS OF JOSHUA AND JUDGES**
>
> This chart outlines the contents of the first two books of the Former Prophets—Joshua and Judges. The content sketches two different views of the Israelite settlement in the land of Canaan.
>
> *Joshua*
>
> | | |
> |---|---|
> | 1–8 | Joshua leads the Israelites into the promised land performing miracles like those Moses performed and laying waste walled cities by means of ritual practices. Those who follow divine commands are rewarded and those who disobey are punished. Several of these stories show Joshua as emulating Moses—crossing water dry-shod (Joshua 3:7–15), having a vision of a supernal being (Joshua 5:13–15), writing out a copy of the law of Moses (Joshua 8:30–35). |
> | 9–10 | These chapters describe the Gibeonite treaty and its binding nature and point to God's miraculous power over nature. |
> | 11–12 | These chapters sketch the battles Joshua fights and the fact that they are the means by which God's power is made known in the world. |
> | 13–22 | The land of Canaan is allotted to various Israelite tribes, to create cities of refuge and to provide cities in which priests (Levites) may dwell. |
> | 23–24 | The book concludes with several (not entirely consistent) reviews of Israelite history, covenant making, and the transfer of priestly power from Aaron's son Eleazar to his son Phinchas. |
>
> *Judges*
>
> | | |
> |---|---|
> | 1–3 | These chapters describe the settlement of the land and set out the theological claim that when Israelites follow God's will they defeat their enemies but when they abandon it their enemies defeat them. |
> | 4–5 | The story of Deborah and Barak is told in prose and poetry. |
> | 6–9 | The stories of Gideon and his bastard son Abimelech are recounted to reinforce a negative view of kingship. |
> | 11–12 | Stories about the folk-hero Jepthah reveal the problems of occasional leadership, including the ritual perversions that can occur. |
> | 13–16 | Tales of Samson reveal how military prowess may not imply spiritual authority. |
> | 17–21 | Strange religious practices become, in these chapters, provocations that lead eventually to sexual abuse and civil war among the Israelites. |

himself in worship, just as Moses did at the burning bush in Exodus 3. In contrast, Joshua 9 records a binding agreement made with the **Gibeonites**. That treaty meant that these settlements should be spared in the midst of the conquest. The Deuteronomic writer comments that the people were to blame in this, since they "did not ask direction from the Lord" (Joshua 9:14), but nonetheless the treaty remained in effect, although the Gibeonites were forced to do menial labor. Much as the Deuteronomic author wishes to insist upon an ethic of exclusion and separation, the evidence points to an alternative use of an ethic of inclusion that accompanied it. These two ethics create a tension in the religious perspectives found in Joshua.

A comparison between the texts in Joshua 23 and Joshua 24 shows some of the tensions involved. Both texts seem to be a "final address" by Joshua to the Israelites. Chapter 23 does not mention the Exodus from Egypt, but rather a long and arduous process by which the Israelites will eventually take over the land in which they are now dwelling. The basis for the process lies in obedience to the laws written in what is called "the Torah of Moses," and one of the most important points made is that disobedience will lead to defeat and exile from the land. This chapter focuses on "loyalty" to the God who has established this predictable pattern of behavior and response. This chapter assumes a natural correspondence between deeds and consequences that has a type of inevitability associated with it. For Joshua 23, history is a consistent development based on the principles of Torah. It is less a matter of telling the specific tale of Israel's development than teaching what has been called Deuteronomic Theology—that obedience to Torah brings success, and disobedience brings disaster. This ethics of distinctiveness characterizes much of the book of Joshua.

Joshua 24, however, introduces a very different model of history. Here God intervenes again and again for the sake of the chosen people. History is a series of discontinuous events, punctuated by great miracles. Joshua reviews biblical history from Abraham through the "conquest" of the land (24:1–13). He portrays the battle for Jericho differently from Joshua 6–7. Beyond that, the review is distinctive because it emphasizes the unexpected and unpredictable. Not only are the victories historical reverses, but enjoying of the land is a "miracle." Such miracles require that the Israelites remain loyal to God's will, especially as Joshua explains it to them.

The ritual declarations in Joshua 24:14–18 continue this theme of the marvels of God's intervention in the world and the loyalty that they demand. Joshua demands that the people serve God "in sincerity and in faithfulness" in order to earn the land promised them. The people respond that they will serve only the Lord who brought them out of Egypt and conquered their enemies. This exchange between Joshua and the people is followed by what looks to be a duplicate account—one in which a witness against the people is established.

Joshua 24:19–28 begins by charging that the Israelites will be unable to prove loyal to their God. The people deny this charge, and Joshua demands that they admit to being "witnesses against yourselves" (vv. 21–23). He then augments the general demand for loyalty with a specific set of commands that are set out on a stone. This entire narrative suggests a detailed covenant that creates a new and predictable pattern for behavior. The covenant that had been called the "Torah of Moses" in Joshua 23 becomes "the Torah of God" in 24:26—a change that suggests that God interacts directly with the people, rather than through a leader who acts as intermediary. Joshua 24:23–28 seems to initiate a new covenant that brings an entire population into relationship with the divinity. Some biblical scholars suggest that non-Israelites as well were "naturalized" and thus incorporated into the new covenant community through this ceremony. Whether that supposition is actually the case cannot be proven. At the least, however, Joshua 24 indicates that God creates new covenantal agreements after having established one with Moses during the Exodus from Egypt.

In contrast to Joshua, the book of Judges relates its ethics of exclusivism without ambiguity; its narratives emphasize how assimilation and ritual are tied together. The book seems a polemic against an inclusive ethics, waged against those who would unite with the culture of the non-Israelite peoples, either through marriage or through imitation of the rituals and practices in the land. Women, almost inevitably, become victimized in these stories.

One tale, that associated with the leader **Jepthah** (Judges 10–12), relates how an outcast son becomes a hero through his victory over tribal enemies. At the heart of the story is a vow that Jepthah makes (Judges 11:29–40). Jepthah is called upon to fight against the army of the **Ammonites**. After "the spirit of the Lord" comes upon him, Jepthah makes an agreement with the Lord: "If you will give the Ammonites into my hand, then whoever comes out of the doors of my house to meet me, when I return victorious from the Ammonites, shall be the Lord's to be offered up by me as a burnt offering" (Judges 11:30). That sacrificial victim turns out to be his daughter; what results is a ritual wailing carried out annually (although neither later biblical texts nor Jewish tradition record any further practice of this ritual).

Whether such a ritual actually arose from this tale, or whether the tale disguises a practice adopted from indigenous groups, is irrelevant. The point of the story is that even the greatest leaders during the time of the settlement of the land eventually brought about assimilation to the customs of that land and, thereby, tragedy to the people. The woman in this story is clearly an innocent victim.

The women who figure in the story of **Samson** (Judges 13–16) are more ambiguous. Certainly Samson's mother appears in a positive light. The angel announcing Samson's birth comes to her rather than to her husband. That angel entrusts her, rather than her husband, with the command that Samson obey the vows of a **Nazirite**, vows that he, in fact, routinely flouts. Although most people remember his violation of the prohibition on cutting his hair, the vows also include restrictions on touching dead animals, on sexual intercourse, and on drinking intoxicating liquids—all of which Samson violates. Samson's mother carries out her task well; she cannot be blamed for his eventual transgression of these vows. While she and the angel seem to trust those vows as a way to ensure Samson's safety, the other women in the story use those same ritual means to ensnare him. The other women of the story are outsiders, **Philistines**, who either try to trap Samson through their own rituals (marriage rites and trials of strength or ingenuity) or through his own rituals (making him violate his Nazirite vows). Samson succumbs. The rituals his mother taught him cannot keep him safe from the attractions of the Philistines. The point here, in contrast to Joshua, seems to be that rituals cannot protect the Israelites against an invasive and inclusive ethics that will undermine Israelite identity. The choice between an idealized exclusive ethics of Israelite purity and the tempting but dangerous inclusive ethics of assimilation dominates the book of Judges.

Women play prominent roles in this choice. Foreign wives, as evidenced in the Samson story, are forces for an inclusive and destructive ethics. Israelite women, by contrast, act for the sake of Israel's distinctive identity. Some women, such as **Deborah** (Judges 4–5), protect the exclusive identity of the Israelites. Although she is said to have been a "a prophet judging Israel" (Judges 4:4), she seems to wield only limited power and must nominate a man, **Barak**, to lead the army in battle (Judges 4:6–10). Some women, such as the woman who inflicts a mortal wound on the royal pretender **Abimelech** (Judges 9:53) are instruments of the divine will. Some are mothers who have a strong influence on their sons (Samson's mother in Judges 13 and Micah's mother in Judges 17). Still others, such as Jepthah's daughter and a Levite's concubine (Judges 19), are victims whose victimization shows the need for a change in the political system.

HISTORICAL PRESENTATIONS OF ISRAEL'S PERIOD OF KINGSHIP

The political structure of the Israelite people does indeed change. The scattered Israelite communities, threatened by the enclaves of sea peoples (Philistines or "Palestinians" who invaded the area about 1200 B.C.E.), banded together into a kingship (see the situation reflected in Map 5–2). The creation of a kingship altered the nature of Israelite self-understanding and challenged a continuous view of its history. The biblical texts from 1 Samuel through 2 Kings struggle with this problem. They also seek to integrate the Deuteronomic thesis of divine response to Israel's ethics and ritual with the new approaches developed in the royal courts by priests and prophets. What follows analyzes various biblical narratives in which views of history, ritual, ethics, and the nature of the divine are all intertwined.

The beginnings of the kingship are traced to an abortive attempt during the time of the Judges. The story of Abimelech (Judges 9) provides a negative view of kingship; only those who are unfit for any useful purpose desire to be king. Just as only the useless bramble consents to be king of the trees, so only the worst human beings consent to being king over other people. God brings violence on people like Abimlech, who have pretensions to royal power. The same negative view of kingship occurs even when the prophet Samuel finally agrees to establish a kingship over the people. 1 Samuel 12 puts the request for kingship into the context of the entire history of Israel.

Samuel declares that the people need no other political authority than that of a seer, and he holds out his own honesty as a model of that type of leadership (12:1–5). He then reviews a history that begins with Moses and Aaron, returns to Jacob, and emphasizes that during the times of the judges the Israelites abandoned the God of the Exodus and therefore suffered defeats until they repented of idolatry (12:6–14). Samuel emphasizes the pattern of idolatry and defeat, repentance and victory, and sums it up by denying that a king will make any difference to that pattern. Having a king will not ensure Israelite victories. Israel's success under a king will depend on whether that king follows God's will. In order to add dramatic

BOX 5–2 THE BOOKS OF SAMUEL AND KINGS

This chart outlines the contents of the four books included in Samuel and Kings. The content sketches the initial rise of kingship, an idealized united kingdom, a divided kingdom with Israel in the north and Judah in the South, and the final destruction of both kingdoms.

1 Samuel

1–3	The story of Samuel's birth and childhood reveals the weakness of priestly leadership.
4–9	The story of the Ark of the Covenant and of the failure of the priesthood of Shiloh suggest the need for a new type of leadership.
10–14	The kingship of Saul, Israel's first ruler, creates conflict over prophetic authority and the appropriate amount of power a king should enjoy.
15–31	David rises to power in King Saul's court, falls out of favor, and confronts Saul on several occasions These stories show again and again how a new type of kingship is needed and how change and innovation mark the development of history.

2 Samuel

1–8	David is described as an exemplary king who is first hailed as ruler in Judah and only later becomes king over a united Israel. Chapter 7 provides an idealized covenant between God and David's family. Other chapters sketch the taking of Jerusalem, the rise of its Zadokite priesthood in Jerusalem and the laying of plans for the building of a Temple.
9–20	These chapters describe David's troubles as a ruler—his adultery with Bathsheba and internal fighting within his own family. Once again the stories express the idea that history entails surprises, that patterns are not predictable, and that change rather than continuity marks human life.
21–24	These chapters focus on various aspects of David's royal activities—his graciousness toward King Saul's family, his covenant with the divine, and concludes in chapter 24 by merging both the story of his punishment for taking a census of the people and his moving the Ark of the Lord into Jerusalem as the central focus of what would become God's Temple.

1 Kings

1–4	Solomon is portrayed as shrewd and pious. His wisdom included marriage to an Egyptian princess (1 Kings 3:1)
5–9	Solomon's building of the Temple and its dedication is described. Important in that description is the inclusion of several non-Israelites such as Hiram of Tyre (1 Kings 5) and the universalism of his dedication of the Temple which he declares a sanctuary to which even foreigners pray (1 Kings 8:41–43)
10–11	These chapters show Solomon's shortsightedness and the criticism given by Ahijah the Shilonite. One criticism was directed against his entanglements with foreign women (1 Kings 11).
12–16	These chapters describe the schism under Solomon's successor Rehoboam that lead to the creation of a divided kingdom between Israel and Judah.

17–22	These chapters describe the Omride Kings and criticism from prophets such as Elijah.
2 Kings	
1–17	These chapters focus on the kings of Judah and Israel through the fall of the northern kingdom to Assyria. Chapter 17 claims that the Samaritans were outsiders who converted to worship of YHWH only by the threat of lions.
17–25	These chapters follow the southern kingdom of Judah in the face of Assyria and Babylonia; chapters 22–23 describe Josiah's reform of Judean religion and chapters 24–25 describe the Babylonian conquest of Judah.

force to this claim, Samuel calls upon God to send thunder and rain. The miracle convinces the people that they have done evil, but it does not dissuade them from choosing a king for themselves, King Saul (12:15–25).

This story expresses views of the divine, of ritual, and of ethics. God clearly takes a hand in human affairs; history reflects divine judgment concerning the way Israel has behaved. The miracle makes this even clearer. Thunder and rain appear unexpectedly during the harvest season. Even the orderly process of nature does not provide an inevitable and reliable basis for prediction of the future. In addition, the ritual process does not, by itself, change reality. Ritual observance may prove obedience to God, or, they may sometimes prove the opposite. The rituals, however, do not bring victory or defeat; only the conduct of the people accomplishes this. This emphasis on correct action points to an inclusive ethics. The destiny of the nation does not rely on the status of one leader, the king. Kingship does not ensure success; the entire population bears the responsibility for national welfare. These views of divine immanence, ritual celebration, and ethical inclusiveness sometimes conflict with other views articulated in the biblical story.

1 Samuel 13 illustrates such a conflict. God rejects King Saul because the king has offered sacrifices on his own, without waiting for Samuel to conduct the ceremonies. Samuel contends that God brings victories not because of sacrifices offered, but because of obedience to the divine commandments. Samuel declares that God has chosen someone else to lead the people (1 Samuel 13:12–14 and 1 Samuel 16:22–23). This rejection of the dynastic principle reinforces the anti-hierarchic bias already found in 1 Samuel 12. That God intervenes in human history to choose a particular person as king also represents divine immanence—God's interest and involvement in mortal lives.

The hero who replaces Saul, King David, represents a different type of leader altogether. Perhaps the portrayal of this hero reflects the political and military victories he achieved. The kingdom he governed had grown into a unified empire by the time of his death (see Map 5–2). The heartland governed by Saul had been expanded to include outlying districts extending in every direction. By the time of David's successor, Solomon, incursions had been made into far-flung territories as well. This success inspired a positive view of kingship.

Not only the story of David himself, but also threads in the story of Saul suggest this different view of kingship. 1 Samuel 10 takes a far more positive view of kingship than does 1

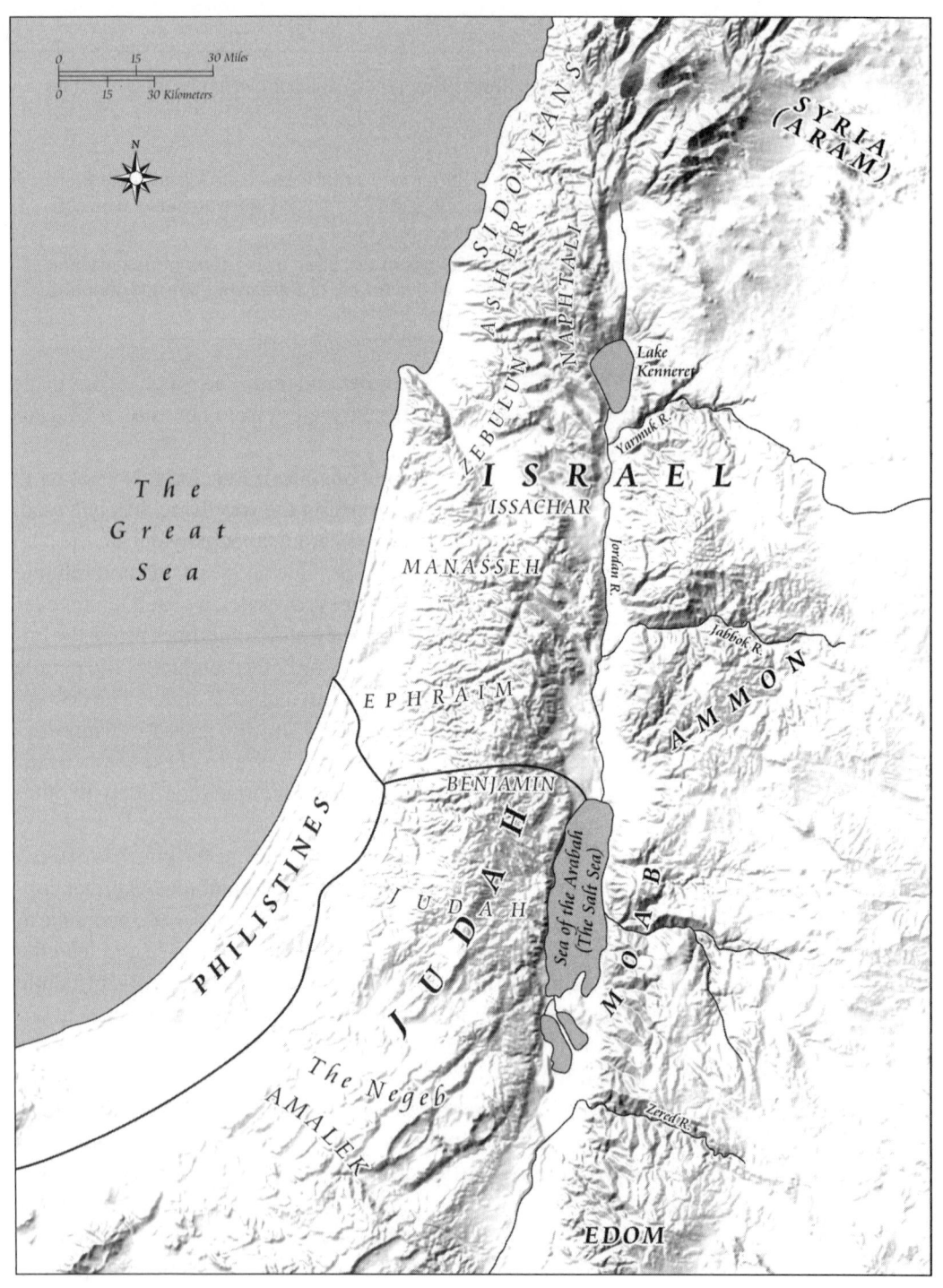

Map 5–2 The United Monarchy

Samuel 12. A second story of the rejection of Saul, 1 Samuel 15, agrees with 1 Samuel 13 that sacrifices are meaningless if they do not reflect obedience to the divine.

The command in question, however, emphasizes an exclusive ethics; the complete destruction of the **Amalekites**. The Torah takes pains to criticize the people of Amalek; they attacked the Israelites when they were weak from the Exodus out of Egypt (Exodus 17: 8–15), and so an eternal hostility begins toward them. This hostility expresses a sense of Israelite distinctiveness, and if the king ignores the command to exterminate non-Israelite nations, he shows he does not follow God's ethical injunctions. In this second strand of thinking, the king is indeed an exemplary figure, one who holds an important hierarchic place in society. This is so much the case that Agag, the king of the Amalekites, is singled out for punishment. History involves a combat among kings, between leaders of different groups. This positive view of kingship combines with an exclusive ethics.

Perhaps the most significant example of this second view of kingship lies in the concept of a royal covenant, a dynastic promise made to a particular ruler. An extraordinary expression of this view occurs in 2 Samuel 23:2–5. David claims to have prophetic power; "The spirit of the Lord speaks through me, his word is upon my tongue. The God of Israel has spoken…he has made with me an everlasting covenant ordered in all things and secure." Both this statement and the hymn that precedes it (2 Samuel 22) emphasize a transcendent view of the divine. God interacts with the king, the representative of the people. While God does govern and shape history, divine deeds respond to the character of the ruler, not of the people in general.

Drawing upon ancient Near Eastern prototypes, the leader of the nation was appointed by divine decree. The divinity intervenes in history to decide who should guide the nation in its civil life. The ritual investing the individual with this power, pouring oil over the head of the selected ruler (the Hebrew word *Messiah* literally means "one anointed with oil" and came to mean the king whom God has invested with authority), transforms the person selected into an instrument of the divine. Thereafter, the king serves as God's emissary and functionary. This creates a substantive ritual, in contrast to the purely celebratory ritualism associated with Samuel and Saul. 2 Samuel 23 continues after David's "last words" to a description of his warriors, including a bodyguard of thirty-seven soldiers with whom he surrounded himself (2 Samuel 23:24–38). They include people such as Uriah the Hittite, who was obviously not an Israelite. Royal ethics tended to be inclusive in ways that the Deuteronomic author found dangerous and problematic.

The story of David's ascent to the throne assumes a contingency not found in 2 Samuel 23. If a king obeys God, then that king succceeds. If a king disobeys God, then no matter what his lineage, his rule has become illegitimate. This paradigm certainly applies the experience of Saul to that of the Davidic kingdom. Royal legitimacy depends on continuity of the obedience to the divine. In contrast, the absolute position argues that no matter what, God cannot intervene and change the shape of history. 2 Samuel 7 struggles to balance these views. David clearly wants to establish a permanent kingship. He seeks to build a central shrine for all Israelite worship. God denies him that privilege, stating that God has never previously dwelt in such a building (2 Samuel 7:7–11). 2 Samuel celebrates God's variety of chosen offspring may need chastisement they will not be rejected the way that Saul's dynasty was rejected (2 Samuel 7:14–16). Significantly, the chapter ends with a long hymn reviewing Jewish history attributed to David (2 David (2 Samuel 17:18–29). Although God (through Samuel) reprimands Saul for playing the priest, David's priestly prayers receive no such criticism. The prayer itself is noteworthy since, unlike the review of history in 1 Samuel 12; it does not mention heroes such as Jacob, Moses, Aaron or even the judges. Instead, it briefly declares that God redeemed the people by using great miracles, establishing the nation, and providing for it. The main point of the prayer is to confirm the dynastic promise to David and celerate the common past that Israelites share and that their king symbolizes.

The later events in the story of David have a distinctive tone; quite different from those told about his rise to power (see Box 5–2).

This contingency anticipates later events in the story of David (see Box 5–2). 2 Samuel 9–20 describe how David commits adultery with the wife of his Hittite warrior, and how **Nathan** the prophet declares that his family will be plagued by fighting among his children. Not only does David face internal dissension in his family—his daughter Tamar is raped by her half-brother, and her brother's vengeance almost destroys the nation—but civil war forces him to flee his capital, Jerusalem. All these events suggest that God, while intervening in national history for the good of Israel, will intervene in private lives to either reward or punish individuals. History may be continuous, but God's immanence makes a person's life unpredictable.

Whatever the accomplishments of David, they were soon eclipsed by the problems that faced the people of Israel. The country soon divided into two nations: Israel to the north and Judah to the south. Israel divided into two kingdoms, both of which eventually fell to enemy armies. (Map 5–3 shows how the nation split into two kingdoms after the time of Solomon; Map 5–4 shows the world during Assyrian domination; Map 5–5 shows the world configuration during the exile of the Judeans to Diaspora lands after the conquest by the Babylonians and during the Persian period.) Books 1 and 2 Kings portray this period as one of almost unrelieved apostasy from God's teachings, filled with the disasters that such apostasy must bring. These texts suggest that most of the kings and priests of this time emphasized the need for innovation during times of discontinuous history, an inclusive ethics, divine transcendence, and transforming rituals. The texts also claim that the opposing views of continuity in history, exclusive ethics, divine immanence, and celebratory rituals were espoused by a group called "prophets" who (in the minds of the Deuteronomic authors) represented the true will of Israel's God.

The story of the Assyrian conquest of Israel and siege of Jerusalem are a case in point. 2 Kings 17 describes how **Sargon the Great** "captured Samaria; he carried the Israelites away to Assyria" (17:6). This occurred "because the people of Israel had sinned against the Lord their God" (17:7). The text details the various infractions of divine law that the northern Israelites carried out, so that "the Lord was very angry with Israel and removed them out of his sight; none was left but the tribe of Judah alone" (v. 18). The land was repopulated by an

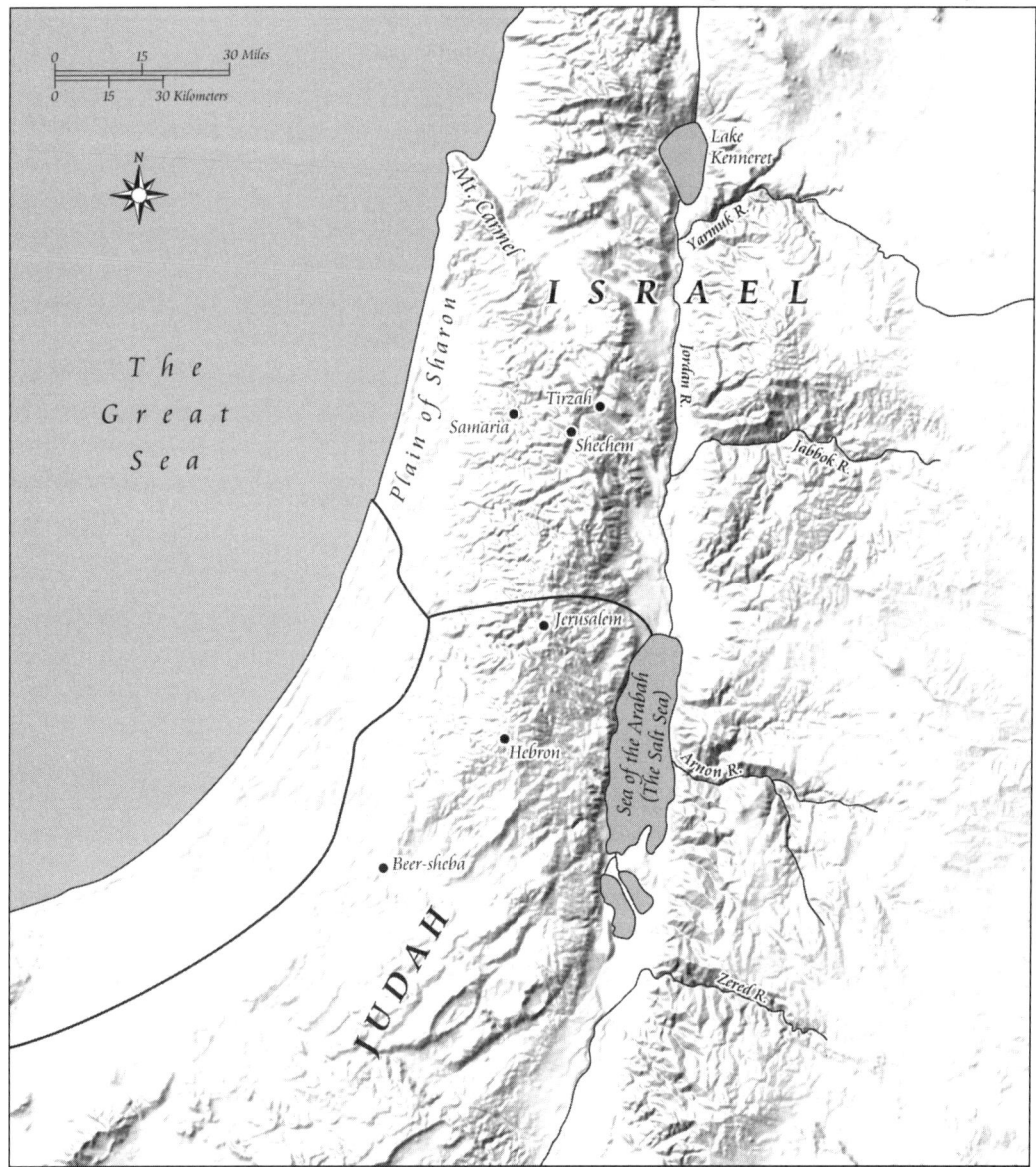

Map 5–3 The Kingdoms of Israel and Judah

alien group of people who came to be called Samaritans (vv. 24–41) and who were untrue to the religious beliefs of the people of Judah. Judah itself, however, was not blameless, so King **Sennacherib** besieged Jerusalem and sought to convince the people to surrender to him. King **Hezekiah** of Judah, however, instituted religious reforms and humbled himself before Israel's God, YHWH. Because of that, the city was spared (2 Kings 18–19).

96 Chapter 5

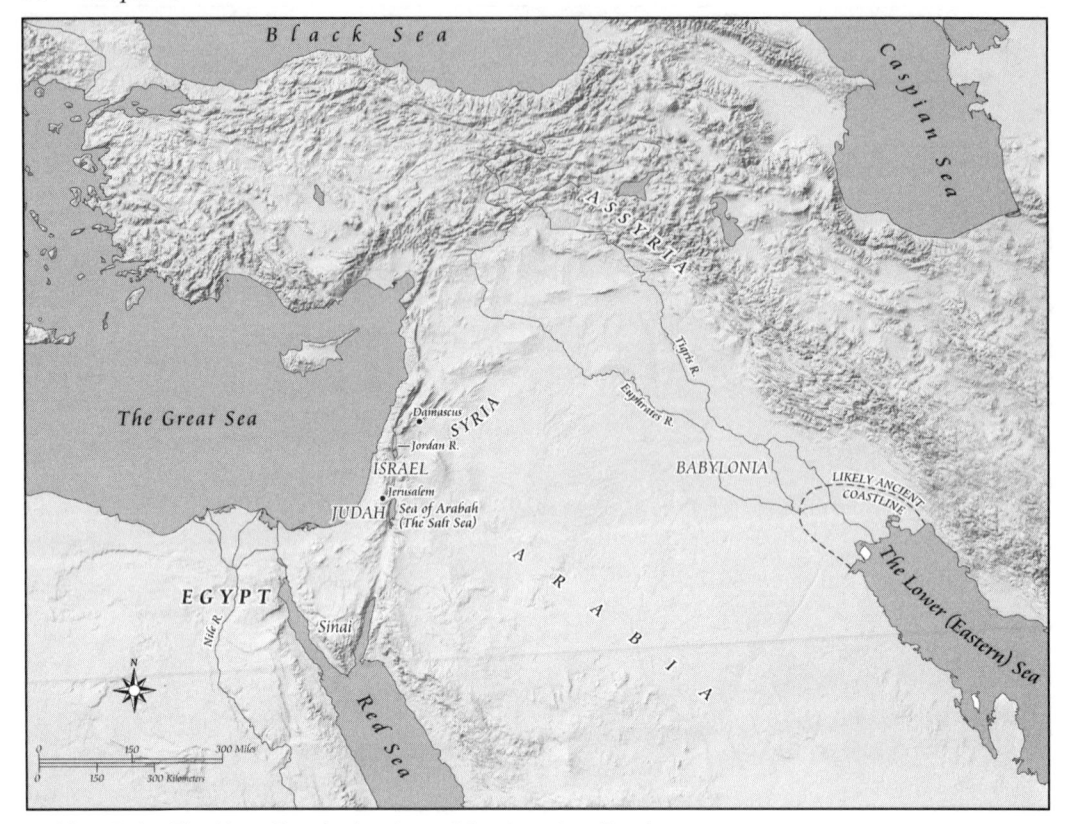

Map 5–4 The Near East in the time of the Assyrian Empire

The story of Hezekiah is one of the rare exceptions to the Deuteronomic history's dismal view of kings. Another occurs in the story of Josiah (2 Kings 22–23), whose establishment of the first biblical canon was mentioned in Chapter One and receives further treatment below. Politically, Josiah sought to expand the power and boundaries of Judah. He initially achieved great success. His reform of Judean religion represents a prophetic triumph: he turns back to the "Torah of Moses" to achieve continuity in history; he institutes a canon that emphasizes God's rewards and punishments of individuals; he destroys all "foreign" worship from Judah, thus showing his ethical exclusivity; and enacts a Passover celebration to symbolize his reaffirmation of ancient traditions. Josiah, however, died while still young. Facing Necho, the Pharaoh who opposed the Babylonians, Josiah died in battle. His reform was overturned by his successor, and the story of the Jewish kingdoms of Israel and Judah concludes with the Judeans being led into exile into Babylonia.

The conquest of Jerusalem by the Babylonian king Nebuchadnezzar in 587 B.C.E. is the culmination of the Deuteronomic history (2 Kings 24–25). All this occurs because the kings of Judah "did what was evil in the sight of the Lord" (24:9). Even after the fall of Jerusalem, King Zedekiah rebelled against Nebuchadnezzar, and God's anger increased: "Indeed Jerusalem and Judah so angered the Lord that he expelled them from his presence" (2 Kings 24:20). That expulsion took the form of an exile from Jerusalem to Babylonia. Most of the population was taken to Babylon, although "some of the poorest people of the land (were left) to be vinedressers and tillers of the soil" (2 Kings 35:12). The Jerusalem Temple was destroyed and ravaged, with its treasures taken away. The final note sounded, however, provides some hope: the Davidic descendant in Babylon is treated with honors and takes up the position that will later be called the **Exilarch** (2 Kings 25:27–30). Perhaps a better future awaits the Judeans.

HISTORICAL VIEWS OF THE BABYLONIAN EXILE AND ITS AFTERMATH

The Hebrew Bible supplements the Deuteronomic History with books such as 1 and 2 Chronicles and Ezra and Nehemiah, extending the historical picture through the Babylonian Exile and the return of Jews from that exile. In 586 B.C.E. the destruction of the Judean Temple and deportation of Judean leaders altered the shape and nature of Judaism. Jews were dispersed to a Diaspora that included Assyria, Babylonia, and Egypt. Among these Diaspora communities new leadership groups arose. Descendants of the Davidic dynasty took on a new role as Exilarch, the leader of the exilic community; priests began planning to rebuild the Temple; prophets advised a new social program. Prophets such as Ezekiel imagined the shape of a reconstruction of the Israelite nation. Later **Cyrus the Great** began a series of conquests that included the taking of Babylonia in 539 B.C.E. (see Map 5–5). As part of his general policy, Cyrus permitted the Jews of Babylonia to return to their homeland, to Israel. Several waves of such return occurred.

The **Cyrus Cylinder**, a Babylonian historical document, tells how Cyrus the Great understood his conquest of Babylon. He claims that his victory derived from a mission that his God Marduk had given him. Cyrus claims that Marduk commissioned him to save all the ethnic groups exiled to Babylonia. He interprets his historical success as proof that Marduk is the most powerful god and has approved of his political campaigns. This view resembles that of Israel's royal leaders who saw in political success a sign of divine authorization. Here again, as in the case of King Mesha's theology (noted in Chapter Four), the view of God emphasizes predictability and the orderly pattern behind history. Given the thinking among the Judean exiles in Babylonia, a return to the ancient heritage was not so much a break with history as a revival of the "true" tradition that had been either lost or corrupted during the period of the kingdoms. From this perspective, the story of Israel's kingship looks like a time of discontinuity with the past that is transcended by a return to the values and practices of the people when the exile ends.

Nevertheless, much of the response to the Babylonian Exile emphasized discontinuity. This is not surprising, since the restored Jewish commonwealth was far reduced from any of the pre-exilic conditions. Israelite religious practice, rituals, and beliefs underwent change. God's actions remained incomprehensible for many Israelites in exile. They would not ac-

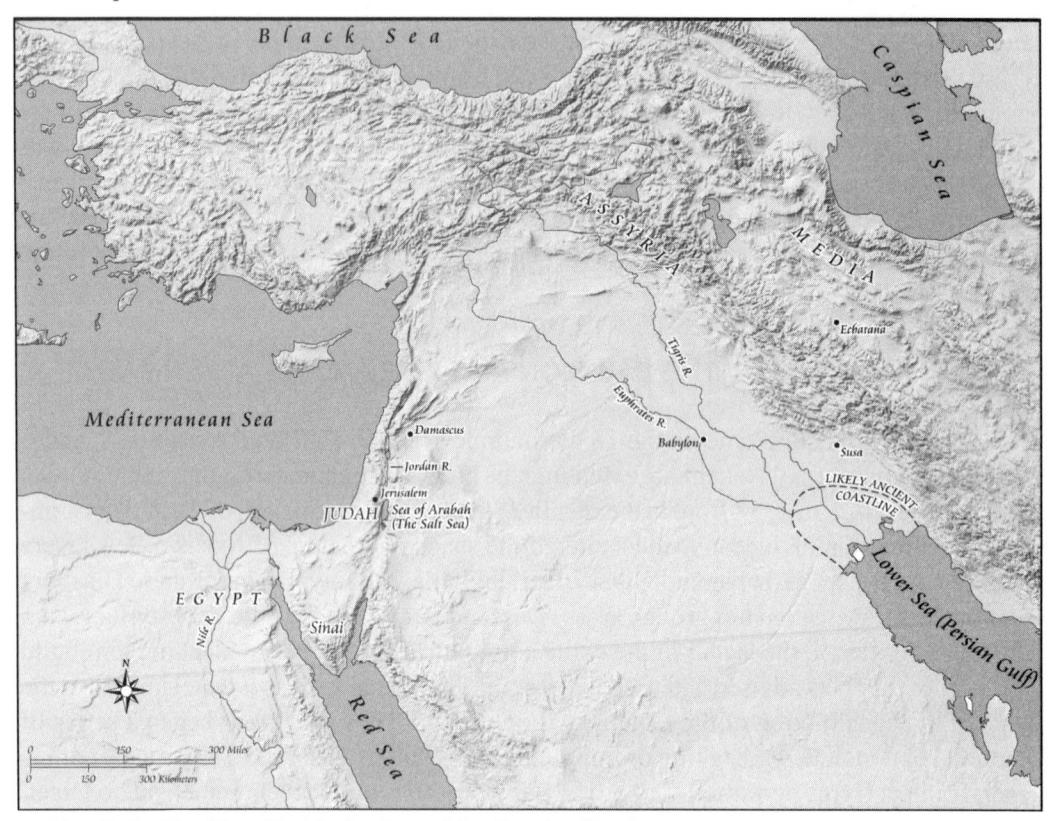

Map 5–5 The Near East in the time of the Persian Empire

cept the explanation that their sins had led to the disasters they experienced. New ideas of how God operated in the world, of the power of angels to introduce chaos and unpredictability in the world, developed to explain what seemed incomprehensible. After the return from the Babylonian captivity, the people of Israel saw themselves as "the Jews" whose history the Bible related, but whose reality comprised a great variety of religious perspectives and actions. The aftermath of the exile also led to a reevaluation of the entire tradition that influenced the way the Jews after the return from Babylonia imagined their previous history, the history of the first kingdoms.

The post-exilic period covers the restoration of the Judean kingdom after the exile to Babylonia. The chronicler who recorded that restoration also retold the stories of Israelite history from the creation of the world through the exile to Babylonia and the return from that exile. Looking at that history retrospectively meant that the writers had a very different perspective from that of the earlier historians. The exilic and post-exilic perspective saw a grand cosmic design stretching from creation through the revival of the Jewish kingdoms. The original period of the kingdoms became for them an ideal prototype made up of glorious models of good leadership. The entire period of the judges was passed over in silence; its chaos and disorder did not fit with the memory of an exalted and exemplary past. Kings such as David and Solomon were understood as ideal priestly figures. Although the tradition that the divided kingdom led to some disastrous rulers could not be expunged from the record, the chronicler who rewrote the history spent little time on these distortions of true religion. Instead, the original leaders were given detailed and loving treatment, and frequent reforms and revivals were highlights in the history. The history of God's holy nation, a nation led either by priests or by kings inspired by priests, became an example of a divine blueprint unfolding.

THREE EXAMPLES OF TRANSFORMED CONSCIOUSNESS: DAVID, PASSOVER, SATAN

Three examples show the change in consciousness experienced by the post-exilic Jewish community. The first focuses on a view of history. Like some parts of the Deuteronomic History, the book of 1 Chronicles considers David a divinely appointed messiah, a leader anointed by the divine for a special purpose (see Box 5–3). The chronicler's retelling of the story of David tends to emphasize the positive and omit anything negative. The narrative of David's census occurs not as an epilogue, but rather as the introduction to a lengthy section (1 Chronicles 21–28) that makes David the true genius behind Solomon's Temple. Not only does David move the Holy Ark and establish its new home, he institutes the priestly worship that will serve in the Temple, he sets out the construction of that Temple, and he instructs Solomon in everything that must be done there. Any negative view of David is carefully hidden in the midst of this description of his greatness.

While clearly the post-exilic period was one of discontinuity with the past, because the messianic kingship no longer ruled an independent Judean state, the chronicler's view emphasizes a different type of continuity. The purposes inspiring David were maintained in the new conditions. The priestly and ritual concerns animating David's career were, according to the picture in 1 Chronicles, precisely reproduced in the post-exilic Jerusalem priesthood. While acknowledging a political discontinuity with the past, the author of 1 Chronicles insisted on a ritual continuity, a continuity that transcended the shifting balance of power that characterizes politics.

A second transformation of data from the Deuteronomic History occurs in the description given to the ritual of Passover as described during Josiah's reformation of Judean religion. The holiday of Passover is described in various ways in the Hebrew Bible (see Box 5–4). Some passages present Passover as a national holiday of Israelite liberation. The ritual of Passover combines a public festival celebrated by the Israelites as a whole through ceremonies at the Jerusalem Temple, with private rituals observed by the family alone (as noted in connection with the holiday of unleavened bread). Joshua 5 connects the holiday with the ritual of circumcision. The Prophet Ezekiel and Numbers 28 understand the holiday primarily in priestly terms.

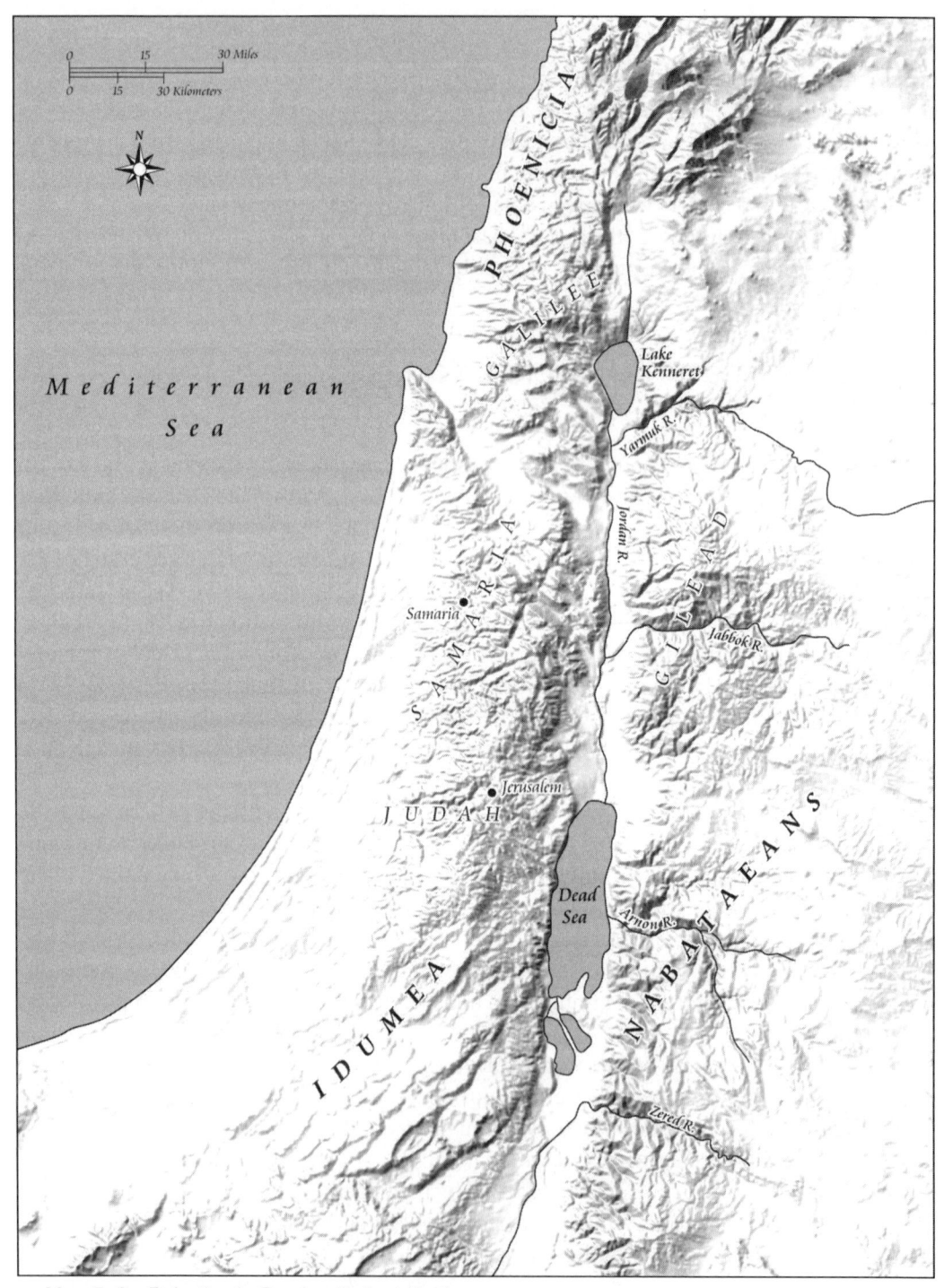

Map 5–6   Palestine in Persian-Hellenistic times

Perhaps the most conspicuous emphasis on Passover occurs during the religious reform carried out by King Josiah in 621 B.C.E. 2 Kings 22–23 describes Josiah's reform of Judean religion. One aspect of that reform included a command to centralize worship in Jerusalem. The narrative in 2 Kings describes how Josiah, fulfilling the injunctions of this book, destroyed the local shrines and gathered all the nation's leaders together in Jerusalem during a celebration of the festival of Passover. With that innovation comes the need to gather all Judeans in Jerusalem. Josiah's reformation creates a series of "pilgrimage" festivals—celebrations in the centralized shrine in Jerusalem at which all citizens are supposed to appear. Here, while the king's leadership is crucial, the text mentions that Josiah brought the priests and prophets to Jerusalem as well, and "all the people" joined in celebrating the holiday (see 2 Kings 23: 1–3, 21–25). 2 Kings emphasizes the Temple aspect of the holiday, celebrating the unity of the nation even while substantively reinforcing it.

Remarkably, 2 Kings says very little about the holiday and its rituals. It remarks that "No such Passover had been kept since the days of the judges," but it describes neither the Temple ceremonies nor any individual practices, although the king commands "all the people" to celebrate it (see 2 Kings 23:21–23). The festival is neither associated with Israel's Exodus from Egypt nor with the practice of eating unleavened bread. The centralization of the ritual in Jerusalem under the command of the king seems the one salient detail that interests the author of this story.

The descriptions of ritual events found in the books of Chronicles, Ezra, and Nehemiah suggest what might very well have been post-exilic practices in the land of Israel after the reconstitution of the Judean commonwealth. These books present a priestly perspective. The leaders of the people are the priests and the Levites, and they, rather than kings, elders, or prophets, shape the ritual observances. Pre-exilic rituals focused on the king and the nation; post-exilic priestly rituals focused on Temple rites. This change is expressed in 2 Chronicles 34–35, which tells about Josiah's reformation, but portrays it in ways more appropriate for post-exilic times than for the times of the Judean kings. While 2 Kings emphasizes that the discovered book led to a centralization of religious worship, 2 Chronicles assumes that Josiah came to this realization on his own; he did not need a book to inform him of its necessity. Instead, the book regulates the detailed practices of the different priestly families.

Passover, in this reading, is a celebration of intricate ritual performances carried out by an official class of priests. The description of Passover in 2 Chronicles combines this holiday with the agricultural "festival of unleavened bread," thereby strengthening its association with priests. The important point is that the priests conduct the ceremonies according to all the appropriate rituals, and the people participate in a state of ritual purity. In both 2 Chronicles 30 and 35, the holiday is not explicitly related to the story of the Exodus from Egypt.

In what way is Josiah's Passover celebration so special that, in 2 Chronicles 35:18, it is called unique among the royal observances of the holiday? Perhaps its importance lies in the

> **BOX 5–3   KING DAVID IN 1–2 SAMUEL AND 1 CHRONICLES**
>
> The portrait of David in the Deuteronomic History differs considerably from that in 1 Chronicles. The list below highlights some of those differences.
>
> *King David's Sins and Errors*
>   2 Samuel 9–20 details how David sins by committing adultery with Bathsheba the wife of Uriah the Hittite, how God s and punishes him, and how his family is plagued by internal divisions. 1 Chronicles omits any reference to any of these events.
>
> *David as King over a United Israel*
>   2 Samuel 2:1 tells how the people of Judah acclaim him as their king upon the death of King Saul. It takes considerably longer before the northern tribes of Israel accept him. Only in 2 Samuel 5:1 do they come to Hebron and declare him their king. 1 Chronicles 11 claims that immediately upon King Saul's death ALL Israel accepted David as king.
>
> *David and Cultic Priorities*
>   1 Chronicles 13–15 reverse the order of 2 Samuel 5–6 to imply that David first turned his attention to building a Temple for God and only then to military matters.
>
>   1 Chronicles attributes several hymns to David not found in 2 Samuel—for example 1 Chronicles 16:8–36 and 29:10–13 .
>
>   2 Samuel 5 only says that David considered building a Temple but that God rejected his idea. 1 Chronicles suggests that David actually planned the Temple and gave the blueprints to his son Solomon (1 Chronicles 22:2–19; 28:1–19).
>
> *David and the Census*
>   2 Samuel 24 claims that "God was angry against Israel" and so incited David to take a census of the people. (2 Samuel 24:1). Thereafter David becomes upset with what he has done and asks God for a way to rectify this error (2 Samuel 24:10). 1 Chronicles 21:1 replaces God's anger with Satan and declares that "Satan stood up against Israel and incited David to take a census." God then becomes angry with David for having yielded to this incitement, and David's regret for his action stems from this divine displeasure (1 Chronicles 21:7).

intricate detail of the priestly activity that took place. For example, in an extraordinary reconciling of differences, the narrative in 2 Chronicles solves a perplexing difficulty in the Torah. Exodus 12.9 declares that the Passover offering shall be roasted and not boiled. Deuteronomy 16.7 instructs the Israelites to boil the Passover offering. 2 Chronicles 35:13 declares that the priests "roasted the Passover lamb according to the law and then boiled the holy offerings in pots and distributed it to the people." From the perspective of 2 Chronicles, the story of Josiah's Passover was the story of a ritual that reminds people of their history,

BOX 5–4 PASSOVER IN THE HEBREW BIBLE

The Hebrew Bible gives many different descriptions of the observance for the holiday of Passover. Sometimes the holiday's association with the Exodus from Egypt is stressed; sometimes its connection to the ritual of circumcision becomes primary; at other times the public priestly performance is emphasized whereas in other case the private home ceremony is considered most essential. The following are some of the primary descriptions of the holiday:

Exodus 12—13
   The celebration is described as a household ceremony by which the participants are saved from the slaughter of the first born that God will bring on the Egyptians. A lamb is selected and roasted—it is not to be eaten raw or boiled (Exodus 12:8–9). The celebration is to be observed with a seven day festival on which no leaven is to be eaten. These passages emphasize the household nature of the festival by suggesting that children will ask about the meaning of the ritual and be told about the events that they symbolize (Exodus 12:24–27, 13:8–10).

Numbers 28:16–25
   The holiday is associated with the eating of unleavened bread but the chief rituals involved are those of public sacrifices performed by the official priesthood.

Deuteronomy 16:1–16
   Passover is described as a sacrifice that must be boiled and eaten in the place of the central sanctuary. It includes a seven day period during which only unleavened bread is eaten. References to "affliction" in Egypt and the departure from there provide an explanation for this festival which seems to be one observed by individual families.

Joshua 5:2–12
   The brief description of Passover —vv.10–12—does not mention the Exodus event and seems to imply that the key idea is that of eating unleavened bread made from the new produce of the field. The chapter gives greater importance to the practice of circumcision (vv. 2–9) which is demanded as a prerequisite for partaking of the Passover meal in Exodus 13:43–49.

Ezekiel 45:21–25
   An earlier passage, Ezekiel 44:9, declares that no uncircumcised person shall enter the sanctuary, since the Passover ceremony described involves only the priests and priestly ritual within the sanctuary, there is no mention of restricting Passover to the circumcised alone. While the Passover is, as in Numbers 28, associated with eating unleavened bread, the ritual is imagined as purely public in performance and not a household ceremony. Unlike Numbers 28, however, Ezekiel focuses on the sacrifices offered by the "princes" of the people.

> *2 Kings 23:21–38*
> This brief mention of the Passover during Josiah's reform remarks that "No such Passover had been kept since the days of the judges." The ritual is merely described as following the rules "prescribed in this book of the covenant," presumably that found in Deuteronomy 16.
>
> *2 Chronicles 35:7–19*
> While this passage does follow 2 Kings in that "The people of Israel who were present kept the Passover at that time and the festival of unleavened bread" and claims that "No Passover like it had been kept in Israel since the days of the prophet Samuel" (vv. 17–18), the emphasis throughout is on the public performance. The priests take up their official positions, the Levites fulfill their appropriate functions, and the Passover offering is BOTH roasted and boiled (thus combining the prescriptions in Exodus and Deuteronomy).

that hearkens back to the earliest times of settling in the land, and that puts into practice the words and instructions of an inherited text. It was unique because it combined and reconciled all the inherited traditions of the past in a single, coherent ritual. Whereas the Deuteronomic History saw the uniqueness of Josiah's Passover as a substantive ritual instituting the centralization of the cult, the post-exilic chronicler understood it as a celebratory ritual that encapsulated and affirmed traditions from the past.

A third example of changes occurring during the exilic and Post-Exilic periods involves views about supernatural beings and, in particular, those about the source and nature of evil. The idea of a supernatural force of opposition, a negative power in the universe, takes shape only after Jews have come into contact with Persian dualism. The influence of the Persians is found in the very name given this figure—that of The Opposer (**Satan**). The symbol of Satan often represents the reality of evil in the biblical tradition. As views of evil changed, so too did the biblical presentation of Satan. In many biblical references, the term *Satan* (Hebrew for "adversary") stands as a title for one of God's angels. This angelic servant of God often substitutes for the divinity when a later writer adapts an earlier story about Israel's kingdoms. A striking example occurs in the appearance of "the adversary" in 1 Chronicles 21.

Contrasting the story of David's census of the people in 2 Samuel 24 with its use in 1 Chronicles 21 suggests how the idea of a Satan became useful for post-exilic Jews (see Box 5–3). 2 Samuel 24 appears as an epilogue to the story of King David. A positive evaluation of that king runs as a consistent thread throughout the two books of Samuel, culminating in 2 Samuel 23, which proclaims a covenantal relationship between Israel's God and the Davidic dynasty. 2 Samuel 24 picks up a different thread, that in which David is hardly an ideal figure and in which his weakness and shortsightedness leads to the separation of the united kingdoms of Israel and Judah and the ultimate collapse of his dynasty. While the covenantal strand emphasizes continuity and an unfolding pattern, this second strand emphasizes discontinuity and the possible reversals that history may hold in store. 2 Samuel 24 begins with the statement that God grew angry with David and therefore inspired him to sin by taking a census of the people. The chapter ends (and the book of 2 Samuel with it) with David's atonement for the census. Strikingly, *he* rather than God recognizes that the census is evil and asks God how to atone for it.

The narrative in 1 Chronicles proceeds differently. The author rejects the idea that God could incite David to sin. Instead, Satan becomes the instigator of the census, and God responds in anger to David's acquiescence to this temptation. These two points suggest an important difference in theology. The Deuteronomic History insists that disasters take place because God punishes apostasy. David's actions become an extension of the divine anger in this case. The author of 1 Chronicles 21 considers God so transcendent as to be beyond instigating evil acts. David could not be more righteous than God. God's pure justice comes out in his rebuke to David. On the other hand, the author of 1 Chronicles 21 realizes that good people sometimes go astray. Bad things happen, and there must be some cause for them; nevertheless, the transcendent divinity cannot be that cause. By creating a figure to take responsibility for evil off of God's shoulders, these Jews maintained that the divine plan unfolds without a wrinkle, that despite some setbacks, nothing will hinder the destiny to which God is leading Israel.

SUMMARY QUESTIONS

1. How do the ideas of covenant and Torah in Joshua 23 contrast with those in Joshua 24?

2. How does the book of Joshua differ from the book of Judges in describing the period of the settlement in the land of Israel?

3. What roles are given women in the views of the ritual and ethics in the book of Judges?

4. How are covenant and kingship intertwined in the stories of Israel's kingship from Saul through Josiah?

5. How does the chronicler transform stories from the Deuteronomic History?

Four Suggested Essay Questions

1. Explain two ways in which a tradition may view history. Show how one story about Joshua (for example, any one of the stories in Joshua 2–8) expresses one way and how one story about King David (for example, any one of the stories of his rise to power in 1 Samuel 15–31 or of his familial woes in 2 Samuel 9–20) illustrates the other.

2. Explain two ways in which a tradition may view the supernatural. Apply one of them to the narrative about the census in 2 Samuel 24 and the other to the narrative in 1 Chronicles 21.

3. Explain two ways in which a tradition may view ethics. Apply one of them to stories about Samson found in Judges (any of the tales about how foreign wives led him into disaster would be useful) and the other to the portrait of Solomon's ethics given in such passages as 1 Kings 3:1–3, 5:7–12; 8:4–43.

4. Explain two ways in which a tradition may view ritual. Apply one of them to the Passover ritual described in Exodus 12:1–13 and the other to the Passover ritual described in 2 Chronicles 35.

Exercise

Read the following paragraph from an answer to Question 4.:

> Religious rituals sometimes seek to transform the world in which the worshiper lives, while at other times they provide public evidence for the loyalty of believers to the religious community. Transforming rituals often seek to protect worshipers from grave danger. Such rituals often focus on the personal life of individuals and the choices they make. Rituals proclaiming public loyalty, however, are most often performed by ritual experts trained in intricate procedures. These rituals affirm the group purposes and solidarity of those within the religious community.

Now answer the following five questions:

1. Write a topic sentence for a paragraph showing that Exodus 12:1–13 illustrates a transforming ritual.

2. Select a verse from Exodus 12:1–13 that illustrates how Passover is a transforming ritual.

3. Write two sentences, one of which either cites the verse you have selected verbatim or paraphrases it, and the second of which explains how it illustrates that Passover is a transforming ritual.

4. Select a verse from Exodus 12:1–13 that illustrates how the Passover ritual focuses on the private life of the individual.

5. Write two sentences, one of which either cites the verse you have selected verbatim or paraphrases it, and the second of which explains how it illustrates that the Passover ritual focuses on the private life of the individual.

FOR FURTHER READING

The books listed below should be a point of departure for your future study. Each includes a bibliography that will guide you beyond its basic information.

1. Ackroyd, Peter R., *The Chronicler in His Age* (Sheffield, England: JSOT Press, 1991).

2. Brettler, Marc Zvi, *Creation of History in Ancient Israel* (London: Routledge, 1995).

3. Davies, Philip R., *In Search of Ancient Israel* (Sheffield, England: Scheffield Academic Press, 1992).
4. Mullen, E. Theodore, *Narrative History and Ethnic Boundaries: The Deuteronomistic Historian and the Creation of Israelite National Identity* (Atlanta, GA: Scholars Press, 1993).
5. Sweeney, Marvin, A. *King Josiah of Judah: The Lost Messiah of Israel* (Oxford: Oxford University Press, 2001).
6. Thompson, Thomas L., *The Mythic Past: Biblical Archaeology and the Myth of Israel* (London: Random House, 1999).

6

Religions of the Prophets

READING ASSIGNMENT

    1 Kings 17–19, 21
    2 Kings 1–9, 18–20
    Hosea 1–7
    Amos 1–5
    Isaiah 6, 7–8, 44, 58
    Jeremiah 17:19–27; 30–31
    Haggai (complete)

LEARNING OBJECTIVES

By the end of this lesson, you will be able to:
- Describe the religious perspectives in the Deuteronomic prophets.
- Describe the religious perspectives in Amos and Hosea.
- Describe the religious perspectives in Isaiah, Second Isaiah, and Third Isaiah.
- Describe the religious perspectives in Jeremiah and Ezekiel.
- Describe the religious perspectives in Post-Exilic prophets.

INTRODUCTION

This chapter looks at the phenomenon of prophecy in the Bible. Ancient Israel had three institutions of leadership—the king, who was authorized by popular acclaim and anointed with oil; the priest, who was born into the family God had designated for the task of carrying

Interpretive Matrix for Chapter Six

View of the Divine: How people interact with God and the supernatural; how God interacts with the world.	View of History: How past, present, and future are related; who controls the shape of events.	View of Ethics: How people behave toward other people; how they behave toward people like themselves and to those who are different.	View of Ritual: How people behave toward the Divine; how they perform religious actions.
The Divine as Transcendent: God communicates to humanity through prophetic intermediaries.	*History as Continuous:* The past creates precedents to be followed in the present. Covenant laws provide continuing guidance for human action.	*Inclusive Ethics:* Royalty and commoners should be treated the same way. God does not favor any particular ritual place. God's covenant is with all human beings.	*Ritual as Transforming:* Ritual can effect a miraculous change in nature. Ritual can initiate an improvement in national fortune.
The Divine as Immanent: God alters natural processes such as rain or prosperity. God will heal people if they repent.	*History as Discontinuous:* God as creator can transform events in unexpected ways.	*Exclusive Ethics:* Members of one group should not follow the practices of another group. God favors one ritual place above all others. God has a covenant with only one human group.	*Ritual as Symbolic:* Ritual is purely a human, not a divine concern; God does not demand ritual. Ritual without ethical action is meaningless. Obedience to ritual may lead to ethical actions.

out sacrifices; and the prophet, whom God chose directly without the need for popular election, family descent, or even special training. Other ancient Near Eastern nations besides Israel had similar types of leaders. A royal court included special individuals who could interpret mysterious signs of nature, decode dreams, and provide advice from supernatural sources to their patrons. This chapter looks at the biblical books in which the prophets figure prominently: first the Former Prophets (the Deuteronomic History) and then the Latter Prophets (the so-called "writing prophets" with prophetic books named for their authors).

These different collections of writings exhibit contrasting views of history, the divine, ethics, and ritual. Diversity also exists within each collection. Perhaps the most famous of the Deuteronomic prophets is Elijah. The stories clustering around this figure often offer contrasting religious perspectives. Sometimes, a narrative about Elijah focuses on miracles and the unpredictability of history; at other times, it emphasizes a continuity of divine intention. Some tales of Elijah make ritual actions substantive means of changing reality, of transforming nature; other tales use ritual symbolically to reinforce an exclusive ethics; still other tales focus on an inclusive ethics in which ritual is secondary.

110   Chapter 6

The Latter Prophets show diverse religious strands as well. The pre-exilic prophets, such as Amos, Hosea, or Isaiah, often criticize all ritual. They claim that God insists on a universal ethical standard to which all people, not merely Israelites or Judeans, must adhere. Post-exilic prophets like Haggai, Zechariah, and Zephaniah express a positive view of ritual and claim that God prefers the Jews to all other peoples.

The book of Isaiah represents the tensions within this collection well. It is a composite work and reflects several different historical periods. Even the opening chapters, however, blend particularism and universalism, transcendence and immanence, a positive and negative view of ritual, and an ambivalent understanding of history. This diversity serves an ideological purpose, that of making the prophet's message less easily understood as a way of fulfilling the text: "Say to this people: Keep listening, but do not comprehend; keep looking, but do not understand. Make the mind of this people dull…so they may not look with their eyes and listen with their ears and comprehend with their minds" (Isaiah 6: 9–10). This verse cautions readers from taking any prophetic statement as a simple or literal pronouncement.

SOME IMPORTANT TERMS

The following terms are important in this chapter Some of them have been listed in previous chapters; in those cases the term is not in **bold** in the main body of this chapter. Where names of books are also the names of individuals (such as Isaiah), the name does not appear in the Glossary.

Ahab	Ezekiel	Malachi
Ahaz	Gad	Mernephta
Ahijah	Former Prophets	Minor Prophets
Alma	Gilgal	Naboth
Amaziah	Haggai	Nathan
Amos	Hesed	Obadiah
Assyria	Hezekiah	Particularism
Baal	High Priest	Prophet
Babylonian Exile	Hosea	Sabbath
Bathsheba	Isaiah	Samaria
Beth El	Jeremiah	Second Isaiah
Day of Atonement	Jerusalem	Solomon
David	Jonah	Third Isaiah
Deuteronomic History	Joshua the High Priest	Universalism
Elijah	Josiah	Uriah the Hittite
Elisha	Latter Prophets	Zerubbabel
Exodus from Egypt	Major Prophets	

WHAT ARE THE PROPHETS?

Of the various leadership groups described in Chapter Five, the prophetic type requires special attention. Earlier students of the Bible tended to think of prophecy as a peculiarly biblical phenomenon. To some extent, this judgment was justified. Biblical prophecy exhibits some unique characteristics. Nevertheless, the figure of the prophet is present throughout the ancient Near East. Ancient Near Eastern leaders often turned to individuals said to be inspired by the divine; they are often called oracles, but the term is also used to describe the message itself. An oracle may be a short proclamation of God's intentions, or it may refer to the person delivering that proclamation. Such people advised kings and priests about what God wanted, about how to perform correct rituals, and about God's plans for history. More often than not, such advice concerned tactics for winning a war, encouragement for military endeavors, and predictions of success. The Hebrew term *navi* often describes this type of an advisor. Ordinarily, such persons operated within the normal ritual process (called the *cult*). They would be summoned from their ritual duties to answer the questions set by the king or the priests.

The biblical corpus, however, takes this general ancient Near Eastern religious form and alters it. In the first place, the Bible emphasizes not the cultic prophet, the prophet associated with an established shrine or political center, but rather the prophet who stands *against* the establishment. Second, these prophets repeatedly denounce their audience and predict disaster for them. Prophetic teachings become the basis from which later Jews learned to understand why Israel had gone into exile, why God seemed to have abandoned the divinely elected nation, and how the people could once again find favor before God.

The prophetic section of the Hebrew Bible divides into three unequal parts. The historical narratives of the Deuteronomic History discussed in the previous chapter are populated with established prophets: **Nathan** and **Gad**, who challenge King David; **Ahijah** who confronts Solomon; and **Elijah** and **Elisha**, during the time of the divided kingdom (see Box 6–1). In some ways, these prophets resemble the general model in the ancient Near East. They are attached to official sanctuaries and serve the royal institution. Nevertheless, they show a courageous boldness in challenging the political leadership. This chapter begins by looking at one characteristic conflict, that between the royal religion and the religion of the prophet Elijah.

The section that follows the Deuteronomic History consists of three books: Isaiah, Jeremiah, and Ezekiel. They are called **Major Prophets** because of their length. Modern scholarship believes that these books have been highly edited and combine texts from several different sources. While Jeremiah and Ezekiel require a complex analysis to reveal their composite nature, the book of Isaiah easily divides into three separate sections; the Isaiah of Jerusalem, **Second Isaiah**, and **Third Isaiah**. Each section has its own distinctive approach to the nature of the divine, and the meaning of history, ritual, and ethics (see Box 6–2). Taken as a whole, however, the book of Isaiah shares a common structure with that of the other two books. The three books taken in sequence move from the time of the northern kingdom's fall, through the fall of Judah, to the exile and the predicted return from it.

BOX 6–1   THE PROPHETS IN THE DEUTERONOMIC HISTORY

The Deuteronomic History or Former Prophets records several conflicts arising between prophets and kings. This chart outlines those conflicts.

1 Samuel 15	Samuel, called a seer and a prophet, confronts Saul for disobeying his instructions demanding the annihilation of the Amalekites.
2 Samuel 7	Nathan the Prophet instructs David concerning God's will concerning the building of a Temple in Jerusalem.
2 Samuel 12	Nathan confronts David and reprimands him because of his adultery with and subsequent marriage to Bathsheba.
2 Samuel 24	The prophet Gad instructs David concerning his reparation for taking a census and tells him to erect an altar in the place that eventually was the site for Solomon's Temple.
1 Kings 11	Ahijah of Shiloh confronts Solomon and predicts that the united kingdom over which he rules will be ripped apart.
1 Kings 13 2 Kings 23	Jeroboam, king of the Northern kingdom of Israel, is admonished by an unnamed prophet who predicts the birth of King Josiah of Judah and the eventually centralization of worship in Jerusalem.
1 Kings 14	Jeroboam's wife seeks help from Ahijah who pronounces God's rejection of Jeroboam.
1 Kings 1	God sends Jehu the son of Hanani against Baasha of Israel predicting that he shall suffer the same fate as Jeroboam.
1 Kings 17–19, 21	These chapters describe several encounters between Elijah the Tishbite and Ahab, king of Israel. The chapters also mention a certain Obadiah who saves a hundred prophets by hiding them in caves.
1 Kings 22	Micaiah ben Imlah provides a prophecy of disaster that is proven correct in contrast to the statements of the prophet Zedekiah ben Chenaanah who predicts success.
2 Kings 2–9, 13	These chapters focus on Elijah's disciple Elisha ben Shafat and his political intrigue with the Arameans and his instigation of Jehu's coup to take the throne from Ahab.
2 Kings 14:25–27	Jonah ben Amitai provides an optimistic prophecy for Jeroboam ben Joash with assurances that God has taken pity and would not utterly blot out the name of Israel.
2 Kings 18–20	These chapters describe the relationship of Isaiah ben Amoz to Judah's King Hezekiah. While some of these narratives overlap with chapters in the Book of Isaiah, they also add some new material.
2 Kings 22	The only female prophet in the Deuteronomic History, Hulda, is called upon to verify the authenticity of the book of Moses that has been found. If that book is identified with Deuteronomy, then there is an irony that Hulda, a female prophet, authorizes the only book in the Torah that prohibits women from being prophets.
2 Kings 24	Nebuchadnezzar destroys Jerusalem and carries away its spoils and its citizens "according to the word of the Lord that he spoke by his servants the prophets" (24:1). No specific prophet is named.

BOX 6–2 THE MAJOR PROPHETS

The three books, Isaiah, Jeremiah, and Ezekiel, that begin the Latter Prophets are called the "major" or "longer" prophets. They are distinguished by their length rather than by their relative importance in the canon. The following outlines chart the development within each of these books. They all move from predictions of destruction for Israel to predictions of revival and restoration and conclude with imprecations against foreign nations. That organization suggests a conscious plan and program of the editors of these works.

The Book of Isaiah

1–6	Prologue including Isaiah's earliest predictions against Israel and his call to be a prophet
7–8	Isaiah's interaction with King Ahaz of Judah during the Pyro-Ephraimite war (743–733)
9–12	Assorted oracles with some predicting disaster and others predicting a future of greatness
13–23	Oracles against foreign nations
24–27	A set of apocalyptic visions about the end of the world and the end of history; these are probably a later addition to the book of Isaiah
28–32	Oracles about Samaria and Jerusalem
33–35	Poetic evocations of the end of the world and eschataology including poetry resembing liturgy used in worship
36–39	Legends concerning the siege of Jerusalem by the Babylonians similar but not always identical to those found in 2 Kings 18–20
40–55	Oracles of redemption for the Judean exiles claiming that God will restore the fortunes of Israel, identified as God's suffering servant, and will work miracles for the Jews
56–66	Oracles reconstituting the Palestinian Jewish community including an evocation of changed rituals and a universal message of God's cosmic power that brings all nations under God's power

The Book of Jeremiah

1–25	A series of sermons, visions, and oracles from between 627–605 focusing on the coming of destruction, infractions of moral and ritual commandments, Jeremiah's emotional response to the situation, and several legends about Jeremiah's behavior to symbolize these ideas (7:1–26;13:1–11; 16:1–9;17:19–27;18:1–11;19:1–13; 20:1–6; 21:1–7; 24:1–10)
26–29	Confrontations between Jeremiah and various Judean kings concerning the siege of Jerusalem, the exile to Babylonia, and Jeremiah's council on accepting the long-term nature of the exile
30–33	The book of Consolation—including predictions of a new covenant between God and Israel and a restored Jewish nation

34–45	Legends on religious life and authority in which Jeremiah interacts with various leaders during the period of exile after the Babylonian conquest of Jerusalem
46–51	Hymns against the nations of the world that include an exilic perspective, a philosophy of history, and mythic eschatology about the end of the world; 51:63 announces that the words of Jeremiah have ended
52	Epilogue that reproduces the description of the fall of Jerusalem and the deportation of its leading members found in 2 Kings 24:18–25:30; Jeremiah is not mentioned in this chapter

The Book of Ezekiel

1–3	Prologue including Ezekiel's inaugural vision
4–14	Oracles predicting the destruction of Judah in general and Jerusalem in particular
15–20	Poetry, images and parables asserting personal responsibility and the dire future of Judah
20	A meditation on the meaning of covenant and ritual
21–24	Predicting and describing the destruction of Jerusalem by the Babylonians
25–32	Oracles against foreign nations such as Moab, Egypt, Tyre, and Babylonia
33–39	Oracles concerning the restoration of the post-exilic Jewish nation and the final conflict that will end history
40–48	oracles describing the rebuilt Jerusalem sanctuary, the ritual calendar and the priestly practices that will be carried out

The final section of the biblical prophetic corpus includes twelve books, extending from Hosea through Malachi. These are called the **Minor Prophets**, not because of difference in importance, but only because of difference in length. The themes, style, and intent of the minor prophets parallel those in the major prophets and trace the same historical trajectory from predictions of disaster, to predictions of a restoration, concluding with works from the restored commonwealth (see Box 6–3). The history of the period has been sketched in the previous chapter (see Box 5–2), and provides background as you read about these prophets.

CONCERNS OF THE DEUTERONOMIC PROPHETS

The prophets, by their very nature, might seem to symbolize a view of unpredictable history. Divinely appointed intermediaries convey God's desires to people. The need for such periodic communication suggests that new commandments arise as new situations demand new responses. Such intermittent messages point to historical discontinuity. Nevertheless, the Deuteronomic prophets often express a view of religious continuity. They rely on the early history of the people—stories of Abraham, Isaac, and Jacob—as precedent for their own times. When King David seeks to build a Temple in Jerusalem, a prophet criticizes him. God announces that "I have not lived in a house since the day I brought up the people of Israel

BOX 6–3 THE MINOR PROPHETS

These twelve books, called the "minor" prophets begin with writings primarily from the pre-exilic period, continue with works from the fall of Israel, move to the fall of Judah, and conclude with prophetic texts from the restored Jewish commonwealth after the return from the Babylonian exile in 538 B.C.E. Each description gives an approximate date for the prophet and a summary of the contents of the book. All dates are before the common era.

Hosea was a pre-exilic prophet; the book uses Hosea's own biography to symbolize Israel's relationship to God; it rejects the leadership of priests and kings and exalts the traditions of Moses rather than of patriarchs such as Jacob. It insists that God loves Israel but that an exile will still take place.

Joel as a book provides no internal basis for dating it. The book affirms God's favor on Zion and predicts divine vengeance on Israel's enemies. In 1:2–2:27 Joel interprets a plague of locusts as divine judgment that provides the basis for an apocalyptic vision. Most modern scholars think of this book as an expression of prophetic ritualism composed during the Persian period (about 400 to 350).

Amos was thought to be a contemporary of Hosea; he was a Judean prophet who went to the north to preach against Jeroboam II, the king of Israel; the book includes legal indictments of Israelite behavior, sermons that emphasize God's desire for ethics rather than ritual, visions indicating coming disasters, and a legend in which Amos opposes Amaziah, the priest of the king's shrine at Beth El.

Obadiah was the shortest book of the prophets, certainly writing during the exile to Babylonia; it has three sections—an indictment of the Edomites for attacking the Israelites when they were in danger, an announcement of God's punishment on foreign nations, and a proclamation that Israel's exiles will return to their promised land.

Jonah is not really a prophetic work but a legendary narrative about a certain Jonah who sought to avoid his task of preaching to non-Jews but who eventually does so. A liturgical hymn is inserted into its second chapter. The book was probably written during the Babylonian or Persian periods.

Micah was prophet about 740–700; the book shares passages with Isaiah. It has an anti-urban bias, emphasizes the doom of exploitation of the poor, corruption among the priests and aristocracy, and hopes for a better future.

Nahum was written at the fall of Assyria and its capital Nineveh (probably 612); the emphasis is on a universal, international ethics; uses liturgical formulas drawn from the psalms; themes other prophets applied to Israel such as false leaders and injustice are now applied to the other nations.

> *Habakkuk* is a form of complaint literature in the shape of a prayer; distinguishes between the godless and the righteous a central feature; 1:2–2:5 a dialogue between the prophet and God; 2:6–20 five woes against a wicked nation; chapter 3 a lengthy psalm-like poem. Probably lived between 608 and 598.
>
> *Zephaniah* was written during the reign of Josiah (640–609); prepares the way for the Josianic reformation; declares the problematic politics of pro-Assyrian strategies of the kings before and after Josiah; includes condemnation of Judean religious practices before Deuteronomy in 1:4–6, 8, 9, 12; 3:1–3, 7, but extends a warning to foreign nations and predicts a day of wrath upon them and a day of comfort and consolation for those who serve God.
>
> *Haggai* was written 520 during renewed efforts to establish a religious community; emphasizes the Temple and its functionaries—both the king, Zerubbabel and its High Priest, Joshua; predicts a glorious future for Judah when the Temple is completed.
>
> *Zechariah* divides into two parts: 1–8 coming from the early Persian period (contemporaneous to Haggai) and 9–14 (which nowhere uses the name Zechariah) that probably derives from the Hellenistic period; 1–8 assert the value of relying on God rather than power and focus on the High Priest Joshua rather than Zerubbabel; Zechariah 3 portrays Satan as an angel subservient to God; 9–14 consist of eschatological oracles and visions culminating in universal worship in Jerusalem; messianic images include riding a donkey, thirty pieces of silver; and the new celebration of Sukkot (the festival of booths) in Jerusalem.
>
> *Malachi* anonymous—the phrase means "My messenger" and is a title not a name; focus is on priestly concerns such as Israel's relationship to God, sacrifices, marriages, tithes, theodicy; 2:10's question "Have we not all one father" refers to the priestly caste and seeks to end their internal disputes.

from Egypt to this day" (2 Samuel 7:6). The verse questions the need to change established practices by building a fixed sanctuary. Actions in the present should continue the practices of the past. Nevertheless, change does occur throughout the period of the kingship, and prophets often adumbrate those changes. When the united kingdom under Solomon is about to split into two kingdoms, a prophet announces that change (1 Kings11:29–36).

The Deuteronomic prophets, such as Nathan, Ahijah, and Elijah (see Box 6–1), stand within the institution of kingship. They address royalty and provide advice on practical matters. When King David wishes to build a Temple, he asks for counsel from a prophet. When God takes him to task for taking a census, again a prophet makes the proclamation. The clear message here is that God interacts with humanity through inspired intermediaries. God is transcendent and aloof. Only through selected individuals does the divine communicate to someone even as exalted as a king.

Prophets, therefore, sometimes represent a transcendent view of the divinity. They bridge the distance between the divine and the human. Most mortals cannot comprehend God's supernatural power. God's reality transcends the ordinary categories by which human beings understand the world; God is beyond human comprehension. The supernatural is so much more powerful than humanity and so removed from humanity that most people cannot grasp the divine essence at all. When contact with God is needed, even the king requires the help of a prophet.

Prophets, however, also view God's power as immanent in the world. God can cause a drought or end it (2 Kings 18). God can heal the sick (1 Kings 17:17–24; 2 Kings 4:11–37; Isaiah 38). In these anecdotes, God enters into human affairs. God has an interest in human politics and human welfare. The Deuteronomic view of the divine emphasizes compassion and concern for humanity—either for all people in general or for the Jewish people in particular.

Just as some aspects of the prophetic writings emphasize transcendence and other aspects immanence, so too some prophetic texts express an inclusive ethics and others an exclusive one. Some passages assume that God makes no distinction between Israelite and non-Israelite when judging human behavior. The famous story about King David and **Bathsheba** reveals this. Bathsheba is married to **Uriah the Hittite**, a non-Israelite who serves in David's army. David pursues an adulterous relationship with Bathsheba, and when he can no longer keep this affair secret arranges to have Uriah killed. God sends Nathan the prophet to David and tricks the king into condemning himself. The ethics in this case demands equal treatment for both the Israelite and non-Israelite.

From another perspective, however, the ethics found in the Deuteronomic prophets is exclusive rather than inclusive. According to that view, ethics distinguishes Israel from its neighbors, and God demands more of Israel because of its relationship to the deity. Covenantal fidelity determines whether the nation will succeed or fail, whether the divine will support or oppose the people.

The Hebrew word describing this idea is "love" or fidelity is **hesed**. The term in itself is neither inclusive or exclusive. It basically means following divine directives, which results in the "good"—that is, in a successful life. Such actions could well apply to all people in all nations and places. In a later period, however, the term took on a particularistic meaning, because the agreement between God and the people became the basis for national identity. It served, as it were, as the constitution of the Israelite kingdoms. God, understood as the protector of the nation, provided the nation with its basic document of incorporation. In this case, doing good implies living up to national ideals, to fulfilling civil responsibilities.

Still later, the agreement with the divine was looked upon as a personal code, a private set of obligations incumbent upon every individual. By obeying this code, people learn what is best for them; the law has been given so that they can realize their highest potential. God, from this perspective, shows covenantal love (hesed) to each person, who then responds with a similar loyalty (again, hesed). Fidelity to covenantal love leads to a distinctive way of life that marks the individual as obedient to God. The demand for and rewards given to such obedience do not depend on a national identity, but extend to include any human being. The differences in how the prophets understand hesed illustrates the ethical divergences in the Former Prophets.

The Deuteronomic prophets also differ concerning ritual. When David proposes to build a sanctuary to YHWH, the prophet Nathan reports that God complains: "Wherever I have moved about among all the people of Israel, did I ever speak a word with any of the tribal leaders of Israel, whom I commanded to shepherd my people Israel, saying, 'Why have you not built me a house of cedar?'" (2 Samuel 7:7). While kings may desire to erect a Temple for Yahweh, this is not God's desire. God seems to reject ritual as a purely human concern.

Another ritual experience seems to reaffirm this. When David commits adultery with Bathsheba, Nathan approaches him and declares: "The child that is born to you shall die" (2 Samuel 12:14). David resorts to ritual actions: "David therefore pleaded with God for the child; David fasted, and went in and lay all night on the ground" (2 Samuel 7:16). The ritual expresses David's repentance and concern, but it does not prevent his child from dying.

Stories about the prophet Elijah, however, suggest that ritual may sometimes accomplish a substantive change in reality. Elijah represents a very strange and ambivalent type of prophetic hero. He is introduced in 1 Kings 17 as a miracle worker whom God uses as his representative before King **Ahab**. This view dominates in the two confrontation stories of 1 Kings 18 and 1 Kings 21. Yet 1 Kings 19 offers a more ambiguous picture of the prophet. 1 Kings 18 makes it clear that **Obadiah** saved at least one hundred prophets. In 1 Kings 19, Elijah claims that he is the only prophet who has been left alive. In 1 Kings 18 and 21, God seems to approve of Elijah. In 1 Kings 19, God seeks out a replacement and actually seems to reject Elijah as his prophet.

The Bible describes two confrontations between Elijah, representative of prophetic leadership, and alternative leaders in ancient Israel (1 Kings 18 and 1 Kings 21). One confrontation (1 Kings 18) portrays a contest between Elijah and the priests of the Canaanite god Baal. From a modern standpoint, the ethics of the story seems rather strange. Elijah demands that the people choose between worshiping Baal and worshiping YHWH, the God of Israel. He claims that one cannot include both types of worship in a single nation: "How long will you go limping with two different opinions? If the Lord is God, follow him; but if Baal, then follow him" (1 Kings 18:21). What follows is a contest. Elijah proves that the priests of Baal cannot succeed in bringing rain. Their rituals are failures. Thereupon he slaughters all the unsuccessful priests and reinstates worship of Israel's God alone.

The story accepts the premise of priestly belief: the proof of religion depends on the efficacy of its rituals. The ethics emphasizes the distinctiveness of the Israelite tradition; the particular culture of the Israelites is made central. Elijah's ritual symbolizes the twelve tribes of this nation and their association with Abraham, Isaac, and Jacob who was called Israel (1 Kings 18: 31–32, 36). He demands that the Israelites affirm their particular identity in contrast to the non-Israelites who serve Baal. He insists that God only helps Israelites when they separate themselves from foreigners. Elijah proclaims **particularism**, that is, God's favoritism toward one national group. This approach differs from **universalism**, an idea that rejects favoritism on the basis of nationality. From that perspective, God makes the same demands for righteousness on all nations of the world. Social ethics unites all people in common interests.

While in 1 Kings 18 Elijah espouses particularism, 1 Kings 21 focuses on a different set of ethics: a social ethics. King Ahab assumes that his will establishes law; ethics depends on what the king decides. According to the tale, **Naboth**, an ordinary Israelite, possesses a desirable garden adjoining the king's property. Ahab wishes to purchase that garden, but Naboth refuses to sell it. The king thereupon claims the right to confiscate the property. Ahab, convinced by his wife, Jezebel, that the king has absolute control over all territory in his kingdom, executes Naboth on a charge of blasphemy. He then appropriates his garden for himself. Elijah confronts him, claiming that God's laws have been violated. Whereas Ahab may think that human beings create the law and can alter it at will, Elijah claims that God promulgates a universal law that all must follow. Elijah raises the claim of hesed, that God demands obedience to ethical principles. Although this ethics of hesed is universalist, Elijah also includes an exclusivist note. Elijah objects that Ahab has assimilated Phoenician ways; he is not being true to the particular rules of YHWH.

The idea of God is different in each tale. Elijah rejects the idea that both Baal and YHWH are divinities; only Israel's God has real power. The tale focuses on a single force dominating all history. God's power over nature expresses a sense of divine transcendence and authority. The second story does not debate the reality or unity of God; both Elijah and Ahab agree that Israel's God has dominion over the king. They disagree about that God's concerns. The question is whether or not God has an interest in mundane human actions. Ahab relegates law to purely human agents; Elijah imagines God involved in daily human behavior.

THE WRITING PROPHETS IN THE DEUTERONOMIC STYLE

The ambiguity noted in the Elijah tales also appears in certain texts of the Latter Prophets. Although, in general, the style, form, and even content of the writing prophets—Isaiah, Jeremiah, and Ezekiel and the twelve minor prophets—differ considerably from that of the Deuteronomic History, there is some overlap. In fact, several chapters in the book of Isaiah report legends also found in the book of Kings. Other books, such as Amos and Ezekiel, also include material that could be called "legendary" and that fit the style and form of the Deuteronomic material. Nevertheless, shaping that material within the context of the rest of these books gives them a very different meaning.

The book of Isaiah displays the variety of content and complex organization of the so-called "writing prophets" (see the outline of the book provided in Box 6–2). Not only does the book divide into several subgroups—one associated with the Isaiah of Jerusalem during the pre-exilic time, another evidently composed during the Babylonian exile, and another written in post-exilic times—but each grouping also includes several genres; oracles, legends, poems, and covenant arguments. The book begins with proclamations made by Isaiah during times of crisis in Judah. The first five chapters outline the social and political failures of the priests, kings, and leading families of the Judeans. They announce the destruction that will follow upon these failures. Isaiah 6 provides the inaugural vision that invested Isaiah with his commission as a prophet. The next two chapters present some prophetic legends much in the style of the Deuteronomic History.

Isaiah 7 tells of a confrontation between the prophet Isaiah and the Judean king **Ahaz** at the time of a crisis in Judah's relationship with the Assyrian empire. Despite its clear setting in a particular time and place, this chapter has often been a central passage for Christian theology, that interprets the prediction of a "virgin" giving birth as an allusion to Jesus. The academic study of this passage begins by rejecting any theological agenda and looking at this text as an expression of a human purpose. The first note to make is that the term *virgin* does not appear in the Hebrew. The Hebrew word used, **alma**, refers to a mature young woman of childbearing age, regardless of her sexual experience. The Greek translation of the Bible, the Septuagint, through its introduction of the term *parthenos*, first suggested the idea of a virgin in the passage.

The content of the chapter divides easily into three parts: verses 1–9 narrate a confrontation between Ahaz and Isaiah in which Isaiah counsels him to avoid entanglement in an alliance against Assyria; vv. 10–17 relate a parallel encounter in which Isaiah gives as a "sign" that, by the time the child of a pregnant young woman grows to maturity, the crisis will have passed; vv. 18–25 describe a terrifying day of disaster that will overpower the nation. What

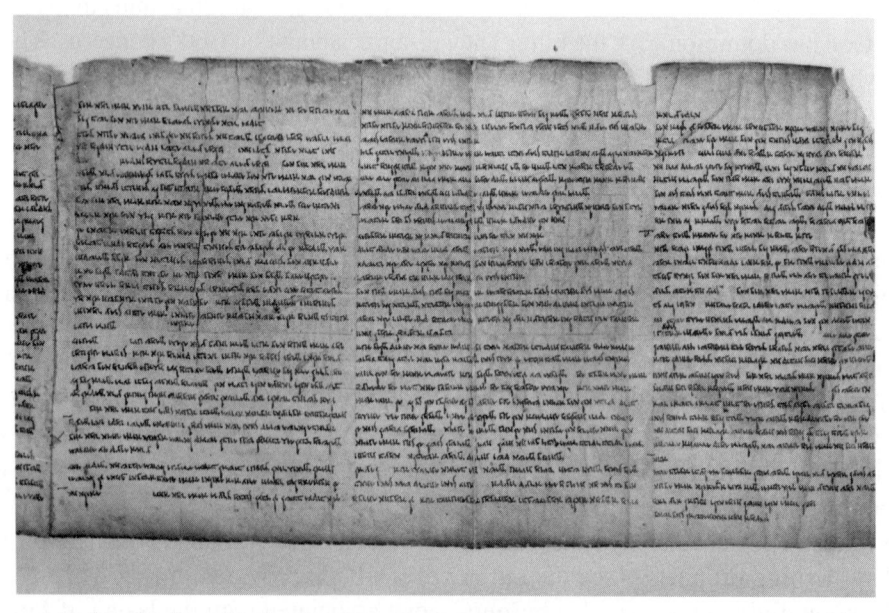

This scroll of Isaiah found in the desert caves near Qumran is part of the so-called "Dead Sea Scrolls" and by its presence testifies to the importance this community gave to prophetic writings.

is striking here is that these are all natural occurrences. The birth of a child to a pregnant woman is not extraordinary. The text emphasizes the situation the child will encounter and the short span of time before it occurs, not the fact of the birth. Isaiah's prediction is that in a very few years people will be living a bare subsistence existence.

Isaiah 7 offers two views of the political future. First, it argues that the nation need not worry about its enemies. It then imagines a period of privation and destruction that is coming. If the king chooses to keep Judah free of foreign entanglements, then the first prediction will come true. If he joins other nations in a futile war, then disaster will strike. This conveys two relevant ideas. The first is that Judah is conceived as a nation; its history is that of a political body, not of isolated individuals. Second, the story portrays the divine as acting in naturalistic ways. God's signs are not miracles that reverse the order of nature. God's predictions do not require some external act to bring them about; they are the natural result of ordinary political processes. The prophet makes predictions and gives signs based on penetrating observation of the sociopolitical realities.

The political message here also has ethical implications. Ahaz is instructed to refrain from international entanglements. This isolationism resembles that advocated by Elijah: the followers of YHWH must remain apart from other nations who have other religious traditions. Isaiah's view seems more extreme. It excludes the politics of the outside world from consideration. This suggests an isolationist ethics in which Judah's political leaders should remain apart from the general culture. As for ritual, Isaiah here demands that political leaders ask prophets for signs and portents; to neglect to do so indicates that they lack trust in the divinity. The prophet is understood as part of the ritual cult, a cult that symbolizes the political reality. In this case, the rituals do not create the predicted future, but rather convey the possibilities inherent in that future and the choices that the leadership must make.

Both the ritualism and ethics of these passages conflict with other texts in Isaiah. Isaiah 6 tells of what is, unarguably, Isaiah's call to be a prophet. It describes how Isaiah stood in the Jerusalem Temple and saw God's presence, noticing how only the "coattails" of that presence filled the sanctuary. At this recognition, Isaiah cries out in alarm: "Woe is me! I am lost, for I am a man of unclean lips, and I live among a people of unclean lips" (Isaiah 6:5). What does that mean? The phrase "unclean lips" suggests that Isaiah has been uttering words that are untrue, that blaspheme God. He has been with a congregation of Israelites proclaiming God's exclusive concern for Jerusalem. His vision has now shown Isaiah the falsity of that declaration. God's presence transcends any single nation. As the chapter continues, God asks for a volunteer to act in the world; that is, the transcendent divinity needs some emissary to perform work in the mundane sphere of human affairs. Isaiah volunteers for that job. His task is to mislead the people by making both optimistic and pessimistic pronouncements. The ethics in this case is inclusive. All humanity comes under divine care; God reaches out to everyone.

Isaiah 37 expresses a view of ritual that challenges the view in Isaiah 7–8. King **Hezekiah** faces a political crisis and uses the ritual of wearing sackcloth and ashes to gain divine favor.

Isaiah seems to approve of this ritual. God indeed looks favorably on rulers who use ritual to solicit divine support and help. Isaiah sees ritual as sometimes celebratory and sometimes substantive, depending on the attitude with which it is performed. The rituals that actually work to the good of the nation are those of humility and self-doubt. Those that work against the nation are those of self-confidence and pride. This insight helps explain the balance between an inclusive and exclusive ethics in Isaiah. When inclusiveness leads to military self-importance, when it supports an international program of national aggrandizement, then Isaiah rejects it. When inclusiveness expresses humility before the divine, then he accepts and affirms it.

RELIGIOUS APPROACHES IN THE WRITING PROPHETS

These themes reappear throughout the rest of the writing prophets. The prophet **Amos** offers a good example of the religious approaches of the writing prophets. Amos emphasizes universalism and an inclusive ethics. He asks pointedly: "Are you not like the Ethiopians unto me, O Israelites?" (Amos 9:7–8). While Israel has a special role in the divine plan, that plan extends to all humanity. Amos enumerates "crimes against humanity" committed, first, by Israel's neighbors and then by Israel and Judah themselves (Amos 1:3–2:8). Prophets such as Isaiah, Jeremiah, and Micah use a single yardstick of justice and righteousness to judge all nations. Perhaps the most extraordinary of the texts illustrating this universalism is the book of Jonah. Not a prophetic collection like other books, this short novella pictures a prophet sent not to Israel, but to Israel's direst enemy, Assyria. **Jonah** seeks to avoid his commission to this nation, but learns that God judges all nations in the same way and waits for all to repent and practice justice and righteousness.

This universalism finds expression in the visions these prophets have for a renewed Israel. Jeremiah 31 imagines a new covenant in which all humanity will have God's law written in its heart. Ezekiel 40–48 imagines a restoration of "the glory of the God of Israel" in which a cleansing spring of water issues from the rebuilt Temple to water the entire world. Isaiah 66 imagines a new creation in which all humanity joins in the religious community of Israel. These visions of the final age expand Israel's horizons to encompass the entire world. What is extraordinary in both of these visions of the end of time is the way they combine a view of Israel's special destiny with the universal concerns of a deity whose interests encompass all reality. While both visions expect the restoration of a Judean kingdom and both expect the misfortunes of the exile to be reversed, the ethics involved is inclusive rather than exclusive. The transformed world envisioned is that in which individual human beings and nations cooperate with one another. God takes action in the world, making nature itself different. This difference affirms the place of God's covenanted people, but also affirms divine transcendence that overlooks particularism in a general concern for humanity as a whole.

Perhaps the most dramatic expression of both universalism and a view of divine activity appears in Isaiah 44. This post-exilic hymn begins (vv. 1–5) with an oracle of salvation. The people of Israel, identified here as God's chosen servant, are promised a glorious future, a future in which they will attract adherents from the rest of the world. This oracle continues with a divine self-disclosure: God's power to make such a promise derives from the nature of the deity as sole creator and controller of the world (vv. 6–8). This deity, whom God's servant Israel proclaims, stands in contrast to the so-called divinities worshiped by other nations, castigated as "idols" in the passage that follows (vv.12–20). While these false gods have no power, Israel's deity is the exclusive force behind all reality.

This view of divinity has important implications for an understanding of history. If God controls all reality, then history unfolds not as the result of natural forces, but because of divine intervention. That intervention occurs in two ways, one of which is "natural" and one of which is "supernatural." The first is evident in the normal course of events. Events often follow predictable patterns and clearly understood causes. Other events seem to occur without any evident cause; they interrupt the predictable flow of events and strike observers as extraordinary. God, therefore, seems to operate in two different ways: either through the continuing patterns of history or through an intervention that introduces discontinuity into events.

The next section of Isaiah 44 builds on this idea and suggests that if this is history, then God expects people to acknowledge the divine role in human affairs. The form of vv. 21–23 has been called a "covenant trial." It includes a call to attention, a review of history, and the consequences of that history. In this particular case, the history reviewed tells of God's relationship to his "servant," the people of Israel, and the consequences are the unexpected forgiveness of the people and their reconsecration to the divine task. The chapter concludes (vv. 24–28) by combining the universalism of God's power and concern for all creation with an exclusivism that sees Israel and Jerusalem as the means by which God achieves goals for the world as a whole.

The covenant trial form suggests an important aspect of the way the writing prophets look at history. God's responses to actions by individuals or nations with whom a covenant has been established go beyond normal historical expectations. Natural events flow from observable causes. Supernatural events flow from God's covenantal response either to obedience or disobedience to the demands of the covenant.

Amos 3 illustrates the supernatural aspects of God's covenantal actions. The chapter begins with a call to attention emphasizing the chosen nature of the people of Israel (vv. 1–2) and the consequences of that choice. The oracle continues by suggesting that the relationship between Israel and its God follows a natural order, analogous to any other sequence of cause and effect (vv.3–8). The final section of the chapter, however, (vv. 9–15) goes beyond what might be expected naturally. The social disorder caused by selfishness, greed, and violence will lead to an unexpected political disaster. God will manipulate the political powers of the world to bring chaos and defeat upon Israel. This relationship between societal inequality and political catastrophe is not natural, but rather covenantal; it springs from disobedience to a divinely given legal system, rather than from pragmatic causes grounded in political theory.

ETHICS, HISTORY, AND BELIEF IN HOSEA AND HAGGAI

The book of **Hosea**—reflecting the same historical background as the book of Amos—mixes ethics, history, and belief in a striking fashion. The first three chapters of Hosea focus on the prophet's life experience. Chapter One provides a third-person account of God's command instructing Hosea to live a symbolic life; he is to marry a prostitute and name his children in ways that will indicate God's rejection of the people of Israel. Here Hosea is shown as living out a history of the unexpected. What covenantal promises seem to project as Israel's future is, according to the symbolism of this chapter, the opposite of what will occur. History will develop in unpredictable ways; Israel will cease being God's people and will be treated without compassion.

The second chapter describes some of the changes involved. Israel's luxury and wealth shall disappear: "I will strip her naked and expose her as in the day when she was born, and make her like a wilderness and turn her into a parched land and kill her with thirst… I will take back my grain in its time, and my wine in its season; I will take away my wool and my flax… I will lay waste her vines and her fig trees… I will make them a forest and the wild animals shall devour them." These disasters take place so that Israel can return to its pristine purity: "Therefore, I will now allure her and bring her into the wilderness…. There she shall respond as in the days of her youth as at the time when she came out of the land of Egypt" (Hosea 2:3, 9, 12, 14, 15). Israel reverts back to her original purity only by being radically stripped of glory and wealth.

Chapter Three seems to reiterate (or give a parallel, duplicate, or second account of) the events in Chapter One. Instead of a third-person narrative, however, the chapter is given in the first person. This short chapter reemphasizes the extraordinary and unexpected nature of life and history. Unlike Hosea 1, Chapter Three portrays the events without giving names and without suggesting that the adulterous wife has borne children whose nature enters into the complex relationship of husband and wife.

God instructs Hosea to love a woman "who has a lover and is an adulteress, just as the Lord loves the people of Israel, though they turn to other gods" (Hosea 3:1). The analogy between Hosea's biography and God's relationship to Israel is clear: just as Hosea must forgive his wife, so God must forgive Israel. Hosea, learning that message, takes her home and sequesters her for many days, just as Israel shall live in exile: "For the Israelites shall remain many days without king or prince, without sacrifice or pillar, without ephod or teraphim" (Hosea 3:4). Just as isolation cures Hosea's wife, so living without royal leadership or priestly functionary will cure Israel.

This reference to a lack of leadership introduces an ethical perspective that animates the entire prophecy of Hosea. An exclusive ethics that emphasizes king, priest, and hierarchy must give way to an inclusive ethics focused on universal concerns for justice, righteousness, and social welfare. Hosea's argument is with the elite, the king, and the priests, as he declares, "Hear this, O priests! ... Listen O house of the king! For the judgment pertains to you; for you have been a snare at Mizpah and a net spread upon Tabor…"(Hosea 5:1–2). The elitism of the society has undermined its social order. Hosea contends that "Gilead is a city of evildoers, tracked with blood. As robbers lie in wait for someone, so the priests are banded together; they murder on the road to Shechem" (Hosea 6:8–9). He observes the corruption and evil of Israel: "for they deal falsely, the thief breaks in, and the bandits raid outside… By their wickedness they make the king glad, and the officials by their treachery" (Hosea 7:1–3). Hosea claims that God will favor Israel only when it abandons its elite leaders to become a cohesive society.

The message of **Haggai** contrasts dramatically with the message of Hosea. Haggai, writing during the reconstruction of the Jewish kingdom after the exile to Babylonia, like Hosea, affirms the discontinuity of history: God will intervene to change the fortunes of the Jewish people. Yet his ethics is one of exclusion rather than inclusion. The book is filled not with common people and those rejected, but with the leaders of society; the governor of Judah and the high priest are central figures. His message is addressed to **Zerubbabel**, the governor and messianic claimant, and to **Joshua the high priest** (Haggai 1:1). He calls upon them not for a change of heart concerning society as a whole or to take care of the poor and needy, but to begin building the Jerusalem Temple: "Go up to the hills and bring wood and build the Temple so that I may take pleasure in it and be honored, says The Lord" (Haggai 1:8).

The rebuilding of this Temple will occasion a restoration of Israel's ancient glory. Haggai addresses Zerubbabel: "I am about to shake the heavens and the earth and to overthrow the throne of kingdoms… On that day, says the Lord of hosts, I will take you, O Zerubbabel my servant, son of Shealtiel, says the Lord, and make you like a signet ring, for I have chosen you" (Haggai 2:21–23). Israel's fortunes are reversed because a Temple is being built with a member of the royal family and the high priesthood in attendance. The idea that history is about to change and God will instigate these changes supports not a universalism, but rather the separate and distinctive national claims of Israel.

RITUAL IN PROPHETIC PERSPECTIVE

The differences between the pre-exilic and exilic prophets, on the one hand, and the post-exilic prophets on the other, occur not only in their views of the divine and history, but also in the views of ritual they hold. While all the prophets declared the necessity of combining righteous deeds with ritual actions, the specific evaluation of ritual and its purpose in each prophet reflects a distinctive and unique response to specific conditions.

The pre-exilic prophets consider moral behavior more relevant than ritual observance for God's response to the people of Israel. Because the nation has sunk into deep immorality, ritual has no effect. Amos, as noted above, exemplifies a call for universal morality and a criticism of Israel's immorality. Amos also offers one of the most explicit condemnations of trust in the power of rituals to bring reconciliation with the divine.

Amos 5 offers a profound criticism of reliance upon ritual. The chapter begins with a formulaic dirge that strikingly resembles the declaration of the Pharaoh Merneptah upon his destruction of Israel: "Fallen, no more to rise, is the maiden Israel; forsaken on her land with no one to raise her up" (5:2). This cultic lament introduces a ritual proclamation of the demise of the northern kingdom because of its sins. Ritual observances offer no solution to the divine anger. The worshipers may well have assumed that if they offered their sacrifices at the official sanctuaries, God would reverse the evil decree against them. Amos rejects this idea. If the worshipers desire life, then they should avoid cultic performances: "Seek me and live, but do not seek **Beth El** and do not enter **Gilgal**" (5:4–5). The priests at Beth El, such as Amaziah (Amos 7), do not appreciate this recommendation; they accuse Amos of both heresy and political instigation.

Amos argues that rituals will not avert the threatened disaster because God rejects the ceremonies that Israel performs. God spurns the festivals, refuses to accept the sacred rites, and rejects the sacrificial offerings. Even such apparently innocuous rituals as prayer and song fall under divine displeasure: "I hate, I despise your festivals, and I take no delight in your solemn assemblies. Even though you offer me your burnt offerings and grain offerings, I will not accept them.... But let justice roll down like waters and righteousness like an ever-flowing stream" (Amos 5:21–24).

Amos 5:25 even denies that God had ever asked such sacrifices from the Israelites. To those who read the books of Exodus, Leviticus, and Numbers as we now have them, Amos' rhetorical suggestion that God never demanded the sacrificial system when Israel left Egypt seems strange, at the very least. Amos, however, is rejecting the priestly retelling of Israel's ancient stories. The text of Amos seems to agree with Hosea 13:13 that the true history of Israel is dependent upon prophetic leadership and not on priestly rituals. Amos does not suggest that rituals might be made acceptable through correct intention. He rejects ritualism out of hand entirely. Ritual must be rooted out; only moral behavior leads to life and success.

Jeremiah offers a more moderated response. Like Amos and Hosea, he attacks priests and prophets alike. He criticizes the lack of justice in the country so that the people "know no limits in deeds of wickedness; they do not judge with just the cause of the orphan to make it prosper and they do not defend the rights of the needy... the prophets prophesy falsely and the priests rule as the prophets direct" (Jeremiah 5:28–31). Jeremiah, however, unlike Hosea and Amos, also traces the disaster he predicts back to ritual lapses. Jeremiah 17:19–27 describes the prophet standing by the gates of Jerusalem and haranguing those passing by about the observance of the Sabbath: "For the sake of your lives, take care that you do not bear a burden on the Sabbath day or bring it in by the gates of Jerusalem" (Jeremiah 17:21). When the people do not heed that warning, Jeremiah proclaims that God "will kindle a fire in its gates; it shall devour the palaces of Jerusalem and shall not be quenched" (Jeremiah 17:27). Ritual here has a substantive effect, or rather the neglect of the ritual has such an effect. It is unclear whether the ritual itself has protected the people. Perhaps obedience to Sabbath law demonstrates acceptance of divine decrees more generally. By performing such a ritual, people declare their intention to place God's will above their own practical necessities. Whatever the case may be, disobedience to the Sabbath rules does bring a substantive response from God—a response of disaster and national catastrophe.

The post-exilic prophets offer a more positive picture, one in which obedience to ritual brings rich rewards. Second Isaiah, Isaiah 40–55, is an extraordinary declaration that God has not forgotten the people of Israel, but will restore them to their former glory. These chapters exalt God's creative control of history. Jerusalem will flourish with righteousness and social justice. Interestingly, unlike Jeremiah 30–31 or the entire last section of Ezekiel, Second Isaiah makes no mention of a restored Temple, of worship, or of ritualism. Israel will be God's servant because it pursues a historic task, because it acts in the world. History, rather than ritual, serves as the basis for the servanthood of God's people.

While the Isaiah of Jerusalem rejects ritual, and Second Isaiah ignores it, the last part of the book of Isaiah, Chapters 56–66 (often called Third Isaiah), strikes a balance between them. Isaiah 58 seems to echo many of the same ideas as does Amos. Fasting before God, the passage claims, has no magical power about it. God does not automatically look favorably on people because they have afflicted themselves. Instead, this chapter, like the book of Amos, argues that they must perform moral acts. The appropriate fast day before God is "to loose the fetters of injustice by sharing food with the hungry, giving shelter to the homeless poor in your house, and clothing the naked when you meet them…" (Isaiah 58:6–7). These actions not only avert disaster; they also bring transformation. Then God will answer Israel's prayers; then Israel's greatness will be reestablished; then Israel will rebuild the ancient homeland. God's immanence will be displayed in Israel's rebirth: "Then your light shall rise in the darkness and your gloom be like the noonday. The Lord will guide you continually and satisfy your needs in parched places…. Your ancient ruins shall be rebuilt" (Isaiah 58:10–12). Ethics, rather than ritual alone, brings about a prosperous change. That prosperity is individual and personal, rather than national. Individuals, rather than kings or priests, enjoy the benefits of such ethical living. For Isaiah 58:1–12, a ritual fast does not, in itself, effect any substantive change in reality; only ethical behavior can influence the future so as to transform ill fortune into good fortune.

Isaiah 58 contrasts vividly with a priestly perspective on ritual. For the priests, fasting before God is of particular importance since through self-affliction a person wins God's favor. Many scholars think that Isaiah 58 may have the fast of the Day of Atonement in mind. This was a priestly ritual of great importance in ancient Israelite and contemporary Jewish life (see Leviticus 16–17).

Once a year all the Israelites would meet at a central place of worship, the great Temple in Jerusalem, and confess what they had done wrong. The special people who worked in the Temple, called priests, would kill an animal and offer it to God. At that time, the most important priest, the High Priest, would speak the special name of God, YHWH. After these actions, the priest would declare that God had forgiven the priests and the people for all their wrongdoing—whether intentional or accidental— in the past year. This complex ritual was meant to transform reality and bring a substantive change to the fortune of individuals and to the nation as a whole. Isaiah 58 rejects this approach to ritual. Ritual fasting, it claims, symbolizes an inner change and a personal commitment to moral actions. If the fasting does not indicate such an internal decision, then, according to Isaiah 58, it is worthless. If the ritual fast does not symbolize an actual personal dedication to right action, then it does not win God's favor.

After its discussion of the "true fast," Isaiah 58:13–14 introduces a discussion of the Sabbath that is both similar and different from that of Jeremiah 17. Isaiah 58, like Jeremiah 17, considers Sabbath observance a crucial ritual, one in which a person places God's interests ahead of personal concerns. For both passages, observance has a value of its own: for Jeremiah 17, disobedience of that observance brings substantive punishments; for Isaiah 58, obedience leads to great rewards. A sincere and honest performance of the Sabbath, according to Isaiah 58, demonstrates willingness to give priority to the divine needs over the human ones and involves "refraining from trampling the Sabbath, from pursuing your own interests on my holy day… from going your own ways, serving your own interests, or pursuing your own affairs" (Isaiah 58:13). The point seems to be that obedience to Sabbath law entails more than just ethical behavior. It demands that people exercise self-discipline, that they devote a day to the divine, rather than to their mundane concerns.

This emphasis on attitude is important. Once people exercise this talent of taking joy in God's desires, they discover a source of happiness that they had overlooked before. When the Jews "call the Sabbath a delight… then you shall take delight in the Lord, and I will make you ride upon the heights of the earth" (Isaiah 58:13–14). In this instance, it looks as if the Sabbath day has a transformative effect. Ritual, when performed with the right attitude, transforms those who observe it so that they become joyful, successful, and reconciled with the divine. This passage moves beyond the clear distinction between ritual and ethics that both Amos and Jeremiah seem to have accepted. A joyfully performed ritual is itself an ethical exercise and brings about a personal transformation.

SUMMARY QUESTIONS

1. How are views of history, God, ritual, and ethics ambiguous in the Former Prophets?
2. How are stories about Isaiah in Isaiah 1–39 ambiguous?
3. What religious ideas are associated with covenant in Jeremiah, Amos, and Hosea?
4. How were the religious ideas of Haggai significant for the post-exilic Jewish community?

5. How are the views of ritual in Isaiah 1–39, Second Isaiah, and Third Isaiah different from each other?

Four Suggested Essay Questions

1. Explain two ways in which a tradition may view history. Show how Elijah's invocation of the tribes of Jacob in 1 Kings 18:30–35 illustrates one way and how Amos' reference to the Exodus in Hosea 2:15 illustrates the other.

2. Explain two ways in which a tradition may view the supernatural. Apply one of them to the narrative found in Isaiah 7 and the other to the narrative in 1 Kings 18.

3. Explain two ways in which a tradition may view ethics. Apply one of them to the prophetic view of Haggai and the other to the narrative in 1 Kings 21.

4. Explain two ways in which a tradition may view ritual. Apply one of them to Amos' critique of Israelite worship in Amos 5:21–24 and the other to the Passover ritual described in 2 Chronicles 35.

Exercise

Read the following paragraph from an answer to Question 3:

> The prophetic book Haggai shows how an exclusive ethics combines with a view of ritual as transformative. Haggai's purpose is to encourage the Jews who returned from the Babylonian Exile to rebuild the Jerusalem Temple and, thereby, to enjoy the blessings of God. Haggai focuses his appeal on those who can help accomplish his purpose—the leading members of society, Zerubbabel, and the high priest Joshua. He reinforces this perspective by applying his view of a stratified reality to the Jewish nation as a whole. For Haggai, God's selection of the Jews indicates that they hold a special place in creation and that God will deal with them in a favored way. He concludes that this has not occurred among the returned exiles because they have not yet rebuilt the Jerusalem Temple. Reestablishing the ritual processes associated with that Temple, he claims, will enable God to provide the special privileges allotted to Jews. In this way, a revival of ritual leads to an experience of Jewish particularity and difference. The exclusive ethics at the heart of Haggai's view of history underlies and justifies his attention to the rituals of the Temple. Haggai's ethics is exclusive in a second sense. The book singles out Jewish leadership as the central players in history. The book specifically addresses Zerubbabel and the high priest Joshua ben Jehozadak. Ethics, in this case, makes special demands on rulers and leaders that are different from those asked of others.

Now answer the following questions:

1. What two religious ideas does the topic sentence introduce?

2. Why does the paragraph mention Zerubbabel and Joshua the High Priest?

3. How does Haggai's view of a rebuilt Temple represent a transforming ritual?

4. How does Haggai's view of a rebuilt Temple represent an exclusive ethics?

5. Write three sentences that introduce the general idea of a connection between transformative ritual and exclusive ethics and that anticipate the ideas expressed in this paragraph.

FOR FURTHER READING

The books listed below should be a point of departure for your future study. Each includes a bibliography that will guide you beyond its basic information.

1. Brenner, Athalya, ed., *A Feminist Companion to the Latter Prophets* (Sheffield, England: Sheffield Academic Press, 1995).
2. Brichto, Herbert Chanan, *Toward a Grammar of Biblical Poetics: Tales of the Prophets* (New York: Oxford University Press, 1992).
3. Brueggemann, Walter, *Prophetic Imagination* (Minneapolis: Fortress, 2001).
4. Carroll, Robert P., *When Prophecy Failed: Cognitive Dissonance in the Prophetic Traditions of the Old Testament* (New York: Seabury, 1979).
5. Grabbe, Lester L., *Priests, Prophets, Diviners, Sages: A Socio-Historical Study of Religious Specialists in Ancient Israel* (Philadelphia, PA: Trinity Press International, 1995).
6. Lindblom, Johannes, *Prophecy in Ancient Israel* (Philadelphia, PA: Muhlenberg, 1963).
7. Petersen, David L., *Prophetic Literature: An Introduction* (Louisville, KY: Westminster/John Knox, 2002).

7

Religions of the Writings

READING ASSIGNMENT

    Ruth (complete)
    Ezra 9–10
    Nehemiah 9
    Esther (complete)
    Daniel 1–6
    Psalms 2, 19, 23, 73, 78, 82, 104
    Proverbs 4, 7
    Ecclesiastes 2–4, 7
    Job 1–3, 38–42

LEARNING OBJECTIVES

By the end of this lesson, you will be able to:
- Describe the views of history, divinity, ethics, and ritual in Proverbs, Job, and Ecclesiastes.
- Describe the views of history, divinity, ethics, and ritual in Ruth, Daniel, Chronicles, Ezra, Nehemiah, and Esther.
- Describe the views of history, divinity, ethics, and ritual in Psalms, Song of Songs, and Lamentations.
- Describe the genre and contents of the Writings section of the Jewish Bible.

Interpretive Matrix for Chapter Seven

View of the Divine: How people interact with God and the supernatural; how God interacts with the world.	View of History: How past, present, and future are related; who controls the shape of events.	View of Ethics: How people behave toward other people; how they behave toward people like themselves and to those who are different.	View of Ritual: How people behave toward the Divine; how they perform religious actions.
The Divine as Transcendent: Nature exhibits a divine order that does not change. Human wisdom can never comprehend the divine. God does not take an active role in human events.	*History as Continuous:* Natural law never changes. Human history is an unfolding of a predetermined divine pattern. Early heroes are examples for later leaders.	*Inclusive Ethics:* Priests have the same obligations as other people. Intermarriage strengthens a community. Minorities should adapt to the ways of the majority.	*Ritual as Transforming:* Ritual must be performed by the authentic priestly leader. Prayer changes reality and can bring national success.
The Divine as Immanent: Human events reflect supernal powers. God performs miracles that change the shape of events.	*History as Discontinuous:* New situations demand new laws.	*Exclusive Ethics:* Women are seen as dangerous and separate from men. Priests must be kept separate from other people. Intermarriage between groups is forbidden. Minorities should maintain their distinctiveness from the majority.	*Ritual as Symbolic:* Ritual cannot protect people from misfortune. Ritual may change attitudes toward reality but not reality itself. Prayer proves loyalty to God but does not change reality.

INTRODUCTION

This chapter looks at those books the rabbis collected as Writings or Ketuvim. They have a primarily liturgical and poetic purpose in the Jewish Bible. While they may repeat earlier narratives (1–2 Chronicles retells the stories from creation through the Babylonian Exile), they expand those stories with hymns and other ritual performances. The narratives of Ruth and Esther are included because they form part of the festival rituals in Judaism. The rabbinic leaders required the reading of these works during the public rituals of the Jews. They added personal meaning to these celebrations.

These writings constitute an important part of the ritual process among the Jews. The Bible acts as a resource for Jewish worship and should be understood as such. These writings also consider the theme of **wisdom**—the knowledge after which human beings seek. Some of the Writings claim that intelligent people can grasp this wisdom; others consider it outside of human reach; still others think of wisdom as a supernal force acting throughout the world.

These stories augment and change earlier stories. The term for such an interpretive rewriting of the past is *midrash*. While this term occurs only in rabbinic writings, scholars have discovered the technique of midrash applied within the Bible itself. This technique becomes clear when comparing the earlier and later versions of narratives found in the Writings.

SOME IMPORTANT TERMS

The following terms are important in this chapter. Some of them have been listed in previous chapters; in those cases the term is not **bold** in the main body of this chapter. Where names of books are also the names of individuals (such as Daniel), the name does not appear in the Glossary.

Abraham	Festival Scrolls	Orpah
Agag	Haman	Parallelism
Ahashuerus	Hesed	Passover
Akhenaton	Isaac	Priest
Amalekites	Jacob	Proverbs
Amenemope	Jehoiakim	Psalms
Augur ben Jakeh	Jehoshaphat	Purim
Belshazzar	Job	Ruth
Boaz	Ketuvim	Samaritan
Chaldean	Levite	Saul
Chronicles	Mashal	Satan
Cyrus the Great	Midrash	Sheol
Daniel	Moab	Song of Songs
David	Mordecai	Tishre
Dietary Laws	Nabonidus	Wisdom Literature
Ecclesiastes	Naomi	Wisdom
Esther	Nebuchadnezzar	
Ezra	Nehemiah	

WHAT ARE THE WRITINGS?

While drawing on material that probably circulated hundreds of years earlier, the books comprising the third section of the Hebrew Bible—the Writings—reflect a post-exilic perspective. Some of these works are wisdom literature—poetry meant to teach lessons or poetry used in a liturgical setting. These works differ from one another but agree on making "wisdom," most often described as "fear of the Lord," the central category of learning (see Box 7–1). This literature uses a special type of poetry, one represented less by rhyme, rhythm, or meter, but by its content. Poetry develops from the structure between verses, a technique called **Parallelism**, in which verses sometimes repeat the same meaning using different words, sometimes set up a contrast between one idea and its opposite, and sometimes establish a sequence in which one theme leads to another. Wisdom works such as Proverbs and Ecclesiastes are as much "poetry" in this sense as are the Psalms or the Song of Songs or Lamentations (see Box 7–2).

Other works are narratives, sometimes retelling earlier stories in new ways or inventing tales about either early or later heroes that reflect the concerns of the post-exilic community. Narrative texts, however, are not exclusively written in prose. Poetic selections, usually prayers, punctuate the stories that are told. These writings are incorporated into the third part of the Hebrew Bible, either because they are resources for liturgical prayers, or because they find a place in public worship during the major festivals, such as the five **Festival Scrolls**. The narratives as well as the poetic literature illustrate views of history, divinity, ethics, and ritual as they imagine new ways of retelling older history (see box 7–3).

The Hebrew word **midrash** offers one way to understand the collection of the Writings. The word means "that which is sought out," and it refers to an investigation of biblical meaning. The term most commonly occurs in rabbinic writings. Ancient rabbis used the midrash to adapt the teachings of the Hebrew Bible to the needs of their own time. Nevertheless,

---

BOX 7–1   WISDOM AND FEAR OF THE LORD IN THE HEBREW BIBLE

Several books in the Hebrew Bible—Psalms, Proverbs, Ecclesiastes, and Job—focus attention on the acquisition of "wisdom." Wisdom is often identified with "fear of the Lord," or better "obedience to divine injunctions." The various sources, however, differ in their characterization of this attribute. All agree that wisdom leads to success and happiness. Several Psalms identify this wisdom with knowing God's commandments; some verses in Proverbs identify it with pragmatic understanding; verses in Ecclesiastes and Job think of it as beyond human reach.

Psalms

14: 4 (=53:4)	Have they no knowledge, all the evildoers who eat up my people as they eat bread and do not call upon the Lord?
19: 7–9	The decrees of the Lord are sure, making wise the simple…the fear of the Lord is pure, enduring forever
112: 1	Happy are those who fear the Lord, who greatly delight in his commandments
119: 22	I run the way of your commandments for you enlarge my understanding

Religions of the Writings

119: 73	Your hands have made and fashioned me; give me understanding that I may learn your commandments
119: 98	Your commandment makes me wiser than my enemies, for it is always with me
128: 1	Happy is everyone who fears the Lord who walks in his ways

Proverbs

1: 7	The fear of the Lord is the beginning of knowledge; fools despise wisdom and instruction
4: 7	The beginning of wisdom is this: Get wisdom, and whatever else you get, get insight
5: 13–14	I did not listen to the voice of my teachers or incline my ear to my instructors. Now I am at the point of ruin in the public assembly
9: 9–10	Give instruction to the wise and they will become wiser still; teach the righteous and they will gain in learning. The fear of the Lord is the beginning of wisdom and the knowledge of the Holy one is insight
10: 27	The fear of the Lord prolongs life but the years of the wicked will be short
16: 22	Wisdom is a fountain of life to one who has it, but folly is the punishment of fools
19: 23	The fear of the Lord is life indeed; filled with it one rests secure and suffers no harm

Ecclesiastes

1: 17	And I applied my mind to know wisdom and to know madness and folly. I perceived that this also is but a chasing after wind
6: 8	What advantage have the wise over fools?
8: 17	However much they may toil in seeking they will not find it out; even though those who are wise claim to know, they cannot find it out
9: 11	Again I saw that under the sun the race is not to the swift, nor the battle to the strong, nor bread to the wise, nor riches to the intelligent, nor favor to the skillful; but time and chance happen to them all
11: 5	Just as you do not know how the breath comes to the bones in the mother's womb, so you do not know the work of God who makes everything

Job

28: 12–13	But where shall wisdom be found? And where is the place of understanding? Mortals do not know the way to it and it is not found in the land of the living
28: 20–21	Where then does wisdom come from? And where is the place of understanding? It is hidden from the eyes of all living and concealed from the birds of the air.

BOX 7-2 POETIC BOOKS OF THE JEWISH BIBLE

The books outlined below are "poetic" in a sense particular to the Hebrew Bible. Since the 18th century that poetry has been designated "parallelism" and the first list here explains that technique. Later biblical studies have supplemented this view with other explanations and commentary on biblical poetry. While all parts of the Hebrew Bible (especially the Latter Prophets) contain poetry, the books outlined here offer the most extended poetic material in the canon.

Parallelism in Hebrew Poetry

Since the 18th century biblical scholars have suggested the biblical poetry is characterized not by rhythm or meter, but by the thematic linking of verses. Verses are put together because they are synonymous, antithetical, or a climactic sequence.

Synonymous Parallelism This type of poetic composition depends on repeating the same idea in different words. Psalm 32, for example, begins by declaring "Happy are those whose transgression is forgiven, whose sin is covered" (Psalm 32:1). The idea of transgression being forgiven is identical to the covering up of sin.

Antithetical Parallelism This approach combines verses that deal with opposing ideas. Proverbs 10:1 declares that "A wise child makes a glad father, but a foolish child is a mother's grief." Not only is the consequence of having a wise child opposed to that of having a foolish one (gladness in contrast to grief) but the parent involved is also of the opposite gender (father in contrast to mother).

Synthetic Parallelism In verses showing this style one image leads to another in a progression of verses; these lead to a climactic conclusion so that this type is also called "climactic parallelism." Ecclesiastes 1:8 declares that "All things are wearisome; more than one can express; the eye is not satisfied with seeing, or the ear filled with hearing." The verse moves from a general comment to discount first speech, then sight, and finally hearing.

The Content of Psalms

The book of Psalms is divided, rather arbitrarily, into five books parallel to the five books of the Torah. Before turning to that content, however, it is useful to look at the types of psalms found throughout each of these books:

Hymns These psalms praise God for creating the world, for historical interaction on behalf of Israel; they also express national thanksgiving and national concerns. They usually begin with a call to prayer, express the reason for prayer, and reach a conclusion associated with Temple ritual. Psalm 27 is an example of this type.

Wisdom Psalms These psalms emphasize the teaching of Torah as a way of life and success. They often take the shape of acrostics or as exhortations to obedience. Psalm 119 is an extended wisdom psalm.

Royal Psalms These psalms are centered on the figure of the king and God's relationship to the nation through the King. The welfare of the king is considered important as is the defeat of the king's enemies. Psalm 2 is an example of such a psalm.

Enthronement Psalms These psalms focus not on Israel's king but upon Israel's God as ruler of the world. Many scholars associate the recitation of these hymns with a ritual in which God is affirmed to sit upon a cosmic throne. Psalm 99 is an example of such a psalm.

Outline of the Book of Psalms

1	This psalm provides a prologue emphasizing Torah as the central value of human life.
2–72	These represent an early collection of cultic materials that assemble several smaller collections together; probably 3–41 was a handbook for private worship; 42–83 were "Psalms of Asaph". That this collection now ends with Psalm 72 probably derives from v.20 that declares "The prayers of David the son of Jesse are ended"—a rather strange statement since later Psalms do claim also to be Davidic (for example, Psalm 86).
73–89	These hymns emphasize God's steadfast love and combine thanksgiving for such love with petition for the display of it. The needs of the kingship are generally prominent, but Psalm 89 gives an extended treatment of the idea of Davidic covenant.
90–106	The seventeen psalms in this collection emphasize God's power and his involvement in Israelite history. Psalms 97 to 99 seem to be a progression of enthronement poems culminating in Psalm 100 in which all nations acknowledge God as king. Psalm 106 sketches Israel's history reaching a climax with the Solomonic Temple.
107–149	This long collection of psalms has several subdivisions—Psalms of David (is a long book (Psalms 107–150) and it has several clear subcollections within it: Davidic psalms (Psalms 108–110; 138–145), Hallelujah psalms (Psalms 111–117, 135, 146–149, and "Songs of Ascents" (Psalms 120–134). The collection emphasizes the Jerusalem Temple and the rituals associated with it.
150	This psalms provides a concluding doxology or collection of praises to God.

Outline of Proverbs

1	The superscription claims that the entire book is the work of Solomon.
2–6	These are pragmatic observations drawn not from books but from an attention to reality; Wisdom entails learning to discern what is useful and not useful in the world (see 4:5–19).

10–22:16	These chapters are explicitly identified as "proverbs of Solomon" and show evidence of a bias toward the upper classes—attention is given to behavior in court, on generosity, good government.
22:17–24:23	These sayings are attributed to "the words of the wise" and teach a general wisdom that often overlaps with teachings in the preceding section. What is particularly remarkable is that many of the sayings included are identical to that given by the Egyptian sage Amenemope (1200 B.C.E.).
25:1–29:27	These chapters are attributed to Solomon, but only through the officials of King Hezekiah who copied them. That they were added at such a late date suggests the stages by which the book of Proverbs was composed.
30	These sayings are attributed to a certain "Augur ben Jakeh" who is associated with "massa"—a term that could either be a place name or a word meaning "oracle." If it is a place name then this is another instance in which a non-Israelite source is used as a basis for biblical wisdom. While the name YHWH is mentioned in the chapter, there is nothing else that would require this to be understood as a specifically Israelite text.
31	King Lemuel, said to be the author of this chapter, is otherwise unknown. It makes sense to consider him another non-Israelite source. The first verse says that this is an oracle "his mother taught him" and the content of this hymn of praise to the industrious woman justifies such an attribution.

Outline of Ecclesiates (Qoheleth)

The opening verse of this book claims it to be written by Qoheleth, a son of David who ruled in Jerusalem. That term "the Congregationalist" is a title and not a name. It refers to someone who offers public teachings. Nothing within the book itself requires it to have been written by Solomon.

1–2	These chapters set the theme of the futility of human aspiration; Wisdom has no value.
3	While God may know the time and season for everything, human beings cannot understand this; God's plan is incomprehensible, even if it exists.
7–11	Life is filled with paradoxes; society lacks lawfulness, death shows life's lack of meaning. Both feasting and fasting are praised; death is better than birth but better a living dog than a dead lion; too much piety is rejected but all people are in the hand of God.
12	Life is meant to be enjoyed and this chapter enjoins such living and offers an extended allegory between the human body and a machine that is soon to become ruined.
12:13–14	These verses probably come as an editorial comment blunting the effect of the book as a whole; Qoheleth, it claims, was wise enough to know that living disciples, not a written record is what is most important.

Outline of Song of Songs

1	The poem begins as a dialogue in which the lover and beloved announce their longing for each other.

4: 1–5: 1	The man's musings about the woman. The image of the woman's breasts as fawns grazing (4:5) is a bit strange since it assumes that the breasts are being nourished rather than giving nourishment.
5: 2–16	The woman's dream of wandering Jerusalem and seeking her beloved.
6: 1–12	The descent here to the valley to see whether the fruits, vines, and pomegranates have sprouted has been understood in the light of the Ugaritic myth—the various items may be assurances of a springtime revival of nature. The term "egoz" for nut orchard in v. 11 occurs only in this passage and may suggest that the poem draws on non-Israelite material.
6: 13–7: 13	As in chapter 1 the poem here becomes a dialogue between the male and female lovers. The term for the female "Shulamit" is unusual. It is perhaps a feminized form of the word "Solomon" suggesting that the woman is the feminine counterpart to the lover Solomon.
8	This concluding chapter insists on love being as strong as love more powerful than "Shalhevet Yah"—often translated "flames of the Lord." A better translation is "raging flame." Note the synonymous parallelism in 8:6 "love is as strong as death, passion fierce as the grave. Its flashes are flashes of fire, they are a raging flame."

Outline of Lamentations

Most scholars agree not only that Lamentations was not written by the prophet Jeremiah but that the individual chapters were probably written by independent authors.

1	This poem takes the form of a dirge over Jerusalem. It is written in the first person and it is unclear whether it is meant as a personal or public lament.
2	Vv. 1–10 describe the situation in Zion after its destruction. vv. 11–22 become a first person lament at that destruction. The chapter treats priests and prophets ambiguously—they have misled the people (v.14), but their demise is the cause of reproach to God (v. 20). The king is mentioned along with the prophets as those who have been exiled, leaving the country leaderless.
3	Unlike the other poems in this collection, this chapter is clearly a personal lament focused only on the individual's suffering. The poem includes a theodicy—"God is good to those who wait for him" (v. 26)— combined with a call for repentance (vv. 40–42), but concludes by calling upon God to exact vengeance for the suffering endured (vv. 64–66).
4	This chapter describes the disaster experienced in Jerusalem and only occasionally (vv. 6, 17–20) interjects a personal pronoun. The political aspect of the chapter appears both in the reference to the messiah who has been taken captive (v. 20) and in the call for vengeance upon the Edomites.
5	The final chapter consists of a petition to God, similar to several found in the Psalms (compare Psalms 74, 79, and 80). Verse 21 rewrites Jeremiah 31:18 "Bring me back, let me come back for you are the Lord God" as "Bring us back, Lord God, let us come back."

> **BOX 7–3 NARRATIVE BOOKS IN THE WRITINGS OF THE JEWISH BIBLE**
>
> The books outlined below are narrative tales, some set in an early time such as that of the Judges and others in post-exilic times, such as Daniel and Esther. Chronicles surveys all Israelite history. The book of Job is both narrative and poetic and is considered by itself in box 6–4.
>
> ### Outline of Ruth
>
> | | |
> |---|---|
> | 1 | This chapter narrates how Naomi and her sons migrate to Moab where the sons marry Moabite women. When the sons die, Naomi returns to Israel accompanied by one of her daughters-in-law, Ruth, who proclaims "Where you go I will go…your people shall be my people and your God my God" (v. 16). |
> | 2 | This chapter tells of the practice of having harvesters leave grain for the poor and has Ruth meet Boaz who is attracted to her as she carries out that practice. |
> | 3 | Naomi advises Ruth to seduce Boaz, which she does and he announces his intention to marry her if he can "redeem" her from the official "next of kin" who should marry her. |
> | 4 | Boaz carries out the act of "redemption" and marries Ruth who gives birth to a son who in turn becomes a progenitor of Jesse, the father of King David. |
>
> ### Outline of Chronicles and Ezra and Nehemiah
>
> *I Chronicles: From Creation through the end of David's Reign*
>
> | | |
> |---|---|
> | 1–9 | Creation and the genealogies of priests |
> | 10–29 | The life and times of David the priest—king |
>
> *II Chronicles: From Solomon through Cyrus's edict for a Return from Exile*
>
> | | |
> |---|---|
> | 1–9 | The splendor of Solomon |
> | 11–12 | The schism between Israel and Judah |
> | 13–33 | Pattern of good and bad kings |
>
> *Ezra: Torah and Religious Reforms*
>
> | | |
> |---|---|
> | 1–4 | The conditions of the return |
> | 4–6 | Prophecy and Zerubbabel's failure |
> | 7 | Ezra's commission |
> | 8 | Ezra's retinue |
> | 9–10 | Marriage reforms |
>
> *Nehemiah: Torah and Social Reforms*
>
> | | |
> |---|---|
> | 1–2 | Conditions in Jerusalem |
> | 3 | The diversity of Jerusalem |

4–6	Political controversy and the Samaritans
7	The diversity of Jerusalem
8: 1–10: 40	Affirmation of Torah
11: 1–12: 26	The diversity of Jerusalem
12: 17–13: 3	Dedication of the house of God
13: 4–33	Coda: the value of Torah

Outline of Daniel

1	The story tells how observing dietary laws brings Jews success in their life in the Diaspora.
2	Daniel interprets Nebuchadnezzar's dream and then Belshazzar's dream.
3	Daniel does not appear in the story that tells how three Jewish boys survive in a fiery furnace because they refuse to worship idols.
4	Although scholars think that the story really concerns Nabonidus, who, rather than Nebuchadnezzar was father to Belshazzar, the tale is not historical. What is remarkable here is that the chapter is written in the first person and claims to be from Nebuchadnezzar himself. After the events Daniel interprets from Nebuchadnezzar's dream come to pass, the non-Jewish king proclaims the greatness of Israel's God.
5	This chapter tells of Belshazzar's sacrilege by using Temple vessels for impure purposes and the punishment for this.
6	This famous story of Daniel in the lion's den emphasizes the importance of following Jewish liturgical practice even when it may be dangerous in the Diaspora; vv.10–11 stress the importance of Jerusalem even for Diaspora Jews.
7–12	These chapters are a later addition to the book of Daniel, probably coming from the time of the Maccabean revolution.
7	While written in Aramaic like the first six chapters, this chapter's content resembles that of the following ones.
8	These visions seem to anticipate the rise of Alexander the Great and the rise of the Seleucid empire.
9	This chapter suggests that Jeremiah had already become a canonical book and is used as a proof text. The chapter suggests that a false priest had been installed in Jerusalem.
10–11: 2	This section enumerates a penitential set of behaviors probably influenced by Ezekiel 1–3.
11: 3–12: 4	These chapters summarize history up to the Maccabees and then imagines a future very different from what actually occurred after the Maccabean revolt. Scholars, therefore, date this work to just before the beginning of that revolution.
12: 4–13	This conclusion emphasizes the authenticity of this document, its importance as a vision of the future provided from ancient times, and the rewards awaiting those who are faithful.

Outline of Esther

1	This chapter tells of the king's first banquet and its consequences—Ahasuerus cannot disobey the rules he himself has created so he needs a new queen.
2	In this chapter, Esther is urged by her cousin Mordecai, becomes queen over Persia.
3	The King's advisor Haman is enraged by Mordecai who does not bow to him and seeks to have the Jews destroyed.
4	Mordecai persuades Esther to entreat the king to reverse the decree and she agrees but asks all the Jews to fast for her.
5	Esther's first banquet with the King and Haman succeeds and she asks the king and Haman to come to a second one.
6	Because the King cannot sleep, he learns that Mordecai has saved his life; he instructs Haman to honor Mordecai.
7	Esther's second banquet with the King and Haman; Esther reveals that Haman has set out to destroy her and her people; the king is upset and threatens Haman.
8	Haman's final destruction is planned; the uprising against the Jews cannot be revoked, but the Jews are given weapons and the non-Jews are disarmed; a slaughter of the non-Jews follows as well as the hanging of Haman and his ten sons.
9	The Jews hold a feast day and banqueting to celebrate the victory and ask the king to give them another day of slaughtering and banqueting—their request is granted.
10	Mordecai and Esther write to all the Jews that they should make these days part of the festival calendar of the Jewish year, and such indeed becomes the case.

contemporary scholars find midrash even within the Bible itself. The Writings consist of an entire biblical section that provides a type of midrashic interpretation of the rest of the canon. The historical books of the Hebrew Bible provide some examples of the priestly liturgical system; the Torah offers rules about that system. The book of Psalms offers, as it were, a handbook of liturgical texts and thus supplements the earlier material in a midrashic fashion. The prophets and the Torah set out rules and regulations as ethical principles to be followed. Writings like Ecclesiastes, Proverbs, and Job offer more abstract reflection on ethics and morality, a type of philosophical midrash on ethics. The narratives of Ruth, Daniel, and Esther offer midrashic expansion and interpretation of themes found in other biblical stories.

HISTORY AND DIVINITY IN THE PSALMS AND WISDOM LITERATURE

This section looks at both the Psalms and the wisdom literature. The Jewish tradition divides the Psalms into five books, a parallel arrangement with the five books of the Torah. Like the Torah and the Bible as a whole, the book of Psalms is an anthology and represents a variety of religious views. The next section, focused on ritual, discusses the uses of the Psalms. Both the views of history and of divinity differ from psalm to psalm.

Psalm 82 is particularly striking. That psalm assumes the polytheistic cosmos imagined throughout the ancient Near East (v. 1). God takes up His throne in the midst of the other divinities and shows His power over them (vv. 5–7). The psalm ends with a plea for God to act on this power to punish the wicked and protect the weak and the needy (v. 8). History apparently is in the hands of divine forces. Were Israel's God to claim the power that is rightfully his, then history would undergo a dramatic change. At that point, apparent injustice would be banished and replaced by compassionate divine intervention.

Psalm 19, by contrast, has a very different view of the divinity. There is no question here that Israel's God is the sole divinity, although vv. 5–6 sound very much like a polemic against people who think that the solar orb is a divinity. God's function in the universe is to set out the patterns of nature, to establish the basic order of the cosmos. The natural world exemplifies this order automatically, involuntarily, and without exception. Without thought, without words, they declare God's greatness.

The human world (vv. 7–10) enjoys a similar plan and pattern set by the divine, but humans must voluntarily accept the duty to follow that plan. The point of the psalm seems to be that just as the order of nature is beneficent, so the order given to human society is for the good of those to whom it has been given. The follower of God will be "rewarded" by obeying these laws, not because God intervenes to give a reward, but because the rules are inherently beneficial.

The final section (vv. 11–14) attributes interventionary power to the divine. These verses appeal for God to do what the individual cannot, to correct human error supernaturally. While these verses ask for divine transformation of reality, most of the psalm uses prayer symbolically to convey the divine pattern evident in the natural world and normative for human society. Using this psalm in liturgy provides a lesson to worshipers about the nature of belief. It uses ritual to teach people how to interpret natural and social life. Reciting this psalm enables people to make sense out of the varied experiences of their lives, rather than to transform them.

That purpose characterizes much of the wisdom writing in the Bible (see Box 7–1). The book of Proverbs exemplifies a teaching meant to explain the workings of the world based on natural experience. The material in this book of wisdom advice takes diverse forms. **Proverbs** may be aphoristic or may involve extended allegories. These different forms convey a single idea: one should learn wisdom through heeding the elders (Proverbs 4:1–4). The Hebrew Bible never make clear who these "elders" might be. Are they priests? Are they scholars? Are they a special class of people? Nevertheless, the various teachings ascribed to them show that they claim to have found "wisdom" through pragmatic learning. They study nature, human behavior, and history to discover the appropriate ways to achieve success.

Experience, rather than revelation teaches the way to success. The book of Proverbs is so sure that nature, rather than supernatural revelation, is the source of truth that it consistently turns to the natural world for its lessons. It urges the audience to observe the ant, the grass-

This ancient Egyptian text closely resembles the contents of Proverbs 22:17–24:22.

hopper, the natural effects of drunkenness, the ways of the king's court, the tactics of a military engagement, since all of them will teach "the fear of God" or "the knowledge of the Lord." Not only Jews but other peoples also discern this wisdom. Even the learning of non-Israelites such as **Augur ben Jakeh** becomes a basis for gaining knowledge (Proverbs 30). Proverbs 22:17–23:11 incorporates writings from an ancient Egyptian scribe. The scribe, **Amenemope** (1200 B.C.E.), claimed that the righteous were rewarded and the wicked punished—an idea that was not restricted to the ancient Israelites, but represents a type of ethical optimism found in many cultures.

In contrast to this optimistic view stands the skepticism of Ecclesiastes. The author of this book (called *Koheleth* in Hebrew) claims that while God may know the reason for everything, human beings cannot. God's ways are so recondite that no mere mortal can figure them out. From the human perspective, everything is merely arbitrary. In sharp contrast to Proverbs 4, Ecclesiastes declares that wisdom has no value. The same fate awaits both the fool and the wise man: "What advantage have the wise over fools?" (Ecclesiastes 6:8). The book argues against the primacy of wisdom by emphasizing the role of chance. Whether someone is wise or foolish depends on happenstance. Ecclesiastes denies that a person can cultivate wisdom. Ecclesiastes 7 is particularly dense and confusing in making this case. It seems to exalt wisdom and the wise, yet it includes statements that claim that there is no difference between the righteous and the wicked, between the wise and the fool. Some wicked people prosper, and some fools succeed. Finally, the author admits that wisdom is "too far away" to be attained (v. 21). The upshot seems to be that history is too complicated to be understood, that God is too unlike human beings for people to comprehend the divine plan.

The conflict between those who think God's ways are comprehensible and those who claim they are beyond understanding finds its best expression in the book of **Job** (see Box 7-4).

The story of Job probably originated as a folktale celebrating the simple faith of a believer who had been subjected to numerous misfortunes. As the book developed, it changed from a folktale into a philosophical meditation. The book as we have it now probably dates from the Persian period of Jewish exile (535–400 B.C.E.) and reflects on the theological contention that Jews suffer because they have done something wrong. In its context, the book launches a polemic against those who would blame victims for their own victimization. Satan in this narrative provides an excuse for the evil that God allows in the world (Job 1:6–12; 2:1–7). The author seems to accept the idea of arbitrary suffering as an inevitable part of life, and, therefore, seeks to remove any stigma attached to those who undergo catastrophes and misfortune.

The tale tells of an innocent man, Job, who performs all the requisite rituals correctly and lives an ethically upright life (Job 1:1–5; 2:3–10). Nevertheless, God arbitrarily allows him to suffer as part of a supernal game. God has tempted Satan to try to corrupt someone to prove the divine omniscience. The first two chapters of Job and its last speak of God as YHWH and possess a vividness characteristic more of folktales than the normal wisdom writings. The author seems to suggest that ritual actions do not perform any substantive function. Offering sacrifices cannot prevent a person from suffering evil. God's will is arbitrary and not determined by the ritual actions of humans.

The poetic section of the book (chapters 3–42) emphasizes an inclusive rather than exclusive ethics. It argues that human beings simply do not know enough about the causes of human misfortunes to draw conclusions from them. The main body of the book denounces the theory that victims deserve their sufferings, as punishment for something they have done. It rejects the notion that those who suffer must be castigated and considered outcast until they repent . Although the character Job begins by patiently accepting all that happens, in this section he becomes angry because his so-called "friends" insist that he must have done something wrong to merit his problems. The more the friends argue for a logic of morality to explain God's deeds, the more Job rejects that logic. The established "values" that justify divine actions are shown to be meaningless and untenable.

The end of the book of Job affirms the worthlessness of conventional ways of judging victims. God speaks to Job out of a whirlwind and overpowers him: "And the Lord said to Job, 'Shall a faultfinder contend with the Almighty? Anyone who argues with God must respond.' Then Job answered the Lord, 'See I am of small account; what shall I answer you?'" (Job 40:1–4). Job learns that God cannot be understood, that anger has no rationale since God and humanity are so far apart that they have no common ground. Nevertheless, the author portrays Job finally accepting things the way they are. His final words are very strange:

BOX 7–4 OUTLINE OF THE BOOK OF JOB

The book of Job offers one of the most challenging texts in the Jewish Bible. It consists of a prologue and epilogue that exalt a person named Job as a righteous and honest person who will not curse God. The central dialogue of the book, however, shows Job doing precisely that—claiming that God is acting in an unjust and cruel way. Job has three friends who try to justify God but eventually God justifies Job rather than the friends. The point seems to be that God's ways are incomprehensible and must merely be accepted rather than understood.

Outline of Job

1–2	These chapters serve as a prologue in which God challenges Satan to show that the righteous man Job will eventually curse him. The text makes clear that Job is not only completely righteous but that he carries out ritual punctiliously. Despite several calamities befalling him he does not curse God.
3	Job laments his fate and seems to demonstrate Satan's point by blaming God for injustice.
4–8	These chapters are the first dialogue in which three of Job's friends—Eliphaz, Bildad, and Zophar— argue that Job should accept the teachings of tradition, of common sense and observation, and of revelation that God is always just. Job rejects each of these arguments showing that they are fallacious.
9–21	These chapters depict a second dialogue in which the same arguments are reiterated.
22–27	These chapters seem to have been a third dialogue that has been distorted in transmission.
28	This chapter offers a meditation on wisdom that seems to interrupt the third cycle of dialogue. It claims that human beings may attain technical knowledge but that true wisdom is the possession of God alone. Human beings must resign themselves to acknowledging their ignorance. This is the major theme of the book of Job.
29–31	These chapters are an extended lament by Job over his situation and a criticism of divine justice.
32–37	These chapters are an intrusion by a certain "Elihu" which rehashes the earlier arguments and may have been inserted by an editor unhappy with the theodicy that the earlier "friends" of Job had offered.
38–42: 6	In these chapters God speaks out of a whirlwind to prove that the way of the divine is incomprehensible—a point that Job has always affirmed. Job seems to accept this argument in 40:3–5, but God continues to demonstrate that the divine power is incommensurate with human knowledge and voices regret for being but dust and ashes (42:6).
42: 7–17	This epilogue rebukes Job's friends rebuked for not speaking well of God, and Job receives a reward from the Lord. Remarkably, the Satan present in the prologue is nowhere in the epilogue.

"I despise myself and regret concerning dust and ashes" (Job 42:6). Many scholars interpret that last phrase as meaning "I repent by wearing dust and ashes." Another interpretation, however, seems more plausible. Job repents—that is, regrets—that he is merely dust and ashes. He has learned that being human means enduring the trials and tribulations of an incomprehensible divine power.

This final point explains why the character of Satan occurs only at the beginning of the book of Job. The term symbolizes the challenges people meet in their striving to do good. When Job turns from considering his problems to arguing against the philosophies of his friends, Satan no longer plays a relevant role. By the end of the book, the point is not whether God or Satan is responsible for evil, but whether human beings can ever understand what happens to them. Nevertheless, the symbol of Satan does play an important role in the book; it personifies human troubles. Since people normally experience difficulties as they pursue their lives, they often project these problems onto a symbolic figure.

DIVINITY AND ETHICS IN THE WISDOM LITERATURE OF THE WRITINGS

One might assume that an activist view of the divine combines with a transforming view of ritual. Ritual, on that assumption, actually changes lives because it stimulates the divine to intervene in history. Psalm 73 seems to disprove that theory. Psalm 73 confronts the same problem as that of the book of Job, the suffering of the innocent. That psalm takes the form of a personal confession. After stating a thesis—that God does good to the righteous—the psalm seems to set up a counter example. Here is a righteous man who has suffered, who has been oppressed by enemies, who has undergone distress. The psalm, however, reaches its climax in a ritual moment (v. 17). When experiencing God's presence in the Temple, the psalmist undergoes a transformation. God is seen as close and reassuring. What has happened is that "good" has undergone a change. The "good" that God provides to the righteous is not that of worldly success, not that of triumph over enemies, but rather "good" means "being close to God" (v. 28). The worshipper, not the outside world, changes because of the ritual.

Psalm 73 is usually known as a wisdom psalm (see the section on types of psalms in Box 7–2). It has as its purpose teaching a general lesson. Ritual transforms by altering consciousness. Other types of transformative psalms have a more activist approach. Psalm 2 is what scholars call a "royal psalm." This type of psalm appeals to God to help the nation by helping the nation's ruler overcome enemies and difficulties. The psalm sets the stage by announcing that the nation is in danger; foreigners threaten the king, and therefore indirectly threaten the nation's divinity (vv. 1–3). The king is reassured in the psalm; he has a special status as God's chosen son (vv. 4–7). All who attempt to attack the nation will find themselves opposing God because the special holiness of the Temple in Jerusalem will protect the king and the people (vv. 8–9). The ritual is clearly aimed at preserving the people of Israel, and it defines outsiders as enemies. This approach represents an ethics of exclusion as well as a ritual of transformation.

An even more dramatic type of exclusionary aspect of transformative ritual occurs in Psalm 23. Understanding this psalm depends on putting it in its context. The poem is part of a liturgical handbook for priests; it represents a priestly perspective. That perspective becomes explicit in v. 5, in which the priest recalls his installation into office during which he was anointed with oil (thus becoming *mashiach* or "Messiah") and his place of service—before the "table" or altar within the divine sanctuary. The recitation ends with a declaration of inherited rights and privileges; this priestly representative and his family will retain the sacrificial office forever, or at least for this priest's lifetime. The psalms that see the divine actively taking part in the world and transforming it understand that transformation as either emphasizing the special status of the nation as a whole or of a special priestly group or family.

The wisdom psalms, on the other hand, generally have a different purpose. They tend to emphasize what is universal and inclusive. From the perspective of wisdom, history is a series of predictable actions and reactions. The history of Israel and the history of the world merge into a single story: the tale of God's manifestations of wisdom in the natural and historical world. These psalms may review Israelite history (as does Psalm 78) or the creation of the world (as does Psalm 104). Psalm 78 serves to unite all Israelites together; Psalm 104 reaches even more broadly to extend to all humanity, since all human beings share in the blessings of creation. Perhaps most extraordinarily, Psalm 104 not only reviews creation as a cosmic event, but also echoes ancient Near Eastern themes found in other, non-biblical texts, even using quotations from an early Egyptian hymn, the hymn to the Sun by the pharaoh Akhenaton (1350–1334 B.C.E.).

Just as some psalms sometimes see ritual as transforming and sometimes as symbolic, so too do other poetic works in the Writings. The same duality toward an ethics of inclusion and exclusion occurs in those works as well. The book of Job seems to assume that ritual does make a difference to God in its prologue and epilogue; the poetic section rejects the value of sacrificial ritual. Job also vacillates between an ethics of exclusion and one of inclusion. God, in the prologue and epilogue, does seem to have "favored" individuals and groups; God in the central portion of the book transcends such favoritism.

Ecclesiastes expresses a similar ambivalence, making an interesting distinction between "the sacrifice of fools" and going to a sacred place to learn and listen (Ecclesiastes 5:1). Sacrifices were often thought of as ways of changing the world, of influencing the divinity. Ecclesiastes rejects that view. In its place, the book offers a view of transformation through education. Effective ritual, according to this view, would be ritual that informs, that teaches, and that draws attention to natural truths. Such a ritual transforms people, but only by symbolizing important lessons and values that they should already have known.

One test of ethical inclusiveness or exclusiveness does not seem tied to ritual. That is the view of sexuality and gender. An inclusive ethics will affirm human sexuality as a positive aspect of life; it will support the independence and equality of both males and females in their relationships to one another. An exclusive ethics will relegate sexuality to a domain of danger; men and women should remain separate rather than conjoined. Men and women have different tasks, different inclinations, and different behavioral expectations. How a text looks at gender differences and at the nature of sexual relationships presents important ethical data.

The general approach of the wisdom literature is to warn against sexuality and the dangers of sexual attraction. Women are looked upon as a temptation, as leading men astray, as subverting wisdom. Proverbs 7 develops this theme extensively. Wisdom should be regarded as a sister, as a friend. Another type of woman comes toward a man "decked out like a prostitute… I had to offer sacrifices and today I have paid my vows, so now I come out to meet you… Come, let us take our fill of love until morning" (Proverbs 7:10–18). Such seduction leads man away from true knowledge: "Her house is the way to **Sheol**, going down to the chambers of death" (7:27). In contrast to this seductive woman, Proverbs envisions the chaste sisterly woman who represents wisdom (Proverbs 8).

This suspicion of sexual attraction contrasts with its celebration in the Song of Songs. Unlike almost every other biblical book (except for Esther, to be discussed later), this poetic evocation of sexual desire makes no explicit reference to God. It does mention that love is as strong as "the flame of Yah" (often translated as "raging flame"), but that attribution does not really involve the divinity in the poem. Instead, the poem is a set of speeches between a male and female protagonist. The female speaker demonstrates as powerful a longing, as cogent an argument, and as clear a sexual response as does the male. The equality between the two seems evident, despite the opening verse that declares the author of the poem (and presumably the male speaker) to be King Solomon. The self-confidence of the woman in the poem argues for her status and position in relationship to the man. Sexual desire, according to this view, is not a war between male and female, not a trap set by one for the other, not a contest to be avoided. Instead, sexual relations establish an equality and a commonality that should be cultivated, celebrated, and enjoyed. The teachings found in Ecclesiastes, Proverbs, and the prologue or epilogue to Job (traditional interpreters were quick to point out that Satan spared Job's wife and note the number of daughters in the epilogue) set male against female in an exclusivist ethics. The poetry of Song of Solomon urges a universalistic perspective in which men and women share in the common experience of love.

HISTORY AND ETHICS IN THE NARRATIVES OF THE WRITINGS

Several books in the Writings offer historical fables as a means of communicating religious ideas and practices: Ruth, Esther, Daniel, and the collection from 1 Chronicles through Ezra and Nehemiah. The entire Chronicle, from creation through the reconstruction of the Jewish commonwealth, moves from universalism to particularism. It begins with the creation of the world and continues with a series of genealogies through the exile to Babylonia, making a few brief asides about individuals, but ignoring most narratives, including those of the Exodus and the revelation at Mount Sinai. The main focus of 1 Chronicles is on David and his establishing the central shrine in Jerusalem. While David's review of history (1 Chronicles 16) mentions Abraham, Isaac, and Jacob and divine miracles, like the rest of 1 Chronicles it does not mention either the Exodus or Sinai. 2 Chronicles establishes the criteria for "good" and "bad" kings: ritual correctness, true prayer, reliance on the priesthood. When good kings remember history, it is that of the sanctuary and of God's promise concerning it (see 2 Chronicles 20). 2 Chronicles ends with Cyrus the conqueror of Persia allowing Jews to return to Israel after their exile in Babylonia (2 Chronicles 36:22–23).

The two books of Chronicles seem to have a universalist approach. They begin with creation and see history unfolding in an inevitable pattern. Although miracles do occur in several stories, the point is less that God intervenes than that God's will dominates all events. Priestly ritual celebrates and maintains this universal order. Just as genealogy leads from one generation to another, so too the priestly worship unites the history of the nation and brings continuity of meaning, despite the fluctuation between righteous and unrighteous kings. The books of Ezra and Nehemiah reverse these perspectives. The historical background suggests that Ezra and Nehemiah represent two attempts at restoring a Judean commonwealth.

As the biblical texts now stand, these two have been conflated into a single restoration. Ezra and Nehemiah introduce religious and social reforms. They bring with them the Torah of Moses, and they make this teaching the basis of their new community. Part of their innovation includes rules about relationships with neighbors—the Moabites and Samaritans in particular. The texts of Ezra 9 and 10 make the basis of this distinction clear. The foreign marriages involved do not necessarily entail religious differences. The claim is an ethnic rather than a religious one: "The holy seed has mixed itself with the peoples of the land" (Ezra 9:2). Not only is intermarriage with such groups prohibited, but those who have already taken wives from such groups are now told to divorce them.

This new ethnic community distinguishes itself by the creation of a historical past and a set of ritual celebrations to remember that past. Ezra 6:19–28 describes a Passover ceremony and a celebration of the festival of unleavened bread. Without explicitly saying so, it implies that the Jews in exile could not observe the holiday since they lacked purified priests and Levites and a Temple in which to sacrifice the offering. Nehemiah 8 and 9 suggest that the introduction of the festivals of the first of **Tishre** and the holiday of Booths took the returned exiles by surprise.

Ezra and Nehemiah rededicate the people to the Torah as the new constitution of the people takes effect as part of a public declaration of identity. Nehemiah 9 attributes a long review of biblical history to a prayer recited by Ezra. This prayer introduces the theme of the Exodus from Egypt; it continues by reiterating the pattern of apostasy and repentance during the early settlement period; it concludes with a confession that priests, kings, and officials have not fulfilled God's covenantal commands. This historical review suggests that God intervenes time and again into the life of human communities, that God has a stake in the distinctiveness of the Jewish community in particular, and that both ethical and ritual behavior

Religions of the Writings 151

have as their aim the ensuring of the continued distinctiveness of the group. The two alternatives established by 1 and 2 Chronicles, on the one hand, and by Ezra and Nehemiah, on the other, reappear in the other narrative texts.

The book of Ruth, for example, seems to be a polemic against the exclusive ethics of Ezra and Nehemiah. (see the outline of the book in Box 7–3). The book tells the story of a Moabite woman during the time of the judges who marries an Israelite man. The story tells how God condemns her husband to die, leaving her, her sister, and her mother-in-law widows who must fend for themselves. **Ruth**, unlike her sister **Orpah**, decides to accept the Israelite identity of her former husband. She tells her mother-in-law, **Naomi**, that she will follow her where she goes, accept her land, and accept her God: "Where you go I will go…your people shall be my people and your God my God" (1:16).

The story concludes as Ruth marries a prominent Israelite and becomes the grandmother of Israel's greatest king—David. This tale introduces a cast of characters not present in either the Deuteronomic History or in 1 Chronicles. It stresses an inclusive ethics; Israelites should bring others into the community, not act to exclude them. Had Ruth been excluded, Israel would never have enjoyed its greatest king. God intervenes in the lives of individuals, but does not seem to be shaping national destinies.

The keyword of the book of Ruth is *hesed*—a term associated with Deuteronomic prophets such as Elijah. The term refers to reciprocity: human beings being loyal to each other; God being loyal to those among humanity faithful to the divine cause. Such fidelity extends beyond any particular religious or ethnic community. It stands for a type of justice or fairness common to all human groups. This universal standard of equity permeates the story and gives it a significance for non-Jews as well as Jews. Just as Ruth and her sister (both Moabites and non-Jews) have acted with hesed toward Naomi's family, so Naomi asks God to act that way toward them (1:8). That Ruth finds shelter with Naomi's relative **Boaz** is understood as a sign of divine hesed (2:20). When Boaz finally accepts Ruth as a "worthy" woman, he declares that her most recent acts of hesed are even more exemplary than her original loyalty to Naomi: "May you be blessed by the Lord, my daughter; this last instance of your loyalty is better than the first" (3:10). The dynamic force in history is that of loving fidelity, of loyalty, either practiced by human beings or by the divine. The pattern of human events, as projected by this book, exemplifies a universal force, the force that arises from actions taken by people loyal to one another.

The book of Esther also emphasizes the importance of human actions. Even more emphatically than Ruth, this book removes God's intervention from all aspects of human life. In Esther, human beings alone control their personal and national futures. The tale takes place in Persia. A Jewish girl, **Esther**, becomes consort to the Persian king, **Ahashuerus**, just when the king's prime minister, **Haman**, is plotting against the Jewish community. Haman is furious because **Mordecai** the Jew has refused to bow before him. Remarkably, the book of Esther does not explain why Mordecai will not bow before the prime minister. Nowhere does it state that any Jew other than Mordecai makes a similar refusal. All the text says (Esther 3:6) is that Haman considered the execution of one person too trivial an act for him to pursue, so he decided to execute all Jews.

The story gives no religious justification for this decision. Haman himself explains to the king that his antipathy comes from the fact that the Jews follow laws that are different from laws everyone else observes: "There is a certain people scattered and separated among the peoples in all the provinces of your kingdom; their laws are different from those of every other people, and they do not keep the king's laws, so that it is not appropriate for the king to tolerate them" (Esther 3:8). This, however, seems to be an arbitrary charge that the book itself seems to refute. When all has been prepared for the destruction of the Jews, Esther informs the king of the plot and saves the Jews.

Mordecai and Esther are said to be of the tribe of Benjamin—the family of King Saul. Haman is said to be an Agagite—a descendant of **Agag** the king of the Amalekites whom Saul mistakenly spares instead of executing. The author seems to be saying that the tale unfolds in an automatic way. It is inevitable that the later descendants of Saul will rectify his error toward Agag by taking vengeance on his descendant Haman. That God never appears in the story suggests that the unfolding of this drama takes place as an inescapable consequence of the past. The continuity of past and present underlie the impetus behind the tale. While the story does single out the Jewish people, it places their story in the context of Persian history in general. Nothing specifically Jewish distinguishes either Esther or Mordecai. Both are clearly at home in the Persian court and its environment. The lesson that Jews are like everyone else underlines the falsity of Haman's claims. The story sees history as a continuous reiteration of basic patterns, such as the conflict between the family of Saul and that of the Agagites, and as one that applies generally without any particularistic emphasis upon the Jewish people and its distinctiveness.

The first half of the book of Daniel (Daniel 1–6) takes the opposite position (see the outline of Daniel in Box 7–3). Daniel and his friends in this story distinguish themselves from other Babylonians in several ways; the text emphasizes their dietary laws and their mode of worship in particular. Because of these peculiarities, Daniel and his friends find themselves threatened by many dangers. They may be thrown into a fiery furnace (Daniel 3, a chapter that does not mention Daniel) or made to face hungry lions (Daniel 6, which focuses on Daniel's fidelity to Jewish liturgical practice). In each of these cases, God intervenes to save the day. Heroes suffer because they refuse to change their distinctive behavior and are then rescued by the divinity.

These stories reinforce commitment to an exclusive ethics. Jewish behavior should set Jews apart from others; they should be easily differentiated from the general populace. The author (or authors) of these stories seems to recognize that such self-differentiation can lead to trouble. While Mordecai and Esther adapted to the customs of the non-Jewish world, the case of Jews who celebrate their distinctiveness is different. These stories claim that there is an advantage to the preservation of ethical difference. Even though the immediate consequence of following such an ethics may produce difficulties, the power of the

Jewish God more than compensates. God will turn what had been a disadvantage into an advantage.

Daniel 1 introduces the themes that resound throughout the first part of the book. The book begins with a historically inaccurate description of a siege during the time of King **Jehoiakim**. This historical inaccuracy arises from a midrashic understanding of the statement in 2 Kings 24:1 and, therefore, alerts readers to the style and genre of this book, a meditation on other biblical texts. Verse 4 refers to the language and literature taught to the captive Judeans as that of the **Chaldeans**. The verse understands this term as referring to a priestly class of magicians or astrologers. Such usage dates the writing of this story to Hellenistic times when that term became popular. As the story develops, Daniel and three of his companions resist assimilation. Verse 7 tells how they are given Babylonian names, names which the book of Daniel will assiduously avoid, so as to emphasize that these heroes maintain their original identity.

The four Judeans refuse to eat food forbidden by their tradition, despite the fears of their Babylonian overseers. The text declares: "But Daniel resolved that he would not defile himself with the royal rations of food and wine; so he asked the palace master to allow him not to defile himself" (Daniel 1:8). Miraculously, eating the plain food allowed to Jews makes them stronger and healthier than those nourished on supposedly better palace provisions: "At the end of ten days it was observed that they appeared better and fatter than all the young men who had been eating the royal rations" (Daniel 1:15). Taking its cue from the story of Joseph in the book of Genesis, the tale goes on to portray these Judean captives as wiser and more discerning than the Chaldean magicians and astrologers (1:17–21).

Three principles derive from this story. The first is that Jewish identity must continue as a distinctive and exclusive one, even in the midst of the exilic community. Behavioral patterns such as keeping one's own name and eating only what is ethnically allowed separate Jews from others. Second, however, those special activities have an advantage, not only for those who follow them, but also for the community at large. By retaining a specific Jewish identity, individuals do not alienate themselves from others, but are better prepared to contribute to the general society and provide it with needed information and leadership.

God interacts with history through the mediation of chosen individuals such as the heroes in the book of Daniel. Finally, God's intervention is often mysterious and hard to comprehend. The non-Jewish characters in Daniel 1 do not, at least at first, recognize that God is manipulating events. Only when empirical evidence shows them that something strange and unexpected has occurred do they acknowledge the wisdom of the Judeans. Paradoxically, by holding on to their particularistic ethics, the Judeans publicize and proclaim a message of God's power over all peoples and over nature in general. The significance of Jewish customs for all peoples is evident in Daniel 5. King **Belshazzar**, whom Daniel 5 views, inaccurately, as the last ruler of Babylonia, misuses the vessels from the temple in Jerusalem. He is given a cryptic message that only Daniel can interpret (Daniel 5:10–29), informing him that his sacrilege will lead to his downfall. Not only Jews must obey Jewish law, but all peoples.

RITUAL AND DIVINITY IN THE NARRATIVES OF THE WRITINGS

These narratives in the Writings share a singular approach to ritual: prayer takes pride of place among the various forms of worship described. While the history in 1 Chronicles through Nehemiah does include references to sacrifice and the sacrificial service, priestly prayer becomes the most important way of expressing devotion to the divine. Usually, such prayer takes the form of public worship. Whether expressed by a king such as David or Hezekiah or a priest such as Ezra, these petitions include several standard elements: they include a call to worship, a review of history, and a request for divine assistance.

2 Chronicles 20 introduces a prayer by **Jehoshaphat** that illustrates this view. It begins by announcing that YHWH is the God of the Judean's ancestors and also the only divinity in heaven who controls all human history (20:6). The prayer continues by reviewing how God gave the land to the Israelites because of a covenant with Abraham, and how the Israelites built a sanctuary with the understanding that God would save the people from disaster (7–9). The prayer concludes with a statement that such a time of disaster is now upon the Judeans. The people do not know what to do, but they trust that God will intervene on their behalf (10–13). The author follows this royal prayer with a prayer attributed to a priestly official, a Levite inspired by God's spirit (13–17). The passage continues with a description of how the people worship by reciting words of praise and rejoicing before the Lord (18–21), an event that culminates in a great victory for the people celebrated with more psalms of praise and rejoicing (22–30).

Ritual appears to be both public and substantive. It recites what God has done in the past, and it stimulates the divine to continue such actions in the present. God intervenes in history when rituals are performed according to their correct procedure. The introduction of the idea of covenant complicates this analysis somewhat. God's actions do not flow from capriciousness; the divine must obey certain rules and constraints. The worship in the Temple is efficacious because God has promised that it would be so. The power of prayer in public worship exemplifies a predictable pattern, no less than it shows the control that the divinity exercises over the world. God's ability to alter reality does not, in fact, make that reality purely arbitrary. Believers can count on prayer because its effectiveness has been embedded in the laws of nature.

The book of Ruth continues this general approach, but modifies the type of ritual it considers efficacious. Prayers in Ruth are uttered by ordinary people, not kings or priests. The absence of kings may be explained by the setting of the story during the time of the judges, but that absence does not explain why no civil or religious leader appears in the tale. There are no judges, no Levites, no priests in the story. Instead, prayers express individual or communal concerns. Naomi prays for God to bless her daughters-in-law (1:8–9). Boaz calls on YHWH to reward Ruth for the good she has done to others and for her decision not to let externals decide her choice for a husband (2:11–12, 3:10). The people of the town act as witnesses to Boaz's acquiring Ruth as a wife and ask God to give her familial blessings

(4:11–12). Here again, God seems to be invoked as a means of continuing the normal course of events. God maintains the correct relationship between what people receive in life and what they deserve from life. At the same time, Ruth focuses on religion as private and personal, rather than public and national. God's concerns are with the needs of individuals who serve as the ritual experts appealing to those concerns.

The book of Esther takes the secularization of rituals to its greatest extreme (see the outline of this book in Box 7–3). The central ritual activity in the book is that of an official banquet. Such banquets punctuate the story at crucial points (1:1–19; 2:18–23; 5; 7; 9:17–18). The plot swings into motion when the king, Ahasuerus, and his queen, Vashti, hold banquets. Later Esther holds banquets that lead to the embarrassment and finally execution of the enemy Haman. Finally, Esther and Mordecai declare that ritual banquets will mark the celebration of the events recorded in the story. These banquets are public rituals, but since the book of Esther does not mention the divinity, they do not invoke God. These rituals provide the occasions for dramatic occurrences. Ritual neither confirms the normal expectations of life nor does it transform them. Instead, it presents an opportunity for historical action.

That historical action derives from human legislation. The key idea of "law" plays a significant part in the book of Esther (see 1:8, 19, 3:3, 8, 4:11, 8:8, 17, 9:29–30). In most of these cases, law arises from the word or will of the sovereign. The laws that Esther and Mordecai promulgate concerning the observance of the holiday of **Purim** take effect only because Ahasuerus has authorized them. The king, however, is also bound by law. He cannot change a regulation that he himself has enacted. This reality leads to a tragic comedy of errors at the conclusion of the book. Haman has convinced the king to promulgate a law proclaiming that Jews will be attacked on a certain day. After Esther reveals Haman's villainy, the king regrets this ruling, but does not have the power to change it. Finally, he decides that the populace still must attack the Jews, but they will be unarmed and the Jews armed. In this way, the intended destruction of the Jews becomes, instead, a Jewish destruction of the non-Jews. All of this occurs because the king is unable to rescind a legal enactment that he has made. The rule of law, apparently, leads to strange consequences. One exception to this rule of royal law occurs—Haman's accusation that Jews live by laws other than those of the king (3:8). Tradition seems to be at least an equal authority to that of the king. By the end of the tale, it seems as if the king authorizes new traditions by allowing Mordecai and Esther to institute Jewish customs.

The relationship of ritual to law seems to hinge upon the relationship between banquets and authority. From the perspective of the book of Esther, ritual does not appeal to God but rather sets the stage for the exercise of authority. God does not appear as the source of power or control over the world. Instead, human leaders—who find their legitimacy through such civil rituals as banquets—take over that role. In this way, the functions of ritual and the divine are transposed from the supernatural realm in which they operate in 1 Chronicles through Nehemiah and in Ruth into the sphere of politics.

The book of Daniel presents a contrast to these previous views. Prayer in this book arises out of a recognition of divine greatness. Prayer, whether by individuals such as Daniel or rulers such as Nebuchadnezzar, expresses a sense of the strangeness of the universe and of the divine's place in the cosmos. Daniel 6 seems almost a reflection on the theme of royal law found in Esther. The premise of the book is that enemies try to rid themselves of Daniel, who as a good Jew prays three times a day, by getting the king to pass a law forbidding such worship. The operative phrase in Esther, that the law of the Medes and Persians can never be revoked, reappears in this story (6:8, 15). Unlike Esther, however, the book of Daniel rejects that idea. God's law, it contends, supersedes any merely human injunction. Daniel continues to recite his prayers as required and consequently is forced into a den of hungry lions. At this point the king, rather than Daniel, begins to utter prayers—prayers for Daniel's safety. When Daniel does emerge from the lion's den safe and unharmed, the king recites a short prayer of gratitude for this event (5:25-27). This prayer, ironically, becomes part of a proclamation that the king makes into a new law of tolerance for the religion of the Jews.

That short proclamation echoes the much longer one that constitutes Daniel 4. The chapter, ostensibly related by Nebuchadnezzar, the Babylonian king, develops a theme from the Joseph stories in Genesis—that of the Jewish advisor who can explain the dreams of a ruler. Nebuchadnezzar has had a terrible dream in which he envisions strange images and a heavenly tribunal judging him. None of his advisors can explain the dream (Daniel 4:4–7). He calls upon Daniel, who indeed decodes the dream. It anticipates a time of trial during which the king will be like an animal (some scholars suggest that the madness said to have afflicted the historical Babylonian king **Nabonidus** underlies this), but after which he will be restored to power (Daniel 4:8–27). Unlike the Joseph story, here the king seems to have converted to Daniel's religion (Daniel 4:1–3, 34–37). The chapter concludes with Nebuchadnezzar's hymn of praise to the Most High and his ability to control all life.

Prayer, in these stories, does not seek to change events. Heroes, such as Daniel or the three other Judeans who face similar dangers, do not pray either for their own personal welfare or for any national purpose (the three lads in the furnace do not pray for God to save them; Daniel does not appeal for divine help in the den of lions). Prayer symbolizes devotion to Israel's God. It affirms Jewish identity, or at least an acceptance of the divine will. Nebuchadnezzar does not pray to ask the God who controls all events to change those events. He merely acknowledges that history unfolds because of divine activity. God is indeed actively involved in the world, but ritual is not the means to influence that activity. Whereas the banquets in Esther were occasions on which power could be manipulated, and the prayers in 1 Chronicles through Nehemiah seek national favor from God, these rituals in Daniel point backward and reflect upon history after it has occurred. Of course, Daniel 1–7 affirms that God intervenes in human affairs; the view of divinity expressed is clearly immanent, and history is unpredictable. That unpredictability, however, does not occur because of human prayer. Such prayer symbolizes faith; it does not alter reality. God informs prophets of the divine plan, but that plan operates without the need for ritual intervention to ensure its success or to initiate its process.

SUMMARY QUESTIONS

1. What examples of *midrash* can be found in Chronicles, Esther, and Daniel?
2. How does the view of divinity in Psalm 82 differ from that in Psalm 19?
3. How does the view of wisdom in Proverbs differ from that in Ecclesiastes?
4. How does the view of ethics in Ezra and Nehemiah differ from those in Ruth?
5. How do the views of ethics and ritual in Esther differ from those in Daniel?

Four Suggested Essay Questions

1. Explain two ways in which a tradition may view history. Show how Job 1–2 illustrates one way and how Proverbs 4 illustrates the other.
2. Explain two ways in which a tradition may view the supernatural. Apply one of them to Psalm 2 and the other to the story in the book of Esther.
3. Explain two ways in which a tradition may view ethics. Apply one of them to the ethics promulgated in Ezra 9–10 and the other to the ethics found in the book of Ruth.
4. Explain two ways in which a tradition may view ritual. Show how Psalm 73 illustrates one of them and Psalm 19 illustrates the other.

Exercise

Read the following paragraph from an answer to Question 1:

> Religions sometimes view history as the result of arbitrary decisions made by supernatural beings; other traditions view history as the result of a planned and purposeful program that human beings can comprehend. A view of history as the product of arbitrary supernatural beings makes the course of events unpredictable. Since God's reasons are inscrutable, human beings cannot comprehend the meaning of events. Those who see history as a series of planned and purposeful actions by a rational deity, however, claim that events are predictable once the divine purpose has been discerned. They argue that since God's reason corresponds to human reason, humanity can comprehend the intentions of the divine.

Now answer the following five questions:

1. Write two sentences showing how Job 1–2 illustrates history as the result of arbitrary decisions.

2. Write two sentences showing how Proverbs 4 illustrates the view of history as a series of planed actions by a rational deity.

3. Write two sentences showing how Job 1–2 views history as incomprehensible to human beings.

4. Write two sentences showing how Proverbs 4 views history as comprehensible to human beings.

5. Write a topic sentence concerning the view of history in Proverbs 4 for the third paragraph of an essay that begins with the cited introduction and continues with a paragraph devoted to the view of history in Job 1–2.

FOR FURTHER READING

The books listed below should be a point of departure for your future study. Each includes a bibliography that will guide you beyond its basic information.

1. Berlin, Adele, *The Dynamics of Biblical Parallelism* (Bloomington: Indiana University Press, 1985).

2. Berqant, Dianne, *Israel's Wisdom Literature: A Liberation-Critical Reading* (Minneapolis, MN: Fortress Press, 1997).

3. Bickerman, Elias Joseph, *Four Strange Books of the Bible: Jonah, Daniel, Koheleth, Esther* (New York: Schocken, 1968).

4. Bloom, Harold, *Where Shall Wisdom Be Found?* (New York: Riverhead Books, 2004).

5. Crenshaw, James L., *Old Testament Wisdom: An Introduction* (Louisville, KY: Westminster/John Knox Press, 1998).

6. Fisch, Harold, *Poetry With A Purpose: Biblical Poetics and Interpretation* (Bloomington: Indiana University Press, 1988).

7. Fokkelman, J. P., *Reading Biblical Poetry: An Introductory Guide* (Louisville, KY: Westminster/John Knox, 2001).

8. Weeks, Stuart, *Early Israelite Wisdom* (Oxford, England: Clarendon Press, 1994).

8

Religions of Hellenistic Writings

READING ASSIGNMENT

Ben Sirah (Ecclesiasticus) 44–50
1 Maccabees 1–4, 14
2 Maccabees 7, 10
Wisdom of Solomon 9, 10, 14
Tobit (entire)

LEARNING OBJECTIVES

By the end of this lesson, you will be able to:
- Describe the impact of the history and culture of Hellenism on the views of history, ritual, ethics, and the divine in the Apocryphal writings.
- Describe the views of history, divinity, ritual, and ethics in the Apocryphal books of 1 Maccabees and 2 Maccabees.
- Describe the views of history, divinity, ritual and ethics in the Apocryphal books of Tobit, Judith, Additions to Daniel, Additions to Esther.
- Describe the views of divinity, history, and ritual in the Wisdom of Solomon and Ecclesiasticus.

INTRODUCTION

This chapter examines those works found in the Greek Septuagint not accepted as canon in Jewish or Protestant Bibles, but accepted in the present Roman Catholic Bible. The history

Interpretive Matrix for Chapter Eight

View of the Divine: How people interact with God and the supernatural; how God interacts with the world.	View of History: How past, present, and future are related; who controls the shape of events.	View of Ethics: How people behave toward other people; how they behave toward people like themselves and to those who are different.	View of Ritual: How people behave toward the Divine; how they perform religious actions.
The Divine as Transcendent: God remains uncontaminated by the physical world. God is accessible through an emanated divine spirit. God sends angels to act in the human world.	**History as Continuous:** Patterns in the present reflect events from the past. Apparently new celebrations echo older holidays. Ancient heroes appear in visions to instruct and authorize later leaders.	**Inclusive Ethics:** Philosophical ideas in the general culture are used to explain a minority's traditional literature. Ethnic and national outsiders can be incorporated into the group if they adopt the group's ideas and practices.	**Ritual as Transforming:** Ritual brings military victory and national success. Ritual observances assure a person of justification after death.
The Divine as Immanent: God rewards and punishes people in this life and in the next. God performs miracles that change the shape of events.	**History as Discontinuous:** Political changes demand new religious responses. New holidays are created to celebrate new events. Laws may be put aside to meet the demands of a new situation.	**Exclusive Ethics:** Special practices such as dietary laws separate one group from another. Intermarriage is discouraged.	**Ritual as Symbolic:** Ritual obedience symbolizes loyalty to the ethnic and national group. Ritual symbolizes personal humility and acceptance of the divine plan.

of this period was marked by a response to Greek culture. The books of the Apocrypha offer one set of responses to Hellenism that influenced views of the divine and ritual processes.

Another set of writings provides some background to the period, those found in the **Talmud**—a text finally compiled about 500 C.E. that expresses rabbinic Judaism and its view of the history that led up to its ultimate success. As you study these books, keep in mind that the religious responses involved differed among Jewish groups. Some emphasized continuity; others espoused discontinuity. Some understood the divine as intervening in history; others took a philosophical position and emphasized transcendence. Some assimilated to the majority culture and developed an inclusive ethics; others contended against that culture and cultivated an exclusive ethics. For some, ritual transformed reality; for others, it symbolized values and ideals.

SOME IMPORTANT TERMS

The following terms are important in this chapter. Some of them have been listed in previous chapters; in those cases the term is not **bold** in the main body of this chapter. Where names of books are also the names of individuals (such as Tobit), the name does not appear in the Glossary.

Achior	Gentiles	Mithras
Adam	Gerizim	Nebuchadnezzar
Alexander Balas	Epicureanism	Nicanor
Alexander the Great	Ethnarch	Onias
Alexandria	Hanukkah	Passover
Angel	Hasideans	Philo Judeas of
Antiochus III	Hasmoneans	Alexandria
Antiochus IV (Epiphanes)	Heliodorus	Platonism
Apocrypha	Hellenism	Pompey
Aristobulus II	Herod Agrippa	Pseudepigrapha
Asclepius	Herod	Ptolemies
Asmodeus	Hezekiah	Resurrection
Bar Kokhba	Holofernes	Qumran
Baruch (Apocryphal Book)	Idumea	Sabbath
	Isis	Samaritans
Bel and the Dragon	Jaddua	Seleucids
Circumcision	John Hyrcanus I	Sennacherib
Dead Sea Scrolls	John Hyrcanus II	Seth
Demetrius	Jonathan the Hasmonean	Shem
Devil	Joseph the Tobiad	Simon son of Onias
Dietary Laws	Josephus	Simon the Hasmonean
Dionysius	Josiah	Sol
Dura-Europos (synagogue of)	Judas Maccabeus	Stoicism
	Judith	Susanna and the Elders
Ecclesiasticus	Letter of Jeremiah	Talmud
Edom	Logos	Temple of Onias
Elephantine	Maccabees	Tobit
Enoch	Martyr	Wisdom of Solomon
Enosh	Mattathias the Hasmonean	Zerubbabel
Exodus From Egypt		

APOCRYPHA AND PSEUDEPIGRAPHA

The Apocrypha designates a variety of texts that include historical writings, wisdom poetry, and additions to canonical books (see Box 8–1). These writings do more than continue the traditions of the Jewish Bible; they also introduce new themes and ideas that form a bridge to the religious traditions that came later—rabbinic Judaism and Christianity. Scholars place their composition during the Hellenistic period, one that extended from the time of Alexander the Great's conquest of the Near East (331 B.C.E.) through the aftermath of the Jewish war against the Romans and the destruction of Jerusalem (70 C.E.). The writings studied in this chapter are those canonized in the Roman Catholic Bible.

Many other documents come from that period. Some of them are apocalytpic and describe a final cataclysm that engulfs the world; others report on geography of the supernal world or on angels, demons, and other supernatural beings. Most are written by later authors using the name of an earlier figure; that form is called *pseudepigraphic*, and the writings are called **pseudepigrapha**.

While this book does not analyze those writings that are outside of the Jewish, Roman Catholic, or Protestant canons, the titles are given in Box 8–2. The period in which they were composed saw dramatic changes in Jewish life and dramatic responses to those changes, both of which this chapter will study (see Timeline 8–1). Some responses emphasized continuity of history; others embraced discontinuity. Some created an inclusive ethics affirming the general culture; others advocated a rejection of that culture and an exclusive ethics.

Hellenism—the acceptance of Greek culture by non-Greeks such as Jews, Syrians, and Egyptians—challenged biblical thought in many ways. Hellenistic philosophy introduced new concepts that augmented earlier biblical ideas; Hellenistic religions offered ritual alternatives attractive to urbanized Jews (see Box 8–3). Some groups accepted the new ideas and integrated them into their traditions; other rejected them and sought to maintain older ways.

HISTORY AND THE APOCRYPHA

The book of 1 Maccabees gives the most extensive historical review found in the Apocrypha, beginning with the conquest of the Near East by Alexander the Great and ending with the kingship of **John Hyrcanus I** over an independent Judean kingdom (135–104 B.C.E.). The account highlights the sense of change and discontinuity prevalent during these years. Alexander the Great swept across the ancient world, bringing both political and cultural changes in his wake. In the lands he conquered, he set up political centers with Hellenized generals to govern them and local priesthoods to authenticate them. The narrative about his relationship to these cities is not always clear. A city gained an advantage by pointing to a charter given it by Alexander.

The Jewish historian Flavius **Josephus** (37–100 C.E.) in his Antiquities 11:304ff (see Box 8–2) portrays a meeting between Alexander and the Jewish high priest **Jaddua**. When conquering Syria and Palestine in 332 B.C.E., Alexander met resistance only from Gaza. After destroying it, Jospehus claims that the general then came to Jerusalem. To the surprise of his followers, Alexander bowed low before the high priest, claiming to have seen him in a vision he had received while still in Macedonia and that had promised him victory in his campaigns.

BOX 8–1   THE CONTENTS OF THE APOCRYPHA

These writings, found in the Septuagint, but excluded from the Jewish Bible, are considered part of the Old Testament in the Roman Catholic canon. They reflect Hellenistic culture and the Jewish responses to it.

Supplements to Canonical Books

Additions to Esther   The Septuagint includes six additions to the Hebrew narrative in the book of Esther (placed by Jerome in his Latin Vulgate at the conclusion of the book of Esther). These include prayers and references to God's ability to intervene in history that provide a pious perspective not found in the original Hebrew text. The additions also stress obedience to Jewish law, claiming that Esther refused to eat the food at the royal court because it did not meet Jewish dietary restrictions.

Additions to Daniel   Three supplemental works are added to the Jewish Book of Daniel. The Prayer of Asariah consists of hymns attributed to the three youths (inserted as Daniel 3:24–90). These psalm-like writings refer to an unjust king and persecution of priestly functions that may refer to the situation under Antiochus IV. The story of Susanna and the Elders is appended as Daniel 13 and tells how God's spirit inspires Daniel, still a young man, to vindicate a woman falsely accused of adultery. A second appendix, Daniel 14, consists of three stories in which Daniel undermines the claims of idolatry—by proving that the God Bel does not eat food left for it, that a dragon is merely a creature of God who can die and not a god, and a second rescue from a lion's den in which the prophet Habakkuk comes to save David.

Additions to Jeremiah   Several works are brought together under the title "Baruch." The book claims to be the work of Jeremiah's secretary (identified in Jeremiah 36:4–10), but most scholars consider that claim unjustified. It opens by claiming to have been written in Babylonia and then sent with a long confession to Jerusalem. That confession (Baruch 1:15–3:8) attributes the Jewish exile and suffering to sinfulness, but requests God's gracious forgiveness and restoration to former glory. The next section includes a hymn to wisdom (3:9–4:4) and then a set of lamentations and words of comfort (4:5–9). The Letter of Jeremiah often appears attached to Baruch, although sometimes it is attached to Jeremiah, after Lamentations) and sometimes placed as a book by itself. The chapter is an extended polemic against idolatry and worship of natural phenomena.

Historical Tales

Tobit   This folktale-like narrative tells about a pious Israelite family living in Nineveh. The hero Tobias, the youthful son of the aged and blind Tobit, negotiates several dangers, is aided by an angel and exorcises a demon, in order to marry the pious Sarah and to cure his father of blindness. In the course of the narrative the author introduces priestly prerogatives, prayers, and popular views about good and evil spirits.

Judith The story takes place during the Babylonian defeat of Assyria, although this is associated with Nebuchadnezzar rather than his father who actually achieved this. Nebuchadnezzar sends his general Holofernes to punish all who had not supported Babylonia. One such place is called Bethulia, although it probably represents Jerusalem. Holofernes is advised by a certain Achior the Ammonite not to engage in fighting the Jews (Judith 5) who recites the history of Abraham's migration to Canaan, the Exodus from Egypt, the Babylonian exile, and the return from that exile. Achior is sent to the Jews in Bethulia. When the besieged city is about to submit, its ruler Uzziah convinces people to wait five days to allow Israel's God to save them. That salvation does occur as the woman Judith seduces Holofernes and decapitates him. The people rejoice, and Achior converts to Judaism through circumcision (Judith 14). The book conludes with Judith coming to Jerusalem and chanting a hymn (Judith 16).

1 Maccabees This history of the Maccabean revolt and its aftermath begins by describing Alexander the Great's conquest of the ancient Near East and the division of his kingdom among his generals. It quickly moves to the Seleucid conquest of Judea followed by Antiochus IV's persecution of traditionalist Jewish practices. It describes the revolt of Mattathias and his sons, the battles of Judas Maccabeus and his establishing of the holiday of Hanukkah, the battles under his brothers Jonathan and Simon, and appointing of Simon's son John Hyrcanus as the first priestly ruler of the Hasmonean dynasty.

2 Maccabees This rendition of the story of the Maccabean revolution begins with a letter addressed to the Jews of Egypt instructing them to celebrate the holiday of Hanukkah. They trace the holiday back to Nehemiah's dedication of the second Temple. The second chapter augments this association with references to Jeremiah and even Moses, and claims that Judas Maccabeus revived ancient customs and collected a library of Jewish books. The story of Judas is then related with several miraculous tales included in the narration. The story concludes as, having decided on the necessity of fighting on the Sabbath, Judas receives a vision in which the former high priest Onias and Jeremiah the prophet invest him with a sword to strike down his adversaries and thereby legitimize that decision.

Wisdom Writings

Ecclesiasticus (ben Sirah) Called "The Wisdom of Jesus, son of Sirah" in Hebrew and "Ecclesiasticus" in Greek, this collection of sayings and aphorisms seems to contrast traditional Jewish learning to Greek thinking. Wisdom describes itself as an emanation from the divine (24:9). The natural cosmos is said to testify to God's greatness (42:15–43:33).

A long historical survey (chapters 44–51) reviews the history of divinely inspired men from Enoch in pre-history through the high priest Simon (about 200 B.C.E.). Although Moses is mentioned, priestly leadership receives the greatest attention and praise.

Wisdom of Solomon This Greek text makes frequent use of philosophical terms and shows an awareness of both Hellenistic thought and religious movements. Wisdom, personified as God's Spirit, is an emanation from the divine and possesses a power with which to invest "holy souls" making them prophets (7:24–27). The book stresses immortality as a reward for goodness, making recompense in eternity more important than earthly success (3:1–10). The book includes a polemic against idolatry—described in terms resembling Greek mystery religions (14:8–15:19).

BOX 8–2 ADDITIONAL WRITINGS FROM THE HELLENISTIC PERIOD

This listing summarizes several texts not found in the current canons but that provide important background for this period.

Histories by Flavius Josephus
This Jewish historian composed several historical works and polemics against anti-Jewish authors. The two most relevant to the discussion of the biblical corpus are:

Concerning the Jewish War: Josephus, writing in Rome, sometime before 73 C.E., presents a version of the events leading up to and including the great war of the Jews against the Romans. He uses the book to justify both the Romans and to excuse the Jews for their decision to revolt.

The Antiquities of the Jews: This twenty volume work narrates history from the creation of the world through the war against the Romans. The early books reinterpret biblical material and use allegory to make much of the Pentateuchal narrative acceptable to Hellenistic sophistication. Although the work draws on non-biblical sources, they do not shape his narrative. Books 13 through 17 are important for giving details about Judean life and history during the Hellenistic period.

Pseudepigrapha
These are books originating from as early as 150 B.C.E. and as late as 130 C.E. These "outside books" or non-canonical works are often written by later authors writing in the name of a more famous earlier figure. This chart merely lists their titles:

The Prayer of Menasseh	2 Enoch
3 Maccabees	The Sibylline Oracles
4 Maccabees	Letter of Aristeas
2 Esdras	Book of Jubilees
1 Enoch	Testaments of the Twelve Patriarchs

Testament of Job
The Psalms of Solomon
The Assumption of Moses
The Life of Adam and Eve

The Lives of the Prophets
The Testament of Abraham
The Apocalypse of Abraham
The Apocalypse of Baruch

The Dead Sea Scrolls

Scrolls have been found, both in Qumran by the Dead Sea and in Masada, a fort destroyed by the Romans in 73 C.E., that include most books of the Hebrew Bible, several works from the Apocrypha and Pseudepigrapha such as Ben Sirah, Jubilees, or Tobit, commentaries on biblical books, and writings found no where else. Most scholars think they were composed between the second century B.C.E. and the first century C.E.

This list contains some of the most prominent of the latter:

The Zadokite Document (also called The Damascus Document)
The Manual of Discipline (also called The Rule of the Community)
The Rule of the Congregation
A Scroll of Benedictions
The Testimonies Scroll
Psalms of Thanksgiving
The War of the Sons of Light against the Sons of Darkness (also called The Rule for the Final War)

TIMELINE 8–1 THE HELLENISTIC PERIOD

This chart traces the development of Hellenistic Judaism in relationship to the shifting power struggles in the Near East.

331 B.C.E.	Alexander the Great conquers the Near East
323 B.C.E.	Babylonia claimed for Seleucid Empire
301 B.C.E.	Land of Israel under Ptolemaic rule
300 B.C.E.	Hellenization of Jews in Alexandria begins
200 B.C.E.	Antiochus III establishes Seleucid rule over Land of Israel
168–165 B.C.E.	Hasmonean (Maccabean) Revolution in Land of Israel
142 B.C.E.	Hasmonean Dynasty begins under Simon the High Priest, declared as Ethnarch in 140
135–104 B.C.E.	John Hyrcanus I rules in Judea
128 B.C.E.	John Hyrcanus I destroys Samaritan Temple in Gerizim and conquers Idumea
103–76 B.C.E.	Alexander Jannaeus

63 B.C.E.	Pompey takes over Judea for the Romans
20 B.C.E.–40 C.E.	Philo Judaeus of Alexandria
40 B.C.E.–10 C.E.	Pharisaic leaders in Jerusalem
37 B.C.E.–4 C.E.	Rule of Herod the Great; repels the Parthians; rebuilds the Temple
4 B.C.E.–30 C.E.	Jesus of Nazareth
10–65 C.E	Paul of Tarsus
41–44 C.E.	Agrippa I
60 C.E.	Establishment of Exilarch position by Parthians
65 C.E.	Nero's persecution of Roman Christians
66–73 C.E.	Judea's war against Rome; destruction of Jerusalem Temple

Another legend (Talmud Bavli Yoma 69a) describes how Alexander had first given preference to the Samaritans and their kingdom in the north, but when they sought the destruction of the Jerusalem Temple and its cult, Alexander investigated and gave authorization to the Temple priesthood to destroy the Samaritans.

These different stories have a similar point: Jewish leadership in Judea received confirmation and acceptance from Alexander the Great. If nothing else, this type of narrative testifies to Jewish assimilation of the general culture of the Hellenistic world and its adulation of Alexander. With his coming, a new cultural tradition began, one that was discontinuous with previous Jewish culture.

At Alexander's death in 323 B.C.E., more changes and discontinuity ensued. His generals divided up his kingdom among themselves, carving out individual kingdoms and principalities (see Map 8–1). The generals did not remain satisfied with the territories allotted to them and came into conflict with one another when their expansionist policies collided. Their internal rivalry created a political tension that sometimes expressed itself as cultural conflict as well. The Ptolemaic Kingdom governing Egypt and the **Seleucid** Kingdom governing Syria are of particular interest. Palestine lay between them, and each kingdom desired its land for itself.

This tension led to internal divisions among the inhabitants of Judea itself. Josephus tells (in Antiquities 12) the story of a certain **Joseph the Tobiad** and his son Hyrcanus. The story traces the rise and fall of a certain family as it negotiates the shifting alliances between Judea, Egypt, and Syria. Joseph rises to power when Judea tries unsuccessfully to use a conflict between Syria and Egypt to gain some independence (probably in the year 242 B.C.E.). Since Egypt remained powerful, Joseph's support of the Ptolemaic rulers wins him privileges that his son Hyrcanus shares. When, however, the Seleucids finally triumph, Hyrcanus commits suicide and his entire possessions are confiscated by the Seleucid king **Antiochus III**. Such volatile political dynamics suggest a discontinuity between the past and future as events quickly reverse trends and interrupt set patterns.

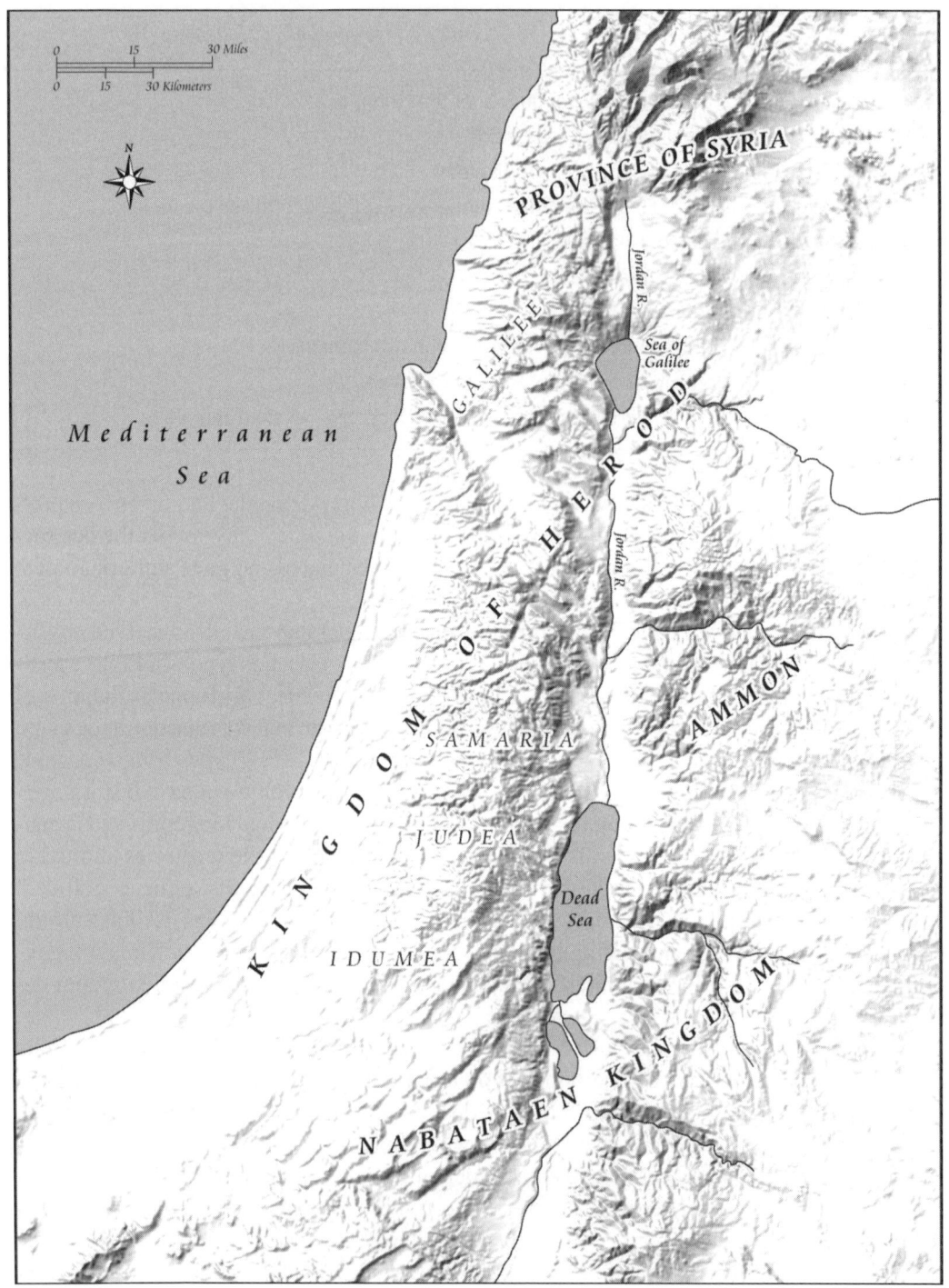

Map 8–1 Palestine in the time of the Herods

The pro-Syrian group that gained power adopted the ways and customs of the Hellenized Seleucids. **Antiochus IV**—called Epiphanes—(175–163 B.C.E.) began an aggressive program of acculturating his holdings. He encouraged the leading priests of Judea to seek the status of Greek City for their capital, Jerusalem. When they did so and installed a Hellenistic gymnasium there, other priestly groups—probably sympathetic to Egyptian rather than Syrian rule—began a revolution. This revolt, led by the Maccabees, eventually installed the **Hasmonean** kings as a new priestly dynasty (see Timeline 8–2). That dynasty began its rule with a call for Jews to return to their traditional laws and customs. Under the military leadership of **Judas Maccabaeus**, the Jews undertook several military campaigns. This endeavor involved a series of sorties, some of which succeeded and some of which were failures. The shifting fortunes of the rebellion led to compromises amidst assertions of independence.

In 152 B.C.E. the revolution reached one milestone. For the first time a Hasmonean priest was installed as high priest (**Jonathan the Hasmonean**). This change in priestly dynasty had political consequences, because from Alexander the Great onwards, Judea's governance had been placed under the control of the holder of this office. A second milestone, in 142 B.C.E. denotes an even greater political advance: **Simon the Hasmonean** was hailed not only as high priest, but also as **Ethnarch**. That title, "leader of an ethnic community," provided Judea with political independence. Simon exercised the powers of a king, combining secular and religious power in a single office.

What was now the Hasmonean kingdom grew and developed, extending its power and control over an ever-increasing territorial expanse. Several extraordinary events occurred under the reign of John Hyrcanus (135–104 B.C.E.). Hyrcanus destroyed the Samaritan capital at **Gerizim** and exerted power over Judea's long-time rival. He also sent his armies into ancient **Edom** (now called **Idumea**) and forcibly circumcised the male inhabitants, convert-

This Greek coin shows Antiochus IV (175–163 B.C.E.), the Seleucid king over Syria against whom the Maccabees arose in revolt.

> **TIMELINE 8–2 THE MACCABEAN REVOLUTION AND ITS AFTERMATH**
>
> This chart traces the rise of the Hasmonean kings, beginning with the Seleucid conquest of Judea.
>
> | | |
> |---|---|
> | 200 B.C.E. | Antiochus III establishes Seleucid rule over Land of Israel |
> | 175–163 B.C.E | Antiochus IV (Epiphanes) favors acculturation throughout his territories |
> | 175–172 B.C.E. | Jason serves as High Priest Hellenizing Jerusalem |
> | 172–163 B.C.E. | Menelaus serves as High Priest and seeks "Greek City" status for Jerusalem |
> | 168–167 B.C.E. | Pietists revolt against Hellenizers and Jerusalem is "desecrated." |
> | 166–165 B.C.E. | Hasmonean (Maccabean) Revolution in Land of Israel led by Mattathias succeeded by his son Judas Maccabeus |
> | 164 B.C.E. | Antiochus ends the persecutions and offers amnesty which is refused; Hannukah inaugurated at the end of that year |
> | 163 B.C.E. | Antiochus IV dies and is succeeded by his son Antiochus V |
> | 162 B.C.E. | A peace treaty and compromise establishes Alcimus as High Priest |
> | 152 B.C.E. | Jonathan the Hasmonean is established as High Priest (but not as ethnarch or king) |
> | 142 B.C.E. | Hasmonean Dynasty begins under Simon the High Priest, declared as Ethnarch in 140 |
> | 135–104 B.C.E. | John Hyrcanus I rules in Judea |
> | 103–76 B.C.E. | Alexander Jannaeus rules Judea |
> | 67–63 B.C.E. | Aristobulus and John Hyrcanus II struggle for control of Judea |
> | 63 B.C.E. | The Romans take over Judea |

ing them to Judaism. The Hasmonean regime adopted Hellenistic characteristics and evolved into a tyrannical despotism typical of the period when Rome was developing as a world power. When rivalry broke out between two Hasmonean brothers, **John Hyrcanus II** and **Aristobulus II**, the nation turned to the Romans to arbitrate the dispute. The independent nation finally fell under the sway of the Roman empire and in 63 B.C.E. lost its independence. The Roman general **Pompey** removed Aristobulus II from the throne and placed John Hyrcanus II on it as his puppet. The Hasmonean reign was nearly over, and Herod the Great, related to the Hasmoneans only by marriage, would succeed John Hyrcanus. Thereafter, Judea was ruled by foreigners (see Timeline 8–3).

Under the Romans, the political and geographical conditions of Judea changed once again (see Map 8–2). The presence of Roman government in Judea did not lessen the instability of historical events. The Romans began by setting up a puppet ruler of their own, an Idumean who had ties to the royal family and who ruled as **Herod the Great** (37–04 B.C.E.). In his wake, however, a series of Roman officials exercised control, sometimes benevo-

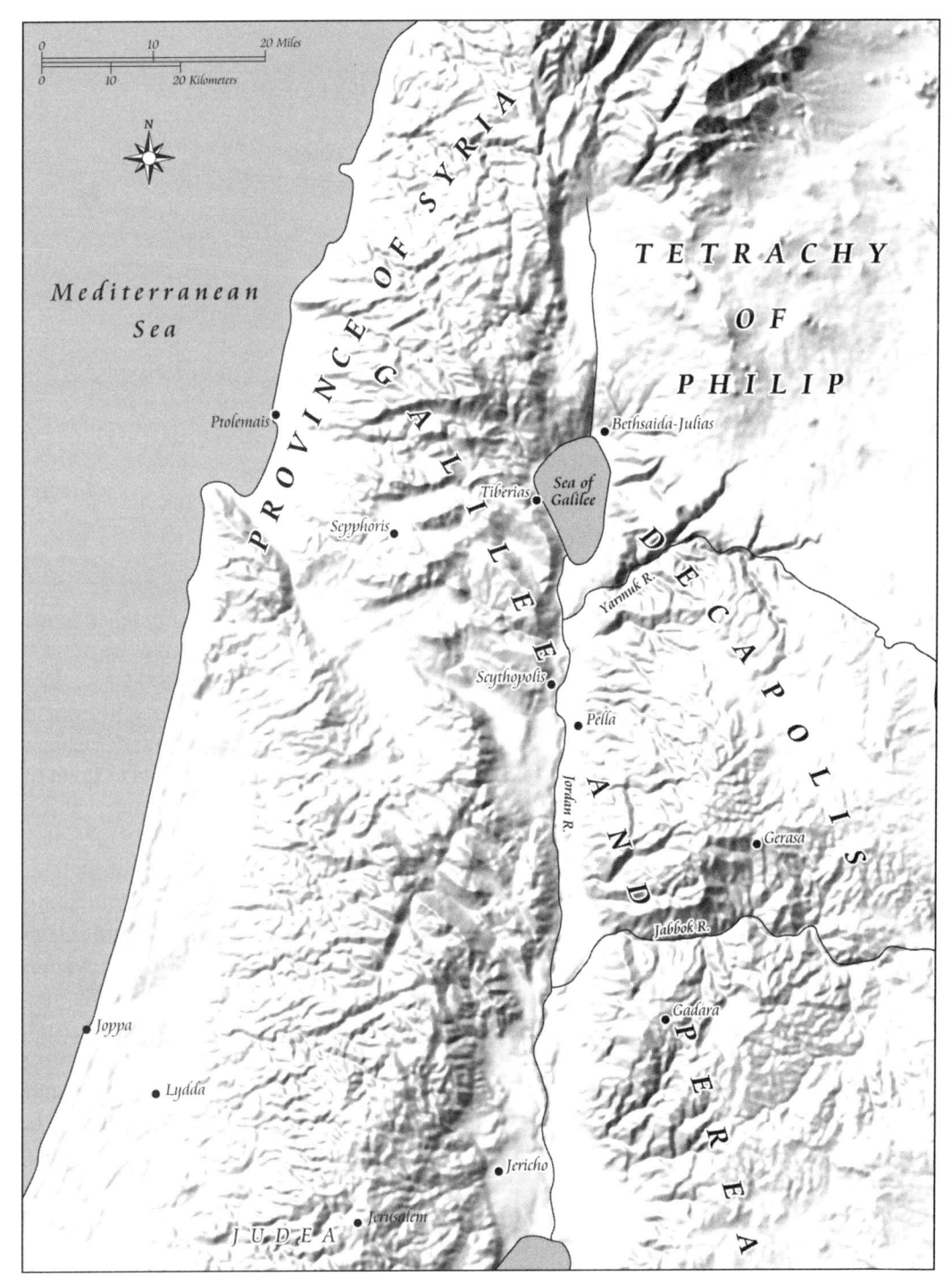

Map 8–2   The Near East in the Hellenistic Period (Ptolemaic and Seleucid Empires)

> **TIMELINE 8–3   ROMAN DOMINATION OF JUDEA**
>
> This chart traces the rulership in Judea from 64 B.C.E. through 135 C.E.
>
> | | |
> |---|---|
> | 63 B.C.E. | Pompey takes Jerusalem |
> | 37–04 B.C.E. | Herod rules Judea under Roman supervision |
> | 04 B.C.E.–41 C.E. | Roman officials govern Judea |
> | 26 C.E. | Pontius Pilate procurator of Judea |
> | 41–44 C.E. | King Herod Agrippa rules Judea |
> | 44–66 C.E. | Roman officials govern Judea |
> | 45 C.E. | Revolt of Teudas the Messiah |
> | 66 C.E. | Gessius Florus, Roman official over Judea |
> | 66–73 C.E. | Judea's war against Rome |
> | 70 C.E. | The Fall of Judea |
> | 132–135 C.E. | Bar Kokhba revolt against the Romans |

lently and sometimes with harsh cruelty. A brief interlude brought a taste of independence and kingship under **Herod Agrippa** (41–44 C.E.), but it was followed by even more repressive Roman rule. This oppression finally drove the Judeans into revolution (66–73 C.E.). Despite the overwhelming odds against them, it took a protracted campaign by several Roman generals to defeat the Jewish forces. The revolt, however, did finally fail, and the Jerusalem Temple was destroyed in 70 C.E. Even the failure of that movement did not lead to quiet in the country. Another outbreak, that of the **Bar Kokhba** rebellion (132–135 C.E.), was the last concerted attempt to attain political independence.

While Judea was in turmoil, Jews had established themselves in other places throughout the Roman world. Jews had long settled in **Alexandria**, Egypt, and had built a flourishing community there. Hellenistic Jews flourished in other venues as well. The **Elephantine** Jewish community (from about 525–400 B.C.E.) had adapted Jewish tradition to Egyptian ways. Evidence of a **Temple of Onias** (about 145 B.C.E.) also testifies to Jewish adaptations of their religious life to fit in more completely with a foreign culture.

Philo Judaeus of Alexandria (20 B.C.E.–40 C.E.) expressed a thoroughgoing Hellenized Judaism. His interpretations of the Hebrew Bible (based on the Septuagint Greek) and his defense of Jewish practice show him not only comfortable in Hellenistic philosophy and political thought, but also able to identify Jewish tradition with it. Flavius Josephus, although born in Judea, illustrates a similar acculturation to Hellenism through the mediation of Rome. Jewish communities throughout the Roman Empire, from Rome itself to Asia Minor, developed Jewish expressions of their own. Discoveries of a third-century **synagogue in Dura-Europos**, Syria, contains murals and manuscripts that show how the Jews in the Diaspora merged their heritage with the cultural and aesthetic conventions they found around them.

This arch, erected to illustrate Rome's defeat of the Jewish revolt (66–73 C.E.), shows the Romans carrying off treasures of Jerusalem.

This history of Hellenization both in Judea and the Diaspora suggests turmoil and discontinuity. Not only do different empires exert influence on Judea (Ptolemaic Egypt, Seleucid Syria, Rome), but internal divisions lead to change and conflict. No single pattern seems dominant; no predictable sequence of events emerges from this history. Nevertheless, the Apocryphal books impose an order and meaning on the past. Some texts reaffirm continuity and argue that change is only apparent. Others admit the presence of discontinuity, but attribute it to the hand of the divine working in history. The flow of historical events just outlined provides the raw material out of which the narratives, wisdom writings, and expansions of biblical texts that make up the Apocrypha wove their religious perspectives.

HELLENISM AND RELIGIOUS VIEWS IN BEN SIRAH

The influence of Hellenistic thinking appears in the way books of the Apocrypha view history. One such book, that of Ecclesiasticus (known in Hebrew as the Wisdom of Jesus Ben Sirah), emphasizes how the priesthood dominated biblical history and continued to be the leading force of Jewish life through **Simon, son of Onias** (a pro-Egyptian high priest 219–196 B.C.E.). The Wisdom of Ben Sirah reinforces a sense of continuity and employs figures of speech and even quotations from earlier wisdom literature. Wisdom is personified as God's first creation who provides the blueprint for everything else that follows (Sirah 1:1–10; compare Job 28 and Proverbs 8). The book reiterates and develops the key idea of "fear of the Lord" as the beginning of wisdom (1:14–20; compare Box 7–1).

BOX 8–3 INFLUENTIAL PHILOSOPHIES AND RELIGIONS OF THE HELLENISTIC PERIOD

This listing summarizes the major philosophical and religious influences that affected writings found in the Apocrypha and in the New Testament.

Philosophies

Platonism   The Greek philosopher Plato (427–347 B.C.E.) emphasized the primacy of the "ideal" over the physical world. He wrote several dialogues featuring the earlier philosopher Socrates as his mouthpiece. Plato's dualistic view as well as his championing the idea of immortality was highly influential. His disciple Aristotle (384–322 B.C.E.) began the process of revising Plato's thought. Between the first and second centuries of the common era this revision continued in what is called "middle Platonism" and is associated with Philo of Alexandria (20 B.C.E.–40 C.E.) who identified the ideal "Good" of Plato with the biblical divinity. Because the "Good" must remain free from contamination by this physical world, Philo imagined several emanations from the divine to this mundane plane, the first emanation of which he called the *logos* or divine Word.

Stoicism   This philosophy is associated with Zeno of Cyrus teaching in Athens about 308 B.C.E.). It emphasizes self-control and strict discipline in the face of life's challenges. It appealed to both Greek and Roman thinkers as a source of personal virtue. It promised immortality and judgment after death. It posited a divine power directing human affairs, a force it identified as the *logos* or universal reason inherent in all things.

Epicureanism   This school of thought is traced back to Epicurus (341–270 B.C.E.) and taught that the pursuit of pleasure—or rather the absence of pain—is the most important moral quest. The philosophy was proudly atheistic, contending that the existence of evil disproves the existence of a benevolent deity.

Religious Expressions

The Cult of Asclepius   Asclepius was the Greek God of healing around whom an impressive following developed about 300 B.C.E.. Worshipers described the miraculous cures—including raising the dead back to life—that their God had accomplished. His sign or symbol was a snake, and snakes were often found in places where he was worshiped.

The Cult of Dionysius   This religious cult exalted a deity born from a virgin impregnated miraculously by the god Zeus after his son Zagreus has been torn apart by the goddess Hera. The cult sought to free its followers—primarily women—from their worries through inducing ecstasy by dancing, drinking, and symbolically consuming the flesh of their divinity. The cult was introduced into Rome about 200 B.C.E. and despite various attempts by the Roman government to repress it, it continued to flourish.

> *The Cult of Isis*   Although originally an Egyptian (and Ethiopian) goddess of fertility, this cult rose to prominence in the Hellenistic world. Although opposed at first, her cult gained popularity. During the reign of Gaius Julius Ceasar (20 B.C.E.–04 C.E.) the festivals of Isis were celebrated in Rome and Isis became a leading Hellenistic goddess. She was said to have gone to the underworld to bring her husband back to life. Portraits of her suckling her son Horus resemble later portraits of Mary and the baby Jesus.
>
> *The Worship of Mithras*   Unlike the previous cults the worship of Mithras eventually became an official religion in the Roman Empire. Mithras was a Persian god who mediated between the creator deity, Ahura Mazda, and human beings. Mithras is a solar deity associated with the twelve signs of the zodiac and his myth tells of his sacramental meal with his twelve associates. He was said to have traveled through the underworld and triumphed over death, being reborn at the winter solstice, December 25th.
>
> *The Worship of Sol Invictus* ("the unconquered sun")   In 270 C.E. the emperor Aurelian introduced the practice of this cult into Roman worship and sanctioned it, even though he did not make it the official Roman religion. He made the sun-god the most important divinity in the empire and took to wearing the god's crown of rays. Many aspects of the worship that Aurelian instituted were identical to those of Mithras including a public festival on the twenty-fifth of December.

Ben Sirah sees God's hand in historical events and asks God to perform wonders for his people in the present comparable to those performed in the past (Ben Sirah 36). Ben Sirah seems to affirm an immanence of the divine in the world. God's presence, manifested as wisdom, touches people, guides them, and brings success. For many Hellenistic authors, God's immanence is not an anthropomorphic one; God does not take on a human appearance or act on the basis of humanlike passions. God, however, is accessible—through the Spirit of the Lord, the Word of the divine—through Wisdom. In this way, the unfolding of history represents the presence of divinity among human beings manifested through divine wisdom (39:32–35).

The most sustained treatment of Jewish history occurs in the final section of the book (chapters 40–50) that traces world history from creation through the high priest Simon, son of Onias. This reconstruction of earlier history selects only those events and heroes the author considered important. Ecclesiasticus 44 describes social leaders who contribute to civilization and society. The chapter highlights figures such as Enoch, Noah, Abraham, Isaac, and Jacob. Chapter 45 focuses on the leaders during Israel's formative time. After a brief description of Moses (45:1–5), the chapter continues with a lengthy description of Aaron and the Aaronide priesthood (6–26). The chapter concludes by suggesting that just as the Davidic covenant ensured that "the king's heritage passes only from son to son, so the heritage of Aaron is for his descendants alone" (45:25). The need to assert this contention suggests that while the Davidic covenant was not controversial, the claim of the Aaronide priests was. Other priestly families may have asserted an equally valid claim to the office of high priest.

The emphasis on the priestly covenant may explain why David's rule is given very little attention (47:1–11) even though God "gave him a covenant of kingship and a glorious throne in Israel" (47:11). Other kings receiving praise are Hezekiah and Josiah. Zerubbabel gets a single verse, although he was "like a signet ring on the right hand" (49:11). After this review of history through Ezra and Nehemiah, Ben Sirah adds a strange comment: "Few have ever been created on earth like **Enoch**...Nor was anyone ever born like Joseph...Shem, Seth and **Enosh** were honored, but above every other created living being was Adam" (49:14–16). Enoch appears earlier in the list (44:16), but the other five heroes, including Adam, have been left out of the account until this point. Why are they introduced here? Perhaps to show that despite a continuity within the divine plan, certain extraordinary individuals do occur and punctuate the otherwise steady unfolding of history.

That realization prepares for Chapter 50 and its presentation of Simon the Priest (Simon, son of Onias). The author portrays him as a civil and military leader no less than a religious functionary. Not only does he function as an exemplary priest (5–19), but he also strengthens the fortifications of Jerusalem as a wise military and political leader (1–4). These two accomplishments suggest that Simon looks forward to a new period of Judean independence. The glories of the priesthood will develop into the glories of national political freedom. History follows a programmed pattern. Nevertheless, important individuals can shape and mold its progress. Ben Sirah moves in Chapter 50 from the inevitable chain of leadership dominating God's history to a new possibility—that God will intervene through this extraordinary priestly leader and work miracles for Israel. The chapter concludes with a prayer for the success of the Israelite nation and an imprecation against its traditional enemies (20–26).

That prayer expresses the ethics animating this exposition of Judaic wisdom. Ben Sirah affirms the special place the Jews hold in God's favor. One Hebrew variant to the Greek version of the book (found among the **Dead Sea Scrolls**) adds the declaration that God "has raised up a horn for his people...for the children of Israel, the people close to him." (See the verses occurring among the scrolls found in a cave in **Qumran** near the Dead Sea cited at the end of Sirah in the New Oxford Bible's translation of the book.) Sirah balances belief in an enduring pattern and continuity in history with a hope for extraordinary individuals who will alter the political realities for the sake of Israel.

Ben Sirah's grandson probably doubted his grandfather's ethics and articulated an inclusive view in which the wise must teach all interested persons. Living in Alexandria and writing in Greek, he translated this book of wisdom not only for Jews who "are disposed to live according to the law," but also "through the spoken and written word to help outsiders" (Sirah, Prologue). The Greek version of the book leaves out the concluding hymn that asserts Jewish chosenness before God, yet the duality toward history remains as an important contribution of the book.

Religions of Hellenistic Writings 177

HELLENISM AND RELIGIOUS VIEWS IN MACCABEES

While Ben Sirah extols the high priest Simon son of Onias, the book of 1 Macabees 14 tells of another Simon, Simon the Maccabee Hasmonean, whose elevation to position of Ethnarch in 142 B.C.E. brought to fruition the prayer that Ben Sirah uttered. That chapter describes Simon the Hasmonean as a Messianic king, applying the ideals of kingship found in prophetic writings such as Isaiah, Joel, Zechariah, and Micah. The land "had rest all the days of Simon" and "He established peace in the land." People are described as sitting under their "vines and fig trees, and there was none to make them afraid" (1 Maccabees 14:1, 11–13). Ushering in such an idyllic period represents a dramatic change from the turmoil and conflict of the Hasmonean wars that came before it. 1 Maccabees sees this innovation as a response to new challenges Hellenization brought to Jewish religion.

1 Maccabees 1 tells of how Alexander the Great introduced Hellenism into the ancient world and how many Jews adopted its ways. The text calls them "renegades" who declared: "Let us go and make a covenant with the Gentiles around us, for since we separated from them, many disasters have come upon us" (1 Maccabees 1:11). Those Jews changed traditional ways by leaving their sons uncircumsised, by abandoning traditional holidays and festivals, and by following non-Jewish practices. Eventually, according to 1 Maccabees 2, Antiochus IV decided to demand that everyone in his kingdom follow the same customs and practices. This meant that Jews would no longer follow their laws of circumcision, dietary laws, or festival observances. The text records that while "Many of the people forsook the law…many in Israel stood firm" (1 Maccabees 2:51–64). This crisis created the need for the Maccabean revolution, a rebellion described from the uprising of **Matthathias the Hasmonean** through the expansionist reign of John Hyrcanus I.

The crisis of Hellenization stimulated many changes in Jewish religious life, all of which 1 Maccabees claims to have been justified by necessity. During the early stages of the resistance to the decrees of Antiochus IV, many traditionalists insisted on following the Sabbath law strictly. Certain pietists (Hebrew *Hasidim* and Greek *Hasideans*) refused to take up arms on the seventh day. Keeping that day holy meant doing no manner of labor or carrying any burden or weapon, even on threat of death. Mattathias rejects that approach. He declares: "Let us fight against anyone who comes to attack us on the Sabbath day" (1 Macabees 2:41). Circumcision, which had been a personal initiation ritual, becomes a public sign of Jewish identity. As such, it may be imposed on others, converting them to Judaism against their will. The warriors led by Mattathias "forcibly circumcised all the uncircumcised boys they found within the borders of Israel" (2:45). The changing nature of the social and cultural environment created a situation in which ritual life would change as well.

One example of such a change was the inauguration of a new holiday, that of **Hanukkah**. The festival commemorates the victory of the Hasmoneans under the leadership of Judas against the Seleucids in 164 B.C.E.. Although this was but one victory in an ongoing conflict (see Timeline 8–2), it was considered an important milestone. Judas won the victory after

These coins from the time of John Hyrcanus (67–40 B.C.E.) and Antigonus (40–37 B.C.E) indicate the religious symbolism and independence of the Hasmonean rulers.

having refused an amnesty offered him by the Seleucid king. It occasioned rededication of the Jerusalem Temple and reestablishment of the priesthood. Never before had such an endeavor taken place. Could the old Temple be utilized after it had been polluted? What new rituals needed to be developed? According to 1 Maccabees 4, the leaders consulted the revealed tradition and followed it wherever they could. When the books provided no answer, they decided to wait until a prophet would arise to tell them what to do (4:41–46). Finally, the leaders of the people—the Hasmonean brothers and something called "the assembly of Israel"—declared a holiday to remember the victory (4:59). Historical discontinuity requires new rituals and practices.

The innovation of this festival brings up certain questions. 1 Maccabees 4 provides a very general description of celebrating "with joy and gladness," of offering sacrifices and decorating the Temple (4:52–59). Other sources include the lighting of lamps and kindling of fires (Talmud Bavli Shabat 21b). Hellenistic rituals of both the sun deity **Sol** and of **Mithras** (see Box 8–3) involved public ceremonies held at the time of the winter solstice. That the Hasmonean kingdom established a similar ceremony at the same season suggests both adaptation to a cultural pattern and a variation on it meant to emphasize difference and national identity. While affirming a culturally prevalent seasonal occasion, Hanukkah makes a statement about Judean independence and difference. It highlights Jerusalem and the Jerusalem Temple and sets their primacy above all other national centers and cultic shrines.

The celebration of Hanukah, however, suggests an important point. God has not entered into history to act on behalf of the Jews. The celebration points to what human beings have done, to the way Judas and his army "removed the disgrace brought by the **Gentiles**"

(4:58). At a later battle, that against **Nicanor**, the priests do indeed invoke God's name. God, however, seems to act through intermediaries, through an angel. When Judas prays, he asks that just as God's angel struck down Sennacherib's army, so Judas' army should act as God's instrument against this foe. When the enemy is defeated, Judas proclaims "Nicanor Day" to celebrate his victory, not an intervention by the divine (1 Maccabees 7). God's transcendent nature precludes his direct participation in human affairs: human armies fight his battles for him.

The transcendence of the divine implies that ritual performances do not directly influence the divine. While 1 Maccabees emphasizes practices such as circumcision and the holiday of Hanukkah, it puts them into the context of national identity and its affirmation. The ethics arising from the view of history espoused by 1 Maccabees insists on Jewish separatism that is not only ritualistic but also political. 1 Maccabees 14, using a Hellenistic model of democratically acclaimed leadership, portrays how the people "elect" Simon as high priest, military leader, and king. This combination of the Messianic ceremonies that appointed both kings and priests into the election of a single person represents a significant innovation in the choice of leadership.

From the Deuteronomic History through the chronicler's writings, the two institutions of priesthood and kingship were kept separate (and not always equal). For the first time (under Simon in 142 B.C.E.), the same person was recognized as both ruler and priest, both anointed to perform sacrificial rituals and to lead the civil government. This new model of leadership, while derived from the Hellenistic environment, articulates an exclusive ethics: the Jews must create their own sociopolitical entity to rival other Hellenistic powers. This ethics allows Jews to make alliances with other nations such as the Romans, whom Judas calls upon as an ally in 1 Maccabees 8, but demands that they maintain their separate identity.

When **Alexander Balas** opposed **Demetrius** as king of the Seleucids, he appointed Jonathan as high priest. Although Demetrius promised the Jews complete religious freedom, 1 Maccabees records that they supported Alexander Balas, who ultimately defeated his rival (1 Maccabees 10). The nationalistic emphasis of 1 Maccabees culminates in the succession of John Hyrcanus I and his father's injunction to him: "Take my place and my brother's and go out and fight for our nation, and may the help that comes from Heaven be with you" (1 Maccabees 16:3). John Hyrcanus maintains the Hasmonean ethics of national identity and independence and expands the nation into foreign lands such as Edom (or Idumea, as it was called at that time).

Second Maccabees portrays events differently. The book implies that every innovation is actually a renewal, that what appears to be new is, in fact, a restoration of what had been previously established. The book begins with a letter (dated in the reign of Demetrius 138–125 B.C.E.) to the Jews in Jerusalem and Egypt reminding them of their common heritage and urging them to celebrate the new holiday of Hanukkah (2 Maccabees 1:1–9). This is followed by another letter addressed to the priest Aristobulus and to the Jews in Egypt defending the holiday of Hanukkah as rooted in ancient tradition, and it is given an ancient pedigree not found elsewhere.

To make its point, the book begins by describing the rebuilding of the Temple by Nehemiah and how that rebuilding exemplified prophecies by both Moses and Jeremiah (2:19–12). Even before the Maccabees, then, this holiday had been authorized. After the Maccabean victory, however, the author invites all Jews everywhere to keep the holiday: "It is God who has saved all his people…We have hope in God that he will soon have mercy on us and will gather us from everywhere under heaven into his holy place" (2:17–18). Ritual helps bring about the salvation of the people. Even an apparently new ceremony actually recalls older holidays and helps achieve a time-honored goal: the ingathering of the exiles. This affirmation of the old receives confirmation when Judas the Maccabee collects all the books that had been lost (2:13–15). Thus the Hasmonean transformation of leadership has restored the Jewish tradition. All that has been scattered has been brought together once again. Continuity, rather than discontinuity, characterizes the view here. These two letters at the beginning of 2 Maccabees appear as introductory material. Following them, the author explains that this book summarizes a five-volume work by a certain Jason of Cyrene (otherwise unknown). The condensation abbreviates the work to entertain and instruct readers (2:19–32). That instruction continues the theme of emphasizing continuity.

When faced with an army of elephants, Judas prays for divine assistance, and an angel answers him in a fashion that resembles earlier stories in Joshua 5, Judges 6, and 2 Kings 19 (2 Maccabees 11:6–9). Reference is made to Joshua's defeat of Jericho (2 Maccabees 12:15–16), to Jeremiah, to Hezekiah, and to the former high priest **Onias** (15:12–24). The treatment of the institution of Hanukkah (2 Maccabees 10) differs considerably from that given in 1 Maccabees. The holiday is not imagined as an innovation celebrating a political victory. Instead, when the Maccabees reclaim the Temple, they purify it and pray that God should be merciful and forgive their sins, rather than punish them in such a way (10:4). They celebrate the purification for eight days because they remembered "how not long before, during the festival of Booths, they had been wandering in the mountains and caves like wild animals" (10:6). The holiday serves two purposes: it seeks to gain God's mercy, and it replaces a festival that had been abandoned out of necessity.

2 Maccabees ends by calling for yet another holiday (the 13th of Adar) as Nicanor Day. That celebration recalls the defeat of the general Nicanor and Judas' hanging his head from the citadel (2 Maccabees 15:35–36). The two public ceremonies described in 2 Maccabees (the institution of Hanukkah and the inauguration of Nicanor Day) illustrate commemorative festivals. These rituals do not change reality. Instead, they point to events that the community shares in common. These are celebratory rituals that remind people of a past that encapsulates their communal memory.

Nevertheless, 2 Maccabees does affirm transformative, substantive ritual in the case of personal prayer. The defeat of Nicanor begins as Judas prays asking for angelic aid and for God's support. He asks that "By the might of your arm may these blasphemers who come against your holy people be struck down" (2 Maccabees 15:24). Judas offers similar prayers before every battle and offers praise to God for answering those prayers by providing victory. Such transformative ritual suggests that God may be immanent in some form, even though God makes use of angels and other intermediaries to perform miracles.

2 Maccabees tells the story of **Heliodorus**, a Seleucid official who tried to confiscate Temple funds. He was rebuked by a frightening vision (3:7–30). God did not intervene directly but sent a vision, rather than appear in person. Another vision, this time with a positive message, also implies divine transcendence. When preparing to fight against Nicanor, Judas tells his troops of a vision he has seen in which both Jeremiah and the former high priest Onias invest him with a sword of victory (2 Maccabees 15:12–16). God sends his messengers to deliver this weapon; he does not appear in person. Historical events display divine transcendence rather than immanence.

God's immanence, however, is present as a response to private devotions. Everything really depends on individual Jews. The author explains the predations of Antiochus IV by saying that the Jews deserved them. The people had descended to a spiritual level such that they did not merit special favor. Why was Jerusalem not protected from the Seleucids? Because Jews had not lived up to the laws God had given them. The author explains this by saying that the nation had been sinful and was, therefore, not deserving of such an act: "But the Lord did not choose the nation for the sake of the holy place, but the place for the sake of the nation. Therefore, the place itself shared in the misfortunes that befell the nation and afterward participated in its benefits…"(5:20).

2 Maccabees understands transformative rituals not only as a means of achieving national goals, but more importantly and more consistently as a way of achieving personal salvation. Personal reward and punishment become more important than national fortunes. When Syrians try to convince the aged scribe Eleazar to eat forbidden food, he rejects their temptation. "Even if for the present I would avoid the punishment of mortals," he tells them, "yet whether I live or die I will not escape the hands of the Almighty" (6:26).

Obedience to ritual commandments has a substantive effect in terms of the actions God takes toward the individual. A mother watches as her seven sons are put to death, rather than betray Jewish ritual law (2 Maccabees 7). The king asks her to convince her younger son to obey him. The mother, however, offers a different argument, one that reinforces disobedience to the king. She advises her son not to abandon Jewish practice because to do so would be to lose the promise of immortality. "Accept death," she tells her son, "so that in God's mercy I may get you back again along with your brothers" (7:29). Obedience to Jewish rituals transforms mortal beings into immortal ones. They become witnesses to God's greatness, as the term **martyr** indicates. Martyrs lose their fear of death because immortality rewards their deeds.

Hellenistic culture stimulated thought about immortality and personal salvation (see Box 8–3). Certainly 2 Maccabees accepts the idea that human beings have an immortal soul. The text goes beyond that philosophical concept to develop a theory of **resurrection**. Not only does the soul survive death, but eventually it will be reunited with the body. 2 Maccabees 7 develops this point in several passages. The second brother martyred declares: "the King of the universe will raise us up to an everlasting renewal of life because we have died for his laws" (v.9). The mother encouraged each son by saying: "The Creator of the world, who shaped the beginning of humanity and devised the origin of all things, will in his mercy give life and breath back to you again since you now forget yourselves for the sake of his laws" (v. 23).

In a similar vein, Judas was said to have sent money to provide for sacrificial offerings in the name of the dead, and "In doing this he acted very well and honorably, taking account of the resurrection," recognizing that the dead would rise again and need to be delivered from their sin (2 Maccabees 12:43–45). In this view of resurrection, judgment, and the effectiveness of prayer and sacrifices, 2 Macccabees goes beyond Hellenistic philosophy to express a substantive view of ritual and a belief in bodily resurrection.

HELLENISTIC PHILOSOPHY, PHILO OF ALEXANDRIA, AND THE WISDOM OF SOLOMON

Hellenistic philosophy influenced Jewish thought in many ways, particularly in urban settings such as Alexandria, Egypt (see box 8–3). Philo Judaeus of Alexandria (20 B.C.E.–40 C.E) defended the sophistication and political loyalty of Jewish citizens both politically and intellectually. He argued that Jews contributed much to the general culture. More than that, he offered striking reinterpretations of biblical stories to show how they fit philosophical ideas, especially **Platonism** and **Stoicism**. He allegorized tales about heroes such as Abraham and Sarah, drawing lessons from them about the struggle of the mind against the body and the need for spiritual discipline from those works. He recognized that the Platonic ideal of a purely spiritual Good, transcending this world of experience, does not fit the biblical portrayal of Israel's God. To solve this problem, he posited that the One God who exists beyond all things interacts with the world only through intermediaries. The first and most important intermediary he called the **logos**—a Greek term meaning "word," but used in the sense of the universal force of Reason that animates the cosmos. Where the Hebrew Bible conceives of God interacting directly with human beings and taking part in the world, Philo pictures the Logos mediating that relationship.

The Apocryphal book "The Wisdom of Solomon" (henceforth referred to as Wisdom) follows a procedure similar to Philo when incorporating into itself an extensive range of philosophical language. It makes use of key ideas from Platonic and Stoic thought, such as the four cardinal virtues of self-control, prudence, justice, and courage (Wisdom 8:7). The book understands wisdom as a type of "world-soul" that pervades all things and holds the cosmos together (1:7; 7:22–23), an idea very close to the Stoic idea of a supernal "reason" or "logos." The book exalts this force of reason as a supernal power of creation that also sustains the world. Wisdom 9:1–4 identifies this "Word" (logos) as God's creative power, as the wisdom that created human beings and that "sits by" God's throne. Here again, the distinctive form of immanence as understood in Hellenistic wisdom literature is manifest. God is present in the corporeal world through the pervasive "Word" that fills the universe.

These philosophical ideas shape the way the book reinterprets the biblical heritage. Wisdom 10–12 retells the Pentateuch's narrative from Adam through Israel's conquest of the nation. The examples of Adam, Cain, Noah, Abraham, Jacob, and Joseph illustrate both the value of cultivating philosophical virtues and the folly of abandoning them (Wisdom 10:1–14). Israel's exodus from Egypt, its wandering under Moses, and its conquest of the land all illustrate divine justice and the working of divine wisdom (10:15–12:18). The most extended rewriting of biblical history comes in a retelling of the plagues leading up to the Exodus from Egypt (they receive brief mention in Wisdom 10:16) as an example of divine justice. Every plague on the Egyptians was paralleled by a blessing on the Israelites. Every plague derived from a flaw in the Egyptian character; every blessing from a virtue in the Israelites (11:5–17, 12:23–27, 15:18–19, 17). This telling of the story serves to prove that the plagues were justified since sinners "justly suffered because of their wicked acts" (19:13).

The most devastating consequence of wickedness, of course, is death. In treating this subject, Wisdom follows Philo and the Stoic philosophers (see Box 8–3) to affirm the possibility of transcending bodily existence. Philosophers like Plato distinguished between the physical world in which all things come into being and go out of being and the spiritual world of the ideals. Stoics sought to cleave to the ideal, rather than the transient physical attractions of this world. Wisdom devotes its first five chapters to a discussion of this idea, and, unlike 2 Maccabees, it ignores the idea of resurrection. Immortality comes to those who transcend the physical world; there is no need for a return to the body. In a curious passage, it associates the choice between immortality and death with a choice between God and the **devil**.

The devil becomes a significant figure only in writings of the post-exilic period. Influenced by Persian thought, that figure takes on many different meanings. Sometimes the term *Satan* (or its Greek equivalent *daemon* or devil) stands for an agent of the divine, sometimes for a supernatural being opposed to the divine, and sometimes for the cause of all misfortune in the world. The term *daemon* also occurs and is translated "devil" in many contexts. For Wisdom, the devil is associated with death. Choosing for the devil means choosing against immortality. Humanity becomes mortal through the "envy of the devil" and regains the eternal life God originally planned for it only through attention to Wisdom (Wisdom 2:21–24). The introduction of the devil, like the figure of Wisdom herself, separates the divine from this material world. By associating the demonic with corporeality, Wisdom distances the devil from God. God has no relationship either to death or to the devil. They are merely manifestations of the temptations and dangers of this world.

Jewish religious groups, however, were not alone in promising relief from the dangers of this world and promising immortality. Mystery religions, drawing on Egyptian myth—such as that of **Isis** or on Greek myths such as that of **Dionysius**—offered similar promises of salvation and eternal life (see Box 8–3). Wisdom seems aware of this ritualistic competition. Wisdom 13:1–15:17 develops a vigorous polemic against "idolatry." While many of the accusations launched against religious perversion here draw on earlier material from the Psalms (such as Psalm 135) and Prophets (see Isaiah 44, Jeremiah 10), other passages seem directed against Hellenistic cults. Wisdom 14:15–21 gives several possible ways in which idolatry begins: from a parent's grief at bereavement, from a king's desire for worship, from aesthetic delight. These motivations often lay behind the successful appeal of one or another of the Hellenistic religions. The author of the **Wisdom of Solomon** may well have written with the intention of lessening the attraction of these cults for Jews. The list of substantive consequences of such false belief astounds the reader: sexual life and marriages become impure; murder, theft, corruption, perjury, and "confusion over what is good and what is evil" follow from idolatry (14:23–27). Just as true ritual leads to a substantive good, immortality, false ritual and false belief lead to every manner of substantive evil.

This Roman statue of Isis, originally an Egyptian Goddess, shows her dressed in royal garments and cosmic symbols that would later become associated with the Christian figure of Mary.

RELIGIOUS PERSPECTIVE IN ADDITIONS TO JEREMIAH, ESTHER, DANIEL

The themes found in the apocryphal additions to canonical books of the Hebrew Bible echo the themes of other works in the Apocrypha and respond to the same Hellenistic background (see Box 8–1). The book of **Baruch** and the **Letter of Jeremiah** attached to the prophetic book of Jeremiah reiterate themes of wisdom, **theodicy** and idolatry. Baruch 1:1 confesses Israel's iniquity and thus justifies what God has done, although it ends by petitioning God for mercy and the creation of the New Covenant described in Jeremiah 32 (Baruch 2:27–35). Biblical history is rehearsed as a story of divine wisdom, culminating in Wisdom's being entrusted to Israel and living with humanity as the book of commandments given to the Jews (3:36–4:1).

The so-called Letter of Jeremiah resembles the Wisdom of Solomon in being an extended polemic against idolatry and may intimate conduct among Jews who followed Hellenistic ways. Verses 4–7 of the Letter of Jeremiah warn against being led astray by foreign religions and their adherents and worshiping in the manner of those among whom the Jews will live in exile. This warning suggests that the author had encountered Jews who had adopted religious behavior from their environment.

The story of **Bel and the Dragon** among the additions to Daniel teaches a similar lesson. Daniel encounters naïve believers who hold to superstitious ideas (Bel and the Dragon 1–6). Daniel unmasks the priests who are eating the food and wine prepared for the God Bel (vv. 18–20); he destroys a dragon by feeding it pitch, fat, and hair, thus showing that it was not a god (vv. 21–27). The final story compiled in Bel and the Dragon emphasizes historical continuity (vv. 33–42). Daniel, while in the lion's den, is visited by the Judean prophet **Habakkuk**, thereby establishing a connection to the Judean homeland and to a part of the Hebrew prophets.

The story of **Susanna and the Elders** teaches a different lesson. In the Hellenistic context, Jewish groups suspected one another of treachery and insincerity. This mutual suspicion finds expression as God calls forth Daniel to reveal how two elders have slandered an innocent woman, Susanna, because she would not grant them sexual favors. That story suggests that God uses human beings to intervene in the world and influence human affairs. Another addition deepens the piety of the boys cast into a furnace by attributing a hymn to them that expresses their humility and acceptance of whatever God wills (The Prayer of Azarich).

Additions to the canonical book of Esther also function to augment biblical passages that appear to lack sufficient piety. The canonical book remains silent about Jewish religious practices and never mentions the divine. The additions make it clear that Esther observed Jewish dietary laws—so important in books like 1 and 2 Maccabees—and both she and Mordecai are said to have offered lengthy prayers that express an exclusive ethics and belief in divine help. Esther tells God that she abhors the sexual union she has with an "uncircumcised alien" (Additions to Esther 14:15–17). These sentiments supplement the biblical book and bring its message into greater harmony with that expressed by other books in the Apocrypha.

186   Chapter 8

THE RELIGIOUS PERSPECTIVES OF TOBIT AND JUDITH

The apocryphal books of Tobit and Judith contain much folklore and indicate some of the changing views of religion among Hellenistic Jews. The story of Judith describes how God answers the prayers of Jews who are besieged by Nebuchadnezzar and his general **Holofernes**. God's intervention takes the form of the inspiration of a heroic woman, **Judith**, who first seduces and then decapitates Holofernes. As a subplot to this story, Holofernes has an advisor, **Achior**, who warns him against attacking the Jews. Achior is packed off to the besieged city where, Holofernes presumes, he will die among the inhabitants when the city falls. Instead, Achior recognizes Holofernes' head, bows to Judith, and converts to Judaism: "When Achior saw all that the God of Israel had done, he believed firmly in God. So he was circumcised and joined the house of Israel" (Judith 14:10).

Conversion in this tale represents a change of heart, a realization of the truth concerning Israel's God. Such a view stands in sharp contrast to the actions of the Hasmonean John Hyrcanus I, who forcibly circumcised the Idumeans. While voluntary circumcision is part of the substantive change by which a non-Jew becomes a Jew, forced circumcision is seen as merely a surgical operation without any sacramental power.

This strand of the narrative makes two points. The first concerns ethics; while celebrating a national victory, Judith is actually an inclusive ethics. The values and teachings of Judaism are open to all who listen to them. Even someone from the enemy camp such as Achior can enter the community of Israel. Second, the view of ritual expressed emphasizes intention, rather than mere performance. Ritual has substantive effect only if carried out with sincere purpose. That perspective echoes prophetic statements and also finds expression in Judith's song of praise. She declares: "For every sacrifice as a fragrant offering is a small thing and the fat of all whole burnt offerings to you is a very little thing; but whoever fears the Lord is forever" (Judith16:16). Although the verse following curses those who rise up against God's people, the intent here is an inclusive ethics. God does not look at ethnic identity, but at an individual's heart. Those singled out are not Jews as such, but rather all who "fear the Lord." Thus the view of ritual and ethics is combined in a universalistic appeal that includes more than just the Jewish people.

The book of Tobit appears more ethnocentric than Judith. Its story focuses on personal piety and its rewards. The tale, as Tobit himself tells it, describes how pious actions lead to suffering. Tobit's acts of charity bring him into conflict with Assyria's king, and he must flee for his life. Later, another act of charity during the holiday of Pentecost leaves him ill and blind. His wife reprimands him, but like the Job of legend, he refuses to blame God and declares: "You are righteous, O Lord, and all your deeds are just" (Tobit 3:1).

The story continues by shifting its focus on a certain Sarah, who is plagued by the "wicked devil **Asmodeus**" who slaughters her husbands on their wedding night (Tobit 3:7–9). This introduction of the demonic (Asmodeus eventually becomes one of the names Jewish tradition uses for the devil) serves a similar function as in Wisdom of Solomon; God no longer bears responsibility for evil.

Other elements in the story reinforce this view of God's transcendent nature. Tobit's son Tobias finally succeeds both in curing his father's blindness and in chasing Asmodeus into the desert through the intercession of the angel Raphael (the Hebrew name means "God heals"). God, however, cures only through the agencies of others. When Tobias is cured, he thanks both God and the angels: "Blessed be God, and blessed be his great name, and blessed be all his holy angels" (Tobit 11:14). The book continues by joining this view of transforming ritual with an ethnocentric ethics. Tobit's hymn of praise includes many ethnically specific passages; God is praised as one who will gather all the Jewish exiles back to their homeland (13:5) and is petitioned to rebuild Jerusalem (13:16–17).

Nevertheless, several verses suggest a more inclusive ethics. Jews are urged to "Acknowledge him before the nations, O children of Israel" (13:3); the prayer asks: "Let all people speak of his majesty and acknowledge him in Jerusalem….A bright light will shine to all the ends of the earth, many nations will come to you from far away, the inhabitants of the remotest parts to your holy name…blessed forever will be all who revere you" (13:8–11).

Two themes unite in this story. The first is that obedience to divine laws and practices will bring healing and success. This idea occurs in many Hellenistic religious traditions, most particularly in the cult of **Asclepius**, the Greek god whose rituals Hellenistic worshipers claimed provided miraculous cures. The universal appeal of healers made the worship of Asclepius extremely attractive. Other traditions, such as the folk tradition recorded in Tobit, responded to this appeal by offering competing claims of their own to counter that of their rivals.

A second aspect of that theme is an explanation of good and bad fortune as deriving from supernatural forces delegated by, but not identical with, the divinity. Angels and demons explain the shifting fate of human individuals. God's transcendent power controls the ebb and flow of world history; the fate of nations lies in God's hands. The impact of angels and demons, however, affects the more mundane concerns of personal life; health and sickness, marriage and death often result from the interference of the lesser supernatural beings.

The story weaves a third theme into these two dominant ones, that of showing obedience to the divine will. Personal prayers punctuate the tale (Tobit 2, 8:5–8, 15–17, 11:14–15, 13). Tobit exhorts his son to observe Jewish laws and morality (4:5–19). These ritual and moral deeds demonstrate the greatness of God to the world. They are celebrations of how Jewish living inculcates basic human virtue. Most of the precepts endorsed are general ones: giving charity, acting benevolently to family and kin, seeking advice from everyone, paying workmen honestly, being disciplined in behavior. Indeed, Polonius speaking to Laertes in Shakespeare's *Hamlet* echoes Tobit.

The one exception might be advocacy of endogamy (4:12–13). The author, however, makes clear that the reason for marrying within the group is not ethnic pride, but rather the opposite. One should not choose exogamy out of embarrassment at one's own kinship; do not refuse to marry within your own group out of an arrogant exceptionalism (4:14). The general theme is one of inclusiveness: Jews are to praise God and live exemplary lives so others will join with them. God acts inclusively as well: "For none of the nations has understanding, but the Lord himself will give them good counsel" (4:19). The book as a whole, then, despite its clearly Jewish content, expresses a universal perspective on life.

SUMMARY QUESTIONS

1. Which elements in Hellenistic Jewish writings emphasize continuity, and which emphasize discontinuity?
2. How did different Jewish leaders respond to Hellenism among Jews during the period following Alexander the Great and his successors?
3. What religious ideas does Ecclesiasticus express?
4. How do the religious ideas expressed in 1 Maccabees differ from those expressed in 2 Maccabees?
5. What views of the divine and ritual are expressed in Tobit and Judith?

Four Suggested Essay Questions

1. Explain two ways in which a tradition may view history. Show how the celebration of the Hasmonean victory in 1 Maccabees 7 illustrates one of these ways and the story of Habakkuk and Daniel in Bel and the Dragon the other.
2. Explain two ways in which a tradition may view the supernatural. Show how 2 Maccabees 15 represents one of these ways and Wisdom of Solomon 9 illustrates the other.
3. Explain two ways in which a tradition may view ethics. Apply one of them to the ethics expressed in Judith 14:1–10 and the other to the ethics implied by the Hebrew additions to Ben Sirah.
4. Explain two ways in which a tradition may view ritual. Show how the use of ritual in 2 Maccabees 7 illustrates one of them and the additions to Esther that emphasize her observance of Jewish dietary laws illustrate the other.

Exercise

Write an introduction for the essay in Question 2 by doing the following:

1. Write a sentence describing the need for intermediaries between the divine and the human indicated by Judas' dream in 2 Maccabees 15 (but do not mention that example since this introduction should remain general).
2. Write a sentence describing the immanence of the divine indicated by Solomon's request to be invested with God's Holy Spirit in Wisdom of Solomon 9 (but do not mention that example since this introduction should remain general).

3. Write a sentence describing God's need for human rulers as illustrated by Wisdom of Solomon 9:7–8 (but do not mention that example since this introduction should remain general).

4. Write a sentence describing the human need for God's intervention based on the miracle during the time of Sennacherib described in 2 Maccabees 15:22–23 (but do not mention that example since this introduction should remain general).

5. Write a topic sentence to put before those four sentences that indicates the contrast between transcendence and immanence, as well as that between the divine need for humanity and the human need for the divine that you will develop in the paragraph as a whole.

FOR FURTHER READING

The books listed below should be a point of departure for your future study. Each includes a bibliography that will guide you beyond its basic information.

1. Bickerman, Elias Joseph, *From Ezra to the Last of the Maccabees* (New York: Schocken, 1962).

2. De Lange, Nicholas R. M., *Jewish Literature of the Hellenistic Age* (New York: Viking Press, 1978).

3. Grabbe, Lester L., *Judaic Religion in the Second Temple Period: Belief and Practice From the Exile to Yavneh* (London: Routledge, 2000).

4. Levine, Lee I., *Judaism and Hellenism in Antiquity: Conflict or Confluence* (Seattle: University of Washington Press, 1998).

5. Tcherikover, Avigdor Victor, *Hellenistic Civilization and the Jews* (Philadelphia, PA: Jewish Publication Society of America, 1959).

6. VanderKam, James, *An Introduction to Early Judaism* (Grand Rapids, MI: William B. Eerdmans, 2001).

9

Introduction to the Gospels

READING ASSIGNMENT

Matthew 14, 26–27
Mark 13, 15
Luke 21–23
John 18:28–19:22

LEARNING OBJECTIVES

By the end of this lesson, you will be able to:
- Describe the Jewish background against which to read the Gospels and the views of history, the divine, ethics and ritual in them.
- Compare the views of history in the Gospels and in Jewish groups.
- Compare the views of the supernatural in the Gospels and Jewish groups.
- Compare the views of ethics in the four Gospels and Jewish groups.
- Compare the views of ritual in the four Gospels and Jewish groups.

INTRODUCTION

This chapter examines the New Testament Gospels in relationship to the Jewish background at the time of Jesus and the early church. Although we will look at specific texts within the Gospels, this chapter will focus on the shape and format of each of the canonical Gospels. The New Testament portrays Jesus as a Jew living in Roman Palestine. The first section here looks at the Jewish alternatives present at that time. The next sections examine the Christian

Interpretive Matrix for Chapter Nine

View of the Divine: How people interact with God and the supernatural; how God interacts with the world.	View of History: How past, present, and future are related; who controls the shape of events.	View of Ethics: How people behave toward other people; how they behave toward people like themselves and to those who are different.	View of Ritual: How people behave toward the Divine; how they perform religious actions.
The Divine as Transcendent: Human actions rather than divine actions influence political life. Access to God is limited to a priestly elite. God interacts with the world through a supernal Spirit.	*History as Continuous:* Older patterns of leadership should not be changed to fit new situations. God's interaction with the world never changes.	*Inclusive Ethics:* All members of the society are "priests" and have the same potential for holiness.	*Ritual as Transforming:* Ritual must be performed by the authentic priestly leader. Prayer changes reality and can bring national success. Miracles indicate a transformation in the world.
The Divine as Immanent: God interacts with the world directly and may even become incarnate in the world.	*History as Discontinuous:* God introduces cosmic changes through new revelations and a new relationship with the world. A new age is beginning in the world.	*Exclusive Ethics:* God prefers one ethnic or national group over all others. A group withdraws from contact with all other groups.	*Ritual as Symbolic:* Holidays symbolize both national history and personal experience.

alternatives as presented in the Gospels. These Gospels use the same basic literary tools: they tell the story of Jesus' career; they tell of his death and resurrection; they recount narratives concerning his confrontations with others, parables he taught, sermons he delivered, and miracles he performed. Scholars of religious studies note that the differences between the way the Gospels are organized and the material they include indicate different views of history, the supernatural, ethics, and ritual (these differences can be deduced from Box 9–1).

The inclusion of four distinct retellings of the Jesus story represents an inclusive ethics, one legitimating a variety of Christian communities. Three of the four Gospels share a similar chronology, tell many of the same stories, and seem to see the events "with the same eye." Thus, Matthew, Mark and Luke are called **Synoptic**, a Greek word meaning "seeing together." The fourth Gospel, that of John, has a very different chronology, tells many distinctive stories, and attributes to Jesus a teaching not found in the other Gospels. (See the summaries of these Gospels in Box 9–1, as well as the different geographical descriptions given of Jesus' career.) This chapter examines some of these clues in greater detail.

192   Chapter 9

SOME IMPORTANT TERMS

The following terms are important in this chapter. Some of them have been listed in previous chapters; in those cases the term is not **bold** in the main body of this chapter. Where names of books are also the names of individuals (such as The Gospel of Mark), the name does not appear in the Glossary.

Aaron	Gospel	Parousia
Abraham	Griesbach Theory	Passover
Baptism	Heresy	Pharisees
Christ	Herod Agrippa	Philo of Alexandria
Crucifixion	Herod the Great	Q Source
Elijah	Holy Spirit	Rabbi
Essenes	Jerusalem	Resurrection
Exodus	John the Baptist	Sabbath
Galilee	Josephus	Sadducees
Gentile	Judas	Samaritan
Gnostics	Kingdom of God	Son of God
Gospel of John	Levites	Son of Man
Gospel of Luke	Logos	Synoptic Gospels
Gospel of Mark	Melchizedek	Tithes
Gospel of Matthew	Messiah	Zealots
Gospel of Thomas	Paraclete	

SECTARIAN GROUPS IN ROMAN JUDAISM

Christianity developed within a Jewish environment and should be understood in relationship to the Jewish movements that arose during the Roman period (see Timeline 9–1). The Jewish historian Josephus (see Box 8–2) speaks of four Jewish "heresies" or parties: the **Pharisees**, **Sadducees**, **Essenes**, and a "fourth philosophy," the **Zealots** (The Jewish War, 2:162–166; Antiquities 13:171–172). This seems a good, even if overly simplistic, way to categorize Jewish differences. By calling them "sects" or "heresies," Josephus did not imply that they were unorthodox or deviants from some mainstream truth.

The Judaism of that time had no absolute standard. Josephus used the term sect to indicate a philosophy or belief as recognized in the Hellenistic world. He recognized that these divisions involved only a few elite leaders who vied for control of the majority population. While Josephus does comment that there were "6,000 members of the Pharisees in Jerusalem" (Antiquities 17), this exaggeration merely reinforces his claim that the Pharisees were the most popular of the groups. The division, artificial as it may be, brings into focus the different religious options during Hellenistic times. The present discussion of the four groups

TIMELINE 9–1   THE DEVELOPMENT OF CHRISTIANITY

This chart traces the development of Christianity in the context of Jewish history. All dates are Common Era.

26	Pontius Pilate appointedRoman Prefect of Judea
27–29	John the Baptist's Mission
27–30	Jesus of Nazareth teaches and gains a following
30	Trial, Crucifixion, and Resurrection of Jesus
41–44	King Herod Agrippa rules Judea; Christian leaders persecuted
41–54	Claudius Emperor of Rome banishes Jews from Rome because of trouble arising from "Chrestus"
47–56	Paul of Tarsus establishes Christian communities among the Gentiles
50–70	Source (Quelle) of Jesus' Sayings probably compiled
54–68	Nero rules Rome; 64 Rome burns and Nero blames and persecutes Christians
66–73	Judea's war against Rome
70	The fall of Judea
66–73	Gospel of Mark is written
80–90	Gospel of Matthew is composed; Gospel of Luke is written
81–91	Domitian is emperor and persecutes Christians
70–90	Rabbis of Jamnia canonize the Jewish Bible
98–117	Trajan is emperor and persecutes some Christians who were "troublemakers"
100–140	Many New Testament Letters are written; The Didache and other non-canonical Christian writings appear
117–138	Hadrian is emperor and persecutes Christians as well as suppressing the Bar Kokhba revolution
132–135	Bar Kokhba Revolt of Jews against Rome
138–161	Antonius Pius is emperor; the church excommunicates Marcion

looks primarily at their views of leadership, and, based on that, their views of history, the divine, ethics, and ritual.

Corrupt leadership led many Jews of this period to look for a new leader who would no longer combine kingship and priesthood, but would exemplify a simpler, more original ideal. A central term expressing these views is that of Messiah. Jews confronted the problem of explaining their self-understanding as a spiritual people, united despite their exile to many different places. Some Jews explained that they were waiting for a national restoration, which would occur under a king descended from King David. Such a king would be recognizable because God would anoint him for that office. The word for "anoint" in Hebrew is Messiah (mashiah), translated into Greek as **Christ**. Jews proclaimed that when this Messiah came, they would regain political independence and national reunification. This belief represents an exclusivist ethics focused on Jewish self-interests. Jews holding this view urged people to fight for liberation, to initiate the messianic period. Scholars call this group the Zealots.

The Zealots sought to establish the Kingdom of God, by which they meant a political kingdom in which Jews would live independently. For them, God's kingdom would be created by human beings working to transform the social structure. They looked back to the independence won in the Maccabean revolution and hoped for a similar miraculous victory. They espoused a view of history continuous with the idea of predictable reward and punishment found in the Former Prophets. Reality makes sense because it follows certain political rules.

The Zealots saw themselves as the heirs of Israel's early kings and political leaders. They understood the story of their people as one in which God appoints heroes to lead the people to victory. While God is supreme, humanity must take the initiative in its own salvation. During Roman times, these Zealots aroused great suspicion. Any attempt by a dissident group to announce a new Messiah, to appoint an official Jewish leader, or to gain independence was looked upon with alarm.

The Zealot perspective caused consternation among the Romans because it argued that the ultimate responsibility for Jewish success lies with its human leaders. From that perspective, God sets the conditions under which the Jews must live. Within those conditions, the Jews are expected to make their own contributions to history. They, rather than the divinity, chart the direction in which history must move. They have the duty of using their gifts to attain the goals that God has established for them. For the Zealots, the Messiah is a human figure who will take those actions that God expects from human beings—actions that the Romans invariably saw as seditious.

For the Zealots, God preferred Israel to all other nations. Eventually, God's choice of the people of Judah would result in the overthrow of the Romans and the restoration of political power to the people. This particularistic ethics excluded both non-Jews (Gentiles) and pacifists who sought to make peace with the Romans. Only militant Jewish nationalists could be loyal Zealots. This view also affected the Zealot approach to ritual. For them, ritual reminded Jews of their past. The sacrificial service did not, in their view, make a difference to God. If, as it occurred, the city was besieged and could find no food but the sacrificial meat, the Zealots could requisition it for the army.

Other Jews, however, argued that the true history of the Jewish people was a priestly history in which the ritual performances offered the best defense of Jewish life. This group can be identified with the Sadducees. These Jews saw a continuous history beginning with Abraham and the priest Melchizedek, who offered tithes in Jerusalem (Genesis 14). They traced their lineage through the priestly activities of Aaron and the Levites to the Zadokite priests of Jerusalem in the time of Israel's kings, David and Solomon. They held that Israel was defined by its continuous history of priesthood, not of politics. They interpreted the idea of the Messiah as a priestly figure. Indeed, in ancient Israel, priests like Aaron had been anointed, just as had royal leaders.

This sense of a priestly hierarchy emphasizes an exclusive ethics. Jewish behavior, for the Sadducees, was determined by the class and lineage of any particular Jew. Taking their name from the early priests, they were called Zadokites, but scholars refer to them as Sadducees. For these sectarians, God is not merely transcendent, but demands some intermediary through which humanity can gain contact with the divine. Ritual satisfies the divine will. By transformative rituals such as sacrifices, Jews come into right relationship with the divine. Only when these rituals are performed by authorized priestly leaders can they work effectively. The true Messiah, from this perspective, is an anointed priest who stands between God and humanity, mediating between them. In this way, God is transcendent, needing a human instrument to work miracles for the world. God, for the Sadducees, however, is also immanent: controlling the rain so that it falls in its season, giving prosperity to the people, preserving Jewish religious shrines. The Sadducees felt that God would protect the Temple and be involved in the politics of the priesthood.

Some Jews disputed the claim of the Sadducees to represent the true continuity of the Jewish people. These Jews attributed the problems of their nation to the fact that the priests in charge had become too Hellenistic, introducing innovations that created a new, inauthentic identity. These Essenes, as scholars identify them, rejected the assimilation among the established Sadducees. They claimed that the Sadducees had forfeited their right to be leaders. Here the ethics of involvement espoused by the leading classes clashes with the exclusivist ethics of the opposition group. While both parties believed that the Messiah would be a priest, they each proposed different rituals and a different priestly leader to fit that description.

The Essenes often withdrew to distant places, caves and deserts, to remove themselves from possible contamination by the false priests. This made their ethics one of the most exclusive of the period. They deduced from the political situation that God was displeased with the Jewish people. For the Essenes, God was intimately involved in the political world and would eventually bring that world to an end.

This view of an imminent end to history imagines the future as discontinuous with the past. A new age is about to begin, and new instructions are needed for this time. The Essenes therefore sought guidance from a "righteous teacher" who could put them on the correct path. The members of the community of that teacher, then, had discovered the one true way that God desired, the rituals that alone could bring salvation, and the meaning of Israel's history. To become a member of the community, a person needed to break off connections with outsiders, undergo a ritual cleansing in water (*baptism*), and engage in such activities as fasting, intense scriptural study, and chaste behavior. Membership in the community, therefore, entailed behavior that limited a person's contact with outsiders.

This exclusive ethics depends upon a view of ritual as substantive, but not for the sake of the nation but for the individual. Rituals either purify or defile. They have a transforming effect on the people who perform them. Because the rituals of the Jerusalem priests were corrupt, those who practiced them were polluted. Only a pure ritual, such as that observed by a community of the holy, could be trusted.

A final group claimed to have inherited the message of the prophets. They were called Pharisees (literally "separaters"), perhaps because they sought to separate themselves from impurity, perhaps because they gave interpretations (*perushim*, in Hebrew) to the Bible, perhaps because they separated tithes from grain before eating it. The members of this group, like the prophets, focused on personal piety and individual character, rather than on either the political success of the royalists or the inherited skills of the priests and actually called themselves "the heirs of the prophets." The Pharisees apparently provided the basis on which the later Rabbis justified themselves.

Rabbinic leaders saw themselves as heirs of the Pharisees, just as the Pharisees were heirs of the prophets. The leaders of both groups considered Abraham and Moses both prophets and rabbis, like themselves. Unlike the biblical prophets, however, these rabbis did not attribute their knowledge to a direct revelation from God. Instead, they taught that, when read correctly, the Hebrew Bible itself directed people to personal ethics and righteous deeds, rather than to reliance on some external hero, whether priest or king. For these teachers, the Messiah was a supernatural hero whom God would send to the people only if they proved themselves worthy. Here again, God acts in logical and predictable ways. Only if individual Jews perform what God expects of them can they expect help from God. God's presence is found wherever Jews engage in righteous actions. God intervenes in each person's private life. When each person allows the divine into that private sphere, God will become immanent in history as well as in personal experience.

The most dramatic aspect of the Pharisees was their open view of social identity. They considered every Jew a "priest" and every human being a potential Jew. Their universal perspective led them to endorse proselytism—the seeking of converts to Judaism. They advanced the view that the teachings of the Torah were the natural rules by which all people should live. The Pharisees dedicated their efforts to following laws by which people could improve themselves and thereby improve the world. This group espoused a ritual exclusivism and an ethical inclusivism. Jews should act ethically for the good of all, learning how to live in a cosmopolitan world. Since this view of improvement suggested that the world is in process, the Pharisees interpreted the laws to fit the changing needs of society. Their reinterpretation of these laws became the basis for future Jewish thinking about Judaism in general and about the idea of the Messiah in particular.

The ritualism of the Pharisees is well expressed in their understanding of the Passover ritual. Unlike the biblical tradition, the Pharisees emphasized both the individual nature of the celebration and its association with the Exodus from Egypt. While the Sadducees emphasized Passover as a celebration of the priestly rulers of the people, the Pharisees saw it as a time for individuals to learn about their past and to apply that past to the present and future. While only those in the land of Israel could frequent the Temple for the Passover celebration, everyone joined in the family rituals. They ate unleavened bread and bitter herbs; they recited prayers, both original ones and the psalms recited by the Jerusalem priests.

The rabbis used these private rituals as the basis for their own new understanding of Passover. The Passover they constructed celebrates the individual's life experience and the personal renewal that occurs every spring. Unlike the priestly ritual, this celebration focused on every person's experience of liberation. The rabbis enjoined the reading of the love poem *Song of Songs* on Passover. This association of erotic love with the holiday of freedom altered the nature of the holiday. Personal liberation, symbolized by erotic love and personal need, described by the psalms, replaced concern with national identity. Ritual at this stage moved from public performance to private devotion. This focus enabled the Pharisees to continue as a viable Jewish group, even after the destruction of Judea by the Romans in 70 C.E.

The Romans could be threatened by Zealots, who demanded an independent state, by Sadducees, who required a national shrine and Temple, by Essenes, who criticized all who lived outside their community. The Pharisees, however, could coexist with an imperial power; they could maintain personal ritualism, even when Temple rituals had become impossible. Rabbinic Judaism could affirm living in the general culture without requiring opposition to it. After the destruction of the Temple in 70 C.E., the Romans favored the Pharisees and, as rabbis, they became the new leaders of Judaism, the Judaism that would continue until the present time. It would seem that the rabbis had no competition.

In fact, however, another group of Jews not only competed with the rabbis, but eventually outdistanced them—the Christians. Christianity began as a Jewish group—a sect or "heresy," as Josephus would put it. It developed its own views of history, divinity, ritual, and ethics, which are discussed below. Nevertheless, the variety of Jewish views suggests that when some writers (such as the Gospel of John) speak about "the Jews," this phrase needs to be put in quotation marks. There were so many different Jewish positions that no single characterization of the Jews makes historical sense.

JESUS IN THE JEWISH CONTEXT

Stories about Jesus, the central figure in the New Testament Gospel, assume the Jewish background given above. The Jesus of the Gospels lived in the Roman context of second temple Judaism (see Map 9–1). Perhaps one of the most debated questions concerning early Christianity focuses on the historicity and significance of Jesus of Nazareth. On the one hand, this quest for the historical Jesus may be irrelevant. Understood as mythology, as stories teaching significant truths about reality, the tales in the Gospels have enduring meaning. The four Gospels project four different visions of Jesus to suggest different approaches to reality. The Gospel of John is perhaps the most obviously theological of the renditions, using the wisdom tradition of the Hebrew Bible and of Hellenistic teachings to expound the story

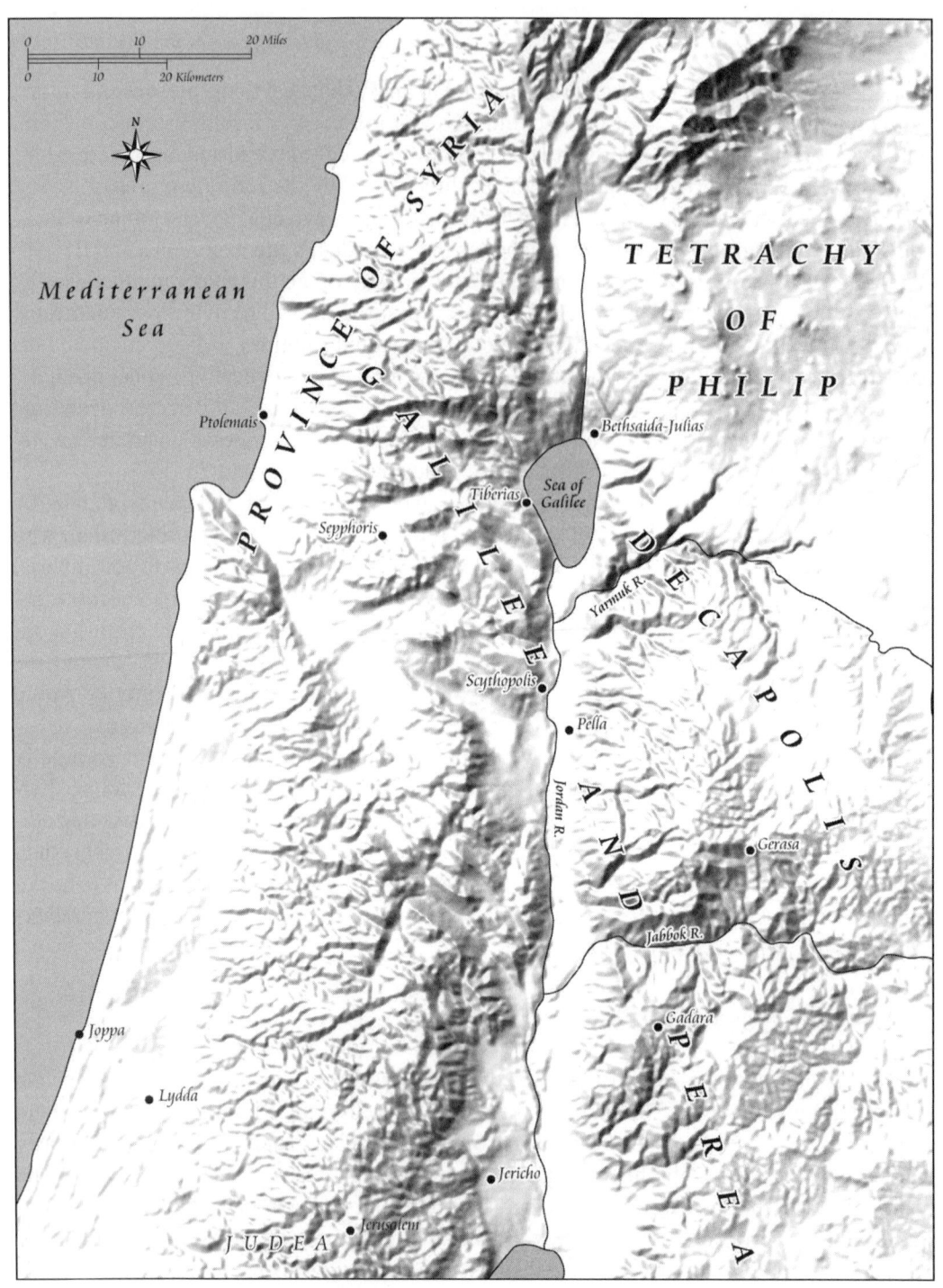

Map 9–1   North and Central Palestine at the time of the Ministry of Christ C.E. 30

of Jesus. In fact, however, each of the Gospels was composed most probably by a community and not by a single individual, and almost certainly not by the specific apostles to whom they are attributed. They are not dispassionate history, but convey a religious message.

Nevertheless, on the other hand, scholars have never ceased in their quest for the historical Jesus. They want to discover what was unique about Jesus' message that sets it apart from what other Jewish teachers may have been writing. Looking at the New Testament within the Hellenistic context helps understand what historicity may lie behind it. Jesus lived and died as a Jew within the context of Roman Palestine. He taught disciples and apparently claimed some sort of Messianic mission. The sources suggest that at least some disciples became disillusioned with these claims. The Gospels tell of the actions of Judas, a disciple who eventually betrayed Jesus. The nature of that betrayal and its significance differs in each telling of the story.

Judas may well represent a broader disaffection among the original followers of Jesus. According to the New Testament he was arrested on charges of both blasphemy and sedition and executed by the Romans (the crime posted on the cross on which he was crucified specified a messianic claim to being "King of the Jews," a claim that the Romans would interpret as political revolution). **Crucifixion** was, historically, the characteristic execution for someone accused of political insurrection. Historically, it would have been impossible for the Jews to have either initiated or carried out such an act. Certainly Passover would have been a time when no executions were allowed by Jewish law. Whatever the historical background may have been, the Romans regularly executed criminals by crucifixion and had a record of executing woul- be Messianic claimants of every sort.

What might such a Messianic claim have meant in its original context? The New Testament itself is divided; it uses the term **"Son of God"** (or sometimes **"Son of Man"**) to describe Jesus but understands that term differently in different contexts. Perhaps the most characteristic, and the most distinctive, usage considered the term an indication of the divine status of Jesus (see Matthew 27:57–64; Mark 14:60–62; Luke 22:66–71; John 19:6–7). Jesus had been sent by a divine father to transform the world. Human nature, the historical relationship between divinity and humanity, would be completely altered by the fact of Jesus' suffering, death, and **resurrection**. That last concept was the crucial one for Christians—Jesus had conquered death by showing that resurrection after dead was possible.

This view of resurrection as an event in the private life of a Messiah differed significantly from the views of either the Maccabean Jews or of the Pharisees. Even more significantly, the term "Son of God" as used by Christians differed from the way Jews used the phrase. For Jews such as the Pharisees, all human beings are identified as "sons of God." To be human means to be created in the divine image and to carry on the divine task. The Christian association of this term with Jesus as Christ drew upon the Hellenistic mystery religions. In these religions, only a special knowledge conveyed by a divine messenger could bring people salvation. The Christian story of Jesus' saving power took on a Hellenistic tone. Jesus the Christian savior differed significantly from the Jewish view of a Christ.

This mosaic found in Ravenna portrays Jesus as a "good shepherd" using a stylized Hellenistic motif often associated with the god Dionysus.

As Christians transformed the Jewish use of the identification "Son of God" into one more common among mystery religions, they changed the way of viewing both the divinity and the Messiah. Now the idea of the Messiah meant a supernatural savior who brought secret (esoteric) knowledge to suffering humanity. God's sending of the Messiah would not result in a social or political change, but rather in a change of human nature. Such a view suggests how the discontinuity of the Christian belief about Jesus as Son of God may have evolved from a continuous set of beliefs in Judaism. The portraits of Jesus often reflect this discontinuity. Jesus is represented using images from portrayals of gods like Apollo, Orpheus, and Dionysius.

The earliest Christian traditions probably saw in Jesus a Jewish leader, not a mysterious divine figure. This view echoes the Hebrew Bible and its implication of a comprehensible universe. The Gospels agree that Jesus was charged with being "King of the Jews" (Matthew 27:27–44; Mark15:1–32; Luke 23:1–5; John 18:33–38, 19:13–16). It is highly probable that Jesus' earliest followers expected him to initiate either an alternative priesthood (such as that described in the Dead Sea Scrolls) or a new political order (such as that for which the Zealots, Jewish revolutionaries, agitated).

The fact that this new movement named itself Christianity, using a messianic title, suggests that it began as an advocate for some sort of new leader, either a new priestly official or a new political leader. Since the Romans recognized the destabilizing effect of such beliefs, they moved forcibly against this Jesus movement and, by executing its leader, hoped to quell its potential threat, as his execution by crucifixion shows. Revolutionaries of various types suffered the same punishment. Insofar as Jesus suffered the same penalty as the Zealots, his movement probably held views comparable to theirs, emphasizing the predictable change that a messianic leader would bring to world events.

The Zealot philosophy emphasizes materialistic success. Jesus' political failure caused some followers to abandon him. Some of his followers may have understood his messianic mission in the way that the Sadducees or Essenes did. Certainly he introduced rituals of personal transformation and sought to bring people to that repentance that would change the nature of the world. Rituals such as baptism were current among the Essenes. Jesus may have been understood as seeking to create an alternative to the Temple ritual. He would destroy false ritualism and replace it with true faith.

The Gospels report that his death and resurrection took place during the Jewish holiday of Passover, the holiday of freedom and liberation. In some of the Gospels, his final Passover celebration became a ritual of liberation, not from physical slavery but from death and the sinfulness of corporeal existence. Certainly the association of Jesus' death and rebirth with Passover's story of gaining liberty from oppression became a symbol of a new type of religious life.

Some New Testament portraits of Jesus resemble descriptions of the type of leaders found among the Pharisees and rabbis. He teaches people how to live as individuals; he gives them private rituals; he offers them advice on every aspect of living. Even some of his most distinctive sayings involving the most important parts of the Hebrew Bible—the necessity to love strangers as well as neighbors, his recommendation to treat others as you yourself would want to be treated—have parallels among rabbinic teachings. His sphere of influence is depicted as focused on Jews primarily in the **Galilee** and Jerusalem.

While some of Jesus' disciples thought of alternative Jewish models, some looked to other Hellenistic religions for guidance. Those who did this transformed his message to suggest that messianic passages in the Bible indicated a spiritual world order symbolized by Jesus' resurrection as the Christ, as a divine rather than political Messiah. Because Jesus' death did not mean that his movement ended, however, his followers needed to remold both his story and their interpretation of it to fit the new facts that confronted them. These followers interpreted Jesus as the harbinger of a new world, and his death only intensified expectations about the end of the present world.

Several Gospel passages suggest that the age is coming to a close (Matthew 24; Mark 13; Luke 21). The earliest disciples reinterpreted the idea of the Kingdom of God, expecting it to come after Jesus' resurrection and, through his second appearance, the Parousia, to usher in the final times. These disciples expected this Parousia during their lifetime as the confirmation of their faith.

THE GOSPELS OF THE NEW TESTAMENT CANON

The New Testament begins with four Gospel accounts that set out a distinctive Christian religious perspective. The genre of Gospel represents a unique type of biography. It is more than history or biography; it is biography told as a story of salvation. Christian tradition associates each of these four biographies with individual people, said to be their authors. Modern scholarship doubts that attribution. The Gospels as we have them now probably reflect the views of a community rather than of individual authors. Although in this lesson we use the traditional names—Matthew, Mark, Luke, and John—we are not referring to individuals but to documents. Mark, for example, refers to the Gospel text bearing that name, not to a person with that name who authored the book.

The three Synoptic Gospels share many similar features. Although scholars have long debated the relationship between these writings, modern scholarship has now reached a general consensus (see Box 9–1). The dominant theory imagines a long period of development from oral teachings by Jesus, to oral and written traditions developed by apostles such as Jesus' first disciples, and then to later teachers such as Paul, culminating in collections of sayings about Jesus, stories about his life and miracle tales, and then the editing of written Gospels as complete and coherent texts. The widely accepted two-source theory believes that the Gospel of Mark came first. It may very well be an abbreviated version of other stories about Jesus that circulated in the early centuries of the Common Era. As it stands now, however, it is the earliest canonical Gospel. Both Matthew and Luke use Mark as the basic framework in which to fit their own expositions of Jesus' life, but these two Gospels share more than just this use of Mark. They both appear to draw on a common source of sayings attributed to Jesus. Early Christians probably had collected books of such sayings.

In fact, scholars have discovered in the Gospel of Thomas a source that resembles that type of book. Since no one has yet found the exact book used by Matthew and Luke, scholars give it a code name, **Q Source**, from the German word *Quelle* for "source." In addition to drawing from Mark and Q, Matthew and Luke added material of their own in fleshing out the story of Jesus. These additions, as well as the adaptation each editor makes in using the common sources, express the unique perspective of each Gospel. In contrast to Matthew and Luke, John (the fourth Gospel) relates the story of Jesus very differently. Since John does not use Mark, its order of events differs from the three Synoptics. It presents a distinctive and unique picture of Jesus' life and teachings, differing significantly from the other Gospels.

In a course devoted only to the Gospel genre, you would undertake an extensive comparison of many different Gospel traditions, not only the four in the New Testament canon, but also those of the Christian Apocrypha. You would make a detailed study of each community that produced the Gospels and review the scholarship that supports the views that dominate the academic study of the Bible. You would also study alternative theories, such as that of Johann **Griesbach** (1745–1812) giving priority to Matthew and Luke and claiming that Mark abridged the other two works. The purpose here, however, is simpler: to discover the differences in views of the divine, history, ritual, and ethics among the four canonical Gospels.

The stories of the New Testament reflect late historical realities. The needs of the early church shaped how Christians recorded, remembered, and interpreted the stories and teach-

BOX 9–1 OUTLINE OF CANONICAL GOSPELS

The following chart outlines the basic contents of the four Gospels and the major differences between John and the Synoptics. Each outline begins with a brief historical sketch of the Gospel.

Mark Scholars agree that this was the earliest written of the canonical Gospels. It was composed about 66–70 C.E. and reflects the background of the Jewish war against the Romans.

1:1–5:43	Jesus' initial appearance: Galilean mission begins
6:1–6, 10:52	Jesus rejected in Nazareth and continues his mission and gives teachings to the disciples
11:1–16:8	Entrance to Jerusalem: trial, dealth on Passover, and empty tomb

Matthew Matthew was written about 80–90 and seems to have expanded Mark in several ways. Taking Mark as a framework, Matthew added "proof-texts" demonstrating that Jesus' stands as the fulfillment of Jewish scriptures. Matthew also added material from a source that scholars call "Q" composed about 50–70 C.E. and attributing teachings and sayings to Jesus. Scholars think of Matthew as being composed in a Jewish–Christian setting.

1:1–2:23	Genealogy and naming of Jesus
3:1–7:29	Jesus' youth exemplifies biblical prophecies
8:1–10:42	Making disciples and church beginnings
11:1–12:45	Teachings of the kingdom
12:46–18:35	Jesus' new family of disciples and his rejection by his family and neighbors
19:1–23:39	Controversies with Jewish authorities
24:1–28:16	Final Days in Jerusalem: trial, death on Passover, resurrection, and world wide mission

Luke Luke, produced about the same time as Matthew and also using Mark and Q, seems to represent a non-Jewish or Gentile background. Scholars think the Gospel was probably written in a Gentile-Christian setting in Asia Minor.

1:1–2:53	Birth tales of John the Baptist and of Jesus
3:1–4:13	John the Baptist's career
4:14–9:50	Jesus' rejection by Jews and his family and his Galilean career
9:51–19:27	Jesus' migration to Jerusalem and his teachings there
19:2–23–53	Final days during Passover in Jerusalem: death on Passover, resurrection, Judean mission

> ***John*** Most scholars think that the Apostle John did not write this Gospel and note that the Gospel itself does not identify the "beloved disciple" said to be the source of the work. The book uses Hellenistic terms and ideas, including the Stoic idea of an eternal "logos" pervading the cosmos. Some of the oldest manuscript fragments of this book derive from about 125 C.E. and most scholars think it was written between 90 and 100 C.E. It differs considerably from the Synoptic Gospels.
>
> | | |
> |---|---|
> | 1:1–18 | Logos prologue; |
> | 1:19–12:50 | Seven signs: water to wine, cure of Centurion's son; cure of invalid; feeding of 5,000; walking on water; cure of blind man; raising of Lazarus |
> | 12–311 | farewell discourses, trial, death on the day before Passover, resurrection, internal mission |
>
> *SOME DIFFERENCES BETWEEN SYNOPTICS AND GOSPEL OF JOHN*
> John includes no record of Jesus' baptism by John the Baptist
> Synoptics include a story of Jesus' temptation by the Devil; John does not have that story
> John has Jesus assault the Temple during a Passover at the beginning of his career (2:13–21) and includes a second Passover in Jerusalem (6:4)—Synoptics have Jesus visit Jerusalem for Passover only at the end of his career.
> John includes several "I Am" sayings but no parables
> John includes no prediction of the fall of Jerusalem
> John omits any reference to a "new covenant" and the consuming of bread and wine at Jesus' last supper

ings of Jesus. The four canonical Gospels represent four ways of presenting the Christian message. Because they are not meant as historical narrative, but as a communication of "good news," they often present conflicting evidence. You may regard them as windows opening to the Jesus of faith, rather than as reports of events concerning the Jesus of history. They offer different but complementary perspectives on how Christians might live a religious life. Reading the Gospels provides information on religious options—options for Christian belief, ritual, and ethics—rather than factual data about a historical figure. The central symbol of Jesus takes on the coloration of four different religious responses to the world through the stories in each of the four documents. While those documents themselves evolved as composite works, each exhibits a characteristic religious perspective of its own.

An outline of the four Gospels shows that, while they follow a similar framework, they have some important differences (see Box 9–1). The first three—Matthew, Mark, and Luke—show strong similarities. John, the fourth Gospel, is set apart from the others by its unique characteristics. Note the distinctive difference between the Synoptics (the first three

Gospels) and John, as well as the differences among the Synoptics themselves. The following sections discuss the important facets of these differences.

Mark begins with Jesus' initial appearance and his mission in the Galilee (1:1–8:33). It continues with anecdotes about Jesus' life and teachings to show that he was a "suffering servant" whose real mission could not be revealed (8:31–10:52). The Gospel ends with Jesus' suffering and crucifixion, but as originally canonized, it did not include stories about a resurrection (11:1–16:8).

Matthew begins with a genealogy and prediction of Jesus' birth and naming (1:1–2:23). It continues with stories of Jesus' youth to prove that he fulfilled predictions in the Hebrew Scriptures, culminating in his baptism and early teachings (3:1–7:29). It then focuses on the selection of disciples and the establishment of a church structure (8:1–10:42), with teachings about the Kingdom of God—the transformed world ushered in by the Messianic appearance—and a manual of discipline for the community (11:1–18:35). The Gospel concludes not only with Jesus' suffering and crucifixion, but also with his resurrection appearance. That appearance takes place in the Galilee as a sign of a worldwide mission.

Luke begins with stories about the births of both Jesus and **John the Baptist** and includes angelic hymns (1:1–2:52). The story then focuses on John the Baptist and on Jesus' mission, but keeps the two tales separate (3:1–4:13). The Gospel then looks at Jesus' ministry in Galilee (4:14–9:50) and Jerusalem (9:51–10:12) and adds unique material about Jesus' ethical teachings (10:13–19:27). The period of his final challenge to Jerusalem, his death, his suffering, and his resurrection—becomes an epilogue to Judaism. Only in the Book of Acts does Christianity become a mission to humanity (19:28–24:53).

What do these three have in common? First, they picture Jesus as a Messiah who brings cosmic change to the world through his death and resurrection. History undergoes radical change because of the events of Jesus' career. In this way, the Synoptic Gospels emphasize a discontinuity between the past and present. A new age has begun. Mark makes this plain by emphasizing the astonishment that contemporaries felt toward Jesus. While Matthew and Luke seem to emphasize continuity with the Jewish past by providing Jesus with a Jewish genealogy and by stressing his fulfillment of Jewish Scriptures, they emphasize discontinuity by displaying Jesus' contemporaries as rejecting his message and failing to recognize the way he stood within the tradition.

Second, all three indicate that God works through history. God's plan unfolds throughout Jesus' life and career. Jesus' actions take place within the framework of a divine program that moves inexorably to its conclusion. God's transcendent meaning and purpose glimmer through various incidents and anecdotes in the stories. Third, Jesus' ethics are open and inclusive. Matthew and Luke, in particular, show Jesus preaching to all who can hear; even in Mark, however, the response of the non-Jews to Jesus' message testifies to the general appeal of his message. Finally, ritual tends to be symbolic, pointing to the new approach Jesus is giving. While some controversy surrounds Jesus' last meal, all three agree that it created a ritual opportunity to symbolize Jesus' life and purpose.

John represents a distinctly different religious perspective (see Box 9–1). John seems to have been influenced by a specific type of Hellenistic religious movement, that of the Gnostics. The term **Gnostic** comes from the Greek *gnosis* meaning "knowledge." In its strict usage, Gnosticism refers to several distinctive Christian groups who claimed that Jesus had initiated a few chosen disciples into certain mysteries meant only for a selected audience. In a broader use, many Hellenistic religions claimed to possess a special knowledge that provided them with a key to human salvation; they know what other people cannot: the path from this world of darkness into the true light. The Gospel of John is not, as it now stands, a Gnostic writing, but it contains elements that resemble the ideas of that movement.

It begins with a hymn to the *logos*, the universal reason, the principle by which many Greek philosophers felt the world had been created (1:1–18). The Gospel of John, unlike Philo of Alexandria or the Stoics, understands the logos as a divine intrusion into the world, a form of immanence rather than transcendence. While Philo and other Platonic philosophers use the idea of a creative power to separate God from mundane experience, for the Fourth Gospel the logos is a divine presence in the world. Because of this stress on immanence, several elements in the early narrative clash with the Synoptic story. Jesus does not undergo baptism, but John the Baptist declares that the Holy Spirit announced Jesus' status as the logos to him. Jesus does not go into the wilderness and face temptations from the devil. The narrative then retells the story of Jesus' life as a series of seven signs pointing to his secret messianic purpose (1:19–12:50).

This presentation differs dramatically from the other Gospels. No exorcisms are reported, and three Passover holidays are celebrated in Jerusalem in John's Gospel, as compared to only one in the other Gospels. In this Gospel, Jesus delivers long, philosophical sermons, not pithy sayings and parables. Many stories are begun and never completed, as if telling stories was not the Gospel's main interest. The concluding narrative about suffering, death, and resurrection is also unique (13–21). Jesus' last meal, a Passover dinner in the other Gospels, is held before Passover in John, but it engenders no specific ritual or memorial, although the washing of each other's feet is held up as a worthy practice (13:3–16). Perhaps most tellingly, the devil plays a central role in causing Judas to betray Jesus (13:2, 21–30). A long list of the problems that true believers will face has been added at this point; this Gospel alone understands the resurrection as a special sign to the elect.

The religious perspective of John contrasts with that of the Synoptics. History is continuous; the story of the logos proceeds from eternity through the present. The Gospel of John transforms historical events into symbols; thus the resurrection of Lazarus is less a "historical" point than a symbolic anticipation of Jesus' own resurrection (11:1–12:11). Second, God is immanent in the world through Jesus. Jesus' divine status is made clear, insofar as he needs no baptism and faces no temptation. Jesus manifests God's presence among humanity. Third, the ethics involved is exclusive. Only those whose philosophical and spiritual natures have prepared them to understand Jesus' esoteric teaching will be able to do so. Finally, ritual plays a transforming role, with Jesus' miracles being the primary example. These signs of the redemptive power of Jesus show his control over nature—turning water into wine (John 2:1–11) or resuscitating the dead (John 11), for example.

This emphasis on immanence through the presence of Jesus raises a problem for the Gospel of John not found in the other Gospels. How does this immanent presence of the divine continue after Jesus has fulfilled his earthly career? The answer is given through the idea of the **Paraclete**, a term found only in the Gospel of John. The Paraclete substitutes for Jesus' presence; it enables the community that follows Jesus to perform works of healing, to gain special knowledge and power. It imbues them with a true understanding of the special meaning of Jesus' life and teachings. As Jesus is about to leave the disciples, he declares: "But the Paraclete, the Holy Spirit, whom the Father will send in my name, will teach you everything…Peace I leave with you; my peace I give to you" (John 14:26–27). That spirit acts for, and in the name of, Jesus, being a transparent medium of the divine. Jesus identifies his own departure with the coming of that spirit: "If I do not go away, the Paraclete will not come to you; but if I go, I will send him to you…When the Spirit of truth comes, he will guide you into all the truth; for he will not speak on his own, but will speak whatever he hears…" (16:7, 13). This view of divine immanence, which begins with Jesus as the logos incarnate and continues with the Paraclete, separates John's Gospel from the Synoptics.

Beyond these differences between the Synoptics and John, other themes distinguish each of the Synoptics. Mark stresses personal purity, internal religious commitment, and sincerity. That Gospel addresses a Gentile Christian community concerned with private individual salvation, rather than with the social agenda of Jewish religion. Matthew and Luke, on the other hand, reflect the ethical sensitivities of the Hebrew tradition. They emphasize the need for communal solidarity and the importance of institutional leadership in shaping a better world. John draws on Hellenistic wisdom teachings. That Gospel explores the mysteries it attributes to Jesus' secret sayings. The Gospels of Matthew, Mark, and Luke sought to bring Christianity out of its narrow, Jewish origins into the wide world of international politics.

The Gospel of John retreats back into a narrower sphere of concern. Exhibiting the concern for private life found in the Greek religions, this Gospel presents a striking contrast to the Synoptic's universalism. Jesus appears to recommend a special set of esoteric actions that require an elite knowledge, a private key to salvation, and passwords for the initiates into a spiritual realm. The needs each Gospel addresses grow out of its social context, and thus there are the Hellenistic elements in Mark and Luke, Jewish concerns of Matthew, and a particularistic interest in John.

Finally, the Gospel of John pays very little attention to ritual. Jesus does celebrate three Passover holidays in Jerusalem, but they do not play a role in defining Christian ritual. For John, the last supper does not occur on Passover; it occurs the day before Passover, the day on which the sacrificial victim is chosen and slaughtered (John 19:14). The symbolism here is clear: Jesus represents the lamb whose death will redeem humanity. The ritual of the meal is not important; the historic event of Jesus outweighs all ritualism.

SUMMARY QUESTIONS

1. How are the religious ideas of the Pharisees, Sadducees. Essenes, and Zealots different from each other?
2. What are some of the various ways Jesus' claim to be the Messiah may have been understood?
3. What different roles does the symbolism of the Passover ritual play in the Gospels?
4. What are some of the major differences between the Synoptic Gospels and the Gospel of John?
5. What distinctive characteristics distinguish each of the Synoptic Gospels?

Four Suggested Essay Questions

1. Explain two ways in which a tradition may view history. Apply one of them to the views of the Zealots and one to the view of the Synoptic Gospels, emphasizing the effect of Jesus' career, death, and resurrection.
2. Explain two ways in which a tradition may view the supernatural. Apply one of them to the views of the Sadducees and one to the views of the Gospel of John.
3. Explain two ways in which a tradition may view ethics. Apply one of them to the views of the Zealots and one to the views of the Pharisees.
4. Explain two ways in which a tradition may view ritual. Apply one of them to the views of the Sadducees and one to the symbolism of Jesus' last meal in the Gospel of John.

Exercise

Write a paragraph about the Zealots for Question 3 by answering the following:

1. Write a sentence describing the Zealot's hostility to Roman domination.
2. Write a sentence describing the Zealot's claim that Jewish independence is demanded by God.
3. Write a sentence describing the Zealot's view that God expects Jews to take an active role in gaining their independence.
4. Write a sentence describing the Zealot's view of the Messiah.
5. Write a topic sentence contrasting the Zealot's views of God and human initiative to that of the Pharisees.

FOR FURTHER READING

The books listed below should be a point of departure for your future study. This chapter looks at books about the Jewish background of Jesus and the Gospels. The next chapter lists books specifically focused on the Gospels. Each includes a bibliography that will guide you beyond its basic information.

1. Bryan, Steven M., *Jesus and Israel's Traditions of Judgement and Restoration* (Cambridge, England: Cambridge University Press, 2002).
2. Crossan, John Dominic, *The Historical Jesus: The Life of a Mediterranean Jewish Peasant* (San Francisco, CA: HarperSanFrancisco, 1991).
3. De Lange, Nicholas R. M., *Jewish Literature of the Hellenistic Age* (New York: Viking Press, 1978).
4. Flusser, David, *Judaism and the Origins of Christianity* (Jerusalem: Magnes Press, The Hebrew University, 1988).
5. Grabbe, Lester L., *A History of the Jews and Judaism in the Second Temple Period* (London: T & T Clark, 2004).
6. Van der Horst, Pieter Willem, *Hellenism, Judaism, Christianity: Essays on Their Interaction* (Kampen: Kok Pharos, 1994).
7. Koester, Helmut, *Ancient Christian Gospels: Their History and Development* (London: SCM Press, 1990).
8. Murphy, Frederick J., *The Religious World of Jesus: An Introduction to Second Temple Palestinian Judaism* (Nashville, TN: Abingdon Press, 1991).
9. Vermes, Geza, *Jesus the Jew: A Historian's Reading of the Gospels* (London: Collins, 1973).

10

Religions of the Gospels

READING ASSIGNMENT

Matthew 1, 3, 5–6, 11, 19, 28
Mark 1, 12, 16
Luke 1, 3, 6, 24
John 1, 3, 11, 20

LEARNING OBJECTIVES

By the end of this lesson, you will be able to:
- Describe the differences between the Synoptic Gospels and the Gospel of John.
- Compare the views of history in the four Gospels.
- Compare the views of the supernatural in the four Gospels.
- Compare the views of ethics in the four Gospels.
- Compare the views of ritual in the four Gospels.

INTRODUCTION

This chapter examines the Gospel stories about the life and teachings of Jesus. An account of the life of Jesus makes a theological statement about the way the world is, the difference that Jesus made to the world, and the things that people should now do because of him. The four Gospels advance four different religious perspectives. As you read this chapter, you will examine how each Gospel treats similar themes and anecdotes in distinctive ways. The mira-

Interpretive Matrix for Chapter Ten

View of the Divine: How people interact with God and the supernatural; how God interacts with the world.	View of History: How past, present, and future are related; who controls the shape of events.	View of Ethics: How people behave toward other people; how they behave toward people like themselves and to those who are different.	View of Ritual: How people behave toward the Divine; how they perform religious actions.
The Divine as Transcendent: God is manifest only to an elite and select group. God interacts with the world through an emanated Spirit. Spiritual reality is higher than physical material reality.	*History as Continuous:* God adds to past revelations but does not reject those revelations. A new leader stands in direct relationship with earlier leaders. History unfolds according to a predetermined plan.	*Inclusive Ethics:* Leaders appeal to people from different social, ethnic, and national groups. Laws are modified to apply to a greater number of people.	*Ritual as Transforming:* Ritual participation makes a person different and alters a person's nature.
The Divine as Immanent: God is manifest physically and materially. Miracles occur from direct contact with the divine.	*History as Discontinuous:* New leaders create new laws for a new religious community.	*Exclusive Ethics:* Extreme religious action is demanded, such as giving up all material goods. Only a select few are allowed to be members of the group.	*Ritual as Symbolic:* Ritual should serve people, people should not serve ritual. Ritual should bend to the needs of human beings. Ritual is not an end in itself but is used to teach a lesson.

cles and parables attributed to Jesus, as well as his conflicts with others, provide further clues to the differences between the Synoptics and John and even within the Synoptic Gospels themselves. This chapter examines some of these clues in greater detail.

Scholars of religious studies have noted the differences between how each Gospel opens and ends. The additions or omissions to the story of Jesus change the message being transmitted. The Gospel of Mark opens with the adult Jesus being baptized by John the Baptist, after which a divine voice proclaims: "You are my son, the beloved," and ends with the discovery that Jesus' burial tomb was empty. On the basis of just this story, readers would conclude that Jesus was adopted as Son of God only at his baptism (Mark 1), and that the disappearance of his body from his tomb was a mystery only some people understand. With the other three Gospels present, however, Jesus' identity as Son of God takes on a very different meaning, and Jesus' empty tomb is only the prelude to his public resurrection appearances. Comparing Mark to each of the other three Gospels, both in the beginning and at the end, illustrates important differences in views of history and views of the supernatural.

The conflicts, miracles, and teachings attributed to Jesus illuminate the ritual and ethical views of the different Gospels. Looking at how each one understands the purpose of miracles, the protagonists in a conflict, and the specific injunctions Jesus gave shows how each Gospel interprets the meaning of ritual and whether it defines community in an inclusive or exclusive way.

SOME IMPORTANT TERMS

The following terms are important in this chapter. Some of them have been listed in previous chapters; in those cases the term is not **bold** in the main body of this chapter. Where names of books are also the names of individuals (such as The Gospel of Mark), the name does not appear in the Glossary.

Abraham	Herod Agrippa	Nag Hammadi
Apostle Peter	Herod the Great	Nicodemus
Baptism	Holy Spirit	Parable
Beatitudes	Jerusalem	Parousia
Beloved Disciple	John the Baptist	Passover
Christ	Judas	Pharisees
Crucifixion	Kingdom of God	Resurrection
Elijah	Lazarus	Sabbath
Galilee	Levites	Sadducees
Gentile	Logos	Samaritan
Gnostics	Lord's Prayer	Satan
Gospel of John	Mary and Martha of	Sermon on the Mount
Gospel of Luke	Bethany	Sermon on the Plain
Gospel of Mark	Mary Magdalene	Son of God
Gospel of Matthew	Mary the Mother of James	Son of Man
Gospel of Thomas	Melchizedek	Soter
Gospel	Messiah	Synoptic Gospels

BELIEFS ABOUT HISTORY AND THE OPENING CHAPTERS OF THE GOSPELS

The way each Gospel opens its story of Jesus' life indicates its interpretation of history. Mark begins not with Jesus' birth, but with the initiation of his career (Mark 1:1–14), declaring, not insignificantly: "The beginning of the Gospel of Jesus Christ, the Son of God: As it is written in the prophet Isaiah—See I am sending my messenger ahead of you." Apparently, Mark links Jesus' beginning to a prophecy of the Hebrew Scriptures. Mark cites a passage that, in fact, conflates Malachi 3:1 with Isaiah 40:3. Nevertheless, after John the Baptist baptizes Jesus, it seems as if a new era has begun. Jesus goes out into the wilderness and is tempted; then before his career can begin as such, John is arrested. Jesus then announces the "good news" (gospel) that the time prophesied is "now fulfilled" (1:14–15).

Mark's introduction suggests both continuity with the past—Jesus fulfills the Old Testament prophecy of Isaiah—and discontinuity with the future—a new era begins with the public career of Jesus. Jesus' baptism symbolizes not only the beginning of a new era, but the transformation that ritual brings about (1:9–11). This act takes place in private, with the voice from heaven addressed directly to Jesus. It symbolizes how people change when they are initiated into Christianity. Such a transformation portrays the ritual by which Christians take on their new identity as discontinuous with their past; a person begins a new life by becoming a Christian. History begins anew for each individual, even if that individual imitates previous generations when fulfilling the ritual.

Matthew's Gospel extends the narrative backward from Jesus' baptism to his genealogy and early years (Matthew 1–2). The first chapter provides a Davidic genealogy for Jesus (1:1–17) and thereafter uses several verses from the Hebrew Bible as proof that Jesus fulfills biblical expectations. Thus his birth is predicted by Isaiah 7:14: "A young girl shall give birth," and his family flees Herod's slaughter of the innocents (for which there is no historical verification) so Matthew can also apply several other verses from the Hebrew Bible to his life (Numbers 24:17; Jeremiah 23:5, 31:15; 40:1; Hosea 11:1). Matthew seeks to show how the Hebrew Bible anticipates every event in Jesus' life.

History, in this case, represents an unfolding of a predetermined plan. Those who hold the key to the secrets of the Hebrew Scriptures can discern the workings of that plan. This explicit link between the Hebrew Bible and Matthew's writings may well explain why the early church placed Matthew at the beginning of the New Testament. The church embraced this view of history as its own; its story was the continuation of that of ancient Israel. The genealogy with which Matthew begins affirms this continuity by showing that Jesus is a Jew whose ancestry stretches back to the first Jew, Abraham.

That continuity and predetermined plan help explain how Matthew 3:13–17 portrays John the Baptist. While John does baptize Jesus, he does so reluctantly, confessing that Jesus should baptize him. The confrontation with Satan (Mark uses this Hebrew title throughout; both Matthew and Luke generally use the Greek term devil, with the exception of Matthew 4:10 and Luke 13:16), which takes only two verses in Mark, becomes an extended chapter (Matthew 4:1–11) in which every test includes a contest between Jesus and the devil to see which one better understands the meaning of the Hebrew Bible. The entire opening section of Matthew presents an unambiguous continuity between Christianity and its Jewish heritage.

The Gospel of Luke puts Jesus in the context of the history of the world, rather than that of Judaism. The placement of Jesus' genealogy offers a crucial clue to the view of history expressed. The Gospel of Luke does not introduce a genealogy of Jesus until Chapter 3. The first chapters remain in a Jewish environment, although unlike the opening of Matthew they are not filled with proof-texts from the Hebrew Bible. Instead, Luke 1–2 offers new hymns and prayers, most probably associated with those in use in the churches Luke knew.

By Chapter 3, however, Jesus (and thus also the story of the Christians) has moved beyond Judaism to a wider community. Luke signifies this by using a genealogy that traces Jesus' lineage not to a Jew, but to Adam, the first human being (Luke 3:23–38). While Matthew views history from a Jewish perspective, Luke focuses on a universal historical panorama. Luke continues this wider historical emphasis by appending the Acts of the Apostles to his Gospel. The story of Jesus requires the fulfillment of the spread of Christianity into the Hellenistic Gentile world.

This historical vision expresses Luke's view of Jesus as "savior" (deliverer), or in Greek, **Soter**, a word that does not appear in any of the other Gospels. Although both Mark and Matthew seem to use a Jewish model of Jesus as Messiah, Luke seems to address an audience more accustomed to Greek and Roman cultural forms of expression. Jesus brings salvation to the world, rather than instruction to disciples (Mark) or deliverance to the Jews (Matthew). While the Christian's identity is part of a continuous human history for Luke, it marks a break with Jewish history.

The distinctiveness of Jesus comes in Luke's view that Jesus and John the Baptist never met; Luke 3:19–20 has John shut up in prison before moving on to describe Jesus' baptism in 3:21–22. The confrontation with the devil uses much of the same material as that in Matthew, but puts them in a different order. That order ends with the temptation that Jesus make use of his miraculous power to save himself (Luke 4:9–13). Luke, unlike Matthew, emphasizes that Jesus' mission is not based on miracles, but on his personal teachings.

The Gospel of John offers an even more strikingly different view from any of the Synoptics. Here, normal history appears irrelevant. John provides Jesus with a cosmic genealogy, not a Jewish or universally human one. Whatever later Christianity decided, John's view of Jesus represents a minority opinion among the Gospels. From John's perspective, history, as normally understood, is irrelevant. The eternal, as incarnated in Jesus, transcends the everyday affairs of human life. The Gospel of John eschews history in favor of the logos, the creative power of wisdom personified, which transcends daily experience and extends from the beginning of creation to the end of time (John 1:1–18).

In this perspective, John the Baptist appears to witness a new phenomenon—the intrusion of the holy into the everyday. He offers an enigmatic statement about Jesus: "After me comes a man who ranks ahead of me because he was before me" (1:30). The descent of the logos into human affairs is both absolute discontinuity—because this had never occurred before—and absolute continuity—since the logos is the primal creative power that has maintained the world since its beginning. In the very opening of this Gospel (as opposed to coming at the conclusion, as in Luke) the disciples recognize Jesus' nature: Philip found

Nathanael and said to him, "We have found him about whom Moses in the law and also the prophets wrote…" (1:45).

That continuity, however, brings with it an appellation strange to the Jewish tradition. Jesus is the Son of God as well as King of Israel (1:49). He is more than a mere human being; he has a cosmic nature that elevates him above mortals. This special nature distinguishes a Hellenistic savior from a Jewish Messiah. The absence of a temptation by the devil underscores the unusual nature of this messianic perspective.

BELIEFS ABOUT THE SUPERNATURAL AND ENDINGS OF THE GOSPELS

Comparing the way each Gospel ends reveals differences similar to those found by looking at Gospel beginnings. Each of the four portrays the discovery of Jesus' empty tomb, but they do so differently (see Box 10–1). The earliest manuscripts of Mark end abruptly with a short scene in which women disciples discover the empty tomb (Mark 16:1–8). The resurrection appearances in our present texts are later additions. Thus Mark, at least as originally canonized, emphasizes the mysteriousness of the divine, the wonder and awe of anticipating what cannot be understood.

Three women—**Mary Magdalene**, **Mary the mother of James**, and Salome—come after the Sabbath ends (on Sunday morning at sunrise) to anoint Jesus' body. They are astounded to find the stone rolled away and a young man dressed in white there. The man tells them that Jesus has been raised, but they are seized with terror and amazement "and they said nothing to anyone" (Mark 16:8). Not coincidentally, Mark emphasizes wonder, awe, and amazement throughout the Gospel. Mark conveys an impression of an unpredictable world in which wonders constantly occur. The divine intervenes in mysterious ways. God is immanent in human affairs, but only some people—usually non-Jews and demon-possessed individuals—recognize that immanence.

Matthew's perspective emphasizes the glory of the resurrection and the potential of the New Jerusalem Church to replace early Judaism. A new day has dawned as the women, without any explicit reason given, come to the tomb and experience a terrifying event (Matthew 28:1–10). Because Matthew sees the rise of Christianity as a miraculous historical event, this Gospel heightens the supernatural element in Jesus' death and resurrection, surrounding the narrative with signs of the wondrous. An earthquake accompanies God's angel who has rolled back the stone. The figure by the tomb appears in a frightening way "like lightning and his clothing was white as snow. For fear of him the guards shook and became like dead men" (Matthew 28:3–4).

The women, however, are strengthened in their convictions as the angel tells them not to be afraid. They do what they are bidden and "left the tomb quickly with fear and great joy" to tell the disciples (v.8). The priests and elders, however, dismiss this miracle and spread a rumor that the disciples have stolen the body (vv. 11–15). The supernatural invades this world in an unmistakable way. When unbelievers seek to discredit this immanent power, they

> **BOX 10–1: THE EMPTY TOMB**
>
> This chart outlines the sequence of events given in each of the four canonical Gospels for the discovery of Jesus' empty tomb and its aftermath.
>
> *Matthew 28*
>   Occurs after the Sabbath (as the first day of the week was dawning)
>   Mary Magdalene and the other Mary are present
>   An angel appears with an earthquake opening the tomb—guards flee
>   The women obey the angel's command
>   A Jewish rumor says the disciples stole the body
>
> *Mark 16:1–8*
>   Occurs after the Sabbath (but early morning Sunday)
>   Three women (Mary Magdalene, Mary the mother of James and Salome) anoint the body
>   An unidentified youth appears
>   The women flee in terror
>
> *Luke 24:1–17*
>   Occurs on the morning of the first day (no mention of the Sabbath)
>   Several women (identified in v. 10 as Mary Magdalene, Mary mother of James, and "the other women") anoint the body
>   Two men in dazzling clothes appear at the tomb and tell the women he has risen
>   The women are terrified but eventually believe the message given them
>   The disciples disbelieve the women until Jesus convinces them of his resurrection by providing physical evidence of his reality
>
> *John 20:1–18*
>   On Sunday morning while it is still dark
>   Mary Magdalene is alone, discovers the stone removed from the tomb, runs to disciples
>   Peter and the beloved disciple believe
>   Mary weeps and is rebuked by Jesus as is "doubting Thomas" who requires physical proof of Jesus' resurrection

spread evil rumors. Unlike Mark, Matthew does not portray the women misunderstanding the divine message given them. When God appears to them, they heed the call.

While Luke, like Matthew and Mark, reports the empty tomb, this Gospel focuses more attention on the disciples and their experience of divine immanence. The women in Luke do indeed tell the disciples, but unlike in Matthew, the disciples do not believe them. They are convinced only when Jesus himself appears and gives them evidence of his reality (Luke 24:13–42). While the resurrected Jesus teaches them the predictions of his death and resurrection, the disciples still do not believe in his immanent presence. Only after Jesus demonstrates his corporeal reality are they fully persuaded. Jesus insists that the disciples test his bodily presence (vv. 36–42). The divine, in this case, shares in all the physicality of the human. Jesus overcomes disbelief and wonder through proof of his corporeality. In Luke, God's presence among humanity is a physical one.

As if to oppose Luke's view, the Gospel of John considers the desire for bodily or physical confirmation of Jesus' presence a sign of weakness. In John 20 the new day does not begin at sunrise; the empty tomb is discovered while it is still dark (20:1). Mary Magdalene, the only woman involved here, who, as in Luke, is given no reason for being at the tomb, is astounded and finally even mistakes Jesus for a gardener (20:15). While the **Apostle Peter** and the **Beloved Disciple** immediately believe and understand what has happened, this is not the case for other disciples. The proverbial "doubting Thomas" in John 20: 24–25 is rebuked because he believes only on the basis of his senses. As in the other Gospels, the resurrection demonstrates the continuing presence of the divine in the world, an emphasis on divine immanence. Yet that immanence is not for all to see. Only those with true spiritual understanding comprehend the divine presence. Unlike in Luke, that presence is spiritual rather than corporeal. Believers who require corporeal proof stand at a lower level than other believers.

Thus Jesus says to Thomas: "Have you believed because you have seen me? Blessed are those who have not seen and yet have come to believe" (20:29). The divine message cannot be understood by everyone; one needs a special insight to comprehend Jesus as divine being. Nevertheless, this Gospel opens the way for disciples who have not known Jesus in the flesh during his earthly career. Those who believe without the experience of the immediate disciples are, according to this perspective, especially precious and blessed.

MIRACLE STORIES AND ETHICS IN THE GOSPELS

The Hebrew Bible often emphasizes divine intervention in the world through telling stories about miracles. The tales of Elijah the prophet, for example, justify his assertion of authority through his ability to control natural events. Elijah shows that the divine determines whether there will be rain or drought, food or famine, sickness or health, life or death. The view of how the divine interacts in the world often corresponds with a type of ethics. If God's intervention over natural causes is clear and unmistakable, then its operation is comprehensible to all. The message that it gives is open to everyone. If, however, a miracle is really a coded message, a secret sign that only those initiated into its meaning can understand, then a miracle points to an esoteric knowledge available only to those within a special community.

The different Gospels tell stories about miracles associated with Jesus for a variety of purposes (see the chart in Box 10–2 that lists the miracle tales for each Gospel and outlines the stories discussed below). Scholars of religious studies interpret stories of miracles by asking

The Dutch painter Rembrandt (1606–1669) suggests the mysterious nature of Jesus' healings in this picture of "Christ with the Sick Around Him, Receiving Little Children."

several questions: When in Jesus' career do they occur, and under what circumstances? What response to the miracle is recorded in the story? How does the story portray Jesus' own understanding of the miracle?

Luke 8:43–48 tells a fascinating story of a woman suffering from a bloody flow for twelve years who had been unable to find a cure from physicians. She touches Jesus and is miraculously cured. Jesus, however, feels a drain of power from him and demands to know who touched him. Jewish law forbids a male from touching any woman who has a blood flow. This regulation may underlie Jesus' response, but the narrative itself does not mention it. All it records is Jesus' accusation that someone intentionally drew upon his power. Everyone denies having done this, and the disciple Peter is singled out as claiming that what Jesus felt could have been an innocent crowding by someone. Jesus rebukes him and announces that he has felt a drain of power. At that point, the woman admits that she has touched Jesus and announces the miracle to everyone. At that point, Jesus tells her, "Your faith has made you well; go in peace" (Luke 8:48).

Several points conjoin in this story. The first is that Jesus possesses a supernatural power that, when tapped, can reverse the course of nature. Jesus exerts a force that countermands natural causes. Second, the text goes out of its way to contrast the denseness of Peter with the

BOX 10–2: MIRACLE STORIES IN THE GOSPELS

This chart outlines a healing miracle found in the Gospels. An asterisk marks stories found in only that Gospel. Miracle stories are a narrative genre found in the Gospels telling of Jesus' power to alter natural law, told to illustrate a view of the new reality experienced after the Jesus event. The first section lists the miracle stories in the Gospels—you should note both which stories are reported or omitted as well as the different order in which they occur; the next section outlines the stories discussed in the textbook.

Miracle Stories in Mark

1:21–28	Commanding demons at synagogue in Capernaum
1:29–34	Healing Simon's (Peter's) mother-in-law
2:1–12	Healing a paralytic
3:1–6	Healing on the Sabbath
3:7–12	Various healings
3:20–30	Questioning the Holy Spirit and Jesus' source of power
4:36–41	Calming the winds
5:1–20	The Gerasene demoniac (My name is Legion)
5:12–43	Jairus' daughter resuscitated
5:24–34	Healing the hemorrhaging woman
6:30–44	Feeding the five thousand with bread and fish
6:45–52	Walking on water
6:52–56	Several healings
7:24	Eventually healing after refusing to heal a Gentile's daughter
7:31–37	Healing the deaf and mute
8:1–10	Feeding four thousand with bread and fish
8:22–26	Healing a blind man
9:14–29	Healing an epileptic child whom the disciples can't cure; only prayer is effective
10:46–52	Healing blind Bartimaeus

Miracle Stories in Matthew

7:28–29	Commanding demons at synagogue in Capernaum
8:2–4	Healing a leper in Galilee
8:5–13	Curing of a Centurion
8:14–17	Healing Peter's mother-in-law
8:23–27	Calming the winds
8:28–34	The Gerasene demoniac (My name is Legion)

220   Chapter 10

9:1–8	Healing a paralytic
9:18–26	A synagogue leader's daughter resuscitated
9:19–22	Healing the hemorrhaging woman
9:27–31	Curing the blind
*9:32–34	The mute demoniac
11:1–6	Miracles are a messianic sign
12:1–14	Healing on the Sabbath
12:15–21	Various healings (cites Isaiah 42:1–14)
12:22–37	Questioning the Holy Spirit and Jesus' source of power
14:13–21	Feeding five thousand with bread and fish
14:22–27	Walking on water
14:34–36	Several healings
15:21–28	Eventually healing after refusing to heal a Gentile's daughter
15:29–31	Healing the lame, blind, maimed, mute, and many others
15:32–39	Feeding four thousand with bread and fish
17:14–20	Healing an epileptic child whom the disciples can't cure; they need faith only as much as a mustard seed
*17:27	Finding a coin in a fish's mouth to pay the Temple tax
20:29–34	Healing of two blind men (unnamed)
21:14	(The only Gospel to include healing in the Temple after Jesus throws out the money changers)

Miracle Stories in Luke

4:31–37	Commanding demons at synagogue in Capernaum
4:38–41	Healing Simon's (Peter's) mother-in-law
*5:1–11	Miraculous catch of fish
5:12–14	Healing a leper in Galilee
5:17–26	Healing a paralytic
6:1–11	Healing on the Sabbath
6:17–19	Various healings
7:1–10	Curing of a Centurion's slave
*7:11–17	Resuscitation of the widow's son
7:18–35	Miracles are a messianic sign
8:33–34	Calming the winds
8:26–39	The Gerasene demoniac (My name is Legion)
8:40–56	Jairus' daughter resuscitated
8:42–48	Healing the hemorrhaging woman

Religions of the Gospels 221

9:10–17	Feeding five thousand with bread and fish
9:37–42	Healing an epileptic child (no mention of disciples' inability to heal)
11:14–23	Questioning Jesus' source of power (but no mention of sin against the Holy Spirit)
*13:10–17	An unsolicited cure of a crippled woman on the Sabbath causing questions about Sabbath observance; Satan causes physical disorders and sickness
*14:1–6	Healing a man with dropsy on the Sabbath
*17:11–19	Ten lepers cleansed
18:35–43	Healing a blind man (unnamed)
*22:47–53	Restoring the ear of a slave (unnamed here, named Malchus in John 18:10, but without a cure)

Miracle Stories in John

*2:1–2	Miracle at Cana—changing water into wine (the First Sign)
*4:46–52	Curing an officer's sick son (the Second Sign)
*5:2–9	Healing a cripple in Jerusalem (the Third Sign)
6:1–13	The feeding of the five thousand (the only miracle recorded by all four Gospels) (the Fourth Sign)
6:16–25	Walking on water (the Fifth Sign)
*9:1–7	Healing a man born blind—not for a sin but so God might be glorified (the Sixth Sign)
*11:1–45	Resuscitation of Lazarus (the Seventh SIgn)

Comparing a Healing in the Four Gospels

Mark 5:25–34

A crowd follows Jesus

A woman suffering from hemorrhages for 12 years touches Jesus' cloak and is healed immediately

Jesus is aware that power had gone forth from him and asks who touched him

The women confesses to him

He says: "Daughter, your faith has made you well; go in peace, and be healed of disease."

Matthew 9:19–22:

Jesus and his disciples get up and a woman suffering from hemorrhages for 12 years approaches him and touches him

Jesus says "Take heart, daughter, your faith has made you well."

Instantly the woman was made well

Luke 8:43–48

Crowds press in on Jesus

> A woman suffering for 12 years with hemorrhages touches the fringe of his clothes and the hemorrhaging stops
>
> Jesus asks who touched him, and tells the disciples that he noticed that "power had gone out of me"
>
> The woman confesses to the entire crowd
>
> Jesus says: "Daughter, your faith has made you well; go in peace"
>
> *John 11:1–45*
>
> Mary and Martha ask Jesus to come to Bethany to heal their sick brother, Lazarus
>
> He answers that the sickness is "for the glory of God"
>
> He goes to Bethany because he knows that Lazarus is dead
>
> Martha declares faith in resurrection
>
> Jesus and Mary weep and people wonder why Jesus could not cure him
>
> Jesus has his burial cave opened and resuscitates Lazarus

honesty of the woman herself (Luke 8: 45–47). Whereas Peter will even try to contradict Jesus, the woman makes full confession of what has occurred. Finally, the story culminates in Jesus' acceptance of the woman's faith. Because she is publicizing his powers, she receives full healing and an affirmation of her faithfulness. Telling this story emphasizes divine control over nature and the ability of Jesus to intervene to change natural occurrences. It also evokes an ethics that places the honesty of a common woman above male leadership. Peter's authority gives him no superiority to the faithful declaration by the woman about what she has experienced. This telling of the tale emphasizes an inclusive ethics that explicitly criticizes the hierarchic leadership.

As told in Mark 5:25–34, the story generalizes this critique of leadership. Peter is no longer singled out. Instead, all the disciples share the inability to understand what Jesus is asking; they all respond when he asks "Who has touched me?" with a rebuke that suggests this is a foolish question. The woman, again, gains favor by giving an honest and truthful report, but without the details found in Luke. Once again, it is the telling of this report that leads Jesus to tell her that her faith has healed her.

This telling omits the idea of a special power within Jesus that can be drained by the performance of a miracle. The healing takes place at the touching of Jesus' garment, but Jesus does not announce that he has felt his power leaving him. The miracle is merely an example of the unexpected and surprising ability of Jesus. Mark emphasizes the amazement at Jesus' power that the miracles bring (5:20, 42).

While other stories put Jesus' miracle working within the context of a conflict between him and other Jewish leaders (see Mark 2:23–28), here merely the amazement is noted. The miracles throughout Mark are not meant to prove Jesus' power or authenticate his mission. Instead, they suggest the inability of others to understand him. Not only in this case but consistently in the Gospel of Mark, the disciples cannot fathom what Jesus means. Miracle tales in Mark tend to emphasize an inclusive ethics. All people, even Jesus' closest disciples, have the same failings; until the resurrection, no one can comprehend or understand what Jesus is about or what he represents.

The story as told in Matthew 9:19–22 shortens the narrative significantly. Matthew is most concerned with establishing Jesus' reputation. The Gospel emphasizes the authority given to Jesus (9:8, 26, 31, 38). Miracles are important because they demonstrate this authority. With that in mind, Matthew changes the order in which the healing takes place. Rather than having the woman's bleeding cease when she touches Jesus' garment, it stops only when Jesus tells her "Your faith has made you well."

The touching in itself seems to accomplish nothing; Jesus does not seem to feel a drain upon his power, and therefore Jesus makes no remark about someone touching him. He only turns and sees her. Certainly Jesus exercises the interventionary power of the divine in this case. The miracle, however, occurs not through a magical power within him, but through the authority of what he says. His miracles are meant for those who accept this authority. In this way, Matthew's telling of the story emphasizes an exclusive ethics in which divine power extends only to those who embrace it.

This story, as such, does not appear in the Gospel of John. Miracles in John are part of an esoteric code: they exist within a symbolic tale of "signs" that the initiated can see as a message concerning the purpose of Jesus as God's logos incarnated. The story of the woman with a bloody flow told by the Synoptic Gospels occurs within another tale, that of the reviving of the daughter of a leader of the Jewish community. The Gospel of John includes a similar resuscitation story (not found in the Synoptics—the famous tale of the resurrection of **Lazarus** (John 11). This story, prefiguring Jesus' own resurrection, is the final "sign" in a sequence of seven miracles occurring from John 2:1–11:57).

The story begins (11:1–6) with two sisters, Mary and Martha, living in a place called Bethany, asking Jesus to heal their brother Lazarus. Jesus, however, claims that no healing is required. Their brother has become ill "for God's glory, so that the Son of God may be glorified through it" (11:4). Although Jesus has said explicitly that "this illness does not lead to death" (11:4), Lazarus does die. At that point, Jesus goes to Bethany with his followers, despite considerable danger in doing so (vv. 7–16). Jesus promises Martha that her brother will live again, and she affirms the idea of a final resurrection and that Jesus is the way to that resurrection (vv. 17–27). The Gospel of John associates the true "life" to which he will be raised is, in these verses, with taking on the identity of being a Christian. As Mary and Jesus lament Lazarus' death, onlookers wonder that Jesus could not have healed him (11:37). Jesus then resuscitates Lazarus, despite his body already having putrefied (vv. 39–45). That act leads to a glorification of God's name and recognition of Jesus' power. John uses the story to symbolize the true rebirth that occurs when one becomes a Christian.

This story differs considerably from the tales in the Gospels. Scholars think that this final miracle may itself be related to a "secret" gospel that understood such resurrection events as part of an esoteric initiation ritual. The outcome of the miracle reinforces the idea that these signs are misunderstood by outsiders. While some Jews believe in Jesus because of the mira-

BOX 10–3: CONFLICT STORIES AND PARABLES IN THE GOSPELS

This chart focuses on two genre—conflict stories and parables. These reveal both the exclusive and inclusive aspects of ethics as expressed in the Gospels. The chart lists important conflict stories and distinctive parables in each of the Gospels.

Conflict Stories in Mark

2:5–10	Conflict with scribes over authority to forgive sins
2:15–17	Conflict with Pharisees over eating with sinners and tax collectors
2:23–3:6	Conflict with Pharisees over Sabbath observances
3:22–27	Conflict with scribes about the source of Jesus' power
7:1–8	Conflict with Pharisees and scribes over dietary rules
7:14–23	Rejects Jewish dietary rules
8:11–13	Pharisees demand a sign
10:2–9	Conflict with Pharisees about divorce
11:27–33	Chief priests, scribes, and elders question his authority
12:13–17	Pharisees and Herodians ask about paying taxes
12:18–27	Conflict with Sadducees over resurrection
12:28–34	Scribes ask him which commandment is the greatest
12:35–37	Scribes misunderstand references to Davidic messiah

Conflict Stories in Matthew

3:7–10	John the Baptist in conflict with Pharisees and Sadducees
9:3–6	Conflict with scribes over authority to forgive sins
12:1–14	Conflict with Pharisees over Sabbath observances
12:22–30	Questioning Jesus' source of power
15:1–20	Conflict with Pharisees and scribes over dietary rules and rejection of those rules
16:1–4	Pharisees and Sadducees demand a sign from Jesus
19:1–12	Conflict with Pharisees about divorce
21:23–27	Conflict with chief prists and elders about his authority
22:15–22	Pharisees and Herodians ask about paying taxes
22:23–33	Conflict with Sadducees over resurrection
22:34–40	Pharisees ask him about the greatest commandment
22:41–45	Pharisees asked about references to Davidic messiah
23	Diatribe and curse on the scribes and Pharisees who "sit on Moses' seat"

Conflict Stories in Luke

3:7–14	John the Baptist in conflict with "crowds"
5:17–26	Conflict with scribes and Pharisees to forgive sins
6:1–11	Conflict with scribes and Pharisees over sabbath observances
10:25–28	A lawyer tests Jesus asking about the greatest commandment
11:14–23	Questioning Jesus' source of power (but no mention of sin against the Holy Spirit
11:37–54	Curse on Pharisees and "Lawyers" (similar to Matthew 23 but different order)
14:1–6	Conflict with Pharisees over healing on Sabbath
15:1–2	Conflict with Pharisees and scribes over associating with sinners and tax collectors
20:1–8	Conflict with priests, scribes, and elders about his authority
20:20–26	"They" send spies to ask about paying taxes
20:27–40	Conflict with Sadducees over resurrection
20:28–47	He said to "them" (Sadducees?) the question about Davidic messiah and tells his disciples to "Beware of the scribes"

Conflict Stories in John

1:19–25	John the Baptist in conflict with "the Jews," priests, Levites, and Pharisees
3:1–21	Conflict with Nicodemus
5:9–16	Conflict with "the Jews" over Sabbath observance
6:41–59	Conflict with "the Jews" over Jesus' claim to be "the Bread of Life"
7:32–37	Conflict with chief priests, Pharisees, and "the Jews" plotting his arrest
8:1–11	Pharisees test him with a woman caught in adultery
8:21–59	Jews who were former disciples claim descent from Abraham makes Jesus' liberation of them unnecessary; they end up trying to stone him
9:1–41	Conflict with "the Jews" surrounding his curing of a man born blind
10:31–39	"The Jews" attempt to stone and arrest Jesus

Parables in Mark

4:1–20	Parables are to confuse rather than to clarify; explaining the parable of the Sower

Parables in Matthew

13:1–23	The parable of the Sower—the disciples understand
13:24–58	Several parables of "the kingdom"
18:12–14	Parable of the lost sheep
24:45–51	Parable of the delayed master
25:1–13	Parable of the wise and foolish bridesmaids
25:14–0	Parable of the talents

> ### Parables in Luke
> | | |
> |---|---|
> | 7:41–43 | Parable of two forgiven doctors |
> | 8:4–15 | Parable of the Sower |
> | 10:3?–37 | Parable of the good Samaritan |
> | 11:5–8 | The uncharitable friend |
> | 12:16–21 | Parable of rich man who wants to store his goods but will die the next day |
> | 12:36–48 | Parable of master returning from a wedding feast and slaves awaiting him—expanded into delayed master parable |
> | 15:3–7 | Parable of the lost sheep |
> | 15:8–10 | Parable of the lost coin |
> | 15:11–32 | Parable of the prodigal son |
> | 16:1–13 | Parable of the dishonest manager |
> | 16:19–31 | Parable of Lazarus and the rich man |
> | 18:1–8 | Parable of the widow and the unjust judge |
> | 18:9–14 | Parable of the Pharisee and the tax collector |
>
> ### "I Am" Teachings in John
> | | |
> |---|---|
> | 6:22–55 | I am the bread of life |
> | 10:1–21 | I am the good shepherd |
> | 11:25 | I am the resurrection and the life |
> | 14:6 | I am the way, and the truth and the life |
> | 15:1–17 | I am the true vine |

cle, others report him to the authorities, using the sequence of signs involved as proof of sedition (11:45–48). Those Jews have misunderstood what the events were meant to show. The Gospel of John understands Jesus' actions as evidence of divine intervention in the world, whether as signs that Jesus is God's logos or as clear reversals of the natural order.

More important, these miracles show why Christianity must create an exclusive community. Only those who are insightful, who have an ability to perceive the meaning of such signs, know what they mean. Everyone else, when confronted by these occurrences, becomes alarmed and feels threatened. Christians differ from others precisely in their recognition of the true meaning and significance of Jesus' miracles.

Several of the miracle stories are also the basis for a conflict between Jesus and his opponents (compare boxes 10–2 and 10–3). The Gospel genre uses several different stylistic forms to convey its point, and these differences will help you discern how a text understands ritual and ethics. The particular styles that developed as the sayings were encased in narrative deserve special mention. The term *paradigm* when referring to a New Testament text, indicates a story used as the setting for a transmitted saying. For example, the phrase "Pay Caesar what is Caesar's and God what is due to God" originally circulated as a saying (or logia) on its own, as the apocryphal Gospel of Thomas found in Nag Hammadi demonstrates. Only later did it become part of an anecdote about how Jesus responded to challenges raised by his opponents.

Mark 12, vv. 13–17, places that saying in the context of a conflict between Jesus and certain Jewish leaders—the Herodians here probably being the supporters of Herod Agrippa, and the question being one of political loyalty. This type of paradigm exemplifies a general form, that of the conflict story. The conflict story claims to describe a dispute between Jesus and one of his adversaries. In fact, however, this type of story focuses on an argument within the early Christian community itself. Conflict stories focusing on Jesus' arguments with Pharisees, Sadducees, and other Jews reflect controversies among later Christians (living a generation or more after Jesus) about dietary laws, Sabbath observance, and inheritance. (See the listing in Box 10–3; notice how the Gospel of John, for example, almost always uses the term "the Jews," while Matthew emphasizes "the Pharisees.") These stories suggest the ethics of early Christianity.

ETHICS AND RITUAL IN THE GOSPEL OF MATTHEW AND THE GOSPEL OF LUKE

All four Gospels present complex ethical perspectives not only in the miracle stories, but also in the teachings attributed to Jesus. Christianity presents itself as a universal tradition, one that invites all people into its community. Jews, Gentiles, men and women, members of both lower and upper classes mingle as followers of Jesus. At the same time, the Gospels make it clear that to become a Christian means to separate oneself from previous connections. While originally a Jew or Gentile, a newly converted Christian severs ties with previous relationships. The varieties of Christianity expressed in the Gospels intertwine an inclusive ethics among believers with an exclusive ethics in relation to other religious communities in Roman times.

The Gospel of Matthew makes this duality clear and provides a good example of both the inclusive and exclusive ethics found in the Gospels. Matthew 10:34–37 explicitly announces that Christianity divides families and sets father against son, mother against daughter, making "enemies out of your kinfolk." This conflict provides the basis for a wider set of concerns that point beyond the narrow duties that bind families together. Christianity displaces the ordinary considerations of family relationship and creates a broader, greater "family" to create a wider sphere of affection, loyalty, and support. This new "family" integrates those who are often marginal to the mainstream society: tax collectors, prostitutes, and sinners of various types. The loyalty demanded by this new substitute for kinship obligations not only unifies a group of previously divided social outcasts; it also creates a sense of being different from others that emphasizes an exclusive identity.

Matthew 5:17–48 makes the exalted nature of this identity clear. Jesus dismisses the idea that Christians need not obey the detailed laws of the Jewish codes. Indeed, breaking even the least of the commandments detracts from a person's status in paradise, and without a righteousness that "exceeds that of the scribes and Pharisees, you will never enter the kingdom of heaven" (5:17–20). Christians must perform more than the most observant Jew. Not only is murder forbidden, but also insults are considered equal to murder (v. 22). Not only should you not commit adultery, but also lusting looks are equally culpable (v. 28). Not only should you not make false oaths, but also you should make no oaths at all (v. 34).

The contrast is made even stronger by misrepresenting the earlier tradition against which Christianity measures itself. Jesus says, "You have heard that it was said, you shall love your neighbor and hate your enemy" (v. 43), although no such verse appears in the Hebrew Bible and does not seem to have been taught by any of the four types of Judaism noted at the beginning of this chapter. Such a statement, however, makes a nice contrast to the next verse: "But I say to you love your enemies" (v. 44), although that verse does, indeed, have parallels in the Hebrew Bible (Exodus 23:4, for example). The culminating verse of this section makes the extreme nature of Christian identity clear: "You shall be perfect as I the Lord your God am perfect" (v. 48). The ideal perfection of Christian ethics seems to exclude those who cannot achieve such a high standard of behavior.

Matthew 19:16–26 expresses this aspect of early Christianity. In the anecdote told there, a rich young man asks Jesus what he needs to do in order to gain eternal life. Jesus queries the man as to whether he has obeyed the basic laws of Jewish morality. On receiving a positive reply, Jesus then adds two more demands: sell all your possessions and give them to the poor and follow me. Here, the detailed law of Judaism is rejected not because it is too stringent, but because it is not rigorous enough. Christian identity demands actions that go beyond what other groups do. To be a Christian means to be an extremist who is necessarily an outsider to normative morality.

This exclusive criterion, however, receives an almost immediate retraction. When Jesus is asked whether anyone can live up to such an impossible standard, he replies: "It is impossible for mortals but nothing is impossible for God." This admission opens the door once again to those who might have been excluded from the community for not adhering to its ideal goals.

The Gospel of Luke resembles Matthew in many ways. It emphasizes a church community with a self-conscious identity. Like Matthew, it gathers together sayings of Jesus and emphasizes both exclusive and inclusive ethics. Luke, like Matthew, contrasts the ethics of Christianity with that of former Jewish religiousness (6:27–38). Both agree that Jesus brings dissension and breaks up family ties (Matthew 20:34–26; Luke 12:51–53). Yet in many ways, Luke emphasizes a universal ethics even more inclusive than the ethics found in Matthew.

Both Luke and Matthew include a set of blessings that detail the ethics of the new community. Comparing the so-called **Sermon on the Mount** of Matthew and the **Sermon on the Plain** of Luke illustrates the different ethical perspectives in each Gospel. Matthew 5:3–12 and Luke 6:20–26 reveal striking points of contrast. Both texts develop a series of **beatitudes** or blessings (statements of good fortune), using a phrase often found in the Hebrew scriptures: "happy are they who" (for example, Psalm 144:15). Luke generates a parallel set of "woes" (statements of misfortune) in the spirit of Deuteronomy 27–28. These various statements may be seen as incentives to persuade people to accept the Christian doctrine; rewards are promised for fidelity to the Christianity of the Gospel authors. When looked at in detail, however, the two are quite different.

In Matthew, the promised blessings all relate to spiritual gain. Those who know their need for God are blessed; those who hunger for righteousness will be victorious; those with pure hearts will see God (Matthew 5:3–10). These are incentives to join a theological community. Those being addressed desire to choose one belief system over another because of their theological concerns. Only the final verses—declaring the good fortune of both peacemakers and those who suffer—point to concrete experiences.

Matthew 5 advocates unity and praises those who reconcile arguing factions. Matthew 5:4–6 promises material rewards for those who suffer. Verses 7–9 promise spiritual rewards for those who practice moral virtues. For Matthew 5, the ethics of Jesus is exclusive, making demands that separate those who perform them from everyone else and addressed specifically to disciples: "Blessed are you when people revile you and persecute you and utter all kinds of evil against you falsely on my account…you are the light of the world" (Matthew 5:11, 14).

Luke 6, however, places ritual and ethics in an economic context. One must choose to associate with the rich or the poor; one must either include the outcasts or side with the oppressors. Rather than focus on the "poor in spirit," Luke 6:20 blesses the "poor." Rather than bless those who "hunger after righteousness" (Matthew 5:6), Luke has Jesus bless "you who are hungry." This Gospel praises those who are inclusive rather than exclusive, for they alone recognize the true human community, or in technical language, God's kingdom. This ethics creates a new social order in which all join in a common cause.

This impression of the Lucan Gospel gains confirmation by looking at its use of parables. The term **parable** translates the Hebrew mashal, referring to a riddle or mysterious tale. Several books of the Hebrew Bible include this sort of material. The book of Proverbs (Hebrew Mishlei, the plural of mashal) contains short pithy sayings, riddles, and questions, and more extended explanatory stories. Scholars of religious studies recognize the variety of purposes for which parables are used. They examine such usage in the Gospels as a way of understanding the message intended. Sometimes parables are meant to clarify difficult concepts; sometimes they are used to illustrate a new idea by relating it to an older and more familiar one.

More often in the Gospels, however, parables either confuse or shock. Jesus must later explain the meaning of the parable to his followers (see Box 10–3 for a comparison of the Gospel usages of parables). Mark 4 provides a dramatic definition of the genre that, while picked up by the two other Synoptic Gospels, is used most consistently throughout Mark. Parables are meant to confuse listeners; not everyone to whom Jesus speaks should be able to understand him. Mark 4:12 quotes Isaiah 6, in which God informs Isaiah that he is to preach so that his listeners will not be able to perceive, "so they may not turn again and be forgiven." This represents an exclusiveness even deeper than that found in Luke or Matthew. Mark believes that during Jesus' lifetime, no one was able to comprehend him or his mission. This predetermined reality meant that even the disciples misunderstood his point again and again.

Luke seems to use the term parable in the more popular meaning of an illustrative story; yet the quality of proverbial riddles continues. The point is lost if the element of surprise, shock, or even obscuring of truth is ignored. Several parables with ethical implications occur only in Luke and in no other Gospel (see Box 10–3). They tend to emphasize the inclusive ethics of Luke, suggesting the priority of the lost who have been found, rather than those who have always been present (Luke 15:3–32), of the poor over the rich (11:5–8, 16:19–31), of the victim over those in power (16:1–13, 18:1–8).

One of the most famous parables concerns the "good Samaritan" (Luke 10:30–37). Samaritans were inhabitants of northern Israel, and the Jews regarded them as descendants of a group of people imported by the Assyrians after they conquered the land. As such, they were interlopers and intruders in Israel. Conflict separated the Jews from the Samaritans, with members of each group hostile toward those from the other group. Jesus, in response to the question, "Who is your neighbor?" tells the story of a Jew whose life was saved by a Samaritan, not by fellow Jews.

Despite the familiarity of the tale, it contains many problems. Jesus does not really answer the question of who is the neighbor, but rather the question, "What is neighborliness?" In fact, the main point of the parable seems to be that the question asked is meaningless. Good ethics implies an unquestioning and indiscriminate inclusiveness in which one does not even raise the issue of who should or should not be included. The oppressed form a single class, whether they are Jew, Gentile, or Samaritan.

The Sermon on the Mount in Matthew leads into a discussion of worship. Matthew 6:1–17 contains the famous "**Lord's Prayer**." The entire passage contrasts ostentatious religious practice with modest practice. Matthew uses this prayer to contrast Christian worship with Jewish ritualism. Jesus admonishes his followers: "Whenever you pray, do not be like the hypocrites, for they love to stand and pray in the synagogues and at the street corners so that they may be seen…do not heap up empty phrases as the Gentiles do, for they think that they will be heard because of their many words" (Matthew 6:6, 7). For Matthew, Christian ritual, like Christian ethics, replaces previous Jewish precedent. The main ritual on which he focuses is that of prayer, public worship. Whereas Jewish worship is public and ostentatious, Christian worship should be private and modest. Second, Matthew, unlike Luke, distinguishes between Gentile worship and Christian worship. Christian worship should be simple and short, unlike the elaborate rituals of Hellenistic religious practice. Christian ritual, especially Christian liturgy, celebrates an individual's attitude, an internal orientation toward God. The important point of prayer in Matthew 6 is that it accomplishes what the worshiper desires. What mode of prayer brings sustenance, forgiveness, and rescue from evil? The type of prayer that Jesus advocates—individualistic, private, and intimate—achieves its aims more effectively than other types.

While Luke 11:1–4 does, in fact, give a briefer prayer than does Matthew 6, Luke generally offers models for precisely the elaborate ritualism that Matthew rejects. The first chapter of Luke provides hymns for the Universal Savior (Luke 1: 46–55). Luke offers several public hymns that, most probably drawn from the liturgical worship of the Lucan community, have become part of Christian liturgy even today.

This Gospel repeatedly describes people praying, singing, and engaging in ritual rejoicing. Unlike Matthew, then, the Gospel of Luke affirms public worship and ceremony. Worship need not be carried out privately and quietly. It can be a visible proclamation of the expectations of the community. This suggests that public prayer functions for Luke much as the Passover did in II Kings 22–23: as a means of strengthening communal ties. Ritual, then, has a substantive effect; it actually binds a community together.

That exclusive perspective, however, is modified by a religious inclusiveness that expands members' responsibilities and affections to include others often excluded by social or familial obligations. Luke's religion is based on the principles of love and acceptance, rather than on a set of rigid expectations and rules. As Christianity developed, this double view of ethics continued. At times Christians focused on an exclusive and legalistic ethics, and at other times they developed an inclusive approach to morality and community.

RITUAL AND ETHICAL ALTERNATIVES IN MARK AND JOHN

The Gospels of Mark and of John offer a very different view of both early Christian religious organization and of the ethics and rituals involved. Both Gospels seem to come from smaller-scale communities, more intimate and close-knit than those reflected in Matthew and Luke. Both focus on personal piety and the Christian individual, rather than on the institutions of Christian life. The miracle and healing tales of the Synoptics draw upon the Gospel of Mark. So too do the conflict stories, but in them the distinctiveness of Mark becomes clearer.

Mark, for example, rejects Jewish tradition entirely, unlike Luke or Matthew, which retain some connection to Jewish practice. For Mark, the observances marking Jewish life are both unnecessary and obstructionist. Jesus sides with various prophetic criticisms of ritual: God requires justice and righteousness, not ritual, a view echoing the ideas of some of the prophets of the Hebrew Scriptures.

Mark 2:23–3:6 takes up the issue of Sabbath observance (see Isaiah 58 as a contrasting text) and argues that various Sabbath prohibitions may be set aside in the name of the greater authority of Jesus. While Jews may not pick grain during the Sabbath, Jesus permits it, since "the Son of Man is Lord of the Sabbath" (Mark 2:27).While the Pharisees permit breaking the Sabbath law only to save a life, Jesus takes the prerogative of doing any healing on that day. Throughout, Mark uses Jesus' rejection of Jewish ritual as proof of his superior status. Mark 7 shows Jesus rejecting the dietary restrictions and demands for ritual purity of rabbinic Judaism (Mark 7:14–23).

Mark 12 provides an extended example of the major themes in Mark. The chapter emphasizes the astonishment with which Jesus' words are received (Mark12:17). Jesus' authority is unassailable, and all who question him are seized by awe and trembling. Mark 12:1–12 describes Jesus castigating his adversaries who are too frightened to arrest him. Verses 13–17 raise the question of obedience to civil authority and Jesus' answer amazes his audience. Verses 18–27 show Jesus refuting Sadducees who deny the idea of resurrection. After Jesus successfully answers a scribal demand to know the most important commandment (vv. 28–33), his adversaries are defeated and verse 34 comments: "After that no one dared to ask him a question." In each of these cases, Jesus articulates an inclusive ethics. Those who seek to exclude him are characterized as evil laborers. Civil authority is affirmed as equally valid as religious authority; the living and dead share in a common future; love of others is the primary commandment.

Mark 12:28–33 considers the important human task to be doing good deeds; it may entail being a loyal citizen and giving to the emperor those things due the civil government, affirming theological ideals that transcend human logic, accepting the principles of biblical law, if not their detailed legal decisions, opposing those who seek to create an aristocracy of the pious, favoring the poor over the rich. Jesus leaves people astounded when he declares that the worth of charity depends not on what it accomplishes, but on how much it represents of the giver's possessions. In this text, ritual is clearly symbolic and not substantial. Ethics emphasizes the unity of all human efforts. This leads to historical discontinuity: the demands of the hour supplant tradition.

Mark 12 begins with a parable, a word for which Mark 4 offers an explanation, suggesting that it is a concept that needs explanation. The parable explained in that context expresses a particularistic and exclusive ethics. Jesus, in Mark 4:3–8, tells of a sower who distributed seed as he went. Some of the seed fell on the path and was eaten by birds. Other seed fell on rocky ground and grew quickly. but without striking deep roots the growth soon died. Other seeds fell among thorny weeds and were choked to death. Only a small percentage of the seed fell into good soil and produced an abundant harvest.

Mark 4:13–20 provides an explanation for that parable. It symbolizes how God sends his word into the world. Satan takes some of the seed and makes sure that it will never grow or flourish. This analogy refers to people who receive the Christian teaching joyfully but eventually fall away from it. Only within the "good soil," those people prepared and able to hear God's word, is that word able to grow and flourish. Christianity, therefore, flourishes only among those ready to receive it.

Mark 8:11–13 expresses a similar view. When Pharisees ask him for a sign, he merely states that this generation is not worthy of a sign. The people of Jesus' time cannot understand him. They are trapped in their own age and are unable to transcend its limitations. Matthew 16:1–4 claims that the lack lies within the Pharisees themselves. He charges that while they claim to interpret the signs of the weather, they cannot "interpret the signs of the times" (Matthew 16:4). Luke 12:54–56 condemns hypocrites who can interpret the weather, but cannot "know how to interpret the present time."

While Luke and Matthew both assume that some signs have been given, even if the crowds or Pharisees cannot interpret them, Mark thinks that the lack of understanding lies in the times themselves. Mark, therefore, has an open approach to ritual. It should not be an obstacle to joining the Christian group. He has a closed approach to membership in the community, since only those specially receptive can perceive the meaning of Jesus' life and teachings.

The Gospel of John presents a complex view of both ritual and ethics that seems different from that of Mark. In John ritual actions performed externally have little significance. This attitude helps explain why, of all the Gospels, only John omits the narrative of the Last Supper and the instituting of the Eucharist. The external rituals of the church are less important for this Gospel than the esoteric meaning of spiritual exercises. Even when John tells of a conflict between Jesus and "the Jews" over Sabbath observance, the Gospel adds that Jesus called himself the Son of God, and that this theological claim, even more than ritual disobedience, caused their animosity: "He was not only breaking the Sabbath, but was also calling God his own Father, thereby making himself equal to God" (John 5:18). Initiation into the mystery of Jesus' nature constitutes the basic ritual for John, but that ritual merely affirms the chosen nature of the initiate.

John 3 seems to meditate on the need for ritual baptism, but actually focuses on initiation as confirmation of a chosen status. The anecdote takes the form of a confrontation between Jesus and a rabbinic questioner (compare Mark 12, Matthew 22, Luke 10:25–28). Here the quest for the Kingdom of God drives a rabbinic sage, **Nicodemus**, to seek Jesus' advice. Rather than welcoming him, however, Jesus comments on his obtuseness. Only those who know the secret rituals and can comprehend intricate mysteries are prepared to enter eternal life. Ritual seems substantial here; it is presented as an initiation, as being "born again." Nicodemus asks: "How can anyone be born after having grown old? Can one enter a second time into the mother's womb and be born?" (John 3:4). The rabbi's inability to grasp this concept proves that he is not ready for Jesus' message: "If I have told you about earthly things and you do not believe, how can you believe if I tell you about heavenly things?" (v. 12).

Jesus' remark that "no one can enter the kingdom of God without being born of water and Spirit" (v. 5) seems to suggest a ritual that transforms the individual from living in the physical mundane world to becoming part of the spiritual realm. The worshiper, reborn, takes on a new identity, becomes a spiritual being rather than merely a corporeal one. Nevertheless, only people with the requisite spiritual nature can receive this ritual. In this way, the ritual is celebratory, rather than substantive; it symbolizes the inner nature of the person undergoing it and affirms that nature. One whose nature is unfit cannot benefit from the ritual. Ritual does not transform human beings; either they are ready for Christianity or they are not. If they are the ritual affirms it; if they are not, the ritual is meaningless.

The Gospel of John records none of the ethical instructions found in the Synoptic Gospels. It replaces the parables of the Synoptic tradition with long philosophical statements focusing on the nature of Jesus. The true believer will know what Jesus means by proclaiming:

"I am the bread of life" (6:48); others, like "the Jews," will fail to understand (6:52–59). Jesus' proclamation: "I am the gate for the sheep...Whoever enters by me will be saved" (10:9) seems inclusive, as does the statement: "I have other sheep that do not belong to this fold. I must bring them also" (10:16). All who enter that gate gain salvation, and all are invited to join the fold.

Nevertheless, not only do people misunderstand what he is saying (10:6), but Jesus turns on "the Jews" and declares: "you do not believe because you do not belong to my sheep" (10:26). Even John's advocacy of love is a restricted one: disciples should love one another to prove that they are disciples of Jesus (13:34–35). The command is that "you love one another as I have loved you. No one has greater love than this, to lay down one's life for one's friends" (15:12–13). This admonition to be concerned with those who are your friends differs from the Synoptic command to love your enemies. This command represents an exclusive rather than an inclusive ethics.

SUMMARY QUESTIONS

1. How do the genealogies of Jesus and the figure of John the Baptist differ among the four canonical Gospels?
2. How does the use of miracle stories differ among the four canonical Gospels?
3. How do the teachings attributed to Jesus in the Gospel of Matthew differ from those in Luke?
4. How does the meaning of ritual in the Gospel of Mark differ from that in John?
5. How does the meaning of parable differ among the four canonical Gospels?

Four Suggested Essay Questions

1. Explain two ways in which a tradition may view history. Apply one of these to the first chapter of Mark and the other to the first chapter of Matthew.
2. Explain two ways in which a tradition may view the supernatural. Apply one of them to Luke 24 and the other to John 20.
3. Explain two ways in which a tradition may view ethics. Apply one of them to Luke 10 and the other to John 3.
4. Explain two ways in which a tradition may view ritual. Apply one of them to Matthew 6 and the other to Luke 11.

Exercise

Write a paragraph about Luke 11 as part of an answer to Question 4:

1. Be sure to begin with a topic sentence that contrasts Luke's use of "The Lord's Prayer" with that of Matthew in terms of prayer as public or private and as a sign of identity or as a means to gain access to the divine.
2. Be sure to use the fact that the disciples ask Jesus for a prayer here, in contrast to his initiating the teaching of the prayer in Matthew.
3. Be sure to use the fact that the prayer is couched in the plural "we" throughout, rather than in the first-person singular used in Matthew.
4. Be sure to include Jesus' statement in Luke 11:9; "Ask and it will be given you; search and you will find; knock and the door will be opened for you."
5. Be sure to indicate whether that statement is dependent on the way prayer is offered.

FOR FURTHER READING

The books listed below should be a point of departure for your future study. This chapter looks at books focused on the Gospels. Each includes a bibliography that will guide you beyond its basic information.

1. Brown, Raymond Edward. *An Introduction to the Gospel of John* (New York: Doubleday, 2003).
2. Burridge, Richard A., *What Are the Gospels: A Comparison With Graeco-Roman Biography* (Grand Rapids, MI: William B. Eerdmans, 2004).
3. Collins, Adela Yarbro, *Is Mark's Gospel a Life of Jesus: The Question of Genre* (Milwaukee, WI: Marquette University Press, 1990).
4. Griffith-Jones, Robin., *The Four Witnesses: The Rebel, the Rabbi, the Chronicler, and the Mystic* (San Francisco, CA: HarperSanFrancisco, 2000).
5. Hengel, Martin., *The Four Gospels and the One Gospel of Jesus Christ: An Investigation of the Collection and Origin of the Canonical Gospels* (Harrisburg, PA: Trinity Press International, 2000).
6. Nickle, Keith Fullerton, *The Synoptic Gospels: An Introduction* (Louisville, KY: Westminster John Knox Press, 2001).

11

Religions Associated with the Apostle Paul

READING ASSIGNMENT

Acts 1–2, 7, 9–12, 15, 17, 19, 22, 26, 28
Romans 9–13
1 Corinthians 6–11, 13–14
Galatians (complete)
Philippians 2
Colossians (complete)
1 Thessalonians 4–5
2 Thessalonians (complete)

LEARNING OBJECTIVES

By the end of this lesson, you will be able to:
- Describe the impact of the Apostle Paul on the history of Christianity.
- Describe the differences between the genuine Pauline letters, the doubtful Pauline letters, and the portrait of Paul in the book of Acts.
- Describe the way the genuine Pauline letters views history, the divine, ethics, and ritual.
- Describe the way the book of Acts views history, the divine, ethics, and ritual.

Interpretive Matrix for Chapter Eleven

View of the Divine: How people interact with God and the supernatural; how God interacts with the world.	*View of History:* How past, present, and future are related; who controls the shape of events.	*View of Ethics:* How people behave toward other people; how they behave toward people like themselves and to those who are different.	*View of Ritual:* How people behave toward the Divine; how they perform religious actions.
The Divine as Transcendent: God encounters human beings in visions and indirectly God is an ideal creator whose mysterious ways cannot be understood.	*History as Continuous:* A new leader has close ties with previous leadership groups. Texts from an older tradition are used by a newer tradition. Older practices are continued by a newer religious group.	*Inclusive Ethics:* A religion explains itself in terms familiar to the general society. Men and women perform the same religious tasks. The virtues espoused by the group mirror those of the general society.	*Ritual as Transforming:* Ritual makes a physical effect on its participants. Rituals initiate a change that brings a person into a new religious group.
The Divine as Immanent: God encounters human beings directly and physically. God takes possession of human beings and is present within them.	*History as Discontinuous:* A new group modifies the practice inherited from an older group. A newer religious group contends that an older group is no longer an authentic expression of God's will.	*Exclusive Ethics:* Certain religious roles are limited to only one gender. Certain behavior is permitted and other behavior is forbidden as criteria for belonging to the group.	*Ritual as Symbolic:* Ritual performances remind participants of a shared history.

INTRODUCTION

This chapter focuses on the picture given in the New Testament of the Apostle Paul, the most important disciple in early Christianity. Paul of Tarsus composed letters to specific Christian communities, instructing them in appropriate Christian behavior. Many early Christian leaders, especially in Jerusalem, questioned Paul's authority, but as his reputation grew, his letters took on an independent power and served as the first distinctively Christian writings to become canon. Paul self-consciously distinguished between his task—that of preaching to non-Jews, the Gentiles—and the task of other apostles, who directed themselves specifically to Jews. The difference between Paul's message to the **Gentile Christians** and that proclaimed by the **Jewish Christian**s often created tension between him and other Christian

238 Chapter 11

leaders. Nevertheless, his Christianity fit the needs of Roman citizens better than did Jewish Christianity.

This chapter looks at three sources in the biblical text. The first consist of letters or epistles scholars think were actually written by the historical figure Paul of Tarsus. Some scholars distinguish between letters, defined as personal communication between individuals, and epistles, communications addressed to a wider audience. This chapter conflates the two. Any document, whether a "letter" or an "epistle" that begins with a greeting, has a central section devoted to a message, and ends with a greeting is designated by either term. This chapter uses the terms interchangeably.

The second source are letters that most scholars think are not from the historical Paul. Differences in vocabulary, style, and doctrine suggest someone other than Paul wrote them and then appended Paul's name to them. An important minority of scholars, however, think of these letters as historically accurate. A person such as Paul might vary his style or change his mind on important issues (see Box 11–1 which summarizes these two groups). A separate chapter of this book examines another group of letters attributed to Paul in the biblical canon, but considered certainly not from the historical Paul (1, 2 Timothy, Titus, Ephesians, Hebrews).

The third source for this chapter is the canonical Acts of the Apostles. This narrative continues Luke's Gospel from the experiences of the risen Jesus through Paul's ministry (see Box 11–2). This work tends to blur the differences between Paul and other apostles, but it represents an important source for reconstructing early Christian history. Still another group of writings associated with Paul did not achieve canonical status at all. One suppressed work, The Acts of Paul and Thecla, advances the cause of women disciples and their prestige within the church. Another, The Letter of Barnabas, offers a dualistic and Gnostic understanding of both the Hebrew Scriptures and of the Christian tradition. This chapter does not examine these non-canonical works.

SOME IMPORTANT TERMS

The following terms are important in this chapter. Some of them have been listed in previous chapters; in those cases the term is not **bold** in the main body of this chapter. The terms may be found in the Glossary.

Abraham	Claudius	Domitian
Adam	Constantine	Essenes
Ananais	Cornelius	Eucharist
Apostle Peter	Damascus	Eve
Baptism	Didache	Gamaliel
Barnabas	Dietary Laws	Gentile Christians
Circumcision	Dionysius	Gentile

Glossolalia	James	Pentecost
Hagar	Jewish Christians	Rapture
Herod Agrippa II	Lord's Day	Sabbath
Holy Spirit	Nero	Sarah
Isaac	Parousia	Silas
Ishmael	Passover	Stephen
Jacob	Paul of Tarsus	Stoicism

PAUL OF TARSUS AND THE GROWTH OF CHRISTIANITY

The book of the Acts of the Apostles traces the growth of Christianity from a Jewish environment into a cosmopolitan and primarily Gentile movement. (see Box 11–2). That transition certainly took place. The evolution of Christian beliefs shows a progressive separation from traditional Judaism to embrace of the general culture of the Roman environment.

The rituals practiced by early Christians reflect both Jewish and Hellenistic influences. The celebration of the Christian communion ceremony emphasizes the continuity between Christianity and Judaism. Using bread and wine to illustrate a historical past echoes the Pharisaic understanding of Passover. Some New Testament books, such as the stories about Paul in Acts, suggest that early Christians also followed Jewish Sabbath laws, although several passages in the Gospels claim that Jesus took a rather relaxed view about Sabbath restrictions.

All these rituals can be understood within the context of rabbinic Judaism as celebratory rather than substantive. (Remember that the rabbis opposed the substantive rituals of the priests.) The earliest Christian groups, called "Jewish Christians," followed Jewish practices and saw themselves as an alternative form of Judaism. Associated with the names of the apostles Peter and James, this type of Christian who followed Jewish observances would be displaced by a Christian religiousness more in keeping with Hellenistic religious influences.

As Christianity developed into a Gentile-oriented religion, its ritualism took on a different tone. The Eucharist, for example, maintained its external Jewish form derived from Jesus' Passover celebration. In significance, however, it took on the meaning of a mystery cult's sacred meal by which worshipers enter a mystic communion with their deity. As such a ritual, it could not be confined to one time of the year; in fact, outside of mentioning Jewish holidays such as the fast of the Day of Atonement, Pentecost, and the Sabbath, the New Testament makes no mention of special calendar festivals in connection with early Christian behavior. One of the earliest books of teaching, the Didache, written about 80 c.e. but attributed to the twelve apostles, gives instructions for baptism, weekly fasting and the practice of the Eucharist, but includes only the **Lord's Day** (Sunday) as a festival bound to a specific calendar date. By focusing on the life of the individual rather than on a calendar date, the celebration of the Eucharist has a personal, substantive meaning for all participants (see l Corinthians 11: 23–34). The ritual

> **TIMELINE 11–1   CHRONOLOGY OF THE APOSTLE PAUL**
>
> This timeline integrates material from Acts with information from Paul's genuine letters. Acts, as noted in Box 11–2, is not always consistent with Paul's actual writinggs. All dates are Current Era.
>
> | | |
> |---|---|
> | 1st century C.E. | Paul is born in Tarsus and educated as a Hellenistic Jew |
> | 30–31 | Paul persecutes Christians |
> | 32–34 | Paul encounters the risen Jesus |
> | 32–34 | Paul travels to Arabic and then Damascus without visiting Jerusalem |
> | 35 | Paul's first visit to Jerusalem |
> | 49 | Paul's second visit to Jerusalem |
> | 50 | Paul writes 1 Thessalonians (2 Thessalonians?) |
> | 54–55 | Paul writes 1 Corinthians |
> | 55–57 | Paul writes 2 Corinthians, Galatians, Romans |
> | 59–62 | Paul is arrested in Jerusalem; writes Philemon, Philippians, Colossians (?) |
> | 64 | Paul is executed in Rome |

proclaims Jesus' death and resurrection. Paul's view of ritual might seem to reject this approach. 1 Corinthians 11:26 considers the Eucharist a way to "proclaim the Lord's death until he comes." This use of ritual to point back to a historical memory is symbolic rather than transforming. 1 Corinthians 11:30, however, claims that consuming the Eucharist with a profane intent makes people weak and ill. Paul, therefore, provides a transformative power to the ritual. A symbolic Eucharist that points to the life of Jesus and its liberating effect parallels the Pharisaic view of Passover. A Eucharist that physically transforms its participants echoes Greco-Roman mystery rituals. In this way, Christian practice moved away from Judaism and closer to the Hellenistic world.

Christians separated themselves from Jews even more radically by their substituting baptism for the Jewish ritual of circumcision. For the Essenes and other similar groups, baptism represented a symbolic ritual, a ritual that pronounced people members of a new community. This initiation, however, did not mean that those who joined the group ceased to observe Jewish rituals. Male children and converts from non-Jewish religions continued to be circumcised. Celebrations such as Passover were still exclusively meant for circumcised males. Christianity altered this.

Baptism became a substantive ritual that transformed people by taking away their sins and initiating them into a new society. This transformation meant that a person no longer was either a Jew or a Gentile, but something entirely new, something that went beyond each of them. This ritual removed people from either the Hellenistic environment of normal Roman life or the Jewish environment of the rabbis. The book of Acts makes clear that this ritual affirms a new way of entering into a holy community, one that supersedes all other rituals (Acts 10:1-11:18). As with the Eucharist, so too with baptism; Christianity moves beyond Jewish practice to embrace a wider cultural tradition, that of Hellenism, the common culture of the Greco-Roman world.

The way Christian identity went beyond either Jewish or Roman culture extended to ethical as well as ritual observances. Early Christians separated themselves from ordinary life and apparently adopted Stoic-like self-discipline as an example of their virtuousness. On the one hand, these disciplines exemplify values that permeated Hellenistic social life; on the other hand, they evoke an extremism that is exclusive rather than inclusive.

The Stoic philosophy claimed that all humanity shared in the single soul of the logos; all people became part of a universal human family. Christians adopted this belief, claiming all their members were part of the single "body of Christ." While clearly utilizing a common and thus inclusive idea found throughout the Hellenistic world, their use of this idea also fostered a greater unity among Christians, setting them apart from others. Their new family originally distinguished itself from the greater family of Hellenistic Rome. The Stoic ideal unified all people; the Christian adaptation unified only those who accepted Christianity.

Despite the particular emphasis found in these adaptations, early Christians showed a willingness to share in the cultural heritage of the Hellenistic world. They were less willing to accept the political practices that unified that world. Roman rulers followed a well-established pattern of identifying themselves with the divine. Christians, as well as other dissident Roman groups, rejected the worship of the Roman emperor as the incarnation of the divine. Roman leaders persecuted those whose religious convictions threatened their imperial unity. Opposing the imperial religion brought with it the charge of political rebelliousness.

The Christians became the object of such a charge, especially because of their association with Jewish messianism. The Romans looked at all messianic claimants as possible rebels. Palestinian "terrorists"—such as the Zealots—often followed one or another hopeful Messiah in a challenge against the imperial government. Seeking an inclusive ethics that would justify their beliefs against charges of insurrection, Christians insisted that Jesus' kingdom would be "not of this world." They developed a paradoxical view of divinity in which suffering became the means to redemption. This view, very similar to those held by devotees of Dionysus, enabled Christians to incorporate an ethic of concern for the poor, for women, and for the outcasts, even while standing aloof from the general society within which they lived. This political strategy led to a universalism that made the Christian message appealing to many people in the Roman world.

As this universalism developed, Christians became more comfortable preaching to the Roman world than to Jews. Their message took root among Gentiles in the Roman provinces and Asia Minor. Success in this outreach brought problems. Christians won adherents, but also opponents in the Roman world. What is clear is that opposition moved from Palestine to the greater Roman world. The emperor **Claudius** (41–54) expelled the Jews from Rome because of the trouble concerning the worship of Chrestus (sic) (Acts 11:28 and 18:2 refer to this event). Later Christians were persecuted not just as a Jewish sect, but as a potential threat to Roman cultural unity by various Roman emperors (**Nero** in 64, **Domitian** in 81–91).

The Christian response to the Jewish war against Rome suggests the orientation they took. Christians remained aloof from the war; they refused to join in the rebellion. This had the effect of alienating Jewish nationalists, but also of ensuring that Christianity, like rabbinic Judaism, would survive after the Romans won the war. Survival did not necessarily bring success, but it did mean that Christianity became more a Hellenistic religion than a Jewish one. Opposition to Christians lasted until the Roman Emperor Constantine (306–337 C.E.)made Christianity the imperial religion of Rome. Then Christianity became the model of licit or acceptable religion. All other forms of religion were now placed in the same vulnerable and uncertain position that Christians had once held. That change meant that the ethics of the Christian church would also need to undergo alteration.

The career of Paul of Tarsus is associated with this development (see Timeline 11–1). Not only was Paul an apostle who took as his purpose preaching to non-Jews, to Gentiles, but Paul was also the earliest apostle who claimed authority without having known Jesus during his earthly career. Paul gloried in the fact that he had been appointed not by one of the disciples who had followed Jesus, but by a visionary experience. He bases his authority on "reve-

Nero (who ruled as Roman Emperor from 54–68 C.E.) shown here on the ancient coin, persecuted Christians and may be the "beast" associated with the number 666 in the Revelation of John 13:18.

This portrait of a contemplative Paul by Rembrandt (1606–1669) evokes his influence as a seminal thinker in early Christianity.

lations" given him and describes being "caught up into Paradise and heard things that are not to be told, that no mortal is permitted to repeat" (2 Corinthians 12:3-4).

This type of authorization was open to all Christians, whether they had been part of the early community around Jesus or not. The priority of the Jewish Christians lay in their historical association with Jesus. When the risen Christ bestowed an equal authority on those living in the Diaspora, that undermined the priority of Jewish Christianity. These themes dominate Paul's writing.

Paul began as a Jew in Hellenized Asia Minor. He was trained in Judaism and defended tradition against Christianity. When a conversion experience convinced him to defect to the Christians, he became their advocate in the Hellenized world of Roman culture. Map 11–1 shows how the book of Acts imagines Paul's travels. Even if, as noted below, Acts is not always accurate, the map does show the expanding Christian presence in the Roman Empire. Paul travels from community to community, from Greece to Turkey to Syria and Palestine. By the end of his career, the center of Christianity moved from its beginnings in Jerusalem to Rome itself, the capital of the empire. Symbolically, Paul stands for the process by which Christianity became a universalist Roman religion rather than a Jewish sectarian group.

THE PAUL OF ACTS AND THE PAUL OF THE LETTERS

Because Paul serves such an important symbolic function, his writings were the earliest to be considered Christian scriptures. As Christianity developed, it became necessary to create

> **BOX 11–1   PAUL'S LETTERS**
>
> This chart describes the letters that scholars think of as either indisputably from the historical Paul of Tarsus or those that while considered "doubtful" may well be from Paul. You should locate the cities indicated on the map of Paul's journeys (see map 10–1) and look at the timeline 10–1.
>
> GENUINE:
>
> *1 Thessalonians*   Thessalonika was the capital of the Roman province of Macedonia. While Acts 17–18 thinks of this as a Jewish environment, this letter makes no reference to a synagogue or to Judaism. Paul expresses his basic view of the Christian message—to turn from idols to God and to wait for God's son, raised from the dead, who will return and bring final deliverance. 4:14–18 describe what has been called the "rapture"—that when Jesus comes again, the dead will rise first "Then we who are alive, who are left, will be caught up in the clouds together with them" (v.17). Paul refuses to predict when this will occur because it will come "like a thief in the night" (5:2–4).
>
> *1 Corinthians*   Corinth was a major port city in ancient Greece. This letter explores "true wisdom" (1:18–3:23), problems in the church such as internal dissension, sexual immorality, ritual performances and true apostleship, and correct procedure in church (11–15) including gender-specific customs and the meaning of the "Lord's Supper."
>
> *2 Corinthians*   Scholars think this work is composed of fragments from at least four separate letters. Chapters 10–13 are a vigorous defense of Paul's claim to being an apostle. The letter develops Paul's view of immortality.
>
> *Galatians*   The exact location of "Galatia" is unclear—either a place in Asia Minor or a Roman province. The letter describes Paul's call as an apostle, his emphasis on faith as the basis of a right relationship to the divine, his view of the relationship of Judaism to Christianity, and his perspective on such Jewish rituals as circumcision and dietary laws.
>
> *Romans*   This letter written about 57 C.E., addressed Christians in Rome before Paul had ever visited there. It opens with a statement of the human situation—sinners in the hands of an angry God. It develops the idea of faith as the only antidote to sin (rather than actions such as those demanded by Jewish law) and uses Abraham, the "father of faith," as his example. Christ is the "new Adam" whose sacrifice redeems the world from the sin of the "first Adam." Paul suggests that the Jewish scriptures, the Torah, had a place in God's plan that is now superseded, but that eventually Jews will be reintegrated into Christianity.

> *Philippians* Writing to the Macedonian city of Philippi, Paul tells of his imprisonment (1:12–26) He interprets suffering as a privilege and uses this occasion to include a hymn (2:6–11) that may well have been used in the early church liturgy.
>
> *Philemon* This letter, written while Paul was in prison, claims absolute spiritual liberty does not require social or political freedom. Paul, therefore, sends Onesimus to return to his former owner.
>
> DOUBTFUL:
> *2 Thessalonians* While, like 1 Thessalonians, focused on the second appearance of Jesus and even using some of the same language, the content of this letter differs considerably from the first. It lists several signs that signify the final age. Unlike the first letter this one does not expect Jesus' return (the Parousia) in the near future. These differences suggest either that Paul changed his mind radically or that a later author wanted to alter the ideas associated with Paul. That suspicion gains strength by a warning that forged letters have been circulating in Paul's name.
>
> *Colossians* Colossae was a small town in the Roman province of Asia. This letter uses greetings and names found in genuine Pauline letters. It offers a view of Christ as divine wisdom in ways not found otherwise in Paul's letters. A hymn in 1:15–20 uses Hellenistic concepts of divine wisdom and applies them to Jesus. The letter describes baptism as a transforming ritual that imitates Jesus' death and resurrection (2:8–15). The letter seems to use the genuine letters as its model (thus 3:11 "In that renewal there is no longer Greek and Jew, circumcised and uncircumcised, barbarian, Scythian, slave and free" seems to echo Galatians 3:28 "There is no longer Jew or Greek, slave or free, male and female").

a portrait of Paul consistent with the developing church. The book of Acts performs this task by continuing the history of early Christianity begun in the Gospel of Luke. Many themes, such as a concern for the poor and egalitarianism, link the gospel narrative and Acts. Acts describes the growth of Christianity into a "church"—that is, an institution with social and communal functions, rather than a message addressed purely to individuals. Acts centers on two heroes, Peter and Paul, understood as the joint founders of Christianity as a church. Much of the book describes the life and teachings of Paul, culminating in his trial before Agrippa, but ending before his judgment in Rome and presumably his death.

There are discrepancies between the Paul of Acts and the Paul of the Letters, both in chronology and substance (see Box 11–2). Even within Acts, the same incident may receive different treatments. Acts tells stories to illustrate theological points, rather than to report mundane details. One example is the way Paul's description of his conversion to Christianity in Galatians 1 contrasts with the story as told in Acts 9. Both narratives tell how Paul,

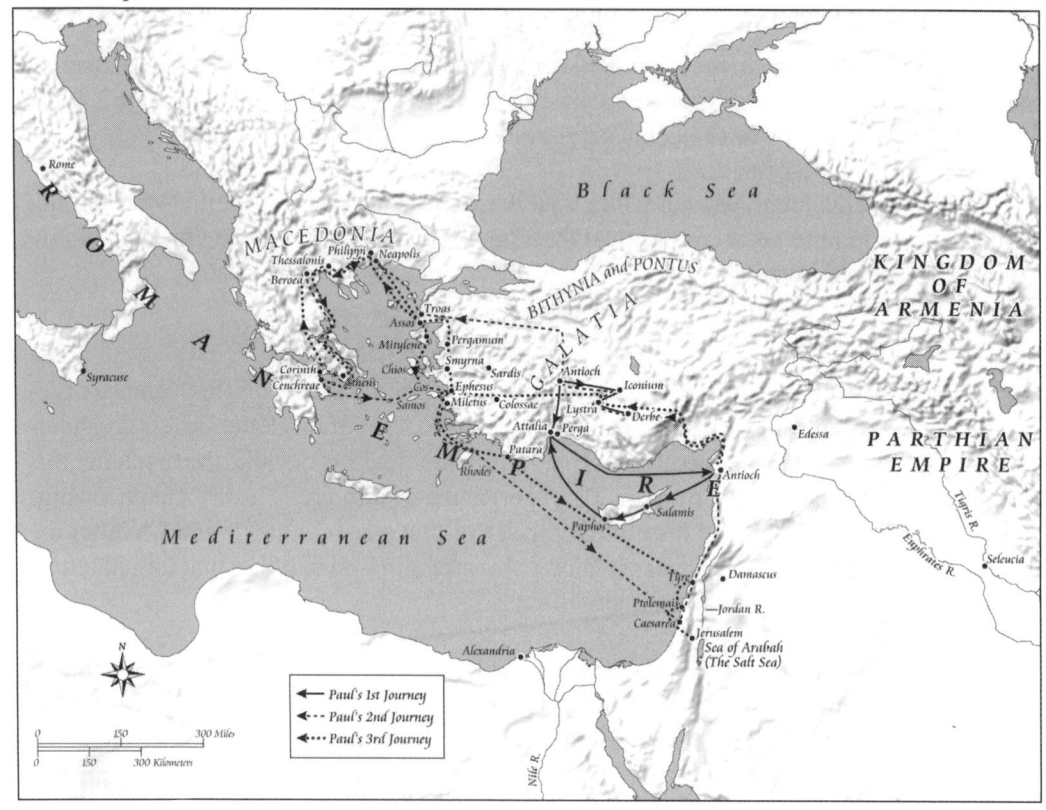

Map 11–1 The background of the New Testament, including Paul's travels

once a fanatical persecutor of Christians, received a vision of Jesus and thereupon became an ardent believer. Both texts agree that Paul had been a vigorous opponent of the Christians. He was a faithful Jew who opposed the new religious sect (Galatians 1:13–14; Acts 9:1–2).

Four major differences separate the two accounts. In Paul's own account, he receives a revelation from the divine (Galatians 1:15–16). He claims that he has been chosen from birth for this task, but he describes no supernatural events or miracles. Acts enhances the story by describing a vision—a blinding light from heaven and a voice telling him what to do. He falls onto the ground and arises blind. He goes immediately to Damascus and meets up with a leading Christian, Ananias, who lays hands upon him, cures his blindness, and baptizes him (Acts 9:3–10).

Paul's own report disagrees with this narrative. Paul claims he went to Arabia before going to Damascus. Paul explicitly claims that he never consulted with Christian leaders and tells of no miraculous blinding and healing (Galatians 1:17). The letter does not include a claim that Paul was baptized, nor that he received an influx of the Holy Spirit.

Acts describes how Paul preached in the synagogue in Damascus and "confounded the Jews" there so that, angered, they sought to kill him. He then escaped the city by being low-

BOX 11–2

This chart outlines the book of the Acts of the Apostles and lists some differences between information in Acts and information given in the genuine Pauline letters.

OUTLINE OF ACTS OF THE APOSTLES

1:1–2:47	The risen Christ and the influx of the Holy Spirit at Pentecost
3:1–5	The work of the apostle Paul and his asociates in establishing the Jerusalem Church (this is usually known as "Jewish" Christianity)
6:1–8:40	The problems facing the early Church—including the trial and martyrdom of Stephen
9	The first telling of the story of Paul's conversion
10–11	Peter learns to compromise on Jewish traditions such as circumcision and dietary laws
12	Persecutions by King Herod Agrippas II
13:1–15–35	Paul's first missionary journey
15:36–18:21	Paul's second missionary journey
18:22–20:38	Paul's third missionary journey
21:1–26:32	Paul's arrest in Jerusalem and speech before King Herod Agrippas (22:4–16, second account of Paul's conversion; 26:9–18, third description of Paul's conversion)
27:1–28:31	Paul comes to Rome, preaches there, and stays there for two years.

SOME DIFFERENCES BETWEEN PAUL'S OWN ACCOUNTS AND THE ACCOUNTS IN ACTS

Only Acts says Paul was named Saul

Only Acts says Paul studied under Gamaliel

Acts has Paul go to Damascus after his vision of Jesus; Galatians 1:12–17 speaks of a revelation of Jesus and of going to Arabia before going to Damascus

Acts 9 has Paul go to Jerusalem after Damascus; Galatians 1:17–20 states that Paul did not go to Jerusalem until three years after his mission to Damascus

Acts associates Paul with Ananias who baptizes him; Galatians 1 asserts that Paul needed no human authorization and never mentions that he was baptized

Acts describes a compromise on imposing Jewish dietary restrictions on Gentiles and forbidding the eating of food sacrificed to idols (Acts 15:19–21)

Acts is filled with miracles and experiences of the Holy Spirit not found in Paul's genuine letters (see Acts 13:4–12; 16:16–34; 19:11–20)

ered down the wall in a basket, after which he went to Jerusalem and was accepted by Peter and the leading Christians there (Acts 9:20–30). Paul's own letters claim that it was three years after his conversion and preaching in Damascus that he visited Jerusalem, and only fourteen years later that he associated with Barnabas there, and then only because a revelation told him that he should do so (Galatians 1:18–2:2).

The tale of escaping Damascus in a basket does occur in Paul's genuine letters, but Paul makes no connection between it and his coming to Jerusalem (2 Corinthians 11:32–34). Retelling of that story in Acts is meant to show that Paul was always a collaborator with the Jerusalem church, and that his teachings correspond to the normative tradition.

PAUL'S RELIGION: THE BOOK OF ACTS

Paul, as presented in Acts, illustrates the view of a continuity of divine intent stretching from the Jewish Bible through Christianity. Acts provides Paul with a pedigree not found in his genuine letters; he has a Hebrew name (Saul) and has studied with a Palestinian rabbi, one whom Acts claims defended Christianity, **Gamaliel** (see Acts 5:34–39, 22:5). This portrait of Paul as standing within the Jewish tradition fits the general contention in Acts that Christianity continues and completes Jewish tradition.

Acts 7 emphasizes the continuity between Jewish and Christian origins, particularly in a speech that recapitulates Jewish history as a prelude to the coming of Jesus. Put into the mouth of the Jewish-Christian **Stephen** as a justification for his martyrdom, Acts 7 takes a very positive view of the early Jewish heroes. Abraham, Joseph, and Moses are treated as worthy figures devoted to God and God's will (Acts 7:2–22). That will seems to demand personal loyalty of his followers, rather than either observance of detailed laws or sacrificial worship. The overriding sin is disloyalty—evidenced in the Golden Calf and in the rejection of Jesus. Acts 7 reserves its wrath for the Jewish people as a whole, for the mass of the nation (Acts 7:23–53). This is a people stiff-necked in nature and "uncircumcised of heart" (Acts 7:51), failing to recognize the duties necessary for serving God. Jesus, in Acts 7, stands within the line of tradition begun with Abraham and carried on through Joseph, David, and Solomon. Jewish history is definitive for Acts 7, even while it points beyond itself. Jews, because they do not see this continuity, cannot understand the new world that Jesus has initiated.

Acts 28 puts the same sentiments into a speech attributed to Paul. Echoing passages from the Hebrew prophets, Paul announces that his message is being sent to the Gentiles because the very nature of the Jewish people prevents Jews from understanding the revelations that they have received. Paul emphasizes that he has "done nothing against our people or the customs of our ancestors" and shows that his task has already been authorized by the Jewish scriptures. He turns to the law of Moses and the prophets to persuade Jews of the authenticity of the Christian mission. These arguments do not convince those who disbelieve, but they do establish Paul as being within the Jewish tradition, as preaching lessons continuous with that tradition, and as meriting the respect and authority associated with traditional Jewish identity. This Paul uses Jewish history as the basis for his claims. Acts pictures Paul beginning with the story of the Exodus from Egypt and continuing with the example of Jesus as "the good news that what God promised to our ancestors he has fulfilled for us" (Acts 13:16–35).

The view of the divine found in Acts emphasizes the Holy Spirit and its mediation between God and humanity. Acts 1–2 describe how the disciples gathered in Jerusalem for the Jewish holiday of Pentecost, the celebration that occurs fifty days after Passover, and therefore, according to Luke, fifty days after Jesus' resurrection. For Jews, this holiday recalls the giving of revelation at Mount Sinai. In Acts, however, the holiday commemorates the influx of the Holy Spirit on Jesus' disciples. This event not only occurs at a time traditionally associated with revelation, but is also explicitly associated with a prophecy in the Hebrew Bible associated with an eschatological fulfillment of God's messianic promise, that of Joel 2:28–32. When the gift of speaking in tongues (technically called **glossolalia**) possesses the disciples, it confirms their authority and validity.

The Apostle Peter contends that people should repent and be baptized in the name of Jesus Christ so that their sins are forgiven, and then the Holy Spirit will come upon them (Acts 2:38). The descent of the Holy Spirit provides tangible evidence that a person has been forgiven and has been accepted as a Christian. God's immanence, in this view, confirms the spiritual power of Christian ritualism. While God is transcendent in power and strength, God is also immanent in the Spirit that informs the personality of believers.

God's power invests his intermediaries with authority. That seems to be the connecting link between the various descriptions of how Saul of Tarsus, a Jew who persecuted Christians, became Paul, the disciple of Christianity to the Gentiles. That tale is told in three versions: Acts 9, Acts 22, and Acts 26. The point in each of these tales is less that God has appeared to Paul, but rather that such an appearance justifies and legitimates his function as a Christian disciple. In Acts 9 Paul is on the road to Damascus (Acts 9:3–9). He sees a vision of Jesus, who commissions him to go to the Christian Ananias. Paul is struck blind, but Ananais restores his sight and baptizes him (Acts 9:10–19). This is a vision meant to convince Paul of his own authority. In it, he alone sees the vision of Jesus addressing him and telling him what to do. Those who are with him hear what is said, but do not know the source of what they hear.

Acts 22 has Paul retelling the story to convince a Jewish audience. In this case, he claims that everyone saw the light, but he alone was blinded, and that he alone heard the words being spoken (vv. 6–12). This way of describing the vision has more in common with a Jewish view of divinity—an emphasis on divine transcendence and the personal nature of revelation—and describes Ananias not only as a Christian, but also as a fully observant Jew (v. 12). These elements show that the vision of the divine combines with the other elements in the story to be a persuasive argument to a Jewish audience concerning Paul's authority.

Acts 26 has a different audience—King **Herod Agrippa** II. For that audience, Paul tells only that God appeared to him and gave him his commission of preaching. God is said to have spoken not in Greek, but in Hebrew, thus echoing the other revelations given to the

Jewish people—a point not made in previous renditions of the story (v. 14). Those accompanying Paul fade into the background; they neither hear nor see anything of the revelation. No miracle occurs. Paul is neither struck blind nor cured of his blindness. His one defense is that he did not disobey the heavenly vision and its instructions. Here, even more explicitly than in the other version, the purpose of a divine revelation is to convey instructions, to commission authority.

Miracles, then, are symbols of authority. When Paul and **Silas** are imprisoned for exorcising a girl suffering from a "spirit of divination," God heeds their prayers and shakes the foundations of the prison with an earthquake that sets all prisoners free (Acts 16:16–34). Paul, in Acts, asserts a view of divine transcendence similar to that of the philosophers. He explains to the Athenians that the divine he worships is identical with their "unknown god" (Acts 17:22–28). He interprets this divinity in a Stoic fashion as a creative spirit that exists in and above all things, a divinity of philosophical dimensions. Although Paul does go on to preach the idea of resurrection (17:31–33), which makes some Athenian philosophers scoff, this philosophical approach complements the intermediary power attributed to the Holy Spirit throughout the book of Acts.

Paul's speech in Acts 17 represents an inclusive ethics. He willingly addresses Jews with concepts drawn from their experience and Gentiles with ideas congruent with their thought. Chapter 19 seems to go even further in this inclusive ethics. The chapter begins by contrasting John the Baptist's rituals with those of the Christians. The former only brought about repentance; the latter invests believers with the Holy Spirit (19:1–9). The chapter continues as Paul performs many miracles. When several magicians passing through begin to use both the name of Jesus and of Paul in their spells, the ritual works (19:11–20). This leads to widespread recognition of the truth of Christianity. Paul's true belief seems to convince even magicians, who abandon their books and practices to join his community. This is an open society in which all types of Gentiles, even philosophers and magicians, find a home.

Paul's willingness to compromise in the name of an inclusive ethics finds fullest expression in the compromises he makes in Acts 15. The chapter sets up a tension between those Christian leaders who accept Gentiles within the church without demanding that they fulfill all Jewish laws, and those who require strict observance of Jewish practice among Gentile converts to Judaism (Acts 15:5 identifies them as Christians who at one time had been Pharisees). Peter testifies in favor of allowing Gentiles in because the Holy Spirit came to them (v. 8). Paul and Barnabas relate the signs and wonders that God had done through the Gentiles.

Finally, the inclusive ethics triumphs, and the word goes out that "it has seemed good to the Holy Spirit and to us to impose on you no further burden than these essentials: that you abstain from what has been sacrificed to idols and from blood and from what is strangled, and from fornication" (vv. 28–29). Gentiles need observe only a minimum of ritual and ethical commandments.

Ethics and ritual intertwine in Acts, as Peter's testimony in Acts 15:8 suggests. The association of the Holy Spirit and ritual performances suggests that ritual has a substantive, transforming effect. Acts 10–11 reinforces this view. Chapter 10 describes how the prayers of a certain centurion, **Cornelius**, reach God so that an angel intervenes on his behalf (10:1–7). The Apostle Peter has a dream indicating an open acceptance of food forbidden by Jewish dietary laws and the command: "What God has made clean, you must not call profane" (vv. 9–16). When Cornelius explains that God has heard his prayers and sent him an angel, Peter exclaims, "I truly understand that God shows no partiality, but in every nation anyone who fears him and does what is right is acceptable to him" (vv. 34–35). As Peter preaches, the Holy Spirit fills both Jews and Gentiles (v. 44), showing the transformative power of preaching. Chapter 11 defends Peter's decision to baptize Gentiles no less than circumcised Jews. The descent of the Holy Spirit as a result of Peter's preaching is the ultimate proof that Peter acted correctly (vv. 17–18). The power of ritual to evoke such a divine experience makes it a transforming, substantive activity.

PAULINE RELIGION: GENUINE AND DISPUTED LETTERS

The genuine and the disputed letters attributed to Paul of Tarsus offer different religious perspectives than those of the book of Acts. The stylistic approach, in and of itself, reflects an ethics of inclusiveness, rather than a separatist ethics. Paul self-consciously uses the Hellenistic style of letter writing. He follows the general format of that style: a prescript, greeting, a message, and a conclusion. While he inserts specifically Christian references in each of them, his choice of form shows his desire to fit into the general cultural context.

This acceptance of a new cultural mode indicates that, for Paul, history advances by stages. The pattern of history certainly fulfills God's intention, but what is appropriate at one stage may not be so in another. Paul's complex discussion of the relationship between Judaism and Christianity makes this clear. Paul's genuine letters stress a decisive historical break occurring with the Christ event (the death and resurrection of Jesus). Just as Adam's sin introduced a drastic change in history, so the Christ—the New Adam—introduces a new age (Romans 5:12–21). This distinctiveness leads to Paul's ambiguity about the relationship between Judaism and Christianity. The Jews seem to misunderstand their own history and how it leads into the new history. Eventually, however, they will comprehend (Romans 9; 11:1–24).

This new historical era marks a dramatic shift from what had come before, a shift that owes everything to the freely given will of God. Romans 4 explains that all history depends on voluntary acts of the divine, and that true religious belief, true faith, lies in accepting that will. Abraham's story as told in the Hebrew Bible, according to Paul, reveals such a faith. Abraham believed God's promise in Genesis 15:5–6 despite empirical evidence that would seem to contradict it. Abraham's saga, therefore, teaches the unpredictability of history and the way its surprises reveal the divine will.

That view of Abraham contrasts with the traditional Jewish understanding of an unchanging covenant given to Abraham and through him to the Jewish people. Paul (in Galatians

3–4) explicitly reflects on the relationship between Judaism and Christianity. Paul recognizes that Jews trace their history back to Jacob, his father Isaac, and his parents Abraham and Sarah.Unlike Acts 7, however, Paul does not accept Jewish history as functional. Indeed, he rejects the idea of a continuous line of leadership, even within the Hebrew Bible. The problem is not that the Jews do not recognize the continuity of this new revelation with their old revelation, but that they do not acknowledge the radical discontinuity that always manifests itself in divine acts. Paul notes that Isaac was the younger of Abraham's sons. The elder, and by law more primary, son was Ishmael, whose mother was Hagar the Egyptian. The son by Sarah was preferred not by any right, but by God's free choice.

Paul emphasizes this story to show that divine will, not historical destiny, determines which group can claim to be God's people. In his own time, Paul insists, Gentiles have come to inherit the mantle of "the chosen people" by the same free will of the deity. Romans 9 uses God's choice of the descendants of Isaac, rather than the descendants of Ishmael, as a case in point (Romans 9:6–9). Just as God decided that only one set of heirs were worthy of the divine message at that time, so in the new era God has chosen that the spiritual descendants of Abraham should replace his genealogical descendants (Romans 9:30–33). This change from one set of heirs to another initiates a new period in human history.

Paul's view of the deity reflects this understanding of history. God interrupts history by intruding into human experience. God is transcendent, and so beyond human experience, but also immanent, as shown by Jesus' crucifixion and resurrection. Christians have an immediate experience of the divine; they live in the Christ, and thus are part of God, as God is part of them. Although historically the incarnation of God in Jesus and the crucifixion and resurrection occurred but once, Paul claims that they constantly reoccur. Every Christian recapitulates the experience of Christ. Each is crucified by discovering the transcendent judgment that renders mere earthly meaning insufficient, and each is resurrected to a new life as part of the extended body of Christ. The Christians have been clothed in God. Galatians 3:27 states that "those of you who were baptized into Christ have put on Christ."

Such a view underlies Paul's perception of his own call as a disciple. Galatians 1–2 justifies Paul's mission in terms of the new program of salvation that God initiated with the Christ event. Rather than speak of a sudden revelation, Paul claims that he had been chosen even before his birth to be part of this new historical moment (Galatians 1:15–16). God has been creating a new reality—the reality of life in Christ Jesus. Paul insists that God oversees the sweep of history as a transcendent force that stands above all mundane history. God works through his chosen servants such as Paul. Paul often speaks of acting on the basis of a revelation and notes that he has been selected for that revelation because he has ascended into the heights (2 Corinthians 12:1–4). That transcendence, however, combines with a sense of divine immanence through the incarnation of God in Jesus.

Whether the hymn in Philippians 2 is actually from Paul or merely quoted by him from Christian liturgy, it still reflects a sense of the immanent divinity. The divine is poured into the human form, the form of a slave (2:7). Divine humility extends even to the experience of death (2:8). That immanence forms the basis for the true exaltation of the divine. God is not only immanent but also transcendent. Using the language of Isaiah 45:23 (cited also in Romans 14:11), the hymn calls upon all to kneel before God and to confess the divine greatness.

In the genuine Pauline letters, then, divinity is intuited through the salvation brought by Christ's incarnation in Jesus. In contrast, Colossians, a letter that shares stylistic and theological similarities with Ephesians, a letter most scholars think is clearly not from Paul, offers a very different Christology, or view of the divine in Christ. Again, this disputed letter has advocates who claim that it represents one of the ways Paul varied his thought. Whether the letter is or is not genuinely Pauline, however, it does present a distinctive view of divinity.

Colossians 1 presents Jesus as the perfect image of the divine creator who has no image. Through Jesus, humanity glimpses the divinity in its truest form. Jesus represents a way to know God, an insight into the nature of the deity. Christ in this letter, unlike in Galatians or Romans, does not stand for divine activism, for an immanent divinity transforming the world, but rather for the ideal creator, for God as the designer of the cosmos. Paul's commission, in this reading, is to convey a mystery that had been hidden previously, to uncover a secret truth that only now is being revealed (Colossians 1:25–26).

One aspect of Paul's view of God's plan for humanity does emphasize the mystery of the divine intention—his expectation of the Parousia—Christ's final appearance. Jesus' returning to earth will, Paul thinks, inaugurate the final age, the concluding stage of history. The Christ event inaugurated the new historical era, but a second revelation, the Parousia, will complete it. 1 Thessalonians 4:13–5:10 develops a theory of this completed history. Those who have died in the time before the Parousia will be joined to those who are still alive. They will all be caught up—**raptured** (the term, taken from the Greek for being taken up, is now used for the event itself)—into heaven, and the final stage in the new history will take place. That event will be the culmination of all actions since the first appearance of Jesus. It is not a strikingly different reality the way the first appearance was. It will happen stealthily, without warning (1 Thessalonians 5:2–4), coming like a "thief in the night." Paul, therefore, cautions his followers to be consistent, to remain awake, to be prepared for that day, which will overtake them as part of a continuous history.

2 Thessalonians challenges that view of history as divided into these two parts: before and after the Christ event. Because this view of history disagrees with 1 Thessalonians, and because of its strange structure and differing vocabulary, many scholars suggest that this work is not a genuine Pauline letter. Other scholars, while claiming that the book is genuinely Pauline, still acknowledge that its content and message differ significantly from the former letter and explain these differences as Paul's later reflections on the subject of the end of time.

For 2 Thessalonians, the Parousia will itself represent a break with history. It will inaugurate still another stage in world history (2 Thessalonians 2:7–12). Whereas the genuine letters see demonic forces already conquered, 2 Thessalonians sees them still at work. The devil has taken charge of this age, so that only Christians have been assured salvation (2

Thessalonians 3:1–5). Even more astonishingly, the author of this letter provides clues and hints by which to determine when the Parousia will occur.

Paul's view of ethics follows from his understanding of the new stage in God's history, begun with the Christ event and preparatory for the final age. Ethical behavior is meant to enable Christians to enter that final age and be redeemed. Paul embraces Roman culture and incorporates the commonly accepted virtues of the Greco-Roman world into his writing. He lists virtues widely accepted in the Hellenistic world—such as love, kindness, goodness, and self-control—as given to Christians as "the fruit of the spirit" (Galatians 5:22). Christians do not need to strive after these virtues; they follow from the reality of being one with God. If people do lapse back into immoral behavior, no exhortation or condemnation will do any good. People cannot heal themselves; they must wait for God's grace. Paul therefore counsels his followers to be patient and gentle to those who are "overtaken in any trespass" (Galatians 6:1). This ethics appears inclusive since it accepts those who fail to meet Paul's high standards. Those high standards, however, are the distinctive mark of the "true" Christian. The distinction between the real Christian who is automatically ethical and the Christian who has strayed shows the exclusive nature of Paul's view of ethics.

At first glance, Paul's ethics seem inclusive because he believes that the event of Christ Jesus, the new stage in world history, has created a new sort of community. God now lives within the Christian, so that each Christian has a new identity—neither Jew nor Gentile, male nor female, slave nor free—but exists as part of the body of the divine. This inclusion of opposites surpasses human understanding and leads to a recognition of the mystery of life. This new community manifests itself in members who perform ethical actions not out of duty or habit, but out of their innate nature (Galatians 3:27–28). The ethical egalitarianism matches a ritual one as well.

Nevertheless, many of Paul's actual inculcations are divisive and exclusive. Paul accepts slavery as part of human society, although he emphasizes that all Christians are equal and "free" in the spirit (see Philemon). Although women lead prayers and offer prophecies, they, unlike men, must cover their heads and, again unlike men, should be veiled. Still, both men and women perform the same functions of leading prayers and offering prophecies. Although men and women are dependent on each other, Paul follows Roman custom in making women subordinate (1 Corinthians 11:1–16). Theologically, he traces the beginning of sin back to Eve, the first woman, and lays on her the blame for Adam's actions (1 Corinthians 2:8–15).

The ethical injunctions in Galatians 5:16–6:10 provide a good example of the content of Pauline ethics. That content affirms general Hellenistic virtues: love, peace, generosity, self-control, and self-criticism. The central principle involved resembles that of the Roman Stoics: avoid the temptations of the flesh and cultivate spiritual discipline. Such behavior, according to Galatians, not only strengthens the virtue of the individual, but also works for the general welfare of all people (Galatians 6:10). The path to these virtues, however, is distinctively Christian. Rules of behavior as such, laws regulating actions, and disciplines teaching self-control are beside the point. These are necessary only for people who are still struggling against the temptations of the body. When a person becomes a Christian, such struggles cease. The Hellenistic virtues appear naturally, not as the result of an athletic or ascetic effort.

Romans 13 expresses Paul's hierarchic view of ethics. People are to be subject to governing authorities because God has set such rulers in power (vv. 1–7). He enumerates Jewish legal prescriptions against adultery, murder, stealing, and covetousness (vv. 8–10). Christians, he insists, should live "honorably," avoiding all sorts of debauchery, quarrels, and other vices (vv. 13–14). This type of a morality, while subsumed under the general principle of loving one's neighbor (v. 13), reinforces the structure of society and the hierarchy of the social order. In this way, Pauline ethics creates an exclusive community, one in which only those who live up to an ideal moral code can participate. Moral behavior limits membership in the Christianity that Paul envisions.

While ethical behavior determines who will or who will not be considered a "true" Christian, who will be rewarded with rapture at the final stage of history, and who must be excluded from the community, Paul has a different view of ritual. Ritual does not accomplish any transformative function. It symbolizes loyalty to a particular group or the ideals held by that group. For that reason, Paul rejects the ritual of circumcision (also rejected in Colossians 2:11, 3:11). Becoming a Christian entails taking on a new identity. This identity transcends the ritual distinction between Jew and Gentile. Paul argues that "neither circumcision nor uncircumcision is anything; but a new creation is everything" (Galatians 6:15). Nevertheless, Paul recognizes that rituals do have significance, even those of Judaism. He notes both that dietary laws have no intrinsic value and that they do have importance for some individuals. While all foods are permitted, if someone informs you that something has been "offered as a sacrifice," then you should not eat it because such an act would disturb the person who informed you (Romans 10:23–33).

Ritual actions, however, do play an important role in the Christianity that Paul imagines. He discusses the reenactment of Jesus' last meal as a crucial practice (1 Corinthians 11). He notes that the ritual does act as a reminder of history and is meant as such a reminder. He goes beyond this, however, to insist that it be consumed in an appropriately solemn manner and with a devotional attitude (11:27–34). These verses imply that there is a substantive power to the ritual. Correctly performed, the rite can strengthen the worshiper; incorrectly performed, it weakens worshipers and leaves them prey to sicknesses. That apparent substantive judgment should be put in the context of Paul's most extended treatment of ritual in 1 Corinthians 12–13.

Paul understands ritual as part of an entire system of Christian life. The body of Christianity, he claims, is composed of many members, each of which has its own function and purpose (1 Corinthians 12:12–13). Some of those functions do seem to illustrate substantive rituals: prophecy indicates a transformed person who has become a vehicle by which God's spirit speaks; gifts of healing and the performing of miracles also operate upon the external world and make it different. At the same time, other types of activity—such as preaching, teaching, and charitable deeds towards others—are indicative rather than transforming; they show the world the nature of Christian life, rather than altering the world or even the individuals involved. 1 Corinthians 13:1–4 makes the extraordinary statement that various transformative activities—speaking in tongues, prophetic oracles, miracle working—are all secondary to actions of concern for others.

By making this claim, Paul suggests that ritual actions have a substantive effect, but only insofar as they transform the social order. Ritual performances enhance the spiritual experience for believers. By doing this, they strengthen the community. The rituals, however, were not taken as ends in themselves, but rather as a means to the final end of creating a true and cohesive religious body. Thus Paul prefers prophecy to speaking in tongues because it, at least, is talking to human beings and may be comprehensible (1 Corinthians 14:2). Whether ritual involves prophecy, the eating of the Eucharist, or the preaching in tongues, the point is not to glorify transformative ritual, but to couch that transformation in terms of a celebration of the unified community created when taking on the identity of being a Christian.

SUMMARY QUESTIONS

1. How did Christianity develop as it adapted to the Hellenistic world?
2. How do the different versions of Paul's conversion, both in Acts and in Galatians, differ in the religious views expressed?
3. What are the ideas of history, the divine, ethics, and ritual expressed in Acts of the Apostles?
4. How do the views of history and the divine differ in 1 Thessalonians and 2 Thessalonians?
5. What views of ethics and ritual are expressed in Paul's letters?

Four Suggested Essay Questions

1. Explain two ways in which a tradition may view history. Apply one of them to the view of the Parousia in 1 Thessalonians and one to that in 2 Thessalonians.
2. Explain two ways in which a tradition may view the supernatural. Apply one of them to Acts 17:22–28 and the other to Philippians 2:5–11.
3. Explain two ways in which a tradition may view ethics. Apply one of them to Romans 13 and the other to Acts 15.
4. Explain two ways in which a tradition may view ritual. Apply one to the view of the Lord's Supper in 1 Corinthians 11 and the other to that of Ananias' laying on of hands in Acts 9:10–19.

Exercise

Write an introduction for an answer to Question 3 by writing the following (you may want to note to yourself, but not in the introduction, which concept applies to Romans 13 and which to Acts 15):

1. Create a topic sentence that contrasts ethics as a set of detailed rules to that of ethics as a minimum standard of behavior for a diverse group of people.
2. Write a sentence explaining the general significance of an ethics of detailed rules.
3. Write a sentence explaining the general significance of an ethics as a minimum standard of behavior.
4. Write a sentence connecting an ethics of detailed rules to the idea of an imminent end to history.
5. Write a sentence connecting an ethics of minimum standards to a view that belonging to a religious group makes all members equal.

FOR FURTHER READING

The books listed below should be a point of departure for your future study. These books are general introductions rather than focused on one specific letter of Paul. Each includes a bibliography that will guide you beyond its basic information.

1. Christiansen, Ellen Juhl, *The Covenant in Judaism and Paul: A Study of Ritual Boundaries as Identity Markers* (Leiden: E.J. Brill, 1995).
2. Gager, John G., *Reinventing Paul* (Oxford, England: Oxford University Press, 2002).
3. Levine, Amy-Jill and Marianne Blickenstaff, eds., *A Feminist Companion to Paul* (London: T & T International, 2004).
4. Malina, Bruce and Neyrey, Jerome H., *Portraits of Paul: An Archaeology of Ancient Personality* (Louisville, KY: Westminster John Knox Press, 1996).
5. Neusner, Jacob, *Children of the Flesh, Children of the Promise: A Rabbi Talks with Paul* (Cleveland, OH: Pilgrim Press, 1995).
6. Park, Eung Chun, *Either Jew or Gentile: Paul's Unfolding Theology of Inclusivity* (Louisville, KY: Westminster John Knox Press, 2003).
7. Patte, Daniel, *Paul's Faith and the Power of the Gospel: A Structural Introduction to the Pauline Letters* (Philadelphia, PA: Fortress Press, 1983).
8. Sanders, E. P., *Paul* (Oxford: Oxford University Press, 1991).
9. Tabor, James D., *The Jesus Dynasty: The Hidden History of Jesus, His Royal Family, and the Birth of Christianity* (New York: Simon & Schuster, 2006).

10. Wasterholm, Stephen., *Israel's Law and the Church's Faith: Paul and His Recent Interpreters* (Grand Rapids, MI: W.B. Eerdmans, 1998).

11. Watson, Francis, *Paul, Judaism, and the Gentiles: A Sociological Approach* (Cambridge, England: Cambridge University Press, 1986).

12

Religions of the Later Letters

READING ASSIGNMENT

Ephesians (complete)
1 Timothy (complete)
2 Timothy (complete)
Titus (complete)
Hebrews (complete)
James (complete)
1 Peter (complete)
2 Peter (complete)
1 John, 2 John, 3 John (all complete)
Jude (complete)

LEARNING OBJECTIVES

By the end of this lesson, you will be able to:

Describe the views of the divine, history, ethics, and ritual in Ephesians and in the Pastoral Letters.

Describe the views of the divine, history, ethics, and ritual in the Johannine letters.

Describe the views of the divine, history, ethics, and ritual in the Letter to the Hebrews.

Describe the views of the divine, history, ethics, and ritual in James, 1 Peter, and 2 Peter.

Interpretive Matrix for Chapter Twelve

View of the Divine: How people interact with God and the supernatural; how God interacts with the world.	View of History: How past, present, and future are related; who controls the shape of events.	View of Ethics: How people behave toward other people; how they behave toward people like themselves and to those who are different.	View of Ritual: How people behave toward the Divine; how they perform religious actions.
The Divine as Transcendent: God is assigned the good in the world and another power is assigned the evil in the world. God acts as a heavenly priest.	*History as Continuous:* References are made to earlier texts as the basis for new ideas. Patterns of events in the present mirror patterns found in the past.	*Inclusive Ethics:* Varieties of belief and action are affirmed. Ethical rules of the group reflect those of the general society.	*Ritual as Transforming:* Ritual conveys holiness to those whom it touches and can invest people with religious authority. Rituals can provide forgiveness for sins.
The Divine as Immanent: God intervenes into human lives to help those who face temptation and persecution. God becomes incarnate in the world. God takes an interest in and judges human actions.	*History as Discontinuous:* A new age will reverse the status of people and justify those who are currently suffering.	*Exclusive Ethics:* Some people are designated people of God and others are designated people of the devil. Men and women are assigned different roles. Heretical ideas and practices are explicitly rejected.	*Ritual as Symbolic:* Rituals distinguish between followers of one tradition and those of an older tradition. Prayers for the welfare of the general culture demonstrate political loyalty and good citizenship.

INTRODUCTION

Christians experienced both success and persecution in the ancient world (see Timeline 12–1). They responded to both experiences in diverse ways. Sometimes Christians affirmed the Roman environment and its basic values; sometimes Christians condemned that environment and considered it evil. This ambivalence toward the non-Christian world in which they lived can be found in the finalized canon of the New Testament. Not only does the canon include the letters of Paul, but also several other letters (see Box 12–1). Most are "pseudonymous" in authorship; later writers composed them using the name of an earlier religious figure. Today we might call such an approach "forgery," but in the first century this practice of **pseudonymity** was both common and acceptable. The authors genuinely saw themselves writing in the spirit of the person whose name they used.

Religions of the Later Letters 261

The books of Ephesians, 1 and 2 Timothy, and Titus all express sentiments steeped in the tradition of Paul of Tarsus. The last three are usually grouped together as the Pastoral Epistles because they display a concern for church organization and shepherding a religious flock. The letters of 1, 2, and 3 John represent a distinctive community within early Christianity. James, Jude, 1 and 2 Peter reflect the approach of other Christian communities. The Johannine letters and those of James, Jude, 1 and 2 Peter, and Hebrews are often linked together as Catholic or General Epistles, addressed to an audience at large rather than specific communities. That the New Testament includes so many distinct communal forms suggests both the diversity and tolerance of early Christianity.

SOME IMPORTANT TERMS

The following terms are important in this chapter. Some of them have been listed in previous chapters; in those cases the term is not **bold** in the main body of this chapter. The terms are also found in the Glossary.

Aaron	Elder (Presbyter)	Melchizedek
Abel	Elijah	Mortal Sin
Abraham	Enoch	Moses
Antichrist	Eschatology	Myth
Balaam	Gomorrah	Nero
Barnabas	Heresy	Noah
Bishop	Holy Spirit	Pliny the Younger
Cain	Incarnation	Pseudonymity
Catholic Letters	Jerusalem Temple	Sabbath
Clement of Rome	Justin Martyr	Sarah
Codex Sinaiticus	Korach	Satan
Deacon	Levites	Sodom
Didache	Liturgy	Trajan
Domitian	Lot	
Donatism	Marcion	

THE HISTORICAL CONTEXT OF THE LATER LETTERS

The later letters in the New Testament were composed during a period of growth and turmoil in the early church (see timeline 12–1). After 70 C.E. and the destruction of the Jerusalem Temple, Christianity developed as a primarily Gentile rather than Jewish, movement. Whereas the Apostle Paul struggled against Christians often called Judaizers who insisted that Christians observe Jewish laws, later leaders confronted heresies, alternative Christian doctrine they considered false and untrue. While some heresies maintained Jewish practice, others rejected Judaism entirely. In 140 the church in Rome expelled a certain leader, Marcion, as a heretic. He continued as a major Christian thinker and leader for several years later. His views have been discussed in Chapter 3.

The letter of 1 Clement, written in about 90–100 C.E., raises the question of true leadership and its continuity that concerned people of this time. The letter is not part of the accepted biblical canon, and it does not claim to be from **Clement the bishop of Rome** or the Clement mentioned in Philippians 4:3. It does, however, purport to be a letter from Rome to the Christian congregation in Corinth and reflects the first-century issues facing Christianity. Leadership is explained using the model of warfare: all divisions have their purposes and functions; all soldiers have their place and their stations. A chain of traditional leadership leads directly from Christ to the Apostles to **bishops**, **deacons**, and **elders**.

The letter claims that scripture already predicted the divisions and conflicts within the church concerning leadership, and that faithfulness and righteousness are the best guides. This declaration suggests that leadership and its authenticity were issues for the early church. The ethics of the later letters focuses on this question of legitimate leaders. The growth and development of the church made deciding between "true" and "inauthentic" leaders an essential process. Who should be included as a true Christian, and who should be excluded?

Ritual matters also developed slowly. The Letter of Barnabas, a text considered authoritative in the fourth-century manuscript scholars call the Codex Sinaiticus, not only rejects Jewish rituals but, citing texts such as Amos 5 and Isaiah 58, contends that God requires moral actions rather than ritual deeds. Equally importantly, the letter defends such customs as the Sunday Sabbath and baptism, suggesting controversy over the place of rituals in the early church. Several documents from this time (the Didache, 1 Clement, the writings of Justin Martyr) make the Sunday Sabbath a central issue. As the church grew and expanded, the questions of which rituals to observe and the manner of their observance became significant.

While Christianity expanded, it also encountered resistance, and the writings of this period reflect this situation. Scholars are unsure when the persecutions mentioned in 1 Clement occurred; they believe those in the Letter of Barnabas should be dated to the time of Domitian (81–96 C.E.). In both cases, the works relate contemporary struggles to suffering undergone by ancient biblical heroes and contemporary ones in which the faithful of God were made to suffer. Christians aroused resistance in the Roman world as they gained more followers and, because of their refusal to accept the imperial cult, raised questions about the established order.

A certain **Pliny the Younger** governed a Roman province, that of Bithynia (in what is now Turkey) and wrote to the emperor **Trajan** (98–117) for advice on dealing with the Christians. His letter reveals the hostility with which the official imperial cult viewed Christianity, a sectarian group that refused to worship the emperor. He considers them a strange and dangerous sect that practices obscure and bloodthirsty rituals; they have a common meal in which they eat their divinity. Trajan responded with moderation. If Christians cause trou-

TIMELINE 12–1   CHRONOLOGY OF THE LATER LETTERS IN THE NEW TESTAMENT

79–81	Titus is emperor of Rome
80	The Didache is written
81–96	Domitian is emperor; persecution of Christians
86–117	Trajan is emperor; persecution of Christians
80–100	Letter of James
65–90	Book of Hebrews
90–100	1 Clement
100–110	Johanine Letters (1, 2, 3, John)
117–138	Hadrian is emperor; Bar Kokhba revolt (135)
100–140	Pastoral Letters: 1, 2 Timothy, Titus, Jude, 1 Peter
100–165	Justin Martyr
130	Letter of Barnabus
138–161	Antonius Pius is emperor
After 140	2 Peter
313	Constantine (Emperor of Rome 306–377) declares tolerance of Christinaity

ble, they should be dealt with; they should not, however, be sought out or persecuted as a general group. That moderation did not prevent Trajan himself from initiating some persecution against Christians.

Confronting this situation, Christian texts developed a dualistic approach, drawing on a rich tradition that goes back to Zoroasterian teachings and early Jewish writings. Both the Didache and the Letter of Barnabas develop a theory of the "two ways" a person can choose: the way of life, light, and goodness is the way of God; the way of death, darkness, and evil is the way of the devil. This dualism pervades history. Sometimes history continues an eternal struggle between good and evil. From creation through the end of history, the two are locked in conflict.

Sometimes history appears discontinuous. A dramatic change will occur soon in which the age of the devil gives way to the age of God. In both these cases, the devil appears as a major figure, becoming prominent as a way of making sense of dangerous times. This has implications for a view of divinity. Experiences of pain and suffering challenge the idea of divine goodness. Would a benevolent God allow such occurrences? The figure of the devil provides an explanation for the problems of the world that justifies the claim of divine love.

The views of history and divinity flowing from a dualistic approach and the views of ethics and ritual associated with the growth of Christianity resonate with the later letters of the

New Testament. The Pastoral letters, attributed to Paul but considered non-Pauline by most scholars (1 and 2 Timothy and Titus), the Johnanine letters, and the letters of 1 and 2 Peter, James, and Jude express the world views held by many Christians in the later part of the first through the second centuries. The terms **Catholic Letters** or **General Epistles** suggest the purpose of such works: to instruct the entire Christian community rather than just particular Christian communities. The themes indicated here find expression in the texts that became part of the New Testament canon.

THE DEVELOPMENT OF VIEWS OF THE DEVIL

The view of the devil developed during this time. Some parts of the New Testament hold a view very similar to that found in the Hebrew Bible, whether in Job or in Zechariah. God controls and even rebukes the devil. That idea finds explicit expression in Jude 1–10. The tale tells how the angel Michael was asked to correct the slander Satan brought against Moses, claiming that as a murderer he did not deserve burial. Michael, angel though he was, refused to take action himself, but prevailed on God to rebuke Satan. The letter of Jude uses this inaction to contrast the angelic fear of being considered a slanderer to the brazen slander practiced by the "lawless wicked." As noted below, when the author of 2 Peter incorporated Jude into the text of that letter, this reference was altered significantly.

The Pastoral Letters reflect a perspective in which the devil plays a major role in history; people must choose between following Satan or following God. Nevertheless, the devil seems more like a natural than a supernatural force. The devil appears in the Pastoral Letters as the alternative master who is seeking to capture and ensnare humanity (see 2 Timothy 2:14–26). Choosing the devil entails giving in to temptations and waywardness, to following a path that leads to self-destruction. The devil is not portrayed as God's great enemy, but rather as the personification of the inclinations leading people astray, urges that eventually destroy a person.

1 Timothy 4 refers to devils as natural inclinations leading people to false belief, particularly the belief that the material world as such is evil. The existence of people who follow such inclinations was already predicted in holy writings: "Now the Spirit expressly says that in later times some will renounce the faith by paying attention to deceitful spirits and teachings of demons" (1 Timothy 4:1). These forces have no independent power, but succeed only insofar as individuals allow them to control their lives. Temptations seem to abound in the world, so that people are "trapped by many senseless and harmful desires" that lead them into sinfulness (1 Timothy 6:9). These are the devil's snares that capture people unawares. Nevertheless, through personal effort, people "may come to their senses and escape from the devil's snare in which they have been caught" (2 Timothy 2:26). When God so wills, Satan punishes sinners, but he has no independent power of his own. Thus Paul, in this letter, turns over backsliding Christians to Satan so they may be punished. Through suffering, they will learn to acknowledge God and return to the true faith (1 Timothy 1:20). The devil symbolizes the eternal temptation besetting human beings.

BOX 12-1

This chart describes the later letters found in the New Testament. They are grouped as Deutero-Pauline (letters using Paul's name and written in his spirit, but most probably not from Paul), as Johanine (those bearing the name "John"), and General. The Book of Hebrews is treated by itself. The term "General" or "Catholic" letters usually applies to seven books—including the Johanine among them, but those three are treated in a separate section here.

Deutero–Pauline
These letters express an outlook very close to that of the historical Paul. They address a more bureaucratically developed Church and a different vocabulary than the genuinely Pauline letters. The three letters 1 and 2 Timothy and Titus are usually grouped together as "Pastoral Letters."

Ephesians Several indications suggest that this letter does not come from the historical Paul—a distinctive vocabulary, a different literary style, and a different theology. The letter also incorporates phrases from Colossians, suggesting an influence of that work on it. The book focuses on the wisdom and mystery of the divine, the ethics and tasks of Christian life, and a supernatural struggle against the forces of evil.

1 Timothy The "Timothy" addressed in both 1 and 2 Timothy is probably not the historical disciple of Paul but rather a symbolic figure representing true church leadership. This letter focuses on the qualifications for Christian leadership, the levels of such leadership, and the ethics involved in being a Christian.

2 Timothy This letter concerns itself with false doctrine and uses common Hellenistic views of virtue and vice to attack its adversaries. The letter also uses references to the Hebrew Bible and to "myth" in arguing against false belief and for true doctrine.

Titus The historical Titus does not appear in the Acts of the Apostles, but is mentioned in Galatians 2:1–3 and 2 Corinthians 7–8. Here as in the Timothy letters, the name is used to represent church leadership as such rather than the historical figure. The letter establishes the qualifications for Christian leaders, prescribes correct Christian behavior based on age and gender, advocates acceptance of civil authority, and warns against internal divisions.

Johanine Letters
Scholars assume that all three letters were written by the same person who, in 2 and 3 John, identifies himself as "the Presbyter" or "Elder." The letters reflect a Christian community from about 100–110 from which several members have defected. The key

ideas in the letters focus on a rise of evil and dissension and an expectation that the final age is about to begin.

1 John This letter begins with a confession of faith, one that distinguishes between those who walk in darkness and those who walk in light. The letter emphasizes an exclusive ethics: No one who denies the Son who has the Father (2:23). This ethics divides the world into those who are disciples of God and those who are children of the devil and advocates a love among members of the community in this time of crisis in which "the whole world lies under the power of the evil one" (5:20).

2 John This short letter personifies the church and writes to her as an "elect lady." Using some phrases echoing 1 John, the letter warns the church of heretics and believers who separated the divine Christ from the man Jesus.

3 John This letter reveals conflict within the community headed by the Elder (Presbyter). He seeks support from a certain Gaius, especially since a certain Diotrephes has rejected both the doctrines of the Elder's community and hospitality to members of his group.

General Letters
The three Johanine letters, James, Jude, and 1 and 2 Peter make up what are usually called the "Catholic" or "General" letters because most are addressed to a wide communal audience rather than to specific situations or specific individuals (although 3 John seems to address Gaius). The section below just treats Jude, James and 1 and 2 Peter.

James This letter first circulated without an ascription and probably was not written by the James, the brother of Jesus, referred to in Galatians 1:19 and (in a passage not accepted by everyone as genuine) in the history of Josephus (Antiquities 20.9.1). The book emphasizes charitable acts and helping the poor, contending that such works bring justification (2:24)

1 Peter This letter, referring to "fiery ordeals" (4:12–13) probably reflects Christian response to persecution (either during the time of Domitian or Trajan (see timeline 10:1). Rome has come to stand for urban debauchery and evil—symbolized by the ancient city of Babylon. The author enumerates an ethics of propriety so that the non-Christians (referred to here as "Gentiles") " though they malign you as evil doers may see your honorable deeds" (2:12). The key to eternal life lies in resisting the devil and the suffering that he inflicts on Christians.

> *Jude* This brief letter (only a single chapter) cites several texts known to be late works such as 1 Enoch and the Assumption of Moses (vv. 14–15, v.9) in the midst of a review of biblical history (5–16) meant to correct false beliefs and encourage Christians to reject those who spread those views.
>
> *2 Peter* This letter betrays its late date of composition by incorporating most of Jude (2:2–17) and apparently familiar with Revelation 21:1–3 (3:13), referring to Paul's letters as "Scripture (3:16), and its wrestling with the long delay of Christ's second coming (3:3 suggests that a second generation of Christians has been raised). Although the author refers to a previous letter (3:1), that does not seem to be the text now called 1 Peter. As with the other General Letters, reference is made here to false teachers, particularly to "cleverly devised myths." Several references, however, including the citation of parts of Jude suggest that there were non-canonical stories on which the author drew.
>
> *Hebrews*
> Many scholars, even in the early church, disputed the attribution of this work to Paul. Its earliest manuscripts circulated anonymously, and today most scholars consider it the work of an anonymous author, writing in a Hellenized culture—probably in Rome since v. 24 sends the greetings of "those from Italy" somewhere between 65 and 90%. The author approaches the Hebrew Bible allegorically rather than literally, drawing from it a world view in which what occurs on earth mirrors events in heaven. The book includes a meditation on the true meaning of priesthood that involves an allegorical understanding of the Jewish ritual of the Day of Atonement as describe in Leviticus 16 (Hebrews 9). It reviews biblical history insisting that previous heroes anticipated the Christ event and were animated by the hope it inspired (chapter 11). Like the General Letters it warns against false teachers and provides moral instructions.

Ephesians, a letter that we generally study in relation to the Pastoral Letters, takes a similar approach. Anger and dissension provide the devil with an opportunity: "Do not let the sun go down on your anger and do not make room for the devil" (4:27). The end of that letter, however, adds a new note: "Our struggle is not against enemies of blood and flesh, but against… the cosmic powers of this present darkness…Therefore take up the whole armor of God, so that you may be able to withstand on that evil day" (6:12–13). That view introduces an entirely new perspective. The authentic Pauline letters had contended that the coming of the Christ had defeated all "powers and authorities," so they no longer held dominion over Christians (Roman 8:38–39). Ephesians imagines a final age in which the war between good and evil, between the followers of God and the followers of the devil, has entered a new and more violent stage.

The letters of John continue this view of an active divinity and an active Satan locked in cosmic battle. 1 John 3–4 portrays a world radically divided between the disciples of Satan and the disciples of God. All lawlessness springs from the devil and his followers: "Everyone who commits sin is a child of the devil; for the devil has been sinning from the beginning" (1 John 3:8). The devil and God are locked in a battle, and people must choose either for God or for Satan. From the very beginning, some people choose the devil; Cain stands for all those who persecute the faithful (1 John 3:12). This historical battle, however, seems to be drawing to a close. It is the "last hour" and "many antiChrists have come" (1 John 2:18). The world at such a time is "full of deceivers," and believers must be wary of those who would mislead them (2 John 7–11). The letters describe a continuous battle between good and evil in which even the "final age" stands as part of a larger pattern evident throughout human history.

God appears immanent here, participating in the cosmic battle that marks the meaning of life. Both God and Satan take active roles in shaping and controlling human history. Since these two figures are commanders of great armies, they wield a transcendent power. God's victory is assured, but the conflict continues. Therefore, God's power seems less important than the comforting realization that the divine participates as the community experiences the tensions of life.

The community of those favored by God is clearly distinguished from the community that is rejected. The test of whether someone is worthy to be part of the true community or not depends on actions. Those who "do good" are part of God's company; one who does not act in the true way "has not seen God" (3 John 11). This approach merges ethics and ritual. Behavior, including ritual actions, determines who is included or excluded from a group. Such a criterion may seem inclusive; anyone whose actions measure up can belong to the group. The standard employed, however, is so strict and demanding that only a few hardy people can actually achieve it. The letters of John use standards of behavior and belief to reject other Christians as belonging to the party of the **AntiChrist**. Ritual practices help determine the party to which an individual belongs.

Other letters continue the theme of an activist Satan, struggling at the end of time to gain power in the final age, an age in which Satan prowls about looking for victims. Only vigilance and alertness will save people from being devoured by the voraciousness of the devil. God apparently no longer steps in to rebuke Satan; when 2 Peter 11 repeats Jude 1–10, it truncates the story (noted at the beginning of this section) and only comments that the angels have not raised an objection of slander when the "wicked" spread lies against them. The devil, however, uses more than just heresy and temptation; by persecuting Christians, Satan hopes to make them lose hope and give up faith. The author of 1 Peter urges his audience: "Resist him, steadfast in your faith, for you know that your brothers and sisters in all the world are undergoing the same kinds of suffering (1 Peter 5:8–9).

The letter of James examines the idea of temptation, particularly the temptation of suffering. Those who withstand this test gain great reward, but God cannot be considered responsible for the test itself. The test comes from "evil" since "God cannot be tempted by evil and he himself tempts no one" (James 1:12–13). How do you avoid temptation? By recognizing it and resisting it: "Resist the devil and he will flee from you" (James 4:7).

While this advice sounds much like that given in the Pastoral Letters, it includes a recognition of the devil's supernatural power and ability to bring pain and suffering. God's transcendence consists in an absolute distance from all evil; nothing connected with evil can be attributed to the divine. Nevertheless, God takes part in human affairs and protects those loyal to Him. God restores, strengthens, supports, and establishes those who resist the Adversary (1 Peter 5:10). Everything depends on what a person does, and this has consequences for ethics and ritual. Faith, according to James 2:19, is universal; even the devil has belief in God. This faith, however, cannot save the devil. Only correct actions can do so. Both ritual and ethics, then, are essential, because only they distinguish the saved from the damned (James 2:14–26).

RELIGION IN THE PASTORAL LETTERS AND EPHESIANS

The collections of later letters reflect views similar to those treated above. Most scholars agree that the author of 1 and 2 Timothy and Titus (the Pastoral Letters) is a disciple of Paul who uses his style and language. They also agree, however, that the ideas are different from Paul's. Scholars also attribute the same characteristics to the letter to the Ephesians. Despite the intention to preserve authentic Pauline doctrine, the authors of these letters respond to the problems of the late first through second centuries: the problems of the growth of Christianity and experiences of persecution.

These authors view history as the unfolding program of God. They look at the divine as purely good, solving the problem of evil by attributing it to a source outside of the divine. They accept an ethics that exemplifies good Hellenistic values and virtues, rather than Jewish concerns, and seek to set up standards by which heresies and deviant communities are excluded. The approach to ritual moves away from Paul's polemics against Jewish practices and provides an allegorical and philosophical explanation for Christian rites and performances. The three Pastoral Letters show these traits clearly, and 1 Timothy in particular (on these letters, see Box 12–1). The section below uses 1 Timothy as the basis for explaining the religious perspectives involved.

1 Timothy views world events as exemplifying a continuous unfolding of the divine plan as set forth in the Hebrew Bible. Seeking to justify the practice of keeping women subordinate, 1 Timothy 2:13–15 retells the story of human beginnings originally told in Genesis 2–4. The same reliance on past tradition occurs in 2 Timothy. Knowledge of the past is the best preparation for good action in the present: "All scripture is inspired by God and is useful to teaching" (2 Timothy 3:16). Even Ephesians agrees with the idea of a consistent, eternal, and unfolding plan. Ephesians does suggest that the Christ event introduced some novelty; Gentiles are now included as part of God's chosen. This had not been recognized before: "In former generations this mystery was not made known to humanity" (Ephesians 3:5–6). The plan, however, is eternal and is now being made clear. The author of the letter, speaking as Paul, proclaims his purpose as that of making a mystery evident to all: "to make everyone

see what is in the plan of the mystery hidden for ages in God who created all things" (Ephesians 3:8–9).

References to the divinity tend to emphasize the majesty and transcendence of this creator. Liturgical praises punctuate the letters, addressing "the King of the ages, immortal, invisible, the only God" (1 Timothy 1:17). That this invisible God becomes visible through the incarnation is "the great mystery of our religion" that portrays how God was "revealed in flesh, vindicated in spirit, seen by angels…taken up in glory" (1 Timothy 3:16). Even the incarnation demonstrates God's transcendence since it remains a mystery. God's transcendence, as evident in divine incomprehensibility, is even more pronounced because the Christ event was a deed of pure grace.

The story of Jesus' incarnation, suffering, and death represents a redemptive mystery, performed out of divine love, and not because humanity has deserved it (Titus 3:14). Jesus Christ provides a bridge between the unknowable divine essence and human beings. 1 Timothy 2:5–6 understands Christ as the intermediary through whom human beings can gain access to the divine. Human beings are workers assigned tasks by a supernal master.

Christians should aspire to become true servants and workers for this master. The Pastoral Letters agree with the author of Ephesians in interpreting the Christ event as an act of divine grace by which God "has made known to us the mystery of his will" (Ephesians 1:9). God remains transcendent and mysterious, but the mediation of the incarnation offers an unmerited insight that renders divine wisdom accessible to human beings. Even after that event, God remains overpowering and inscrutable.

1 Timothy 6:16 describes the overwhelming power and transcendence of God by declaring: "He alone has immortality and dwells in unapproachable light, whom no one has ever seen or can see." The Pastoral Letters look forward to Christ's return as a manifestation of this powerful and unapproachable deity. Christians "wait for the blessed hope and manifestation of the glory of our great God and our Savior" (Titus 2:13).

This act of grace creates an ethical community—one marked by virtuous action and unblemished behavior. Ephesians and the Pastoral Letters emphasize general Hellenistic virtues, such as honoring power relations between children and parents, slaves and masters, wives and husbands (Ephesians 5:25–6:9; 1 Timothy 2:8–14; 1 Timothy 6:1–2; Titus 2:9; 3:1). The desire to emulate the good manners of Hellenistic society manifests itself in the ethics of the Pastoral Letters. The often-misquoted 1 Timothy 6:10 suggests the nature of this ethics. The teaching does not call money the "root of all evil"; rather, "the love of money," or in a more colloquial rendering, "the passion for wealth," is the root of all evil. The author affirms the importance of wealth, position, and possessions. This importance, however, lies in the opportunity for doing good that wealth brings. The conventional morality inculcated includes respect for the elderly (1 Timothy 5:1–2), avoiding both ostentatiousness and self-indulgence (1 Timothy 6:17–18; 2 Timothy 2:22–25).

In 1 Corinthians 12, Paul compares the Christian community to a single body in which every limb has its own task to perform. He enumerates apostles, prophets, teachers, miracle workers, healers, interpreters, and "other types of leaders" (vv. 28–30), without creating a fixed bureaucratic structure. The authors of Ephesians and the Pastoral Letters, however, provide a more static model. Strict criteria are set up by which to evaluate and select bishops, deacons, and elders (presbyteros, in Greek) (1 Timothy 3:1–13; 1 Timothy 5:17,1–22; Titus 1:5–9). Ephesians 4:11 explains the necessity for a fixed leadership of "apostles, prophets, evangelists, pastors and teachers" to counteract the proliferation of false teachings, of "people's trickery" and "craftiness in deceitful scheming."

The impetus for an exclusive ethics derives from the threats of dissension, conflict, and divisiveness in the Christian community, particularly in the second century. 1 Timothy begins by explaining the purpose of the letter: to instruct leaders which doctrines to reject, to advise them against "myths and endless genealogies that promote speculations," and "meaningless talk" coming from people who preach "without understanding either what they are saying or the things about which they make assertions"(1 Timothy 1:3–7). 2 Timothy offers more concrete examples of such false doctrines that bring about conflict. Some people claim that the resurrection has already taken place (2 Timothy 2:18); others raise questions about the true leaders (2 Timothy 3:2–9).

The author of Titus rails against "Jewish myths" and "commandments of those who reject the truth" (Titus 1:14). 1 Timothy 4:7 warns that Christians should "have nothing to do with profane myths and old wives' tales," clear signs that some Christians were indeed listening to independent teachers. Although the term *myth* as such merely means "story," as understood in these letters it clearly refers to an untrue story, a tale that has no basis in the tradition or the inherited beliefs of the community. The Pastoral Letters create an exclusive community by excising certain teachings and stories they consider dangerous.

Ritual controversies, no less than theological ones, concerned the author of these letters. Some groups apparently demanded sexual abstinence and specific dietary laws, practices rejected by the established leadership (1 Timothy 4:3–4). Jewish practices such as circumcision were rejected, and those teaching them were branded as "rebellious, idle talkers and deceivers" who must be "silenced since they are upsetting whole families" (Titus 1:10–11). Rituals symbolically reinforce communal identity, and these letters emphasize how correct performance at prayer leads to communal solidarity.

Prayer fulfills a social and political function, demonstrating Christian patriotism by soliciting the welfare of the government and its leaders. Christians demonstrate good citizenship by mentioning the government for special blessings (1 Timothy 2:1–7).

Prayer should mirror good etiquette, with men and women acting in an appropriate fashion—with men demonstrating self-control (v. 8), and women dressing modestly and learning quietly (vv. 8–12). The silence and subordination demanded of women (1 Timothy 2:11; Ephesians 5:22–33) contrasts with Paul's comment in 1 Corinthians 11:5 that assumes women can both pray and prophesy, although they should do so with veiled heads. The difference suggests that the later author, again unlike Paul, wants to minimize such scandal and so emphasizes the correspondence between Christian worship and good Hellenistic etiquette.

Ritual also conveys authority. The ritual of "laying on of hands," for example, conveys spiritual gifts that change those who receive them. Nevertheless, this investiture of power needs rekindling. It is less a permanent transformation of a person than an indication of the powers already available as a gift to that person. The maintenance of those gifts is considered essential (1 Timothy 4:14–15). This ritual has special significance since it rededicates people to a life of discipline and action (2 Timothy 1:7). These rituals bind the church together in a bureaucratic unity and, as such, possess a substantive power that Paul himself denied to ritualism.

RELIGIOUS PERSPECTIVES IN THE JOHANNINE LETTERS

The Johannine tradition (see Box 12–1 on these letters) emphasizes continuity—a continuity extending backward into primal history as found in the Jewish Bible and forward to the second appearance (the Parousia) of the Christ. 1 John 1 achieves this sense of continuity through style and content. It opens with an echo of both Genesis 1:1 and the Gospel of John 1:1. It emphasizes the continuity of the message preached with that which has gone before. 1 John 2:7–8 makes continuity explicit; what is being explicated is an "old commandment," but it is attached to a "new commandment."

Other later letters also emphasize a continuity of history. Jude in verses 5:1–15 reviews Jewish history in a strange sequence, beginning with the Exodus from Egypt, returning to the story of Sodom and Gomorrah in the age of Abraham, jumping forward to the time of Moses, and backward to Cain, then forward to **Korach**, and back again to Enoch. What this suggests is that neither "before or after" are essential frames of reference. All history teaches the same lesson. The identical paradigms occur again and again: faith wrestles with faithlessness, obedience with disobedience, godliness with devilish wiles.

The history within which Christians stand seems, from this perspective, to be a history in which good battles evil, in which the divine and the devil are locked in conflict. God is present in the world, just as is the devil. God is involved in the struggles of the world. The true Christian has a fellowship with God: "Truly our fellowship is with the Father and with his Son Jesus Christ" (1 John 1:3). In some ways, God is transcendent. God stands against the materialistic world; God does not love the world or the things of the world (1 John 2:15–16). God's presence in the world is part of the cosmic battle between the spiritual and the material. God is spiritually present in the fellowship of Christians.

Keeping this distinction clear was not always easy. 2 John:7–11 mentions Christians who deny that Jesus came in the flesh; they advocate a purely spiritual incarnation. Several official heresies such as **Donatism** fit this description (see 1 John 2:22–23, 4:2–3). The Johannine letters create an ethics to safeguard against such false belief. Those letters make it clear that Christians may be misled; God is present in the world, but not everyone claiming to be a spiritual leader speaks for the divine . The author warns: "Do not believe every spirit, but test the spirits to see whether they are from God" (1 John 4:1). Not every revelation can be trusted. The letters make a demand for an exclusive community with rigid criteria of membership: acceptance of the Gospel of John as the standard of belief. While proclaiming a message of love, the author of the letters nevertheless introduces the first Christian standards to distinguish "the spirit of error" from "the spirit of truth" (see 1 John 5:6–12). 1 John 2:3–11 makes caring for the welfare of the community the crucial test. A Christian who rejects another believer "is in darkness, walks in darkness, and does not know the way to go."

The Johannine letters respond to conflict and suffering. Not only do Christians suffer from internal divisions, but they also suffer from rejection by the outside world. Why are Christians being persecuted? "The reason the world does not know us is that it did not know Him"(1 John 3:1). The Christian community the Johannine letters have in mind is exclusive because it must reject heretics within and because the world outside has rejected it.

That recognition tempers the view of ritual espoused in the letters. The author recognizes the power of baptism, but reminds his audience that not only baptism by water but trial by blood and suffering are the legacy they have (1 John 5:6–8). The ritual cleansing by Jesus' blood becomes a substantive act for this community. Through such actions, sins are forgiven and suffering takes on meaning (1 John 1:5–10). While distinguishing between **mortal sins** and other sins (1 John 5:14–17), the Johannine letters do not make clear what rituals remove the non-mortal sins. Prayer seems the key point since "There is sin that is mortal; I do not say you should pray about that" (1 John 5:16). Thus prayer seems, in general, to transform the worshiper, cleansing sin. In cases where that is impossible, prayer, apparently should be avoided.

RELIGIOUS PERSPECTIVES IN JAMES 1, 2, PETER, AND JUDE

While the Johannine and Pastoral Letters emphasize continuity, other letters focus on discontinuity (see Box 12–1 on those letters). Persecutions made some Christians think that the promise of redemption in the near future appeared empty (look at Timeline 12–1 to see some of those persecutions). History may well be continuous—a continuous story of failure and disappointment. 2 Peter 3 takes up this issue. That letter probably comes from a later time than 1 Peter and focuses on the belief that history will have a cataclysmic final time. Scoffers deny that the world was created and can be destroyed, emphasizing instead its eternality (2 Peter 3:3–6).

The author goes on to say that while the coming of the final day may appear no different from what went before, stealing up on people like a "thief in the night," once it arrives, dramatic changes will take place, accompanied by a "loud noise" and a fiery end to all things (v. 10). When this dramatic end comes and everything melts and dissolves in fire, then God will provide a "new heaven" and "new earth" in which the good are rewarded because "righteousness is at home" (2 Peter 3:11). Other letters reinforce this sense of imminent change and historical reversal. 1 Peter 4 remarks on the Judgment Day and its effect not only on the living, but also on the dead. All action should be oriented toward that final test because "The end of all things is near" (1 Peter 4:7).

The idea of divine judgment suggests that God has an interest in human deeds and beliefs. Such concern testifies to divine involvement with humanity, to an immanence that arises from God's desire that people act in a certain way. God enters human affairs to show favor to the humble and to humiliate the proud (James 4:6; 1 Peter 4:4; compare Proverbs 3:34). Those who disobey God "stumble because they disobey the word," but a chosen people enjoy a special enlightenment (1 Peter 2:8–10). 1 Peter 5:6–7 exhorts Christians to humble themselves under God's hand "so that he may exalt you in due time," and to unburden themselves to God since "he cares for you."

Both Jude and 2 Peter (a letter incorporating much of Jude) bolster these claims for divine involvement with humanity by pointing to historical precedent. God took action in the time of Noah and brought a flood on the world, but spared one righteous man. Angels condemned Sodom and Gomorrah, but Lot was rescued (2 Peter 2:5–8). The Israelite Exodus from Egypt testifies to God's saving power, just as the destruction of grumblers in the wilderness shows the power of God's anger (Jude 5–6).

God's judgment on the world necessitates correct living and moral behavior; only those who act righteously will merit a reward on the final day. 2 Peter 2 describes teachers who promulgate "immorality." Such teachers, compared to **Balaam** in the book of Numbers, lead people astray by tempting them with material pleasure and self-indulgence. The author turns to examples from Genesis of how immorality leads to destruction (the great flood, the destruction of Sodom and Gomorrah) and the rewards for morality (the saving of Lot). 2 Peter 3 moves beyond this generalized lesson to introduce **eschatology**. Obedience to ethical precepts will hasten the coming of the final appearance of the Christ. That final appearance will bring with it judgment against the immoral and reward to the moral.

The most important moral quality seems to be both humility and an awareness of the transciency of human plans and expectations. Making long-range plans ignores the possibility that the world will end tomorrow: "Yet you do not even know what tomorrow will bring" (James 4:14). Rather than arrogantly assert what one intends, a person should recognize that God determines everything. Instead of arranging for the future, the author urges saying, "If the Lord wishes we will live and do this or that" (v. 15). Such an approach leads to patience, consideration of other people, ability to bear with social conventions, and hope for the future.

Does this produce an exclusive or inclusive ethics? 1 Peter 2:13–3:7 seems to differentiate ethical obligations based on social status as master or slave or on gender differences as husband or wife. Nevertheless, the letter advocates "genuine mutual love" and unity of spirit (1 Peter 1:22). Although social distinctions exist and must be respected, they should not be used to alienate one member of the community from another. The detailed list of the ethics that binds all Christians together does affirm the social stratification underlying Hellenistic society (see 1 Peter 2:11–3:9).

Nevertheless, that list also emphasizes that just as slaves must obey their master, so the master has obligations to the slave, and husbands and wives have duties toward one another (1 Peter 3:7). It concludes with a call for "unity of spirit, sympathy, love for one another, a tender heart, and a humble mind (v. 8). Ethics does not divide one Christian from another but unites them all. James 2:8–10 emphasizes the general principle of loving the neighbor and criticizes any partiality in judgment. That love takes shape only through actions, not just through belief alone (James 2:14–36). Such actions have as their purpose uniting the community: showing wisdom through gentleness, lack of envy, truthfulness, refusing to speak evil of others (James 3:13–18, 4:11–12). The test of ethical behavior is whether it enhances or detracts from the unity of the community.

This idea of a new community and its unity underlies the view of ritual found in these letters. 1 Peter 2:5 describes that community as "a spiritual house, a holy priesthood, offering spiritual sacrifices acceptable to God through Jesus Christ." These characterizations emphasize personal actions and deeds of piety, rather than official rituals. That emphasis is reinforced when 1 Peter 3:20–21 interprets baptism not as an automatic cleansing of sin, but rather as an appeal to God "for a good conscience through the resurrection of Jesus Christ." Prayer and appeal, rather than formal rituals, create substantive transformations.

Ethical infractions can impede the power of prayer. Husbands must ensure domestic tranquility "so that nothing may hinder your prayers" (1 Peter 3:7). Prayer has a power to transform reality, a power rooted in communal faith. Prayer alleviates suffering and saves the sick (James 5:13–16).

James 5:17–18 uses the example of Elijah to prove this point. Just as Elijah's prayers could end a draught, so too prayer by Christians can bring healing and salvation. With an eye on that final desire and a belief that the Judgment Day was coming soon, Jude enjoins its audience to "build yourselves up on your most holy faith; pray in the Holy Spirit" (Jude 20). While many interpreters see in Jude 20–21 a reference to the three persons of the Trinity—praying in the Holy Spirit, keeping oneself in the love of God, and looking forward to the mercy of Jesus—the point to note here is the emphasis on prayer. Just as love of God and hope for the future provide substantive strength to the Christian so too does prayer and its gift of the Holy Spirit.

RELIGIOUS PERSPECTIVES IN THE BOOK OF HEBREWS

The book of Hebrews differs from the other letters discussed previously. Most scholars consider it an allegorical text written by an anonymous author, probably after the destruction of the Jerusalem Temple in 70 C.E. The author concentrates less on the priestly practices in Jerusalem than on the description of the tabernacle in the wilderness and the Levitical provisions made in Exodus 24–25. Hebrews addresses neither heresy nor the problems of persecution so prominent in the other letters. The exception is the closing chapters; the style in these chapters changes, so that many scholars consider this section a late addition meant to make the work sound more like the genuine letters.

The devil appears briefly as the cause of death (Hebrews 2:14), recalling a Jewish text that claims: "The devil, the evil inclination, and the angel of death are identical" (Talmud Bavli Baba Batra 16a). The letter nowhere claims that it is addressed "to the Hebrews," but is filled with references to the Jewish Bible and to the history and narratives in it.

That use of the Jewish Bible shows the emphasis on continuity found in the letter to the Hebrews. Throughout the author uses quotations from Jewish scriptures to prove his point (Hebrews 1:5–13 alone contains seven citations!). Jesus is compared to Moses (Hebrews 3:3), to Melchizedek and Aaron (Hebrews 5:4, 6, 10). History illuminates, justifies, and verifies the claims of Christianity. Hebrews 11, for example, reviews Jewish history as a litany of the faithful. The heroes of the Jewish past anticipate the ideal of Christianity:

vv. 1–3	Faith is defined as belief without sufficient evidence.
4–7	Early heroes, such as Abel, Enoch, and Noah, display such faith.
9–12	Patriarchs and matriarchs lived not for themselves, but for the future.
13–16	These heroes hoped for the kingdom of God, not earthly kingdoms.
17–22	Patriarchal hope went beyond earthly hopes.
23–27	Moses' biography suggests a rejection of earthly hopes.
28–31	Israel's redemptive history points to a hope beyond that of Israelite nationalism.
32–38	Time and again, leaders protested the nationalism that focused only on this world and not the next.
39–40	The real goal for which these leaders hoped was Christianity.

This passage enumerates several Jewish heroes in order to show that even Judaism and its leaders hoped for a goal that transcended nationalism and material good. The theme of faith as belief in the unseen in verses 13–16 points beyond faith to the theme of suffering and hoping beyond earthly hope. Hebrews 11 expresses a Hellenistic understanding of faith that reshapes early Jewish belief and makes it more acceptable to a Hellenistic audience. This view of faith as hope differs from Paul's understanding of faith as trust in Christ. The historical summary in Hebrews 11 appears to offer an identity continuous with the Jewish tradition, but, in fact, it emphasizes discontinuity by its interpretation of that tradition.

While the stories of faith in Hebrews 11 suggest that miracles occur because of divine action, the retelling emphasizes the human actions involved: Abel's offering a sacrifice, Noah's building an Ark, Abraham's obedience, Sarah's trust, Joseph's belief in an eventual return to the promised land. God does have a concern for human beings beyond the concern given angels (Hebrews 1:5, 2:5–9). Nevertheless, that concern expresses itself through intermediaries, particularly the mediation of Christ. That emphasis suggests a view of God as transcendent, standing outside of the immediate context, remaining part of a heavenly rather than earthly battle. That battle, soon to be ended with God's final triumph, takes place in heaven, not on earth.

The true conflict is occurring in a supernal sphere. Perhaps the most extraordinary description of this occurs in Hebrews 7–9. Those chapters contrast the earthly rituals of Leviticus with the supernal rituals performed by Christ. God carries out rituals on high; human priests and rituals are irrelevant. The crucial change in history took place with the substitution of heavenly rituals for earthly ones. The truly transformative ritualism is not that performed by humanity, but that performed in the celestial spheres (Hebrews 7–9). Hebrews 9 describes how God influences history through the supernatural ritual carried out on high.

The combination of citations from the Jewish Bible with allegorical interpretations of those passages implies that the author of Hebrews felt equally at home in Jewish and Gentile cultures. Hebrews 4:2 notes that God's message came to the Jews no less than to the Gentiles, but the Jews did not benefit from the message "because they were not united by faith with those who listened." Unity serves as the highest ethical ideal, a unity of faith and harmony. Peace with others and holiness lead to God. Only a "root of bitterness" may cause trouble and dissension (12:15).

The most striking part of Hebrews concerns ritual processes. Hebrews is the only book in the New Testament in which Jesus appears as a priestly Messiah, carrying out the sacrificial ritual in his own person on a supernal plane. Observance of the Sabbath plays an important symbolic role in Hebrews 4. Sabbath rest was not actualized by the Jews; Psalm 95 suggests that Joshua could not win it for them. It therefore waits for the Christians to enjoy its fullness (4:3–11).

Christians actualize the ritual experience promised in the Hebrew Bible because they have a heavenly ritual leader, Jesus Christ. Jesus is a supernatural High Priest who, nonetheless, understands and has compassion for human beings and their sins. Like humanity, Jesus was tested and faced temptation. He suffered and, thereby, became the perfect intermediary between humanity and the divine (Hebrews 4:14–5:10).

Hebrews 7–10 contrast the spiritualized ritual of Christ with the materialistic ritual described in the Jewish Bible. One contrast lies in the way offerings are made. The Jewish high priests offered sacrifices daily; they renewed the covenant with the divine again and again. They performed rituals at prescribed times and could come before God only on certain occasions. Jesus, on the other hand, offered a single sacrifice and remains accessible to all people at all times. As a spiritual priest, "He is able for all time to save those who approach God through him…Unlike the other high priests, he has no need to offer sacrifices day after day…this he did once for all when he offered himself" (Hebrews 7:25, 27).

Earthly priests follow the law that was given them. They must atone for themselves as well as for others. Jesus, however, represents a different ministry and "is mediator of a better covenant," the covenant indicated in Jeremiah 31:31–34 (Hebrews 8:1–13 and 10:11–17). The earthly rituals emulate the heavenly ones and are less effective than the originals they imitate. The Jewish High Priest enters God's sanctuary only one day of the year—the Day of Atonement. That imperfect ritual demands several actions—offering blood sacrifices, imersions in water, bodily restrictions—indicating the ineffectiveness of the rite, and making clear that "the way into the sanctuary has not yet been disclosed" (Hebrews 9:8).

The ritual of Christ, however, is supernal and not bound by human material considerations. While the human priesthood required blood as purification, the heavenly rituals required different sacrifices that are spiritual rather than material (9:18–14). The criticisms of sacrifice found in biblical passages such as 1 Samuel 15:22, Isaiah 1:10–17, and Jeremiah 7:21–26 become a basis for replacing external rituals with spiritual ones performed by Jesus in a heavenly context (Hebrews 9:5–10). What is the ritual Christians must perform? Hebrews seems to identify it with true faith: "Let us hold fast to the confession of our hope without wavering. And let us consider how to provoke one another to love and good deeds" (Hebrews 10:23–24).

SUMMARY QUESTIONS

1. How did Romans view Christians, and how did Christians respond to their view?
2. How does the view of Satan in the Pastoral Letters compare with the view in the letters of John?
3. How do the Pastoral Letters view God's presence in the incarnation?
4. How does the view of ethics in the Pastoral Letters differ from the view in the letters of John?
5. How does the view of ritual in the letters of Peter, James, and Jude differ from the view in the Letter to the Hebrews?

Four Suggested Essay Questions

1. Explain two ways in which a tradition may view history. Show how 2 Peter 3:1–13 illustrates one way and how Hebrews 11 illustrates the other.
2. Explain two ways in which a tradition may view the supernatural. Apply one of them to Ephesians 1:3–10 and the other to Jude 5–16.
3. Explain two ways in which a tradition may view ritual. Show how Hebrews 10:5–10, 19–25 illustrates one of them and James 5:13–15 illustrates the other.
4. Explain two ways in which a tradition may view ethics. Apply one of them to the ethics expressed in 1 John 2:3–11 and the other to the ethics found in 1Peter 3:8–12.

Exercise

Read the following introduction to an essay answer to Question 1:

Religions sometimes view history as culminating in a dramatic and unpredictable change; other traditions view the culmination of history as effecting an already anticipated and expected result. A cataclysmic view of history often holds that dramatic changes occur because of supernal influence. Human events reflect divine decisions influencing human life. Another way of understanding a dramatic event in history, however, suggests that it occurs as part of a pattern anticipated and understood by at least some human beings from the beginning of time. From that perspective, the final event of history is not really unpredictable. To those who truly understand the past, the present and future fulfill their expectations.

Now write the following paragraphs to finish the essay:

1. Write one paragraph describing the changes that 2 Peter expects in the world and how they illustrate God's unexpected intervention into human life. Be sure that you write a topic sentence that introduces at least two sentences on the type of world transformation expected and at least two sentences concerned with the nature of the divine intervention and its unexpected nature (you may want to use an exact citation here).

2. Write one paragraph describing the view of history expressed in Hebrews 11 and how it had been anticipated by heroes in the past. Be sure that you write a topic sentence that introduces at least two sentences focused on continuity of history in the past (you may want to identify this as a continuity of faithfulness) and at least two sentences describing the predictability of that history, despite its being a matter of faith rather than of knowledge.

FOR FURTHER READING

The books listed below should be a point of departure for your future study. Each includes a bibliography that will guide you beyond its basic information.

1. Aitken, Ellen Bradshaw, *Jesus' Death in Early Christian Memory: The Poetics of the Passion*, Novum Testamentum et orbis antiquus, 53 (Guttingen: Vandenhoeck and Ruprecht, 2004).

2. Brown, Raymond Edward, *The Community of the Beloved Disciple* (New York: Paulist Press, 1979).

3. Harding, Mark, *What Are They Saying About the Pastoral Epistles?* (New York: Paulist Press, 2001).

4. Harner, Philip B., *What Are They Saying About the Catholic Epistles?* (New York: Paulist Press, 2004).

5. Harrington, Daniel J., *What Are They Saying About the Letter to the Hebrews?* (New York: Paulist Press, 2005).

6. Hengel, Martin, *The Johannine Question* (London: SCM Press, 1989).

7. Pietersen, Lloyd, *The Polemic of the Pastorals: A Sociological Examination of the Development of Pauline Christianity, Journal for the Study of the New Testament. Supplement Series, 264* (London: T & T Clark, 2004).

8. Schenck, Kenneth, *Understanding the Book of Hebrews: The Story Behind the Sermon* (Louisville, KY: Westminster John Knox Press, 2003).

9. Van Neste, Ray, *Cohesion and Structure in the Pastoral Epistles*, *Journal for the Study of the New Testament, Supplement Series, 290* (London: T & T Clark, 2004).

13

Apocalyptic Religions

READING ASSIGNMENT

Isaiah 24
Ezekiel 38–39
Daniel 9, 12
Amos 8, 9
Matthew 24–25
Mark 13
Luke 21:5–36
The Revelation of John of Patmos 1–3, 12, 19–22

LEARNING OBJECTIVES

By the end of this lesson, you will be able to:

- Describe the characteristics of apocalyptic writing.
- Describe the views of the divine, history, ethics, and ritual in apocalyptic writings of the Hebrew Bible.
- Describe the views of the divine, history, ethics, and ritual in Mark 13, Matthew 24–25, and Luke 21.
- Describe the views of the divine, history, ethics, and ritual in the Book of Revelation.

Interpretive Matrix for Chapter Thirteen

View of the Divine: How people interact with God and the supernatural; how God interacts with the world.	View of History: How past, present, and future are related; who controls the shape of events.	View of Ethics: How people behave toward other people; how they behave toward people like themselves and to those who are different.	View of Ritual: How people behave toward the Divine; how they perform religious actions.
The Divine as Transcendent: Earthly reality reflects heavenly reality. God communicates with humanity through heavenly intermediaries.	*History as Continuous:* Images and terms from older literature reappear in newer writings.	*Inclusive Ethics:* Images and ideas from several different traditions are used together in the same writing.	*Ritual as Transforming:* Ritual action creates a new reality. Ritual transgressions lead to punishment.
The Divine as Immanent: Heaven descends to earth. God judges human actions with rewards and punishments.	*History as Discontinuous:* A new age is predicted that will reverse the reality of this age. History will culminate in a cataclysmic event.	*Exclusive Ethics:* Disagreement is labeled heresy and rejected as inauthentic. Only the elect are promised salvation. God separates the saved from the damned.	*Ritual as Symbolic:* Ritual displays the inner working of the participants.

INTRODUCTION

Both the Jewish Bible and the New Testament contain what are called "apocalyptic" writings. This chapter focuses on those writings. The word **apocalypse** itself means literally "vision" or "revelation" and is used in Galatians 1:1 to refer to the commission that Paul receives from the risen Jesus. This chapter will use apocalypse and revelation interchangeably, sometimes calling the final book of the New Testament the "Revelation of John" and sometimes the "Apocalypse of John."

The first section of this chapter defines and explains the usage of the term apocalypse in the context of the Bible. Apocalyptic writing, like the prophetic sections of the Jewish Bible, makes predictions about the future. Apocalyptic visions, like many visions in the Jewish Bible, often portray the end of history. Despite these similarities, however, prophetic and apocalyptic styles differ in content and purpose. Apocalyptic texts emphasize a dualistic worldview not found in what is called prophetic writing. Apocalyptic authors demand that their audience decide between being part of the "good' community that will be saved or part of the "wicked" community that will be destroyed. Even when embedded in a prophetic book in the Jewish Bible, texts demonstrating this dualism are identified as apocalyptic rather than prophetic. The only extended apocalyptic texts in the Hebrew Bible are found in the book of Daniel; only the book of Revelation in the New Testament devotes itself solely to apocalyptic messages. This chapter reviews some of the apocalyptic writings of the Hebrew Bible as a background for understanding the images and symbols of the apocalyptic parts of the New Testament. It then compares apocalyptic passages in the three Synoptic Gospels. It concludes with an extended treatment of the Revelation of John. Pay attention to the different characteristics of apocalyptic writing and how the shaping of those characteristics indicates views of history, the divine, ritual, and ethics.

SOME IMPORTANT TERMS

The following terms are important in this chapter. Some of them have been listed in previous chapters; in those cases the term is not **bold** in the main body of this chapter. The terms are also found in the Glossary.

Amaziah	Domitian	Muratorian Canon
Angel	Eschatology	Nero
Apocalypse of Peter	Gog	Noah
Apocalypse	Heresy	Parable of the Talents
Armageddon	Isis	Parousia
Babylon	Jezebel	Satan
Balaam	Josiah	Synoptic Gospel
Day of the Lord	Magog	Widow's Mite

UNDERSTANDING APOCALYPTIC VISIONS

The history of Christianity as outlined in the previous chapter (see Timeline 12–1) combined growing membership with persecution as a minority within the Roman Empire. Perceived as a threat to the establishment, Christians suffered from rejection and ridicule. During this period, Christians turned with hope to the idea of a better future, of a dramatic shift in their fortunes. The world would be transformed so as to vindicate their faith. This perspective, that of apocalypticism, makes sense on the part of a small, powerless group of believers.

When Christianity became the official religion of Rome with Constantine the Great, one of two possibilities could be imagined: some believers claimed that the predictions in the apocalyptic literature had come to pass; others felt that since Christianity was identified with the established religion, apocalypticism should be relegated to a minor place. One early work from the second century, the Apocalypse of Peter was mentioned in an early canon (The Muratorian Canon) but was kept outside of what became the official Christian Bible.

The Revelation of John became the only entire apocalyptic book included in the final New Testament canon.

A dualistic view of history and reality form the matrix of the apocalyptic mentality. According to the apocalyptic world view, history follows a predetermined design of apparently dramatic changes that actually exemplify a continuing pattern. At the beginning of human history, the world fell into the hands of the powers of wickedness. Since then, time and events have been moving steadily toward redemption. An apocalyptic writer seeks to reveal the imminent realization of that redemption, which takes the form of an eschatological vision.

The word eschatology, literally "knowledge of the end," describes the type of writing found in the apocalyptic genre. An apocalypse is a "revelation" (as the word literally means in Greek), a disclosing of hidden things. More often than not, the hidden things uncovered concern the end of time (eschatology). Apocalyptic literature usually includes a description of a time of chaos and catastrophe when history comes to a close. It also possesses the characteristics of dualism and dense literary symbolism.

Apocalyptic eschatology may emphasize either the continuity of a predetermined pattern or the discontinuity that will follow the end of time. Both Jewish apocalyptic visions, as in Daniel, or Christian visions, as reported in the Apocalypse of John, may stress a sense of discontinuous identity. The writers of these works see themselves living in a singular time, at a crucial point in history. They are on the brink of a new world order. As such, they identify themselves in new and startling ways. Some apocalyptic writers, however, emphasize continuity. They not only use symbols derived from past writings, but use quotations from earlier scriptures to prove their authenticity. Common symbols—such as the **Day of the Lord** (from the Hebrew prophets' Day of YHWH), the desolating sacrilege of the Temple (from Daniel 9:27), **Armageddon** (from references to where two kings of Judah died), **Amaziah** and Josiah (in 2 Kings 9:17, 23:29–30), and the war between **Gog** and **Magog** (Ezekiel 38)—testify to a continuous historical tradition predicting this final end.

Some scholarly interpreters, particularly in the nineteenth century, attributed these visions to an overactive imagination, a strange psychology, and a disoriented view of reality. More recent scholarship, particularly since 1980, has discovered that those images draw on a rich literary background. That background helps provide the sense of historical continuity by linking one text to earlier texts accepted in the tradition.

The New Testament Revelation of John of Patmos, for example, echoes the symbols used by Isaiah, Ezekiel, Zechariah, Joel, and Daniel. Both the Hebrew Bible and the New Testament draw on ancient conventional images when developing this genre, especially those from Canaanite and Persian mythology. These symbols include fantastic animals conventional in Canaanite and Mesopotamian religious imagery. The portrayal of the devil, originally a Persian creation, links Revelation to passages in Hellenistic writings and passages in the Old Testament. Even Hellenistic divinities provided a model for the author, such as the woman crowned with stars who is drawn from portraits of Isis (see Revelation 12:1–6).

Apocalyptic dualism also has implications for views of the divine. Dualism enters biblical literature through the influence of Zoroastrian religion. According to this religion, the world is governed by two powers: one of good and the other of evil. Although the good power will eventually triumph over the evil deity, this present world is caught in the conflict between the two gods. Only at the end of time will this conflict cease. Until then, human beings must choose sides, deciding whether to fight with the power for good or to accept the leadership of the power of evil.

When Diaspora Jews first encountered this dualism during the Babylonian Exile, many of them rejected it out of hand. Prophets such as the Second Isaiah write polemics against this dualism, proclaiming that Yahweh is responsible for both good and evil (Isaiah 44:5–7). Other Jews, however, accepted this idea, perhaps because they experienced isolation and conflict. They associated this experience with a cosmic reality. When people suffer persecution and deprivation, they may explain it in terms of a struggle between supernal rather than merely earthly forces. God, the symbol of good, is locked in a mortal battle against Satan, the symbol of evil. This vision of a world at war exemplifies the belief that the end of time has come; soon, the believers hold, their righteousness will be vindicated and the evil of those who oppose them exposed. Since God will inevitably triumph over Satan, the group explains its suffering as only temporary. This approach suggests a transcendent image of the divine. God is not intervening in the world directly, but rather has implanted a design that inevitably works its way out in history. In the current period, this view suggests, God has temporarily relinquished control over the events of history and given it over to demonic intermediaries. Only the chosen few recognize this truth and ally themselves with the truly divine and reject the rulers of this corrupt age.

Apocalyptic writings often mention those actions for which people will be punished or rewarded when God judges humanity. This "Judgment Day" is an extension of the Day of the Lord (in the prophets, the Day of YHWH). Sometimes avoiding the impending doom involves practicing rituals such as prayer, rebuilding a Temple, or observing special festivals. In other cases, survival depends upon moral actions: on correcting abuses, fostering peace, and ending quarrels. Ritual may serve a symbolic purpose: signifying membership in a group that is either acceptable to God or unacceptable. Ritual may also serve substantive and transforming uses: hastening the final day or protecting those who endure the suffering that accompanies the final times.

Apocalyptic dualism would seem to imply an exclusive ethics. The elect and the damned form two distinct groups; belonging to one of them excludes membership in the other. Many apocalyptic writings do make such a claim. They castigate outsiders for their heresies, their lack of ritual observances, their persecution of the just and righteous. Other writings, however, take a broader view. They stress the universal nature of the crisis that will alter cosmic reality. Rather than divide the world between the elect and the damned, they address their message to all who will face the impending doom.

APOCALYPTICISM IN THE HEBREW BIBLE AND LATER JEWISH WRITINGS

Since the New Testament Revelation of John is the latest, most developed example of this form, it helps to look at the evolution of the genre from the Hebrew Bible to the New Testament. The book of Amos offers some dramatic visions of God's judgment on the people of Israel. Many Israelites apparently hoped for the day when the Lord (YHWH) would take arms on their behalf. They longed for the Day of the Lord, when God would enter into the fray to fight for Israel against its enemies. Amos 5:18 warns them: "Alas for you who desire the Day of the Lord. Why do you want the Day of the Lord? It is darkness and not light." Amos 8 describes the terror of that final day on which "I will make the sun go down at noon, and darken the earth in broad daylight. I will turn your feasts into mourning and all your songs into lamentation" (8:9–10). Amos 9 augments the dire predictions of Amos 8 with a vision that, while not eschatological or apocalyptic in the strict sense, establishes some of the themes taken up by later writers.

Imagining what the Day of the Lord will be like, the passage envisions the pillars of the Temple shaking so that they shatter "on the heads of all the people, and those who are left I will kill with the word" (9:1). The earth melts and the seas flood (vv.5–6). Israel will be treated no better than any other nation on earth when the time of testing comes (vv.7–8). Sinners will be destroyed, but the Davidic kingdom will be restored and the fortunes of the righteous will flourish (Amos 9–15). The key idea here of a time of destruction and chaos, culminating in judgment of the wicked and just, echo throughout the apocalyptic tradition. Perhaps not coincidentally, v. 3 pictures the people fleeing in distress and being bitten by the "sea serpent"—the great "dragon" of ancient mythology. That symbol recurs in later works.

Amos 8–9 makes a distinctive use of ritual. Ritual processes display the inner orientation of the worshipers. When the catastrophe strikes, the rituals change from being signs of rejoicing to signs of sorrow (Amos 8:10). It may be more than just coincidence that the destruction begins with God striking the pillars of the altar (Amos 9:1). One reason for the destruction is that the Israelites have followed the external practices of ritual without taking their meaning to heart. They have chafed under the restrictions of the New moon and Sabbath celebrations, anticipating their illegal profits when the workday begins again (8:5). Because the rituals belie the inner reality of the people, they are changed, and "The songs of the temple shall become wailings in that day" (8:3). Rituals, in this vision, have a symbolic, celebratory purpose. When their form differs from the intention motivating them, they testify to the moral bankruptcy of the people.

Isaiah 24 adds some other elements present in apocalyptic writing that augment the themes of the punishment of the wicked and the reward of the righteous. Ritual and moral transgressions are cited for having brought about this curse (24:5–6). Ritual actions provide a false sense of security that contrasts with the desolation that the prophet sees about to occur (vv.14–16). Most significantly, however, the situation is universalized. Not only Israel, but both international and supernatural powers are involved: "On that day the Lord will punish the host of heaven in heaven, and on earth the kings of the earth…the moon will be abashed, and the sun ashamed" (vv. 21–23). The cosmic scope of God's punishment does not make it any less a political one; God's glory is revealed precisely in Zion (also called Jerusalem; v. 23).

Ezekiel 38–39 has influenced apocalyptic writing even more than the passages in Amos and Isaiah. Scholars debate the authenticity of these chapters, many claiming that they were not originally part of Ezekiel and may have been written by a separate author. Nevertheless, they have played a decisive role in the development of apocalyptic literature. Following a positive vision of a rebuilt Jewish state, they depict a great war in which the nations of the world, led by the powerful secular hero Gog, who comes from the place of Magog, attack Jerusalem, win a few battles, and are then themselves conquered (Ezekiel 38:1–3). The great victory will prove to the nations that Israel's God reigns over the world: "I will bring you against my land, so that the nations may know me, through you, O God, I display my holiness before their eyes" (38:16). The resulting chaos echoes verses from Amos and Isaiah: "There shall be a great shaking" (38:19). There will be sword against sword, suffering, destruction: "With pestilence and bloodshed I will enter into judgment with him; and I will pour down torrential rains and hailstones, fire and sulfur upon him…"(38:22). The righteous also receive a reward, and Israel is restored to its land and receives spiritual blessings. God is portrayed as saying, "I will never again hide my face from them, when I pour out my spirit upon the house of Israel" (39:29).

The dualism here, in which the nations of the world stand on one side and Israel on the other, is even more striking than in Amos and Isaiah, in which Israel no less than the nations receives some punishment. Here the attack on Israel is understood not as punishment, but as a way to publicize divine power. The section contains only one, very strange ritual reference. When the victory occurs, the animals are to enjoy a "sacrificial feast" on the victims of the war. Sandwiched between two sections that do have extensive ritual discussions (Ezekiel 36–37, 40–48), these two chapters do not discuss human ritual. God performs a ritual sacrifice by slaughtering Israel's enemies.

Daniel 9, in contrast to Ezekiel 38–39, makes ritual practice a central concern. A sign that the final age has come is that the Temple has been polluted, a desolated sanctuary (9:18–19). The people have turned aside from the ritual commandments given them (vv. 10–13). In response to Daniel's prayers (apparently effective as ritual), the angel Gabriel reveals a cryptic message about what will occur in the future: the Temple will be rebuilt; an anointed priest will rule; the Temple will be made desolate; sacrifices will cease; but eventually those who carried out the destruction will be punished (vv. 25–27). Ritual practice, then, is the cause that hastens the final times, just as prayer effectively brings visions to reveal the truth. Substantively, ritual practice can bring either help or disaster.

What follows is an apocalyptic eschatology. History will be coming to an end. A dramatic discontinuity will occur. A new reality will emerge after the final judgment. Daniel 12 hints cryptically at when the final events will occur: "It would be for a time, two times and half a time, and when the shattering of the power of the holy people comes to an end, all these things would be accomplished" (12:7). History will be altered so drastically that Daniel himself does not understand what is being said. God has a plan that unfolds, but not everyone should know that plan. Even the revelation to Daniel must be kept secret until the time is right for it (12:4). Prior to the final judgment will be times of trouble and tribulation.

Eventually, however, the judgment will take place, and "Many of those who sleep in the dust of the earth shall awake, some to everlasting life, and some to shame and everlasting contempt" (Daniel 12:2). The idea of a bodily resurrection for some of those who have died, as well as a judgment on them, occurs only here in the Jewish Bible. It does reappear in apocryphal works such as the books of Maccabees and in the New Testament. Later writings such as 2 Maccabees 7 often expand the concept and insist that *all* people and not just some will be resurrected. God will judge every human being and reward or punish each according to that person's actions while alive. This concept, combined with the idea of a final judgment on the wicked and just, emphasizes an exclusive ethics, one in which the "wise" or the "elect" survive and are rewarded, and the "wicked" or "foolish" are punished.

Daniel receives this information from supernatural sources. Angels such as Michael and Gabriel and unnamed figures such as a man "clothed in linen" (12:5–12) provide him with explanations for what he envisions. The angel Michael reveals to Daniel that the war he thinks is being fought on earth is actually a contest among the supernal beings. The use of angels, a depiction of God as an old man seated on a throne (7:13–14), the title "the Most High" throughout Daniel 7 suggest divine transcendence. This understanding of history as reflecting a cosmic battle reoccurs in later writings, as do several of the images that appear in this book.

The book of Daniel represents an early Hellenistic apocalypse written either just before or during the Maccabean revolution. Later apocalyptic writings reflect life under the Romans. 2 Esdras, probably written around 100 C.E., justifies God's actions toward human beings with an apocalyptic vision. As in Ezekiel 38–39, Israel's tribulations are not due to their sinfulness, but to God's desire to become manifest to the world as a whole. The fate of souls in the afterlife solves the problem of their suffering in this world. Among the ideas adumbrated in 2 Esdras that find expression in later works is the locution of Babylon to stand for Rome, vivid descriptions of the suffering of the wicked and the happiness of the saved, and the image of Jerusalem both in mourning and as a restored and glorious new Zion.

Another apocalyptic work, 1 Enoch, clearly influenced the New Testament tradition. This work seems to conflate several originally independent materials, many from the period before the great war against the Romans. It describes a tour of heaven, a narrative about fallen angels and Satan, the way in which the Son of Man (never identified by another name) will judge the righteous and wicked, and the final conflict in which the world is destroyed and the Messiah appears as a sacrificial lamb. The influence of this work on the New Testament is clear, since Jude 8–9 quotes from it.

APOCALYPTICISM IN MARK 13, MATTHEW 24, AND LUKE 21

Several passages in the New Testament contain apocalyptic elements. Paul's letters—1 Thessalonians, 1 Corinthians 15—express a belief in the immediacy of the end of the age and describe it in visionary terms. The Synoptic Gospels each have a section in which Jesus describes the end of time, the Day of Judgment, and the significance of this vision. Comparing the different versions shows how, despite sharing some basic convictions, each of the Synoptics does indeed have a distinctive religious perspective.

Both Matthew 24 and Luke 21 rely on Mark 13 for the general structure and content of their apocalypse. All three portray the end of the age as a time of conflict, struggle, and great changes that is marked by both social and natural disasters (Mark 13:3–8; Matthew 24: 4–7). God seems immanent in these drastic changes. When the Son of Man appears, it is often with angels, as in Mark 13:16–27, but making the sun dark and shaking the heavens shows the power of a transcendent divinity before whom humanity must tremble. The description of Jesus' coming infuses the world with divine holiness—a clear statement of immanence (especially in Matthew 24:30–31 and Luke 21:25–28). Ritual gets very little mention in Matthew and Mark. Matthew (24:15) and Mark (13:14) make use of Daniel 9:27, referring to the Jerusalem Temple, yet this is described only as a "sign." It has no transforming effect since it is not a cause of the cataclysmic change. Matthew 24:20 mentions the Sabbath as an observance that would make bearing the suffering harder, but again gives no details and makes no clear connection between Sabbath observance and the final days.

Matthew 24–25 adds an emphasis on the nature of the elect and the actions they must do to merit salvation. Both Mark 13:20–22 and Matthew 24:22–27 mention the elect and their tribulations and their being tested by a proliferation of false messianic claimants. Matthew continues this theme with several parables in Chapter 25 that show the value of being awake, aware, and alert when the Parousia, the second coming of Jesus, arrives. That coming will be sudden and surprising, so Christians must ready themselves for that day. While these parables also occur in Luke, they are not put in the context of requirements for being saved at the end of time (compare the **Parable of the Talents** in Matthew 25: 14–30 to Luke 19:12–27).

These preparations are moral and ethical rather than ritualistic. Jesus insists on caring for the poor, the sick, the naked, and the stranger since "just as you did not do it to the least of these, you did not do it to me. And these will go away into eternal punishment, but the righteous into eternal life" (25:45–46). This represents an exclusive ethics; only those who live up to the highest standards of moral responsibility, who have used their talents wisely and who have been prepared for the final day—are justified. The exclusive ethics finds its expression in the image of a shepherd who separates the sheep from the goats in his herd: "All the nations will be gathered before him and he will separate people one from another as a shepherd separates the sheep from the goats" (25:32).

This image (found only in Matthew) draws on an extended metaphor in Ezekiel 34. God appears as the shepherd caring for his flock. Israel is often ungrateful, so God declares: "I

This early sixth century mosaic from Ravenna pictures the apolcalyptic scene at which Jesus separates sinners (goats) from the blessed (sheep).

shall judge between sheep and sheep, between rams and goats" (Ezekiel 34:17). That allusion to a passage in Ezekiel reflects the traditionalism found in Matthew's apocalypse. Matthew 24–25 adds several touches that emphasize continuity in history and tradition. Only Matthew 24:15 cites Daniel by name. Matthew 24:36–39 refers to Noah's flood as a prototype of the destruction and salvation that will come during the Parousia.

While Matthew 24–25 emphasizes an exclusive ethics, Luke 21 evokes an inclusive one. The chapter begins with Jesus' approval of the poor widow who only donates a "mite" (the smallest coin of the realm) to charity—the anecdote of the **Widow's Mite**. Her contribution is more acceptable than the greater largesse of others since "she out of her poverty has put in all she had to live on" (Luke 21:1–4; Mark 12:42–44 leaves this as the conclusion of the previous chapter, rather than attaching it to Chapter 13). While retaining the description of the suffering that the disciples will face at the end of time (Luke 21:12–19; compare with Mark 9–12), Luke omits references to the elect for whom the suffering will be shortened (Mark 13:20; Matthew 24:22). Luke ignores the reference to the desecration of the Temple prominent in Daniel 9:27, focusing instead on the common predicament that faces all humanity. Whereas Matthew 24:39 claims that "all the tribes of the earth will mourn," Luke 21:25–27 notes the "distress among nations confused by the signs and portents," and people who "faint from fear and foreboding of what is coming upon the world," expressing a more universal concern and compassion.

Rather than setting out a long list of required actions to determine who are "sheep" and who are "goats," Luke 21:28 merely tells people to "stand up and raise your heads because your redemption is drawing near." When Luke does make recommendations for behavior that will lead to survival on the Judgment Day, the text recommends avoiding "dissipation and drunkenness and the worries of this life" (21:34). Even more important, Luke 21:26 advocates praying to have the strength to escape what will take place. While Mark 13:33 and the entire collection of teachings in Matthew 25:1–30 stress the need to be alert and awake, only Luke emphasizes the power of prayer. Luke develops a view of substantive ritual that can save a person from cosmic disaster.

THE APOCALYPSE OF JOHN INTRODUCED

The Apocalypse of John, the final book of the New Testament, illustrates the basic concerns of apocalyptic writers. The book itself fits strangely in the New Testament canon. It uses Greek in a distinctive, if awkward, style. Its view of Jesus, or Christology, is very different from that of the other New Testament books. While the name of the book has led some critics to think that the author of the Apocalypse may have had some connection with the Johannine community, too many differences exist in style and philosophy to identify this author with the writer of either the Gospel of John or the letters attributed to John.

The title of the book expresses its purpose: the revelation of the meaning of history and of the final events that will usher in a new age. The context of this book appears to be an early Christian community—a community that was perhaps persecuted by the emperor Domitian—that existed at a time when the Gospels were already established and that was organized in a hierarchic structure.

The book expresses several different views of the meaning of human events and the nature of history. Chapters 2–3 focus on the seven churches that have engaged in some type of backsliding. These chapters maintain historical continuity by using images from the Hebrew Bible to describe the errors of these churches or the benefits they will receive: Balaam (2:14), Jezebel (2:20), manna (2:17), Key of the House of David (3:7). The end of history, however, introduces discontinuity as a "new Jerusalem" descends from heaven and a "new name" is bestowed on the prophet (3:12).

This ambiguity continues through the book. Sometimes "history" consists of God's actions controlling all events. Sometimes "history" consists of choices made by individuals deciding between the way of God and the way of Satan. Sometimes Revelation envisions discontinuity with the past. Sometimes it describes the "new" reality in images drawn from earlier texts. Sometimes it uses material clearly derived from Jewish sources. Parts of the book may well have been a "Jewish apocalypse," that is, a dualistic view of history culminating in the triumph of the Jewish people over all other nations. Other parts of the book reject such a Jewish orientation. Those parts draw on ancient Near Eastern, Greco-Roman, and Persian mythology. As a composite work, the Revelation of John combines continuity and discontinuity, Jewish and non-Jewish elements, and universal and parochial themes.

This eclectic use of images sometimes leads to strange consequences. The author apparently misunderstood the reference in Ezekiel where Gog is from a place called Magog (Ezekiel 38:2), because in Revelation 20:8 the two represent different nations. This final conflict becomes a symbol of the mysterious but predetermined fate of the good and the wicked in apocalyptic writings. Here the conflict does not depend on human actions, but on the unfolding of a plan already prepared from the beginning of creation. Thus the apocalyptic world view emphasizes the incomprehensibility of the world, the unpredictability of the future.

Chapters 4–11 are probably a Jewish apocalypse, interpreting the way in which earthly conflict mirrors a heavenly struggle. Chapters 12–18 portray a graphic battle between the forces of good and evil—both in heaven and on earth—using vivid images to describe the evil kingdom and its fall and emphasizing the motif of trust in God despite persecution. This motif culminates in Chapters 19 to 22:5, which depict the final days of the "old age," the defeat of Satanic forces, and the judgment on humanity, to be followed by a "new heaven and new earth" that replaces the old reality.

The ambiguous view of history expressed in the Revelation of John is echoed in its mixed view of divinity. Revelation 1:7–8 seems to imagine God's immanence: the Almighty will come and all the nations will mourn. Yet throughout, the vision describes God's transcendence and difference: the Son of Man has royal clothing, looks like the transcendent judge in Daniel 7, and speaks with the transcendent roar of Ezekiel's vision (1:12–16). It continues with a criticism—now rather obscure to modern readers—of heresies against which the community launches an attack. Heretics will suffer for their errors, the author contends, and describes in loving detail and metaphor both the error and the coming punishment.

The end of the book returns to the theme of heresy. The entire book concludes by declaring the book itself a canonical text to which nothing can be added and from which nothing should be removed. This means that traditional behavior, whether ethical or ritualistic, determines who is among the elect and who is not. The structure of the book, as now composed, represents a circle; it begins and ends with considerations of heresy. This suggests an important point: the images, use of tradition, and vivid language reinforce the author's conservatism. The author urges readers to maintain their loyalty to traditional beliefs, despite their suffering and doubts. This injunction to loyalty evinces an exclusivist ethics. The Apocalypse of John insists that Christians maintain their separation, that they distance themselves from the communities in which they live. Even nominal Christians, according to this text, often constitute a polluting and foreign influence on true Christians. The search for purity of doctrine, no less than purity of action, characterizes the ethics of this book.

FURTHER REFLECTIONS ON THE REVELATION OF JOHN

The central theme of the book arises from an expectation of apocalyptic catastrophe. This cosmic disaster will justify the few elect who have obeyed the "eternal commandment" of loyalty to the hidden truth and will punish those who have followed heresy. The Apocalypse of John envisions a dramatic confrontation in which the forces of Satan battle the forces of God and are eventually defeated. Reality itself is split, with John of Patmos and his followers alone knowing the truth. In this text, apocalyptic dualism—drawing inspiration, perhaps, from the Zoroastrian religion prevalent in Persia—attributed to Satan a power nearly equal to God's. God has his forces—the children of light—and Satan has his army—the children of darkness. The ideology of an apocalyptic vision divides the world into the true and the false, the blessed and the cursed, the saved and the damned. Satan becomes the symbol of the latter in each of these dichotomies. Thus, the world of evil becomes the creation not of God, but of the devil. Those who are children of light belong to God; those who are representatives of evil have been spawned by, are enslaved to, and will ultimately be destroyed together with their master Satan.

The book develops the idea of Satan in various ways. All who oppose Christians or who introduce heresy or innovation, are, thereby, members of Satan's army. Pergamum is the place "where Satan's throne is," perhaps because of its association with worship of the Roman emperor as a divinity (Revelation 2:13). A recurring phrase speaks of "the synagogue of Satan who say that they are Jews but are not" (2:9, 3:9). The overriding symbol, however, is that of "the beast." This image, drawn from Daniel and from ancient Canaanite mythology, arises from the deeps ("the bottomless pit") to war against the righteous (11:7). Identified in 12:3 and 9 as Satan, the devil, this beast attacks "a woman clothed with the sun, with the moon under her feet, and a crown of twelve stars" (12:2). According to this chapter, the woman stands for God's people, both regal and victimized. The symbolism of the woman draws on many sources. Her celestial dwelling recalls the Babylonian and Canaanite goddesses, and her crown of stars reflects Hellenistic motifs, particularly the cult of Isis. In biblical traditions, the figure merges with the symbolism of the Song of Songs, traditionally interpreted as a reference to Israel as the bride of God, and with the New Testament presentations of the Church. In its portrait of the holy community, the text uses older symbols and gives them a new meaning.

Satan persecutes the woman and God protects her, hiding her until her time of triumph comes. The dragon, according to the vision, may try to destroy her, but will not succeed (12:10–12). These hints of salvation punctuate references to persecution. While Satan may succeed in harassing the elect for a short time, he cannot triumph in the end.

Revelation 13 portrays two other beasts accompanying the dragon. The first has features combining the four beasts described in Daniel 7, perhaps suggesting the Roman Empire (13:1–10). The section ends by noting that this "is a call for the endurance and faith of the saints" (v. 10). The second beast exercises the power of the first and performs miracles (vv. 11–18). A cryptic allusion to "wisdom" and calculating "the number of the beast," which names "a person," concludes this section. Several scholars think this person is the former emperor Nero, widely believed not to have died but to be about to return to take control once again.

Several ideas intertwine here. The Satanic figure of a beastly antichrist, who contrasts with the redeeming figure of Jesus, takes on various forms and has various aliases and accomplices. Suffering and persecution is a fate the faithful must endure, but evil will not ultimately triumph. The relationship between the supernal dragon and the earthly beasts suggests that what happens in the human sphere mirrors and echoes events in the heavenly world. That idea finds confirmation when seven angels pour out plagues on various earthly powers, including the throne of the beast, the beast and the false prophets, and Babylon (Rome). The sixth plague takes place at Armageddon, where the armies of God, the Lamb, and of the beast fight a final battle. The forces of God defeat the beast and its "false prophets" who are thrown alive into "the lake of fire that burns with sulfur" (19:17–21). Earthly defeat occurs when cosmic powers are defeated.

Satan's defeat occurs in Revelation 20. The dragon—who is the serpent, the devil, and Satan—is thrown into a pit and bound for "a thousand years" (20:1–3). Nevertheless, after those thousand years, Satan will arise again. The war of Gog and Magog takes place, the final victory takes place, a general resurrection occurs, all are judged, and then: "Death and Hades were thrown into the lake of fire. This is the second death..."(20:14). Here again, that connection between earthly warfare and the battle on high becomes clear.

History, then, depends on the changing influence of heavenly forces. Discontinuity rather than continuity reigns. Not only are events shaped by divine power, but that shaping is unpredictable, except for those who have received a special revelation. While the devil may be bound in chains for a while, he may arise once again. No natural set of causes and effects coordinates historical events. Such a view of historical determinism might indicate divine immanence. Nevertheless, Revelation abounds in angels, demons, and other intermediary figures. This suggests divine transcendence. The final chapters of the book reinforce this view. A new heaven and a new earth descend upon the world (21:10–14); a new reality appears in which God becomes the temple of the world: "I saw no temple in the city, for its temple is the Lord God the Almighty and the lamb" (21:22). When the vision has been accomplished and the final judgments made, then God will become immanent. Until then, the divine remains transcendent. The future descent of the holy into this world suggests that in the present time God remains distant and aloof, hidden and revealed only to the chosen ones.

Revelation espouses an exclusive ethics in which the chosen who understand the meaning of history, who serve God alone, and who will survive the final judgment are contrasted to the wicked, immoral, and powerful who now control earthly affairs. The book portrays the persecution of the righteous, whether described symbolically, as the attack of the dragon on the woman clothed with the sun, moon, and stars, or referred to directly, as being "slaughtered and by your blood you ransomed for God saints from every tribe and language and people and nation" (5:9) as a sign of election. Those who "listen to what the Spirit is saying to the churches" have an advantage over all others.

This constitutes the basic demand for those wishing to belong to the community. The recurring phrase "Let anyone who has an ear listen to what the Spirit is saying" (2:7, 17, 28;

3:6, 13, 22) suggests that paying attention to a message, rather than carrying out a ritual deed, is paramount. The question of authority is prominent. The opening sections of the book do not focus on ritual errors as such. They do suggest that certain Christians have gone astray after false leaders, that they have accepted the authority of people who are unworthy. The writer proclaims: "I also received authority from my Father... Let anyone who has an ear listen" (2:28).

The consequences of belonging to the elect are significant. Chapter 21 provides a graphic vision of those consequences. The present and corrupted world will be replaced with a supernal ideal, an ideal pictured as descending upon, and being superimposed over, this current reality. This new creation will transcend the limitations of mortality, of suffering, and of time. The righteous will enjoy eternal bliss; the wicked will suffer eternal punishment (21:1–8). Choosing to accept the teaching of the true visionary entitles a person to membership in the saved community. Revelation 21:1–4 suggests the transformation of history; 21:5–8 spells out the differences in that history for two types of people. The righteous will receive "water as a gift from the spring of the water of life," and those in the right camp will receive gifts (vv. 5–6). Those belonging to the other camp—who are polluted, idolaters, and liars—will suffer punishment "in the lake that burns with fire and sulfur" (v. 8). Revelation 22 records the final vision of the book and continues the dualism and exclusive ethics found in the previous chapter. The central concern is with the preservation and publication of the prophecy itself. This is a vision not to be ignored or kept hidden.

Ritual in the Apocalypse seems symbolic, rather than substantive. Revelation 19:17–18 reiterates the idea of a "sacrificial feast" carried out by the birds of prey found in Ezekiel 39. Heavenly matters, rather than earthly rituals, concern the author of this text. Ritual, when described, is that of the angelic hosts, drawing on images found in Isaiah 6:2–3 and Ezekiel 1:26–28. These rituals emphasize divine transcendence and power: "Holy, Holy, Holy is the Lord God Almighty...You are worthy, our Lord and God, to receive glory and honor and power" (4:8–11). While the transformed reality presents an immanent divinity who resides among human beings—"See, the home of God is among mortals"—the liturgy before the final transformation emphasizes divine distance. Perhaps this explains why human rituals have little interest for the author, except insofar as they maintain a strict monotheistic worship to God alone. When the visionary seeks to worship his angelic mediator, the revealing angel forbids it (22:8–9). All who keep the words of the book are equal. Worship is God's alone; it is a symbol and signifies purity. The book concludes with injunctions reminding people of the absolute demands given by God.

SUMMARY QUESTIONS

1. What are some distinguishing marks of apocalyptic writing?
2. What historical conditions often produce apocalyptic works?

3. How do the apocalyptic texts in the Hebrew Bible show similarities to and differences from each other?

4. How do the apocalyptic passages in the Synoptic Gospels show similarities to and differences from each other?

5. What are the basic characteristics of the Revelation of John and some examples of them?

Four Suggested Essay Questions

1. Explain two ways in which a tradition may view history. Show how Matthew 24:36–39 illustrates one way and how Revelation 21:1–4 illustrates the other.

2. Explain two ways in which a tradition may view the supernatural. Apply one of them to Isaiah 24:21–23 and the other to Revelation 19:1–6.

3. Explain two ways in which a tradition may view ethics. Apply one of them to the ethics expressed in Luke 21: 25–28 and the other to the ethics found in Revelation 21:5–8.

4. Explain two ways in which a tradition may view ritual. Show how Ezekiel 39:17–20 illustrates one of them and Daniel 9:15–19 illustrates the other.

Exercise

Answer Question 2

1. Be sure that your first paragraph defines two ways of viewing divine power, especially one that requires intermediaries between God and humanity and one that does not. A key idea—that of divine judgment on the world, for example—could serve to unify the introduction and also prepare for the rest of the essay. Another key idea might be whether the divine and the human have anything in common.

2. Be sure that your paragraph on Isaiah 24 includes the fact that God punishes both heavenly and earthly powers and that Zion and Jerusalem are emphasized.

3. Be sure that your paragraph on Revelation 19 includes a reference to how Babylon has corrupted the world and how Revelation 19 emphasizes God's heavenly court.

FOR FURTHER READING

The books listed below should be a point of departure for your future study. Each includes a bibliography that will guide you beyond its basic information.

1. Bauckham, Richard, *The Fate of the Dead: Studies on the Jewish and Christian Apocalypses, Supplements to Novum Testamentum*, v. 93 (Leiden: E. J. Brill, 1998).

2. Collins, Adela Yarbro, *Crisis and Catharsis: The Power of the Apocalypse* (Philadelphia, PA: Westminster, 1984).

3. Collins, John Joseph, *Seers, Sybils, and Sages in Hellenistic-Roman Judaism*, Supplements to the Journal for the Study of Judaism, v. 54 (Leiden, The Netherlands: E. J. Brill, 1997).

4. Cook, Stephen L., *The Apocalyptic Literature: Interpreting Biblical Texts* (Nashville, TN: Abingdon Press, 2003).

5. Friesen, Steven J., *Imperial Cults and the Apocalypse of John: Reading Revelation in the Ruins* (Oxford, England: Oxford University Press, 2001).

6. Lewis, Scott M., *What Are They Saying About New Testament Apocalyptic?* (New York: Paulist Press, 2004).

7. Schüssler, Fiorenza Elisabeth, *The Book of Revelation—Justice and Judgment* (Philadelphia, PA: Fortress Press, 1985).

8. Thompson, Leonard L., *The Book of Revelation: Apocalypse and Empire* (New York: Oxford University Press, 1990).

14

Review Summary

LEARNING OBJECTIVES

By the end of this lesson, you will be able to:

- Describe three ways views of history may be continuous and three ways they may be discontinuous.

- Describe three ways views of the divine may be transcendent and three ways they may be immanent.

- Describe three ways view of ritual may be transforming and three ways they may be symbolic.

- Describe three ways views of ethics may be inclusive and three ways they may be exclusive.

INTRODUCTION

This chapter reviews both the textual analysis and the modes of interpretation used throughout this book. It does not look at every text previously studied, but it seeks to put previous studies into perspective. By comparing differences among similar types of views, this chapter hopes to inspire you to look for variety, difference, and nuance in biblical interpretations. Take the ideas given here as suggestions, as imaginative possibilities, rather than absolute guides to the "true" meaning of any particular text. You may want to go back through this book to find new ways of understanding the examples discussed. Instead of using the same categories as those given in this chapter, you might want to try to emulate the process used here. The purpose of this chapter is not to show the definitive meaning of any passage, but

Interpretive Matrix for Chapter Fourteen

This matrix has been left blank so you can fill it in on the basis of your reading of this chapter.

View of the Divine: How people interact with God and the supernatural; how God interacts with the world.	View of History: How past, present, and future are related; who controls the shape of events.	View of Ethics: How people behave toward other people; how they behave toward people like themselves and to those who are different.	View of Ritual: How people behave toward the Divine; how they perform religious actions.
The Divine as Transcendent:	History as Continuous:	Inclusive Ethics:	Ritual as Transforming:
The Divine as Immanent:	History as Discontinuous:	Exclusive Ethics:	Ritual as Symbolic:

rather the open-ended nature of reflection on those passages. To further this process, the exercises at the end of this chapter are not drawn from the discussion in the chapter itself. They offer new selections for you to analyze freely.

This chapter does not present a list of terms to know. You may want to review the terms in the previous chapters and look at the definitions for them in the Glossary. Try to put biblical texts into their historical and canonical contexts. You also may want to review the timelines in previous chapters and the chapter boxes as a background against which to understand biblical passages. As you experiment with interpretation of biblical texts, test those interpretations to see if they are plausible and reasonable in their contexts.

CONTINUITY IN HISTORY

This book has shown how some biblical passages understand history as made up of events that exemplify enduring patterns and consistent lessons. These passages, however, often mean something different by "history" from one another and often see the meaning of history very differently (see Box 14–1). One example of a continuous view emphasizes history as the events in which the people of Israel figure prominently. Psalm 78 illustrates this view. The psalm relates several divine actions for the sake of the Israelites: saving them from Egyptian slavery, performing wonders in the wilderness, saving them from the Philistines, establishing the kingship of David. It also reports continuing Israelite rebelliousness: attempting to leave Egypt before the time was right, rejecting Mosaic leadership, accepting the idolatrous practices of the Canaanites. The narrative suggests two basic lines of continuity, one human and the other divine. God continually offers gracious gifts to Israel, and Israel continually fails to make good use of these gifts. Perhaps this continuity legitimates the Davidic dynasty and its royal leadership. The choice of David as king represents the final gift God gives Israel. The power and success of that kingship provides a structure and order that keeps the Israelites from rebelling.

Matthew 1 presents another view of continuity in history, one based upon ethnic and textual tradition. The story of Jesus continues the story of the Israelites from two perspectives. First, Matthew 1:1–17 offers a genealogy from Abraham through Jesus. By going back to the first Jew, the Gospel emphasizes an ethnic continuity stretching through Jewish history and culminating in Jesus. This genealogy of Judean kings from David to Solomon to Josiah and through the Zadokites, legitimates Jesus' claim to messianic standing. A second basis for continuity lies in Jesus' biography, presented as fulfilling predictions from the Hebrew Bible. Matthew claims that Isaiah 7:14—"this young woman shall bear a child"—actually foretells the birth of Jesus to a virgin mother. If this claim is true, then tracing Jesus' messianic lineage through Joseph in 1:16 seems irrelevant, but the point is not to offer logical argument. Instead, Matthew 1 intends to show that whether continuity is understood according to ethnicity or according to scriptures, Jesus exemplifies it.

Jude, vv. 4–7, portrays a very different type of consistency, that of divine punishment meted out to evildoers of every sort. One might think that members of the chosen people would be exempt; Jude 5 notes that unbelievers among those rescued from Egypt were destroyed. One might think that angels could escape divine judgment; the case of those who fell and were sent to damnation proves otherwise. Perhaps wealth and riches bring salvation? The fate of the cities of Sodom and Gomorrah teaches otherwise, since these rich and powerful urban centers suffer eternal burning in fire because of their sexual immorality and lust. These warnings suggest that within Christian communities such unbelievers exist. Christians should be wary of the "intruders" who have "stolen among you" (Jude 4) who represent the same type of fifth-column problem as the evildoers found among those rescued from Egypt, among the angels, or among the inhabitants of Sodom and Gomorrah. Historical continuity teaches the lesson that the danger of having evildoers in your midst continues unabated.

BOX 14–1: BIBLICAL VIEWS OF HISTORY

This chart summarizes passages revealing views of history. The summaries point to the views of history indicated in the text of this chapter. Remember that the same texts may be interpreted in different ways depending upon the emphasis chosen.

Views of History as Continuous

Psalm 78 This Psalm reviews Israelite history from claiming that it reveals "the glorious deeds of the Lord." It describes God's continuing graciousness and the continuing rebelliousness among the Israelites. God performs wonders for the people, the people show their lack of steadfast loyalty. The establishment of the Davidic dynasty is the final stage depicted in this history.

Matthew 1 This chapter links the story of Jesus to the story of Judaism in several ways. It begins with a genealogy connecting Jesus to Abraham through the royal family of David, Solomon, Josiah, and Zadok. It continues by applying the text of Isaiah 7:14 to Jesus' birth.

Jude 4–7 These verses remind the reader of how God punishes those who fall away from true belief. Continuity in history reflects God's pattern of executing judgment against human unbelievers, angels, and deviants such as those in Sodom and Gomorrah. God's principle of giving "measure for measure" provides the continuity in history.

Views of History as Discontinuous

Genesis 2:4–4:1 The description of the creation of the world shows several elements of discontinuity: names change over the course of the story—"the woman" becomes "Eve"; animals get names; the punishment threatened for disobedience does not occur but another is substituted; and the roles of men and women have changed by the end of the tale. The key to this discontinuity lies in God's changing intentions; God acts experimentally—creating a world, a man, animals, and a woman in order to see what will happen.

Job 1–2 This "prologue" to the book of Job suggests that history reflects the divine whim. What happens to Job occurs because God taunts Satan with the example of Job and then allows Satan to try a series of escalating catastrophes as a way of testing Job's loyalty. Neither Job's piety nor his ritual practices influence what happens to him. Everything depends on an arbitrary divine decision.

1 Thessalonians 4:13–5:10 Paul, in these verses, describes a cataclysmic end of history in which "the dead in Christ will arise" and the living be "caught up in the clouds" (4:16–17). The result will be a radical change in which those who live in security will suddenly find themselves destroyed and those who are "the children of light" will enjoy the new "day" that has come after a long "night" (5:5).

DISCONTINUITY IN HISTORY

Just as passages viewing events as inherently linked together differ from one another, so too do views of history as a series of discontinuous events (see Box 14–1). Genesis 2:4–4:1 illustrates a type of discontinuity dependent on the changing responses of the divine. God experiments with creation. After creating a world in which nothing grows, God sets a man down to cultivate it. When the man gets lonely, God creates animals and then a woman to solve that problem. This basis for discontinuity continues in other ways as well. God threatens the man with death for disobedience, but when the man and woman disobey, they receive exile instead. More than that, this exile entails a new division of labor. One divine decision leads to another, eventually transforming the nature of reality entirely. Neither God alone nor humanity alone create this discontinuity; it arises from the interplay between them, from the dynamics of God's creation and the response of that creation to the divine. Because the relationship between God and the world constantly changes, so too the nature of that world changes and is unpredictable.

Job 1–2 indicates a different basis for unpredictability: God's whims. The prologue to the poetic dialogue between Job and his friends sets up the situation of Job's utter righteousness and blamelessness. The disasters that befall Job occur only because God has drawn Satan's attention to him. God allows Satan increasing control over Job's fate, not for any sin Job has committed, but because of a wager between these two supernatural beings. Nothing Job does can make a difference. Various modes of behavior usually offer predictable success. Different groups advocate hard work, religious loyalty, or ritual observance as the road to a good life. The case of Job proves each of them inadequate. Job's diligence cannot bring success; Job's piety cannot bring him divine favor; his sacrifices cannot intercede for his family. The natural conditions for success and failure do not prevail when God's arbitrary whim comes into play.

The Apostle Paul also rejects the common formulae for success of his times. Eventually the rich will become poor and the poor rich, the successful will fail and the failures will triumph. This will take place when history comes to an end and the Christians are vindicated. 1 Thessalonians 4:13–5:10 describes this transformed reality. The dead will be resurrected; the living will be taken up alive into heaven. Jesus' second coming, the Parousia, discontinued present history. The experience of Christians under the hostility of the Roman Empire seem to disconfirm claims that a new world is about to begin. Paul insists that such an impression is wrong. It arises from an assumption that everything will continue in the future as it has in the past. His view of the end of history counters such an expectation; those who think everything will remain the same are mistaken.

These examples suggest that students must do more than merely distinguish between views of history as continuous or discontinuous. They must also look for the reason for this view. Does continuity lie in a continuing pattern of divine action? Does it lie in ethnic genealogy? Does it lie in scriptural texts? What determines discontinuity? An interaction between God and the creation? The whims of the divine? An impending end to history? Other texts point to still other causes of both continuity and discontinuity. What is important is to look beyond simple dichotomies.

IMMANENT VIEWS OF THE SUPERNATURAL

Views of the supernatural often differ over the sphere in which the divine appears most clearly. 1 Kings 18 advances an immanent view of divinity; God is present in the miraculous occurrences in the world. Elijah moves with miraculous mysteriousness in this chapter. God summons Obadiah to find him, and Obadiah objects because Elijah is so elusive. Nevertheless, Elijah is found. At the end of the story, Elijah runs before Ahab's chariot—a feat of miraculous speed and power. Other examples of divine intervention occur in the story: God has caused a drought in the land; God accepts a sacrificial offering by consuming it in flame; God dramatically ends the draught with a thunderstorm. All these events show God at work in the phenomenal world in which human beings live. One sphere of immanence, then, is the world of nature in which God overturns what appear to have been natural laws.

A second sphere is that of political life and leadership. Isaiah 24:13–42 describes God's intervention into world affairs. The earth suffers destruction; human beings feel terror at the sociopolitical chaos. Not only human beings, but angelic powers suffer as well. The kings of earth and the celestial beings are put to shame and made to recognize their limitations. When God enters the arena of the powerful, no other entity can compete. The destructive effect of the divine strikes fear into both mundane and celestial beings. The presence of God in Jerusalem, in Mount Zion, makes a political statement that renders all human politics irrelevant.

A final sphere is that of the personal. An immanent divinity meets individuals and interacts with them directly. Luke 24:28–42 describes the disciples' encounter with the risen Christ. They do not recognize Jesus, but are amazed at the interpretations of the Hebrew Bible given them. They perceive something strange and marvelous, but do not understand it. The disciples remark: "Were not our hearts burning within us while he was talking to us on the road?" (24:32).

Finally Jesus enlightens them and, despite their misgivings, they recognize that God has joined them. The text emphasizes that Jesus, while divine, also provides a physical presence that brings God into direct relationship to human beings. Jesus breaks bread with the disci-

BOX 14–2: BIBLICAL VIEWS OF THE SUPERNATURAL

This chart summarizes passages revealing views of history. The summaries point to the views of divinity indicated in the text of this chapter. Remember that the same texts may be interpreted in different ways depending upon the emphasis chosen.

Views of the Supernatural as Immanant

1 Kings 18 This chapter describes how God intervenes in history for Elijah the prophet. God sends Obadiah to Elijah. God causes Elijah to move in strange and mysterious ways. God brings a drought, accepts a sacrifice by consuming it with fire, and finally ends the drought.

Isaiah 24:1–13 God's involvement in the world has some dire consequences. Destruction and fear take hold of both the earth and the heavens. God's punishment extends to angelic and earthly powers alike. God's presence is located in Israel—particularly Mount Zion and Jerusalem.

Luke 24:28–43 This account of the disciples' meeting with the risen Jesus, emphasizes the physical presence of the divine among human beings. Jesus' exposition of the Hebrew Bible amazes them. They are encouraged to touch him. He even shares in a meal and eats a boiled fish to show the physical reality of his presence.

Views of the Supernatural as Transcendent

Psalm 19:1–10 God is made known through various intermediaries. The lawful order of nature discloses the reality of God. The social laws of human communities reveal the principles God has implanted in the world. The pragmatic consequences of following or disobeying God's commandments show the divine element within the world. In these cases God does not need to intervene directly since the indirect influences of God's creations provide enough guidance in the world.

Wisdom 9: Wisdom is a supernal power that God used to create the world. Its reality surpasses ordinary mortals. God entrusts wisdom to certain special individuals such as Moses and Solomon. Only the intermediary power of God's Holy Spirit can convey supernal wisdom to human beings.

John 20:24–29: This tale of the disciple Thomas and the risen Christ emphasizes the superiority of the transcendent to the physical. Thomas will not believe that Jesus has really been resurrected until he touches the wounds in his side. Jesus allows Thomas to do this, but reprimands him claiming that those who believe without having seen are higher than those who need physical proof.

ples and blesses it. He has them touch him to prove that he is not a ghost. He even demands that they give him food to eat, and he eats a broiled fish in their presence (24:36–43). Divine immanence in the sphere of the personal seems to imply a physical manifestation. This view of immanence differs significantly from that found in Isaiah's emphasis on God's intervention into political life.

TRANSCENDENT VIEWS OF THE SUPERNATURAL

The same sort of distinctive spheres mark views of divine transcendence. Psalm 19 portrays God's transcendence of the natural world. Through nature, human beings learn about the divine; the heavens and earth proclaim God's reality without words merely by exemplifying divine purpose (19:1–6). God sets the parameters of the human task. As creator and architect of cosmic reality, the divine establishes the basic framework within which humanity lives and carries out its ultimate purpose. Yet this divine architect seems remote. Humans can intuit the divine through a study of divine law, not through direct experience (19:7–10). God transcends the world of both human life and the natural world, but can be deduced from those.

The Wisdom of Solomon offers an alternative view. God's wisdom is not deduced from nature, but exists independently as a supernatural being itself. That wisdom was the tool by which God created the world, judges humanity, and organizes life (Wisdom 9:1–4). Human beings require that God provide that wisdom to them as a gift; it comes from the divine through a choice that God makes (9:5–9). The knowledge of building a sanctuary for God comes not from studying the world, but through divine inspiration (9:8). Wisdom, viewed as a woman to be won, cannot be wooed by human beings directly. Instead, human beings should petition God to learn from her (vv.10–16). When that wisdom comes, it is an inspiration from the transcendent, a gift of the Holy Spirit (v. 17). Here transcendence is not related to implanting a structure in the world, but in providing a political advisor, a supernal ally for the leader of a people.

A final sphere of transcendence is in the personal. John 20 addresses this through an account of the disciples' encounter with the risen Christ. In many ways, the portrayal of that encounter is written as a direct repudiation of Luke 24. Those disciples who seek physical confirmation of Jesus' resurrection are reprimanded. John 20 portrays a spiritual basis for the divine kinship to humanity. God transcends the physical, and human beings who seek a connection with the divinity must also learn to transcend the desire for evidence from sense data. In this case, not only is God transcendent, but this transcendence has consequences for human beings. If people wish to understand the divine or be acceptable to the divinity, they must emulate God's transcendence. Any attempt to grasp God's nature based on physical or corporeal evidence indicates a lack of faith and an insufficiency of religious insight.

These differences show the importance of distinguishing between a specific type of religion—one of transcendence or one of immanence—and determining the actual message that a text seeks to communicate about the nature of the divine. Where is God active? Iin the personal, political, or natural realms? How does immanence or transcendence become evident in each of these spheres? Try to organize views of the divine not only in terms of the nearness or distance of the divine, but also in terms of the contexts in which the divine can be found.

TYPES OF ETHICAL EXCLUSIVISM

While types of ethical religions differ depending on whether they are exclusive or inclusive, they also differ in terms of the communities included or excluded (see Box 14–3). Ethics refers to norms governing how people behave. While this behavior sometimes serves to open up a community to wider membership, at other times it serves to narrow the confines of the community. The nature of community, however, also differs. It can refer to members of an ideological group, of a particular subgroup, or a cultural community.

1 Kings 18 describes a confrontation between the prophet Elijah, who follows YHWH, and prophets of the Phoenician divinity Baal, a situation that expresses an exclusive ethics. Elijah contends that Israelite culture cannot include the worship of both gods. He bases his demand of an exclusive community of believers on the historic precedent of Israel's twelve tribes and their covenantal relationship to YHWH. Clearly, community in this context refers to members in a religious culture. Elijah's rejection of syncretism (which he characterizes as "limping between two opinions" in v. 21) reveals a religion of exclusive ethics for a cultural community.

Matthew 10:34–37 imagines a very different type of community, one that is chosen freely and that rejects the ties of past, history, and kinship. Jesus declares that he has come to bring war and not peace. He is to set family members against other family members. Loyalty to this ideological community severs ties with the "natural" communities established by history and birth. Jesus' new family cuts its members off from the world that they had known before. They have an adopted home, an adopted culture, a new reality. This community centers around a central figure—Jesus. Within that community all are united. Nevertheless, between the members of that community and outsiders stands a wall of hostility and opposition.

A very different sort of community emerges out of the instructions given in 1 Timothy 2:8–15—a liturgical community made up of worshipers. That worshiping community takes stratification of society as a cultural given. There are kings and political officials for whom prayers should be recited. Men have specific duties at prayer, including preaching and conducting the religious worship. Women have separate duties that are focused on the home and on childbearing. They are forbidden authority, teaching, and leadership and are bidden to be silent. This worshiping group is, therefore, made up of several subcommunities divided by gender and status.

BOX 14-3: BIBLICAL VIEWS OF ETHICS

This chart summarizes passages revealing views of ethics. The summaries point to the views of ethics indicated in the text of this chapter. Remember that the same texts may be interpreted in different ways depending upon the emphasis chosen.

Exclusive Ethics

1 Kings 18: Elijah, in this chapter, makes several demands associated with an exclusive ethics. He demands that the people choose between one God and another, that they reject the institutions for a "foreign" God, and that they affirm the history associated with the twelve tribes of Israel.

Matthew 10:34-37: Jesus, in these verses, demands that followers choose between loyalty to their families and loyalty to him. He comments that he has come to bring the sword and not to bring peace. Fidelity to a message transcends other ties and creates a new and more exclusive community.

1 Timothy 2:8-15: These verses create two exclusive communities of prayer divided by gender. Men have the obligation to lift up their hands without anger or argument, they are to the leaders and spokesmen of the community. Women, on the other hand, are to remain silent, dress modestly, and may neither teach nor have authority over men.

Inclusive Ethics

1 Kings 21: Elijah in his encounter with Ahab over the seizure of Naboth's garden, emphasizes that rich and poor, royalty and commoner, all must live under the same law. He argues for an inclusive social order in which economic or political distinctions do not translate into either favoritism or discrimination. Legal obligations must be the same for every member of the society.

Psalm 104: This striking psalm draws on an Egyptian model—as if to emphasize its universalism. It emphasizes a community of creatures, bound together because they all represent and depend upon divine wisdom. Human beings, sea creatures, land animals and even plants and trees look to the same source for their sustenance.

1 Timothy 2:1-7: This section of 1 Timothy emphasizes a unified community of believers. Whether Gentile or Jew, all are united in having one mediator between them and the divine. That unity of concern means that Christians must pray for the social order, even if it is a non-Christian one.

INCLUSIVE TYPES OF ETHICS

While Elijah seems to support exclusive community in 1 Kings 18, the story in 1 Kings 21 emphasizes an egalitarian notion of communal duties. The king has taken possession of a neighbor's vineyard. Elijah confronts him and declares that the king must act under the same laws and rules as any other member of society. That story unites king and commoner under a single judicial order. The community involved is still that of the political order and its religious standards. These standards, however, are now applied over a broader range of citizens than before. This community embraces all subgroups, no matter their social, political, or economic status.

Psalm 104 represents an inclusive community made up of all natural creatures. Such a view moves beyond ideological specificity. The psalm evokes divine transcendence, perhaps to show that God's reality extends to all creatures (104:1–4). This natural, not cultural, community focuses on those functions all living beings have in common. For human beings in particular, it refers to their general activities: cultivation of food and drink (vv. 14–15), daily toil (v. 23), and commerce on the sea (vv. 25–26). No specific occupation or activity divides one group of humanity from another. No specific history defines one human community and sets it off from another.

Belonging to this community does not require specific beliefs or practices. All are united through their natural inclinations. The psalm strikingly addresses the worshiper: "Bless the Lord, O my soul." It does not demand that others give up their convictions or that the true believer must sever ties with everyone outside. Indeed, the opposite seems the case. The psalm implies the need to recognize that all people are members of a wider community, one that exists naturally and without ideological specification.

1 Timothy 2:8–15, as noted above, creates an exclusive liturgical community. The same chapter opens (vv. 1–7) by invoking an inclusive political community. Christians, even during a time of persecution and intolerance, are to pray for the government and the social leaders. The redemption brought by Christ mediates between humanity and God, not just between Christians and the divine. God, according to this text, "desires everyone to be saved and to come to the knowledge of the truth" (v. 4). Differences between cultures—Jews and Gentiles, Christians and other Romans—are subsumed under this open communal concern. While these verses do suggest an ideological community, one that believes in a particular story of salvation, and eventually distinguishes among subgroups based on gender, their politics are universal. The cultural community embraced is wide and unbounded.

TRANSFORMATIVE TYPES OF RITUAL

Transforming rituals perform several different functions (see Box 14–4). Sometimes worshipers use a ritual to alter the material world in which they live; parts of the harvest ritual in

Deuteronomy 26:12–19 serve this function. The ritual, in these cases, represents the human part of an agreement with the divine. The worshiper announces the fulfillment of all commandments, the lack of transgression, and obedience to divine decrees. The ritual then seeks God's response: prosperity and a good harvest. God influences the natural cycle, and rituals ensure the beneficence of that cycle. God also controls the external civil and political realm. Another transformational consequence of the ritual of the First Fruits in Deuteronomy 26 is political success; God will "set you high above all nations that he has made…to be a people holy to the Lord your God" (26:19).

Other rituals seek to transform the worshiper. Matthew 6:1–17 describes a ritual carried out in private—not ostentatiously in public—and with brevity—not extended as in prayers uttered by other religious groups—that will succeed in bringing the worshiper near to God. Some parts of that prayer seem to focus on the external world. Asking for "daily bread" may seen to be demanding a change in the "real" physical world. Other requests—for the coming of God's kingdom, for forgiveness, for God's will to be done—are more personal and private. The prayer as a whole has as its purpose creating a bond between the divine and the human. The various requests seek to facilitate that relationship, as do the instructions about how to perform the ritual action itself.

A third type of ritual lifts the worshiper outside of that reality entirely. Not only does the worshiper undergo change, but the ritual removes the worshiper from one context into another. John 3 presents such a view of ritual. Those who see ritual in purely physical terms, such as the Jew Nicodemus, misunderstand what it means to be a Christian. Christian identity derives from a spiritual rebirth, the acquisition of a new personality through the ritual of baptism. The chapter emphasizes that God's sending of Jesus into the world brings redemption to the world—but also contends that this redemption applies only to those who have been transformed, who have transcended their mundane physicality to become purely spiritual. The ritual here indicates a transformation beyond that of the external world or the individual's relationship to God. Ritual marks a rebirth into a transcendent existence that goes beyond any mundane reality.

TYPES OF SYMBOLIC RITUAL

The types of symbolic ritual parallel the types of substantive ritual. A frequent prophetic theme articulates the inability of ritual to effect changes in the world. Hosea and Amos both claim that God despises the sacrifices and prayers of the Israelites. 1 Samuel 15:22–23 introduces this motif. King Saul has disobeyed Samuel's orders because he wishes to preserve animals for sacrificial purposes. Samuel declares that God does not desire offerings or sacrifices, but rather obedience to divine commandments. Ritual does not bring success; at most, ritual can symbolize the obediential spirit and attitude of a person. Ritual does not change external reality; only changed actions in the outside world can achieve such transformations.

BOX 14–4: BIBLICAL VIEWS OF RITUAL

This chart summarizes passages revealing views of ritual. The summaries point to the views of ritual indicated in the text of this chapter. Remember that the same texts may be interpreted in different ways depending upon the emphasis chosen.

Transforming Ritual

Deuteronomy 26:12–19: These verses emphasize that carrying out the ritual of the first fruits of the harvest will have a beneficial effect. If the person removes the sacred portion, takes care of Levites, aliens, orphans and widows, and does not commit any ritual impurity, then God will "look down from heaven" and make the ground productive. The ritual also ensures political dominance and power.

Matthew 6:1–17: Jesus, in this version of the Lord's Prayer, gives advice on how to have one's prayers answered. The various conditions—that it be done in private and whole-heartedly—are meant to ensure its success. The prayer is to bring material well-being (daily bread) and spiritual well-being (forgiveness).

John 3:1–10 A certain rabbinic leader, Nicodemus, meets with Jesus at night and acknowledges Jesus as a teacher who has "come from God." Jesus informs Nicodemus of the need to be "born of water and Spirit," but Nicodemus cannot understand what he means. Jesus articulates surprise that someone could be a "teacher in Israel" and not understand these things.

Celebratory Ritual

1 Samuel 15:22–23: When King Saul disobeys Samuel in order to procure an offering for God, Samuel replies that God does not desire sacrifices. God wants obedience and loyalty, not ritual offerings. In this way ritual does not affect the external reality but expresses the attitude of the worshiper.

Daniel 4:34–35 This extraordinary prayer put into the mouth of the Babylonian king Nebuchadnezzar expresses his thanks to God. The chapter relates an incident that occurred to the king. It does not seek to change that episode or influence future life. It merely gives voice to gratitude and acknowledgement. This ritual celebrates the lessons that the worshiper has learned.

Revelation 19:17–18: This passage, developing a motif in Ezekiel 39:17-20, imagines God creating a sacrificial feast for the animals out of the destruction of the wicked. God's ritual, rather than human ritual, takes place in the sweep of history. Human beings are not part of this supernal ritual, but they need to recognize it and understand it as testimony to the substantive ritualism of the divine.

Many passages argue the same point in relation to personal change. Ritual acknowledges a person's inner nature, but it does not change that nature. Ritual expresses a relationship with the divine, and if that relationship is not actual, the ritual has no purpose. Daniel 4:34–35 presents an interesting example. The chapter claims to be a document written by the Babylonian king Nebuchadnezzar. Addressing the nations of the world, he praises God and tells how he had a dream that only Daniel could interpret. The dream meant that he would be stripped of his power, go mad, live like an animal, and then finally be returned to his throne. The dream comes true. When Nebuchadnezzar regains his mental faculties, he offers a prayer to God. The prayer praises the "Most High" who rules forever, before whom mere mortals are "accounted as nothing," and whose will none can oppose. Nebuchadnezzar has learned his lesson; he now has a humble relationship with the divine. Of interest is the fact that his mind has already been restored to him (v. 34) before he offers the prayer. He has already rectified himself for the divine; his relationship with God has been established. Prayer celebrates this new relationship; it testifies to a personal change that has just occurred.

Sometimes rituals need not be performed, but merely recognized to be effective. Revelation 19:17–18 describes the great sacrificial meal that God will prepare for the animals once the wicked have been destroyed. This portrait of God's ritual preparation, echoing a description found in Ezekiel 39:17–20, suggests that historical events are actually a working out of a divine ritual. An invitation is given to God's "great supper." The slaughter of the beast takes place, those who follow the beast are defeated, and their remains presumably make up the ritual meal on which the animals will feed. Human beings do not perform any ritual. They should, however, be aware of the ritual implications of the history they witness. John's message warns them ahead of time of the meaning and significance of the events they will see.

Once again, despite the differences between types of ritual, broad areas of agreement exist. Both Deuteronomy 26 and 1 Samuel 15 seek to establish the links between ritual and practical reality. Both Matthew 6 and Daniel 4 look at ritual in the context of personal relationships with the divine. Both John 3 and Revelation 19 look at ritual in the context of a supernal, cosmic drama.

EXERCISES IN BIBLICAL INTERPRETATION

The following are meant both as a review of this chapter and as a review of the content and techniques in this book as a whole:

1. Explain two ways in which a view of history may be continuous. Show how the description of the holiday of Hanukkah in 1 Maccabees 4:54–59 illustrates one way and the use of the Hebrew Bible in the Mark 1 illustrates the other.

2. Explain two ways in which a view of the supernatural may emphasize transcendence. Show how Isaiah 6 represents one way and John 1 illustrates the other.

3. Explain two ways in which an ethics may be exclusive. Show how Christian opposition to the cult of the emperor illustrates one way and 1 John 3–4 illustrates the other.

4. Explain two ways in which a view of ritual may be transforming. Show how the Passover described in 2 Kings 23 illustrates one way and the Lord's Prayer in Luke 11:1–4 illustrates the other.

Glossary

The names and terms here are those emphasized in the textbook. Names of biblical books are not included. Where an individual's name is identical with the name of a book (e.g. Amos, Jonah, or Nehemiah) students are expected to be able to define both the book and the individual whose name it bears only on the basis of the discussion in the text itself.

Aaron The brother of Moses, Aaron was anointed as the first of the high priesthood (Leviticus 8). His descendants were considered the only true priests although other priestly families such as the Hasmoneans actually served in this capacity.

Abel The second son of Adam and Eve, Abel was murdered by his brother Cain (Genesis 4).

Abimelech Several biblical figures bear this name—a king of Gerar interacting with either Abraham or Isaac (Genesis 20–21, Genesis 26) or a son of Gideon who makes himself king of Shechem (Judges 9).

Abraham The story of this biblical hero is told in Genesis 12–26. This name is an expansion of an earlier name Avram (Genesis 17). He is considered the "founder" of Judaism—God's covenant with him becomes the basis for Jewish identity.

Achior According to the book of Judith, This Ammonite leader defects to the Jews when his general, Holofernes does not take his warning that he cannot defeat the Jews. He eventually converts to Judaism.

Acts of Paul This example of Christian Apocrypha includes tales of a pietistic woman, Thecla, who acted as a Christian leader. Perhaps her prominence led to the exclusion of this book from the New Testament canon.

Adah The wife of Lamech who bore Jabal, the first shepherd and Jubal the first musician (Genesis 4:20–21).

Adam The Hebrew word "adam" means "human being." Scholars debate as to when the word becomes a personal name in Genesis 1–4.

Agag Agag was an Amalekite king conquered by the Israelite King Saul. Saul was reprimanded for allowing Agag to survive (1 Samuel 15).

Ahab Ahab was an Israelite king (869–850 B.C.E.) married to a Phoenician queen, Jezebel, who had a contentious relationship with the prophet Elijah (1 Kings 17–22).

Ahashuerus According to the biblical book of Esther, Ahashuerus was king of Persia. Scholars identify him with Xerxes I (486–465 B.C.E.).

Ahaz This king of Judah (733–716 B.C.E.) ruled during a time of Assyrian domination and ignored the counsel of the prophet Isaiah (Isaiah 7).

Ahijah This prophet was active during the time of King Solomon ((961–922 B.C.E.) and was instrumental in the division of the nation into a northern and southern kingdom after Solomon's death.

Akhenaton This Egyptian Pharaoh (1364–1347) is accounted one of the first monotheists because he established the worship of the god of the sun, Aton, as the single cult of the nation.

Akkadian This term refers to the people and language of a Semitic dynasty arising in Babylonia and finally conquering not only Mesopotamia but eventually an extensive empire. The language became the common tongue of the ancient Near East until it was replaced by Aramaic and was in use until the first century before the common era.

Alexander Balas This contender for the Seleucid throne (150–145 B.C.E.) posed as the son of Antiochus Epiphanes, was recognized as legitimate by the Romans, competed with Demetrius, a son of Antiochus Epiphanes, for Jewish favor and appointed Jonathan the Hasmonean as High Priest of Judea.

Alexander the Great This son of Phillip of Macedonia (356–323 B.C.E.) conquered the ancient world and introduced Greek culture to the ancient Near East. Upon his death his conquests were divided up among his generals.

Alexandria A major Egyptian city during the Hellenistic period where Philo-Judaeus flourished and a prominent Jewish community integrated Jewish and Greek values.

Alma This Hebrew word literally means "woman of marriageable age," but as used in Isaiah 7 has been interpreted to mean "virgin" (see Isaiah 7:14 and Matthew 1:23).

Amalekites These traditional rivals of ancient Israel were said to be descendants of Esau, the brother of Jacob—the progenitor of the Israelites. They were finally defeated by King Saul.

Amarna Letters This collection of commercial and legal materials from ancient Egypt have been assigned to the period 1300–1200 B.C.E. and contain information that sheds light on the legal system found in the Hebrew Bible.

Amaziah This priest of Beth El in the northern kingdom of Samaria opposed the prophet Amos who asserted God's rejection of priestly sacrifices (Amos 7). Also the name of one of Judah's kings (see 2 Kings 14).

Amenemope This ancient Egyptian scribe (1300–1200 B.C.E.) wrote a series of wisdom sayings that seem to underlie the teachings found in Proverbs 22:17–24:33).

Ammonites The term refers to the inhabitants of Ammon, a country bordering on Israel. According to the Bible, the Ammonites were related to the Israelites through Lot, the nephew of Abraham (Genesis 19).

Ananais This name is given to an otherwise unknown Christian leader who cured the Apostle Paul of blindness and baptized him (Acts 9).

Angel This term renders the Hebrew word "malakh," or "messenger," and usually refers to divine agents who communicate with human beings. The Hebrew Bible (Daniel 12), the Apocrypha (Tobit) and the New Testament (Revelation) name angels such as Gabriel, Michael, and Raphael.

AntiChrist This term is given to the leader of the forces of evil who fight against the forces of God at the end of time. Although the term is used only in the letters of 2 and 3 John it underlies the figure of the "beast" in Revelation 12–13.

Antiochus III This Seleucid ruler seized control of Palestine from Egypt in about 198 B.C.E. and, according to the Jewish historian Josephus, was widely accepted by a pro-Syrian group among the Jews.

Antiochus IV (Epiphanes) This successor to Antiochus III who ruled from 175–163 B.C.E. sought to introduced Greek culture throughout his kingdom. This led to the Maccabean revolution among the Jews that installed the Hasmoneans as high priests and kings.

Apiru This term means "landless class" and is a rendering of the term "hapiru." Many scholars think that both the term and the description fit the biblical Hebrews.

Apocalypse This Greek word means "revelation" or "disclosure," and usually refers to visions and reports of the end of time. The literary style of such a disclosure uses symbols, images, and mysterious allusions. Apocalyptic writings in the Bible include Daniel 7–10 and the book of Revelation.

Apocalypse of Peter Although mentioned by early sources, this book (probably from the second century of the common era) was rejected by the finalized Christian canon. It offers detailed descriptions of the punishment of sinners in Hell.

Apocrypha This term from the Greek literally means "hidden" and refers to books that appear in the Septuagint Greek Old Testament but not in the Hebrew Bible. Roman Catholics accept many of these books as part of their Old Testament. Protestants often consider them "inspired" works but list them separately from the Old Testament.

Apostle Peter This disciple of Jesus is given pride of place in the Gospel of Matthew where he is made the foundation of the church (Matthew 16:16–20). In Acts of the Apostles he is portrayed as the leader of the Jewish Christians who eventually realizes that Jewish practice is no longer required of Christians (Acts 10–11; 15:6–11).

Aramaic This West-Semitic language became the primary mode of communication throughout the ancient Near East. It was made the official language of the Persian language in about 500 B.C.E. and was most probably the language Jesus spoke.

Aristobulus II This Hasmonean was the younger sibling of John Hyrcanus II who established himself as king and high priest (69 B.C.E.). Pompey placed John Hyrcanus II on the throne.

Armageddon This Greek rendering of the Hebrew "Har Ha Meggido—the Mountain of Meggido" is understood in Revelation 16:16 as the place where the final confrontation between the forces of God and the forces of Satan occurs.

Augur ben Jakeh This name is given to a putative author of Proverbs 30, a fact that suggests the anthological nature of the book of Proverbs.

Asclepius This Greek god of healing became the focus of a Hellenistic religious cult that claimed miraculous cures for its followers. These types of miracle stories are similar to those found in the Apocrypha and the New Testament.

Asmodeus This demon, mentioned in the Apocryphal book of Tobit, eventually comes to be identified with the Devil and Satan as a leading demon opposing God.

Assyria This nation that eventually destroyed the northern kingdom of Israel in 721 B.C.E. and besieged Jerusalem, ruled the territory between the Tigris and Euphrates river in Mesopotamia.

Athanasius This church father (295–272 C.E.) participated in the Council of Nicea and, in 367, wrote a letter listing the books of the New Testament identical with the canon now in use.

Baal The term "Baal" means "master" and was applied to a Canaanite divinity against whose worship many Israelite prophets warned despite the protection given it by many of Israel's kings.

Babel In the Hebrew Bible (Genesis 11)This term refers to a tower whose building was interrupted when God confused (Hebrew—Balah) their languages. Babylonia had such a tower called "Bab-El" or "Gateway to God" at which sacrifices were offered to the god Marduk.

Babylon An ancient city in Mesopotamia that served as the capital for several empires. Nebuchadnezzar II (602–562 B.C.E.) conquered Jerusalem and deported its inhabitants (587 B.C.E.). The culture of Babylonia had a continuing influence on biblical writings. Its mythology shaped stories like that of the Tower of Babel. Its culture became synonymous with decadent urban living so that it became a metaphor for the corruption of civilized life (see Revelation 17–18).

Babylonian Exile From 587 to 538 B.C.E.. the Judeans lived in Babylonia before Cyrus the Great initiated a return to the land of Israel. While in exile Jews consolidated their traditions and created what became the Torah of Ezra.

Balaam The Hebrew Bible tells of this prophet who is hired to curse the Israelites and eventually corrupts them (Numbers 22–24, 31:8, 15–17). Archeologists have found an inscription from about 700 B.C.E. mentioning this prophet.

Baptism The New Testament associates this ceremony of immersion in water with John the Baptist as a ritual of forgiveness. Other Jewish groups such as the Pharisees and Essenes used such a ritual for attaining ritual purity or initiation into a group.

Bar Kokhba This title was given to Shimon Bar Kosiba who led a revolt against the Romans (132–135 C.E.) that ended with a Roman victory.

Barak This Israelite soldier was summoned by Deborah to lead the Israelite forces against Sisera. When he refused to go without her, she denounced him and declared that Sisera would die at the hands of a woman rather than by Barak's. Although Judges 5:12 mentions both Deborah and Barak, the key figure in the poetic telling of the story is Jael, the woman who eventually does kill Sisera (Judges 5:6, 34–27).

Barnabas Both the Acts of the Apostles (e.g. 9:26–30) and Paul's genuine letters (e.g. Galatians 2:1–13) mention this early church leader in Jerusalem. The later letter the "Epistle of Barnabus" is ascribed to him. This letter contrasts the way of Judaism to the way of Christianity.

Bathsheba This woman, said to be the daughter of a certain Eliam, married a Hittite, Uriah, who was a mercenary to King David. She had an affair with the king and, after David had disposed of her husband, married him. Bathsheba was instrumental in having her son, Solomon, named David's successor. Jesus was said to have had her as one of his progenitors. (2 Samuel 11–12; 1 Kings 1:15–17; Matthew 1:6).

Beatitudes This term, literally meaning "happinesses" lists the rewards for several types of people. Both Matthew 5:3–12 and Luke 6:20–23) attribute such a list to Jesus.

Beloved Disciple This figure appears only in the Gospel of John (see John 13:23) and appears to have a special relationship to Jesus—being favored even above the Apostle Peter. While the Gospel could imply that its author was that disciple, that identification is not certain.

Belshazzar The book of Daniel considers him the last king of Babylon, although in fact his father Nabonidus was that king.

Beth El This shrine bears the name of "House of God" and is associated with Jacob's vision of a ramp uniting heaven and earth (Genesis 28:11–13). Later it became the central sanctuary of the northern kingdom of Israel (1 Kings 12:32); the prophet Amos criticized the shrine and admonished the priests there (Amos 5:4–5;7:10–17).

Bishop This term is used to describe an "overseer" – a position indicating a high ranking church official during the early church (see 1 Timothy 3:1–7).

Boaz According to the book of Ruth, Boaz was a relative of Naomi, the mother-in-law of Ruth. Eventually he take pity on the widowed Ruth and marries her.

Booths This refers to the holiday called in Hebrew Sukkot. It was a thanksgiving festival held in the autumn and was one of the "pilgrimage" holidays during which Israelites were to go to the centralized sanctuary in Jerusalem (see Exodus Exodus 34).

Cain The eldest son of Adam and Eve received his name because Eve declared that she had "acquired a son from The Lord." He later murdered his brother Abel, was given a protective mark by God, and established the first cities.

Calendar The Hebrew Bible contains many different types of calendar. Some, like that in Exodus 23:12–19, are based on the movement of the sun and depend on seasonal conditions to set the time of holidays. Others, like that in Leviticus 23, are based on the moon and count months as the basis for setting festival times. The names of the months differ. They may be expressive, such as "Ethanim" or the month with continual flows (1 Kings 8:2) or they may borrow Canaanite names such as Bul (1 Kings 6:1, 37). Sometimes the same month is given different names in different books—the first month is sometimes called Aviv (see Exodus 13:4;23:15;34:18) and sometimes called Nisan (Nehemiah 2:1; Esther 2:7). Scholars try to reconstruct the earliest Hebrew calendars but the data is incomplete—there is no complete rendering of the names of all the months for any calendar, for example.

Canaan This name, given in the Bible to the land that the Israelites finally conquered, refers to the territory west of the Jordan River, bounded by Moab, Ammon, Edom, and Phonecia. The name was said to derive from Noah's grandson—probably an illegitimate child spawned by his youngest son Ham. Ironically, the language of Canaan was what eventually came to be known as "Hebrew," a clearly Semitic language and not a Hamitic one!

Canon This term derives from the Greek for a standard or measure and refers to the writings that a religious group considers authoritative. The Hebrew Bible developed slowly into the present canon accepted by rabbinic leaders in about 70 C.E.; several books included in previous collections such as the Septuagint were reject. The New Testament as well developed its present canon slowly only being finalized around the time of Athanasius.

Catholic Letters This refers to certain later letters in the New Testament addressed to a general audience (the three Johanine letters, James, Jude, and 1 and 2 Peter). Of these the first three and the last four belong as separate collections.

Chaldean The term refers to Babylonians from Chaldea. As used in the later books of the Bible such as Daniel, however, it means "magician"—and such a usage dates a passage to Hellenistic times.

Christ This term translates the Hebrew word Mashiach (Messiah) and refers to a leader anointed as a sign of appointment to a special office. As used in much of the New Testament, including some of Paul's letters, it becomes a personal title for Jesus of Nazareth.

Christian Apocrypha This term refers to books appearing in some early collections of Christian Scriptures but eventually rejected from the final canon. Books such as the Didache, 1 Clement, and the Letter of Barnabas are examples of such writings.

Circumcision This ritual of cutting off the foreskin of the penis is given various explanations in the Hebrew Bible (see Genesis 17, Exodus 4, Joshua 5) and caused a controversy in early Christianity (see Acts 15 and Galatians 2). Eventually the ritual operation became a way of identifying Jews from Gentiles.

Claudius This fourth Roman emperor (41–54 C.E.) was said to have expelled the Jews from Rome (see Acts 11:28 and 18:2).

Clement of Rome This first century bishop was thought to have authored the letter 1 Clement, a work that describes Christian beliefs and practices such as Sunday worship and considers the criteria needed for legitimate Christian leadership.

Codex Sinaiticus This manuscript of the Septuagint includes several Christian writings such as the Letter of Barnabus that were later rejected from the canon.

Constantine This Roman emperor (306–337 C.E.) legitimated Christianity, made it the official religion of the Roman Empire, and called the Council of Nicea in 325 to create a unified Christianity.

Cornelius This Roman centurion appears in Acts 10–11 as an example of God's choice of Gentiles and the movement of Christianity out of the Jewish context.

Covenant This term translates the Hebrew word "brith" and the Greek term for testament. It refers to an agreement generally, and more specifically to an agreement between the divine and human beings. The Hebrew Bible describes covenants with early heroes such as Abraham and Noah, later kings such as David and Josiah, and a "new covenant" to be made after the Babylonian Exile (Jeremiah 30–31). The New Testament sees Jesus' suffering, death, and resurrection as this "new covenant" or "new testament" (Mark 14:22).

Crucifixion This mode of execution was used by the Romans as punishment for political criminals. Jesus of Nazareth was executed in this manner because he was considered a revolutionary "King of the Jews" capable of instigating a rebellion against the Romans.

Cyrus Cylinder This cylinder created to celebrated Cyrus the Great's conquest of Babylonia describes how the Babylonian God Marduk inspired him to restore the various local gods and their peoples to their lands. This ideology differs from that of the Hebrew Bible that attributes Cyrus' actions to the will of the Jewish God, YHWH.

Cyrus the Great This Persian king who conquered Babylon in 539 B.C.E. allowed the Jews to return to the land of Israel and restore their worship of their own God.

Damascus This major city in Syria figures prominently in biblical stories. Abraham has a servant from Damascus (Genesis 15:2) and the Apostle Paul spends time there (Acts 9).

David This king of a united Israelite nation (1000–962 B.C.E.) is credited with rising to power from humble beginnings and gaining a covenant with God for an eternal royal dynasty (2 Samuel 7). He was also considered fallible and liable to sin (see 2 Samuel 12 and 2 Samuel 24).

Day of the Lord This phrase originally entailed an expectation that YHWH (the Lord) would punish Israel's enemies. The prophet Amos warns people against desiring that day (Amos 5:18–20). Later the phrase suggests a cataclysmic end of time (Zephaniah 1:14–19).

Day of Atonement This most solemn day in the festival calendar in Leviticus 16 was a time for forgiveness of sins for the nation, the priests, and individuals. In post-exilic and Hellenistic times this was the one time that the High Priest would recite the actual name YHWH. Hebrews 9 claims that Jesus' supernal ritual sacrifice replaced that ritual.

Deacon The term literally means "servant" and was used in the early church to refer to lower orders of Christian leadership (see 1 Timothy 3:8–13). Romans 16:1–2 mentions a woman, Phoebe, as deacon of the church.

Dead Sea Scrolls These were manuscripts and other types of written material found in caves at Qumran, a settlement near the Dead Sea. These manuscripts seem to come from the first century of the common era and include texts of the Hebrew Bible, Apocrypha, and material found nowhere else.

Deborah This "judge" in Israel is associated with the military figure of Barak. The story of how she rallied Israelite tribes against the Canaanites is told first in prose and then in poetry in Judges 4–5.

Demetrius This son of Seleucus IV reigned from 162–150 B.C.E. and, because of his contentiousness with other claimants on the Seleucid throne, made concessions to the Hasmonean priests, allowing them a large degree of independent political power.

Deuteronomic History This description of what can also be called the "Former Prophets" emphasizes the theology behind the books from Joshua through 2 Kings. That theology builds on the ideas found in the book of Deuteronomy and claims that Israel's apostasy from YHWH leads to defeat and failure while obedience to God leads to success. Scholars think both Deuteronomy and the books of the Former Prophets were produced under King Josiah of Judah after his reformation of religious life (621 B.C.E.) and were then revised during the Babylonian Exile.

Devil This term that translates either "diabolos" (opposer, Satan) or "daemon" (demon) refers to a supernatural force working for evil in the world. Compare Satan.

Diaspora This Greek term meaning "dispersion" or "scattering" refers to Jewish settlements outside the Land of Israel. The Jewish term for this dispersal is "galut" or "exile" implying a forced rather than voluntary scattering.

Didache Discovered in 1883, this "teachings of the twelve" apostles was an early Christian moral text from the first century of the common era. It preserves Jewish moral rules but dispenses with the ritual commandments. It portrays two ways—the way of life and the way of death—between which a person must choose. Its 16 chapters discuss Christian rituals such as baptism, fasts, and the Lord's Day as well as moral and theological issues.

Dietary Laws The Hebrew Bible contains several regulations about diet and food consumption (see, for example, Leviticus 11). Early Christianity rejected most of these, but only after considerable controversy (see Acts 10–11; Acts 15:19–29).

Dionysius This Greek God was the center of a Hellenistic cult advocating freedom and liberty—especially for women—and was outlawed in the Roman Empire. Its myth and ritual included a tale of a God who died and was reborn that some scholars think influenced Christianity.

Documentary Hypothesis Julius Wellhausen in the 19th century analyzed the Pentateuch and discovered it to be composed of four primary documents—the Yahwist, the Elohist, the Priestly, and the Deuteronomic. He related each of these to different historical periods. While scholars have modified this theory in more recent decades, the recognition that the Bible is composite and draws on materials from very different times has become the accepted view.

Domitian This Roman emperor (81–96 C.E.) persecuted Christians. Many scholars see that persecution underlying much of the writing in the book of the Revelation of John.

Donatism This movement claimed that Christ only appeared to take on human form and did not really suffer and die on the Cross. Several books of the New Testament, especially the letters of John seem written to refute such a view.

Doxology This literary form, found often in Psalms and in parts of the New Testament, is a short prayer of praise for God, usually functioning as a concluding coda to a longer prayer, but sometimes existing independently.

Dura-Europos, Synagogue of Discovered in 1932, this ancient Hellenistic synagogue (built about 240 C.E.) in Syria displays murals with biblical portraits showing clear influence of Greek thought and aesthetics. It provides evidence of the integration Diaspora Jews had in the cultures in which they lived.

Edom This ancient Near Eastern country south of the biblical nation of Judah, also bordered Moab, and the Sinai desert. The inhabitants were portrayed as being descendants of Esau, the brother of Jacob the progenitor of the Israelites, and therefore related to the Judeans.

Egypt This ancient land of the Nile river, southwest of Israel, exerted both cultural and political influences on biblical authors. The story of an enslavement in Egypt and an escape from Egyptian slavery dominates the Torah. The attractions of Egypt and the dangers of that attraction are discussed in the prophets. Hellenist Judaism drew much of its culture from Egyptian influences.

Elder (Presbyter) This term referred generally to a Christian leader (see the letters of 2 and 3 John). They are "rulers" but seem to have less specific duties than deacons or bishops (see 1 Timothy 5:17; Titus 1:5–9).

Elephantine This island in the river Nile in Egypt included a significant Hellenistic Jewish population that even established its own Temple. Several papyri documents from this community (from 450– 399 B.C.E.) have been discovered that shed light on the cultural traditions of Hellenistic Jews.

Eli The priest officiating at the shrine of Shilo during the time of Samuel the Seer (1 Samuel 1–4). The corruption of his sons led to Samuel superseding them in the priesthood. During his time the Holy Ark was captured by the Philistines, only to be returned when it brought plagues upon those who had captured it.

Elijah This Israelite prophet and priest (see 1 Kings 17–19, 21;2 Kings 1–2) confronted King Ahab of Israel and demanded that he choose between the God of Israel (YHWH) and the Phoenician deity Baal. Stories of his miracle working became models for later narratives.

Elisha Elisha ben Shafat inherited the mantle of Elijah (2 Kings 2:1–15) and continued his tradition of integrating religious and political concerns. He not only engineered Jehu's coup over King Ahab (2 Kings 9), but was also involved in Syrian politics (2 Kings 8).

Enki This Sumerian god, known in Akkadian as Ea, favored humanity. One Sumerian version of the great flood story claims that Enki warned the one person who would survive the flood.

Enoch The Hebrew Bible provides two anecdotes about this early figure. Genesis 4:17 associates him with Cain's establishing of the first city. Another, Genesis 5:21, tells that he "walked with God" and was taken from earth at the age of 365 years. Later tradition developed that latter tale and reported the visions he had received when entering heaven.

Enosh The Hebrew Bible never develops narratives about this descendent of Seth (Genesis 5:6–9) whose name in Hebrew is often used to mean "human being." The appearance of his name in Ecclesiasticus 49:14–16 suggests that stories about him circulated in ancient times.

Enuma Elish This term refers to an Akkadian creation epic that begins with "Enuma Elish" (Once, on high…). The narrative bears a striking resemblance to the Genesis creation narratives. Several versions of this epic exist. The most familiar is the one written in the twelfth century B.C.E. that adapted the poem to the cultic practices of the god Marduk in Babylonia and ends with the construction of the great "Gateway of the God" or Tower of Bab-El.

Epicureanism This school of thought is traced back to Epicurus (341–270 B.C.E.) and taught that the pursuit of pleasure—or rather the absence of pain—is the most important moral quest. The philosophy was proudly atheistic, contending that the existence of evil disproves the existence of a benevolent deity.

Esau This eldest born son of the patriarch Isaac was said to be the progenitor of the Edomites. The Bible claims that he despised his privileges as first born and that Jacob, his younger brother, took his blessing from him by treachery.

Eschatology This term literally means "knowledge of the end" and refers to texts that purport to describe the end of the world. When that description includes catastrophic and cataclysmic changes it is also apocalyptic.

Essenes The Jewish historian Josephus describes the Essenes as one of the major groups in Roman Judea. He claims that they led ascetic lives of self-restraint and piety. Many scholars think of them as Hasidim or pietists and associate them with the writers of the Dead Sea Scrolls.

Esther The biblical book of Esther gives this as a Persian name for the Jewish girl Hadassah who saves the Jewish people from destruction when threatened by Haman, the advisor to the Persian king. The name probably derives from the ancient Babylonian goddess Ishtar, just as her cousin Mordecai's name probably derives from the ancient Babylonian god Marduk.

Ethnarch This title translates as "Leader of the community" and, in the Hellenistic world, was applied to any appointed head of a country who, nonetheless, did not have the status of an independent ruler. 1 Maccabees 14:28 gives this title to Simon the Maccabee who also was invested as high priest. Later Hasmonean rulers took the title king, but under the Romans only a few Jewish leaders were kings, most were considered ethnarchs.

Eucharist This Greek term meaning "thanksgiving" was applied to the ceremony that Jesus inaugurated as a sign of his "new testament" at his last supper (Mark 14:22–25). Church leaders as early as Justin Martyr use this expression for that ritual, although Paul merely calls it "The Lord's Meal" (1 Corinthians 11:20) and Jude 12 calls it an "agape" or "love feast."

Eve This name is given to the first woman when she becomes "the mother of all who live" (Genesis 3:20). Before this she was merely "woman"—the one taken from the male.

Exilarch This title translates the Hebrew words "Rosh Galut"—the head of the exile (the word is usually translated as "Diaspora" but in Jeremiah 29:22 the negative connotations of the word is made very clear). The first historical references to this title comes from the period of the Parthians in Babylonia (247 B.C.E.. to 228 C.E.). The office itself, however, may be traced bac to 2 Kings 25:27–30).

Exodus From Egypt The Hebrew Bible describes how the Israelites were enslaved in Egypt, freed by God's miracles worked through Moses and Aaron, given the law of the covenant, and brought into the land of Canaan (see Exodus through Joshua and Judges; see the retelling given in Deuteronomy 26, Joshua 24, and Psalm 78).

Ezra This scribe came to the land of Israel from Babylonia bringing the "Torah of Moses" as the law of the land (425–400 B.C.E.). He introduced new religious festivals and a more restrictive marriage policy among the Jews who settled the land.

Festival Scrolls These are the five scrolls—Song of Songs, Ecclesiastes, Ruth, Lamentations, and Esther—read at five Jewish festivals—Passover, Booths, Pentecost, the Ninth of Av, and Purim. The Rabbinic teachers put these books in the Writings part of the canon and used them to provide a personal and individual dimension to public festivals.

Former Prophets See Deuteronomic History.

Gad A prophet mentioned in 2 Samuel 24 who advises King David

Galilee A region in the north of Israel adjacent to the Sea of Galilee (in Hebrew "Kineret" or "harp"

shaped). According to the Synoptic Gospels this is where Jesus grew up and began his preaching.

Gamaliel This name was taken by several leading rabbinical figures in Palestine under the Romans. Rabban Gamaliel I was prominent just before and after the Jewish war against the Romans. This was probably the figure that Acts 5:34–40 and 22:3 associate both with the Apostle Paul and with advocacy of tolerance for Christians.

Gentiles The term translates the Hebrew word "goyyim" meaning "the nations" (Psalm 9:17—"All the Goyyim forget God") and is used to refer to non-Jews.

Gentile Christians The New Testament describes many non-Jews who convert to Christianity. The early church debated whether these "gentile Christians" should be asked to follow Jewish rituals such as circumcision and the dietary laws (see Acts 15).

Gerizim This mountain, name as a holy place in Deuteronomy 27:12, was part of a complex of places making up the ritual center of Shechem (see Joshua 8:30–35). In later times it became the capital of Samaria.

Gibeonites These inhabitants of Gibeon were Horites who tricked Joshua into making a treaty with them rather than destroying them. The town itself became a ritual center during the time of the kings David and Solomon (2 Samuel 21:1-9; 1 Kings 3:4–5).

Gideon According to Judges 6–8 this early Israelite leader resisted the temptation to become a king even while organizing the disparate tribes for self-defense.

Gilgal The Hebrew word "Gilgal" means a heap of stones. It is used to describe Joshua's memorial to the circumcision of the Israelites coming into Canaan (Joshua 5:8–9), is associated with Beth El as a northern shrine visited by prophets (2 Kings 1–4) and is criticized along with Beth El by Amos (Amos 5:4–5).

Gilgamesh An ancient epic about this Sumerian King of Uruk developed in several versions—both Sumerian and Akkadian. The Akkadian version includes a story about a great flood that resembles the biblical story of Noah.

Glossolalia This term means "speaking in tongues." In Acts 2 the disciples speak in such a way that foreigners hear the words in their own languages (so what is Greek to the Greeks is Arabic to the Arabs and Aramaic to Syrians, for example). When Paul of Tarsus declares that although he speaks in tongues, he prefers clear speech instead (1 Corinthians 13:1–3) he seems to be thinking of a different types of speech in which "those who speak in a tongue do not speak to other people, but to God, for nobody understands them, since they are speaking mysteries in the Spirit" (1 Corinthians 14:2). This appears to be a different phenomenon than that described in Acts 2.

Gnosticism Technically this term refers to various Christian movements, eventually considered heretical, claiming a special knowledge (gnosis) granted to an elite membership. These movements often emphasized a dualism—differentiating between a benevolent and demonic deity, between the children of light and the children of darkness, and between the forces of good and the forces of evil. n general, many Hellenistic movements, including Jewish mystical ones, also demonstrate these characteristics of Gnosticism.

Gog According to Ezekiel 38, Gog was the leader of the enemies of Israel whose attack on the Jewish people will lead to the final war between good and evil. This image reappears in Revelation 20:8.

Gomorrah One of two cities whose ruins lie by the Dead Sea, this ancient town was said to have been destroyed by God in retribution for their evil. Genesis 19 suggests that this evil was one of inhospitality. Jude 7 suggests that immorality and "strange lust" led to its destruction.

Gospel The term "Gospel" is an English rendering of the Greek "evangelion" meaning good message. It has been interpreted as "God's Spell" or "Good Spell." The New Testament includes four books called gospels. These combine a biographical narrative about the career of Jesus of Nazareth with saying attributed to Jesus. The term may be used to describe either narratives alone or sayings alone.

Gospel of Thomas This gospel takes the form of a list of sayings attributed to Jesus. These sayings tend to be Gnostic and preach a hidden message. The work is extant now only in manuscripts from the fourth and fifth centuries in the Coptic language. The original work may well have been written in the first century of the common era.

Griesbach Theory Originally proposed by Johann Griesbach in the 18th century this theory denies the commonly accepted explanation for the Synoptic Gospels. While the consensus follows a "two source" theory in which Luke and Matthew drew on the Gospel of Mark and a common group of sayings attributed to Jesus, this theory thinks of Mark as a condensation of Matthew and Luke.

Habakkuk A prophet in pre-exilic Judea. In the story of Bel and the Dragon (an apocryphal addition to Daniel) Habakkuk comes to save the hero.

Habiru This term for an ancient Near Eastern group of nomads appears in several Egyptian monuments. Scholars suggest that this group may resemble the organization and landless status of the early biblical heroes such as Abraham.

Hagar This Egyptian woman was Sarah's handmaid who became Abraham's wife. When Hagar gave birth to a son Sarah insisted that she and her son be cast out (contrast Genesis 16 and 21). Paul of Tarsus uses this as a sign of God's arbitrary choices of favorite people (Galatians 4).

Ham This son of Noah was said to have dishonored his father (Genesis 9:22) and, therefore, had his son cursed (that son, Canaan, was a particular rival of the Israelites). He was said to be the progenitor of the Egyptians and the non-Semitic groups in Canaan (Genesis 11:6–10).

Haman This villain of the biblical book of Esther was said to be a descendant of the Amalekite king Agag just as Mordecai, his opponent, was a descendant of Saul, the king who had spared Agag.

Hammurabi This Babylonian king (1728–1686 B.C.E.) ruled a vast empire. His law code, written in cuneiform resembles many of the legal portions of the Pentateuch.

Hanukkah This festival of "dedication" was instituted by the Maccabees, although 1 and 2 Maccabees tell the story differently and Josephus offers a third version of the tale. It is an eight day festival involving lighting of lamps and general rejoicing and may be related to non-Jewish celebrations observed during the winter season.

Hasideans This Greek form of the Hebrew word Hasidim means pietists. These were devout Jews who followed Jewish law to such an extent that they would not even defend themselves against Hellenistic armies when attacked on the Sabbath.

Hasmoneans This name taken from Mattathias the Hashmoni denotes the dynasty begun by Simon the Maccabee. Although originating as a protest against Hellenization of Jewish religion, the Hasmoneans eventually became Hellenistic themselves. They ruled Judea from the time of Simon (about 145 B.C.E.) to the Roman conquest by Pompei (63 B.C.E.).

Hebrews This term is used in the Bible to indicate the early leaders of the group that eventually became "Israel." The genealogy in Genesis 10:21–31 traces Ever (the first "Hebrew" back to Noah's son Shem. Genesis 14:13 identifies Abraham as "Abram the Hebrew."

Heliodorus According to 2 Maccabees 3 this representative of King Seleucus of Syria sought to despoil the wealth of the Jerusalem Temple for his master. A miracle occurred and Heliodorus was frightened away by a supernatural apparition without accomplishing his task.

Hellenism This term refers to the acceptance and imitation of Greek language, thought, and culture by non-Greeks. Alexander the Great brought Hellenism to the ancient Near East. Hellenism influenced Jews in Egypt, Rome, and even in the land of Israel.

Heresy As used in the New Testament the term refers to beliefs that oppose "true" Christian faith. According to Acts 24:14, Paul defended himself against the charge of heresy. As Christianity developed alternative Christian views became branded as heresy (see 1 Timothy 1:3).

Herod Agrippa The grandson of Herod the Great was made king over Palestine by Claudius and had a short reign (41– 44 C.E.) and, according to Acts 12:1–23 was punished for his appropriation of divine honors by a horrible death.

Herod Agrippa II This son of Agrippa I was made king of the territory of Chalcis in 50 C.E.. Acts

25:13–26:32 pictures Paul of Tarsus defending himself before this king.

Herod the Great Married to a Hasmonean princess, Herod, an Idumean, was appointed king of Judea and ruled from 40–4 B.C.E.. While admired by Diaspora Jews, Herod was detested by Jews in Palestine.

Hesed This Hebrew word means "loving kindness" and refers to the virtue of steadfast loyalty to God and other human beings. It was a primary concern of prophets such as Elijah, Amos, and Hosea.

Hezekiah This king of Judah (715–686 B.C.E.) survived the siege of the Assyrians by Sargon II and then Sennacherib. He is credited with having introduced religious reforms into Judean worship (2 Kings 18–20) and legends connect him with the prophet Isaiah (Isaiah 36–39).

High Priest Although this title appears in some pre-exilic stories (2 Kings 12:10, 2 Kings 22–23 where the term may have been slipped in by an editor who inserted the title from the parallel accounts in Chronicles), most scholars think it is a product of post-exilic Judean religious life. (see Haggai 1:12 and 2:4 and Zechariah 3:1). In post-exilic times the office was the main administrative leader of the Judean people. When, under the Hasmoneans, a kingship was reinstated, the king also served as High Priest.

Historical Criticism This modern approach to the Bible began in the seventeenth century with the writings of Baruch Spinoza. It reads the Bible as any other piece of literature, understanding it in terms of the context in which it was produced, analyzing its claims scientifically, and comparing biblical passages with other writings contemporaneous to them. It was opposed by "Fundamentalism" that gave priority to the truth of certain biblical doctrines rather than to scientific investigation.

Holy Ark Sometimes called "Ark of the Covenant" this chest contained the tablets of the Law said to date from the time of Moses (Exodus 25:10–22). Joshua 3–4 and 6 associate miracles with the presence of the Ark, but the Philistines managed to capture it (1 Samuel 4) although they suffered because that act. King David moved the Ark to Jerusalem (2 Samuel 6:1–15), and King Solomon placed it in the Temple he built there (1 Kings 8).

Holy Spirit This New Testament term derives from the Hebrew Bible's claim that eventually all humanity will be filled with the spirit of God (Joel 2:28–30). In the New Testament Jesus receives such inspiration and passes it on to others (John 1:29–34). In John 14:24–30 the spirit is identified as the "Paraclete" or "advocate" who substitutes for Jesus after he has ascended to heaven. In other parts of the New Testament being the recipient of such spirit is demonstrated by speaking in a strange language that everyone understands and by making prophetic statements (see Acts 2; 1 Corinthians 13).

Hyksos This is the name given in some ancient Egyptian writings to a Semitic group of invaders who, briefly, took control of Egypt from the Egyptians (1720–1570 B.C.E.). Some scholars think that this might have been the time that the Hebrews entered Egypt.

Hymn This literary form of poetry applies to an extended poem praising God for actions in the past and present—often historical, but also daily activities such as feeding the hungry—and includes a call to worship God, the reasons for the worship, and a conclusion.

Idumea This Greek rendering of the name "Edom" refers to the population to the north of Israel the inhabitants of which were forcibly converted to Judaism by John Hyrcanus I (128 B.C.E.).

Incarnation This idea claims that the divine takes on a human body. John 1:1–18 construes Jesus as the embodiment of the divine logos.

Inanna This Sumerian goddess figures prominently in the story of the great flood as well as in the retelling of that story in the Babylonian Epic of Gilgamesh. That epic tells of how "the great goddess" appears to Utnapishtim (the hero of the flood) and flings her necklace into the sky to make the rainbow. In a Babylonian context the "great goddess" was certainly presumed to be Ishtar, but on the basis of the Sumerian original her identity was probably Inanna.

Isaac This son of Abraham and Sarah was preferred over his half-brother Ishmael, the son of Abraham and Hagar (Genesis 16 and 21) and nearly sacrificed by his father at God's command (Genesis 22).

Ishmael The eldest son of Abraham, Ishmael is considered the progenitor of the Arabs and of twelve princes (Genesis 25:12–16).

Ishtar This Babylonian goddess was prominent in Persia, and her name seems to lie behind that of the heroine of the book of Esther.

Isis This ancient Egyptian goddess was the wife of Osiris and mother of Horus and was worshiped in a Hellenistic ritual cult. Portrayals of Isis and Horus resemble the later iconography of the virgin Mary and Jesus.

Israel This name is found as early as the 13th pre-Christian century, but is associated in the Hebrew Bible with the early figure of Jacob (the son of Isaac and grandson of Abraham). Two different stories tell of Jacob's change of name to Israel (Genesis 32:28 and 35:10). Jacob's descendants became known of "Israelites" – a term that led to the land being called "Israel." While a united kingdom of "Israel" seems to have existed from the time of King Saul to King Solomon, after 922 B.C.E. the land was divided into two kingdoms with Israel (or Samaria) being the northern kingdom and Judah being the name of the southern kingdom.

Israelite Although generally applied to all descendants of Jacob, it is more narrowly used to describe citizens of the northern kingdom in the land of Israel.

Jacob The young twin of Isaac and Rebekah (Genesis 25:21–26), Jacob acquired his brother's blessing and birthright (Genesis 26–27), fled to his mother's relatives where he married Rachel and Leah, had children, gained wealth, and returned to homeland (Genesis 29–32). His twelve sons are considered progenitors of Israel's twelve tribes. Eventually he followed his son Joseph to Egypt, where he died although he was buried in his ancestral burial cave in the land of Israel.

Jaddua This priestly leader was claimed by Flavius Josephus to be the High Priest in Judea during the time of Alexander the Great. After conquering the city of Gaza, , Josephus reports, Alexander marched on Jerusalem. Jaddua went to meet Alexander. The great warrior was impressed by the priestly leader and granted him and Jerusalem a charter of independence.

Jafet This son of Noah was said to be the ancestor of Hittites, the "sea people" from the Aegean, and, by extension, the Greeks. Genesis 9:27 suggests a coalition between this group and the Semites—perhaps referring to the co-existence of Israelites and Philistines during the time of the Judges. Later interpreters explained the passage to refer to the Hellenistic tradition that combined Jewish and Greek culture.

Jamnia This independent Roman village became the seat for a rabbinic assembly led by Yohanan ben Zakkai who had escaped from besieged Jerusalem and surrendered to the Romans. What became rabbinic Judaism, including the canonized Jewish Bible, was established at Jamnia (called in Hebrew Yavneh).

Jehoiakim This king of Judah was placed on the throne by Necho of Egypt in 609 B.C.E. and rebelled against Babylonia, expecting Egyptian support that was not forthcoming.

Jehoshaphat This king of Judah (873–849 B.C.E.) is given only 10 verses in the Deuteronomic history (1 Kings 22:41–51). Nevertheless, the Chronicler augments the tale of his reign and even provides him with religious reforms and a hymn to God (2 Chronicles 20).

Jepthah This illegitimate son of the Judge Gideon eventually sacrificed his daughter after securing a victory for the Israelites (Judges 11)

Jericho This ancient city was said to have been destroyed by Joshua (Joshua 2 and 5:13–6:26) but archeological discoveries show it to already have been in ruins at the time attributed to Joshua.

Jerusalem This ancient city originally was a Jebusite city that King David captured (Joshua 18:28, Judges 19:10, 2 Samuel 5:6–10).

Jerusalem Temple King Solomon is said to have built the first Temple in Jerusalem (1 Kings 5–7), while King Josiah centralized Israelite worship there (2 Kings 22–23). That Temple became regarded as the only appropriate place for Jewish worship (although Jews on the Egyptian island of Elephantine had constructed their own Temple). It was destroyed by the Babylonians (587 B.C.E.), then by the Romans during the great Jewish war (70 C.E.), and finally after the Bar Kokhba rebellion (135 C.E.).

Jesus of Nazareth The name given to the hero of the four Gospels and to the messianic figure or Christ throughout the New Testament. The name Jesus was a common one, a Greek form derived from the Hebrew "Joshua" or "Saving Hero." The association of Jesus with Nazareth is complex, associated both with a city in the northern part of Israel-the Galilee- (see Matthew 2:23, Luke 1:26; John 1:46) and with being an ascetic Nazirite (see Matthew 2:23 and Acts 24:5).

Jew This term translates the Greek Ioudious referring to inhabitants of Roman Judean and is found in the New Testament Gospels. It has become the term describing followers of the Rabbinic traditions developed after 70 C.E.)

Jewish Christians This term refers to Christians who demanded that conversion to Christianity entailed an obedience to all Jewish practices.

Jezebel This Phoenician queen of King Ahab supported her own religious traditions rather than those native to Israel (2 Kings 16–21). She met her death with steadfast courage, dressed for the occasion (2 Kings 9:30–37). The scorn cast upon her by the Hebrew Bible is reflected in Revelation 2:20 where she symbolizes false religion.

John the Baptist This ascetic was said to be a preacher during the first century of the common era who predicted a coming judgment and immersed Jews in water for the sake of purification from sins. Each of the biblical Gospels portray a different relationship between John the Baptist and Jesus of Nazareth (see Mark 1:2–8; Matthew 3:1–12; Luke 3:7–22; John 1:29–34)

John Hyrcanus I This Hasmonean King (134–104 B.C.E.) extended the boundaries of the Judean kingdom and forcibly converted the Edomites (Idumeans) to Judaism. He followed a policy of Hellenization.

John Hyrcanus II This Hasmonean high priest was a puppet of the Roman government (63–40 B.C.E.) and was succeeded by Herod the Great.

Jonathan the Hasmonean This son of Mattathias, one of the Maccabean revolutionaries, became the leader of the revolt after the death of his brother Judas. He defeated Bacchides, the head of the Syrian army and "began to judge the people; and he destroyed the godless out of Israel" (1 Maccabees 9:73). He was appointed high priest over the nation (1 Maccabees 10:21).

Joseph The eleventh son of Jacob whose rise to power in Egypt led to the migration of the Israelites to that country and eventually to their enslavement there and their ultimate escape.

Joseph the Tobiad This tax-collector for the Ptolemaic rulers of Palestinian supplanted his father and brothers who supported the Seleucids. The intrigue behind the two parties lay the foundation for the Maccabean revolution (see 2 Maccabees 3–4).

Josephus, Flavius This Jewish writer (37–100 B.C.E.) wrote several polemics and historical works in Greek defending the Jewish people. His *Antiquities* and *The Jewish War* provide background on Jewish life in the land of Israel during the Hellenistic period.

Joshua the High Priest Both the prophet Haggai and Zechariah speak of this post-exilic figure upon whom they fixed their hopes for a renewed Jewish nation. His prominence shows how an anointed "messiah" could be a priestly and not merely a royal figure.

Josiah This king of Judah (640–609 B.C.E.) is credited with a religious reformation (in 621) that centralized worship in Jerusalem and made the "Book of the Law of Moses" the canon of the nation. He was killed attempting to defeat Necho, the Pharaoah of Egypt.

Judah This name, originally one of the twelve sons of the patriarch Israel, came to be applied to the southern kingdom in the Land of Israel. This kingdom survived a siege by the Assyrians who had destroyed the northern kingdom of Israel, suffered exile to Babylonia, and returned from that exile to create a new nation that was known as Judea.

Judas This Greek rendition of the Hebrew name "Judah," was popular among Hellenistic Jews. The name occurs in the Gospels (see Luke 6:16 where "Judas son of James" is distinguished from "Judas Iscariot, who became a traitor"). The most famous of these, Judas Iscariot, is portrayed as betraying Jesus to the Roman authorities, sometimes because of greed (Matthew 26:14–16) and sometimes because of Satan (Luke 22:3–4).

Judas Maccabeus This Hasmonean hero led the revolt of the pietistic Jews against the Hellenizing pro-Seleucid priests. His war against Antiochus IV (168–165 B.C.E.) included the capture of Jerusalem and the establishing of the holiday of Hanukkah.

Judea This is the name given in Hellenistic times to the province that included Jerusalem and its environment. It was not identical to ancient Judah and did not include the northern section of the land of Israel which was the province of Samaria.

Judean This term, strictly speaking, refers to inhabitants of the southern kingdom in the land of Israel. After the reign of King Solomon, the united Israelite kingdom divided into two different independent states—the northern state called Israel or Samaria and the southern state called Judah.

Judges This term refers to a type of decentralized leadership associated with Israel's entrance into the land of Canaan and its fight against the Philistines (1220–1000 B.C.E.). Judges such as Jepthah and Samson are thought of as often instituting illegitimate religious practices.

Justin Martyr This early church leader (100–160 B.C.E.) provides insights into the canonization process and the development of early Christian liturgical practice,

Ketuvim This Hebrew word meaning "writings" refers to the third part of the Jewish Bible, including the books from Psalms through 2 Chronicles.

Kingdom of God A term referring to the idealized world that will follow the destruction of this mundane historical world. This idea can be revolutionary—referring to a political transformation, or spiritual—focusing on a change within human beings.

King Lemuel This king is said to have authored Proverbs 30. Such attribution is a sign that biblical wisdom literature saw itself as universal and not merely Hebraic.

Korach This priestly leader rebelled against Moses' leadership during the wandering in the desert before reaching the promised land. He and his followers were swallowed up by the earth (Numbers 16–17).

Lamech A descendant of Cain who demonstrates the violence of civilization. His wives bear the ancestors of civilized life while he boasts of his killings (Genesis 4:18–24).

Latter Prophets This term refers to the prophetic books Isaiah, Jeremiah, Ezekiel, Hosea, Joel, Amos, Obadiah, Jonah, Micah, Nahum, Habakkuk, Zephaniah, Haggai, Zechariah, Malachi. The designation "latter" refers to their placement in the Hebrew Bible after the Deuteronomic History and not to their historical period.

Lazarus In Luke 16:20–25 This name is used in a arable about a beggar who receives rewards in the world to come. In John 11:1–12:10 it is the name of the brother of Mary and Martha whom Jesus revives after he has died.

Leah This first wife of Jacob was considered "unloved," nevertheless of her six sons Reuben was the first born and Judah became the leading tribe because King David came from there.

Levite Levi was also a son of Leah. The tribe was designated the priestly tribe (Numbers 3) and did not inherit land with the rest of the Israelites.

Lex Taliones This "law of the limb" requires exact retaliation of "an eye for an eye" for a few selected legal infractions such as harming a pregnant woman (Exodus 21:23–25), human injury in contrast to animal injuries (Leviticus 24:17–22), or false witnessing (Deuteronomy 19:21).

Liturgy This term means the actions and words used in public worship. Liturgical controversies in the Bible included prophetic criticisms of prayer and sacrifice, Christian debates about the day on which the celebrate the Sabbath, on the necessity of circumcision and dietary laws for Gentile Christians, and on the meaning of baptism and the Lord's Meal.

Logos This Greek term literally means "word," and was used by philosophers like the Stoics to denote the universal force of Reason that permeates the world. Philo Judaeus identified this logos as God's eternal Torah. The Gospel of John 1:1–14 identifies it as incarnate in Jesus.

Lord's Day This celebration of a Sunday Sabbath was controversial in the early church. Some early writings, like the Didache supported such an observance.

Lord's Prayer This short prayer, versions of which appear in Matthew 6:9–13 and Luke 11:2–4. Both versions emphasize God's material and spiritual sustenance of those who worship truly.

Lot This nephew of Abraham migrated with him from Ur to Canaan but finally settled in Sodom. After God destroyed Sodom, Lot was saved but incestuously fathered two nations the Moabites and Ammonites (Israel's traditional enemies).

Maccabees This was a title given to the Hasmonean Judas the Maccabee (the Hammer) and extended to his father and brothers who joined in the fight against the Seleucids. The Maccabees finally gained independence for Judea and established the Hasmonean dynasty.

Magog According to Ezekiel 38:2 this is the land from which Gog the leader of the forces of evil in the final confrontation between the wicked and the good comes. In Revelation 20:8 this is interpreted as another leader of the forces of evil.

Major Prophets This term refers to the longer books of the prophets—Isaiah, Jeremiah, Ezekiel. "Major," in this context, means longer rather than more important.

Marcion This second century C.E. Christian leader who rejected the Jewish Bible as the product of a demonic deity. He created his own Bible—composed of a single Gospel and several of the Pauline letters. He was expelled from Rom3 in 140 C.E., but continued to exert an influence on the early church.

Marduk The Babylonian deity was chief god in Babylonia and the hero of the Babylonian epic the Enuma Elish. His name seems related to that of the Jewish hero of the biblical book of Esther, Mordecai.

Martyr This word means a "witness," and in particular a witness to God through willing self-sacrifice (see Acts 22:20). 2 Maccabees tells stories of Jewish martyrs (see 2 Maccabees 7) and the martyrdom of Stephen (Acts 7) is a prominent example in the New Testament.

Mary Magdalene This woman, often incorrectly identified as a former prostitute, was exorcized on demons by Jesus and became one of his disciples. According to the Gospels was one of the first to see the risen Jesus.

Mary and Martha of Bethany These women are identified in Luke 10:38–42 and John 11:1–12:8 as followers of Jesus.

Mashal This Hebrew word translates as "proverb" but also means "parable." It refers to a short statement that conveys a wisdom teaching. This may be an aphorism or it may be an extended allegorical narrative.

Mattathias the Hasmonean This old priest is credited for beginning the revolution against the Jewish priests who had accepted Hellenistic ways and Seleucid rule. His family eventually became a dynasty of priestly kings, the Hasmoneans.

Melchizedek This priest in Salem to whom Abraham paid a tithe of his spoils of war (Genesis 14:17–20) became a prototype of the ideal priest (Psalm 110:4; Hebrews 7)

Merneptah This Pharaoh of Egypt (1224–1211 B.C.E.) erected a victory stele in which he declared Israel destroyed never to rise again.

Mesha This king of Moab (849–820 B.C.E.) erected a stone declaring that when his God Chemosh was angry Moab suffered defeat by Israel and when Chemosh was no longer angry Moab defeated Israel.

Mesopotamia This name refers to the land between the Tigris and Euphrates rivers – what is now modern Iraq. In ancient time it was the locus of several important civilizations—the Sumerian, Akkadian, Assyrian, and Babylonian.

Messiah This term renders the Hebrew "Mashiah" or "anointed" and refers to a leader invested with his office by having oil poured on his head and beard. Two figures in the Hebrew Bible—the king and the high priest—were anointed. After the destruction of the Jerusalem Temple and the loss of national independence both positions were abolished. Jewish tradition claims that eventually God will restore the Temple and independent Jewish leadership. Hope for such messianic leadership animated many Jewish revolt movements. The Greek translation for this term, Christ, was applied to Jesus of Nazareth.

Midrash This Hebrew word means "that which is sought out." Midrash refers to a technique used by Jews since at least the Hellenistic period for discovering new meanings in the Bible by analyzing textual hints, anomalies, and other overlooked possibilities in selected passages.

Minor Prophets As used in this term "minor" means "shorter" rather than "less important." The twelve prophetic books from Hosea through Malachai constitute the "minor prophets."

Mithras This Persian God was said to have been born on December 25 and inspired a religious group practicing many rituals similar to those found in later Christianity.

Moab The inhabitants of Moab, a country bordering on ancient Israel, were considered related to the Israelites through Lot, the nephew of Abraham (Genesis 19). Ruth, an ancestor of King David, was said to be a Moabite (see Ruth 4:13–22).

Mordecai The hero of the book of Esther, Mordecai, was said to be his adopted daughter and cousin. His name resembles that of the Persian god Marduk.

Mortal Sin According to 1 John 5:14–17, certain sins may be forgiven through prayer. Prayer cannot remove other sins, and these are considered "mortal" sins.

Moses Moses is the leading figure in the story of Israel's Exodus from Egypt through their reaching of Canaan, the promised land (Exodus through Deuteronomy). He is credited with transmitting the Torah to Israel, establishing courts of law, and investing the priests with their sacred duties.

Muratorian Canon This list of "official" books in the Christian canon occurs in a fragment of a Latin document dating from the eighth century. Most scholars think it represents a translation from a much earlier Greek document, coming from as early as the fourth century.

Myth The word myth comes from a Greek term meaning story. As used by modern scholars it refers to a story that functions to convey a view of reality or an approach to the world rather than a report primarily meant to transmit factual information. In the New Testament the word is used to characterize false stories, heretical narratives, or beliefs rejected by the author (see 1 Timothy 1:3–7; 4:7; Titus 1:14).

Nabonidus This final king of Babylonia (556–539 B.C.E.) does not appear in the Hebrew Bible—often being replaced by his son Balshazzar.

Naboth This Israelite owned a garden coveted by King Ahab (1 Kings 21). When the king decides to have Naboth executed and then confiscates the garden, Elijah the prophet opposes him and expresses a universalistic ethics in which the king is no better than a commoner.

Nag Hammadi In 1945 several ancient manuscripts were found in Nag Hammadi, a village in Egypt. These manuscripts include Coptic writings of which several are non-canonical Christian texts. One of these, the Gospel of Thomas, collects Gnostic-like sayings attributed to Jesus.

Naomi In the book of Ruth, this Jewish woman goes to Moab where her sons marry Moabite women and die. Naomi returns to Israel with one of her daughters-in-law, Ruth, who marries Boaz and becomes an ancestor of King David.

Nathan This prophet in King David's court promises him that his dynasty will last forever (2 Samuel 7) and also upbraids him for his sin with Bathsheba (2 Samuel 12).

Nazirite A person vowing to refrain from imbibing intoxicating drinks, eating impure food, engaging in sexual relationships, and cutting his hair was known as a "Nazir" ((Numbers 6:1–21). The most famous of such Nazirites was Samson (Judges 13–16), although he eventually disobeyed each of these prohibitions.

Nebuchadnezzar This name represents a common biblical misrepresentation of Nebuchadrezzar (see Jeremiah 39:2 for the correct reading), the powerful Babylonian king (605–562 B.C.E.) who defeated Egypt and Judah, finally deporting Judah's elite to Babylonia in 587 B.C.E.

Necho This Egyptian Pharoah (610–594 B.C.E.) attacked Josiah of Judah, killing him and gaining Judah, but was defeated by the Babylonians.

Nehemiah This Jewish official at the Persian court is credited with going to Judea and spearheading the rebuilding of the Jerusalem Temple.

Nero This Roman Emperor (54–68 C.E.) was reputed to be ruthless and to have persecuted Christians.

Nevi'im This Hebrew word means "Prophets" and refers to the second section of the Jewish Bible. The Nevi'im comprise both the "former prophets" from Joshua through 2 Kings and the "latter prophets"—including both the "major" and "minor" prophets.

Nicanor This Seleucid general was defeated by the Maccabees who thereupon instituted a holiday to celebrate the victory (1 Maccabees 3:38; 7:26–32; 2 Maccabees 14:12–15:36).

Nicodemus According to the Gospel of John, Nicodemus was a leading Pharisee who visited Jesus and performed other actions showing his respect for him (John 3; 7; 19).

Noah The hero of the biblical story of a great flood (Genesis 6–9), upon the instructions given by God, Noah builds a wooden boat that enables the world to continue after a divinely inflicted flood kills all other living beings. This story bears resemblances to tales in Sumerian (Atrahasis) and Akkadian (Gilgamesh) literature.

Obadiah While Obadiah names the shortest of the Minor Prophets, it is also the name of an associate of King Ahab who saved 100 prophets from persecution and acted as intermediary between Ahab and Elijah (1 Kings 18).

Omri This king over the northern kingdom of Israel (876–869 B.C.E.) led that kingdom to great heights. Even after his dynasty ended, Assyrian records consider Israel "the land of Omri."

Onias This name was held by several Jewish High Priests, probably translating the Hebrew name Honi. These priests were usually pro-Egyptian, and the last of them, Onias IV fled upon the Seleucid conquest of Judea and built a temple of his own in Egypt in the year 169 B.C.E.. He was said to have appeared in a vision to Judas Maccabeus (2 Maccabees 15:12–24).

Orpah In the biblical book of Ruth, Orpah marries one of Naomi's two sons but unlike Ruth does not follow her mother-in-law from Moab to Israel.

Parable The term from the Greek for a "comparison" seems to translate the Hebrew "mashal," meaning a riddle, striking saying, or proverb. It is used in the New Testament to refer to stories told to shock, surprise, or startle the reader. Parables often, following the injunction of Isaiah 6:9–12, seek to confuse, disguise, or obscure meaning so that only the elect can understand (see Mark 4:10–12).

Parable of the Talents This story found in Matthew 25:14–30 and Luke 19:12–17 suggests that Christians must improve on what they have been given or suffer dire consequences. What is shocking in both versions (although more elaborated in Luke) is that the master—a symbol of the divine—is described as harsh and opportunistic.

Paraclete This term, found only in the Gospel of John, means "advocate" or "intermediary." The Gospel claims that after the death of Jesus this intermediary will convey the divine will to Christians.

Parallelism This literary style indicates Hebrew poetry and is based on patterns in the writing rather than rhyme or rhythm. Successive verses may repeat the meaning of the first verse, reverse that meaning, or develop it further.

Parousia This Greek word meaning "being near" is used to indicate Jesus' "second coming" or "appearance," that will indicate the conclusion of history and the beginning of the new age. At the Parousia God will judge humanity—giving out eternal rewards or eternal punishment.

Particularism This way of looking at the world emphasizes the individuality and difference of a particular group. It often imagines the group as chosen and elect—as more beloved by God than any other people.

Passover This Jewish festival commemorating the Exodus from Egypt is described in many different ways in the Hebrew Bible (see Exodus 12–13; Leviticus 23:4–8; Deuteronomy 16:1–6). The festival entails sacrificial offerings, priestly rituals, and often home rituals that including eating unleavened bread and bitter herbs and the drinking of wine. It acts as a symbol of liberation and freedom. The three Synoptic Gospels claims that Jesus' last supper was a Passover meal.

Paul of Tarsus Paul of Tarsus (10–65 C.E.) is credited with spreading Christianity through the Hellenistic world. The New Testament contains several letters attributed to Paul and a history, the Acts of the Apostles, that purports to record the events of his life.

Pentateuch This term, literally meaning "five scrolls" in Greek, refers to the first five books of the Hebrew Bible—Genesis, Exodus, Leviticus, Numbers, and Deuteronomy.

Pentecost Literally meaning "50 count," this term refers to a holiday occurring 50 days after the Jewish holiday of Passover. Although originally celebrated as a holiday of the wheat harvest, rabbinic Judaism understood it as a festival of the giving of the Torah. In Christianity the holiday falls 50 days after Easter and commemorates the influx of the Holy Spirit that occurred among the Apostles on the Pentecost after the Passover on which Jesus was crucified and resurrected.

Pharisees This is a name Josephus uses for one of the "Jewish sects" he describes. They are said to have been popular with the people, to have been lenient in applying Jewish law, and creative in adjusting to the changing needs of the nation. Rabbinic Judaism traces its origins back to the Pharisees. The New Testament singles them out for criticism, especially the Gospel of Matthew (see Matthew 23).

Philistines These "sea-peoples" as they were called, invaded Canaan from the Aegean Sea. From about 1200–1000 B.C.E. they proved an intractable foe, more dangerous than the native peoples the Israelites had originally faced. The Israelite kingship began as a response to this threat, and King David eventually conquered the Philistines. The Philistine name, however, remained in the designation of "Palestine" for this region.

Philo Judeas of Alexandria This Alexandrian Jewish philosopher (20 B.C.E.–50 C.E.) worked to reconcile Jewish tradition and Platonic philosophy. His philosophy emphasized God's transcendence and claimed that the "logos" or divine Word had emanated from God and, in the form of Torah, continued to mediate between the divine and the human.

Platonism This Greek philosophical tradition traced itself back to the philosopher Plato (427–347 B.C.E.). It emphasized a dualism between matter and form, body and spirit and believed in a single supernal divine Mind that Jewish and Christian scholars identified with the biblical God.

Pliny the Younger This official in the Roman Empire was administrator of Bithynia during the reign of Trajan as emperor Trajan (98–117 C.E.). He wrote for advice on how to deal with Christians who seemed to be trouble makers in his realm.

Pompey This Roman general conquered Judea in 63 B.C.E., thereby ending the independent kingship of the Hasmoneans.

Post-Exilic This term refers to the Jewish settlement in the Land of Israel that occurred after Cyrus the Great allowed Jews to return to that land (537 B.C.E.). The biblical religion that developed in this period differed significantly from that of previous biblical religions.

Priest In the Hebrew Bible two tribal groups make up the priestly families—the Kohanim and the Levites. The primary task of the priest was to offer sacrifices in the Jerusalem Temple. Some of the Psalms seem to have been composed by priests for use in the sacrificial service.

Proverb This term refers to a short wisdom saying, translating the Hebrew "mashal."

Pseudepigrapha This term literally means books ascribed to ancient heroes but actually written by more recent authors. It technically refers to a set of books excluded from both the Hebrew Bible and the Apocrypha although considered as canonical by some early collections of sacred writings.

Pseudonymity This refers to the practice of a later author taking on the name and persona of an earlier figure and writing in that figure's name. Often this tactic should be contrasted with forgery since the author sincerely believes that the new writing springs from the same ideas and consciousness as that of the older author to whom it is attributed. Several books in the Hebrew Bible such as parts of Isaiah and Daniel and several books in the New Testament such as the Pastoral Letters exhibit this feature.

Ptolemies This dynasty of Hellenistic rulers in Egypt descended from Ptolemy I who ruled Egypt (323–285 B.C.E.) after the death of Alexander the Great. One of his successors, Ptolemy II (285–246

B.C.E.) is credited with having authorized the writing of the Septuagint. The dynasty continued until the Roman conquest of Egypt in 31 B.C.E.

Purim This Jewish holiday, described in the biblical book of Esther, is said to commemorate a victory of Jews in the Diaspora over a plot to kill them. Many of the characters in the story bear the names of Persian deities, and the story itself lacks historical plausibility.

Q Source Scholars analyzing the Gospels of Luke and Matthew have isolated a set of "sayings" attributed to Jesus that these two have in common. They have labeled that "quelle" or "source" and abbreviate it as "Q." No documentary evidence for such a source has been discovered, but the non-canonical "Gospel of Thomas" presents a collection of sayings very much like those thought to have comprised Q.

Qumran In caves near this village near the Dead Sea scholars found a horde of scrolls that included early manuscripts of canonical biblical works, apocrypha, and other previously unknown material. Scholars think that a community of pietistic Jews lived here before it was destroyed by the Romans about 68 C.E..

Rabbi This term literally means "my master" in Hebrew. It was used after 70 C.E. as a title for the leading religious leaders authorized by the Roman government.

Rachel This daughter of Laban the Aramean was beloved of Jacob who served Laban seven years for her hand in marriage. When Laban gave him Leah instead, he served yet another seven years. Rachel's son Joseph was especially favored by Jacob.

Ras ShamraTablets These ancient writings from an ancient Canaanite city (from about 1600–1400 B.C.E.) preserve Ugaritic mythological and religious texts. These show how the idea of a covenant with the divine developed in Canaan—an idea found also in the Hebrew Bible.

Rebecca This wife of Isaac, procured for him by his father Abraham's servant Eliezer, comforted him on the death of his mother Sarah and took an active role in determining that Jacob rather than Esau would receive Isaac's blessing.

Glossary 331

Resurrection This term refers to a bodily revival after death. Several late texts from the Hebrew Bible use the idea metaphorically referring to the rebirth of the nation (Isaiah 26:19; Ezekiel 37). The first explicit mention of a literal resurrection occurs in Daniel 12:2–3. The idea is expressed throughout 2 Maccabees and figures in several New Testament passages (1 Thessalonians 4; 1 Corinthians 15; Matthew 25:31; Revelation 20:13).

Sabbath The Hebrew Bible declares the seventh day a "Sabbath" to God—that is a day of sacred resting (see Exodus 31:12–17)—that the Israelites must observe as a sign of their relationship with the divine. New Testament evidence suggests that early Christians also celebrated a seventh day Sabbath (Acts 13:44). Controversies in the early church over whether to have a Saturday or Sunday Sabbath were finally settled in favor of the Sunday date.

Sadducees This sect, one of those described by Josephus, was a priestly group that denied the idea of a literal resurrection of the dead and held to a strict interpretation of Jewish law.

Samaria This name for the Northern kingdom comes from the capital city built by King Omri. Although the city was destroyed by the Assyrians in 721 B.C.E., the name continued in use for that region even through Roman times.

Samaritans The term refers to the post-exilic inhabitants of the north of Israel. The Hebrew Bible (2 Kings 17) considers them descendants of non-Jews who were imported into the area by the Assyrians. After Nehemiah and Ezra (about 400 B.C.E.) rejected Samaritan offers to help in establishing a common Temple, the Jews regarded the Samaritans as non-Jewish rivals.

Samson This "judge" in Israel fought against the Philistines but was led astray by various women, the most famous of whom was Delilah (see Judges 13–16) revealing the weaknesses of the leaders of the pre-monarchic period.

Samuel This seer and prophet helped establish the first kingship in Israel (that of Saul) and its replacement (by David). He acted as both priest and prophet.

Sarah Sarah was Abraham's wife who bore him Isaac. She convinced Abraham to exile her handmaid Hagar who had borne Abraham a previous son, Ishmael. (Genesis 12–23). God's preference for her and Isaac is used to show God's ability to reject one group and choose another (see Romans 4:9).

Sargon the Great This king of Assyria (722–705 B.C.E.) captured Samaria and exiled its inhabitants in 721 B.C.E..

Satan The Hebrew Bible uses this term to describe an angel whose task is to accuse human beings of error before God (Job 1–2, Zechariah 3:1–3). He occurs only in later books of the Bible (contrast 2 Samuel 24:1 and 1 Chronicles 21:1). He appears in the New Testament tempting Jesus (Mark 1:13, Matthew 4:10) and is identified with the serpent in Eden (Revelation 12:9).

Saul This first king of Israel (1020–1000 B.C.E.) was installed by the prophet Samuel (1 Samuel 10–12) who later rejected his legitimacy (1 Samuel 13–15). He had a tempestuous relationship with David, who could succeed him as king (1 Samuel 15–24) until his death during the Battle of Gilboa against the Philistines (1 Samuel 31).

Second Isaiah Scholars regard Isaiah 40–55 as the product of an anonymous prophet who lived during the time of the Babylonian Exile. These chapters include polemics against idolatry, an affirmation of YHWH as the only divinity, and references God's chosen servant (passages that are ambivalent and hard to interpret; scholars divide in identifying that servant as the people of Israel, as the prophet himself, or as some other figure).

Seleucids This Hellenistic dynasty begun by Seleucus I (312–280 B.C.E.) after the death of Alexander the Great ruled Syria and sought to expand its territory—eventually seizing Palestine from Egypt in 198 B.C.E.. Under the Seleucid Antiochus IV the Maccabees led a revolt leading to an independent Judean state.

Sennacherib This son of Sargon II ruled Assyria (704–681 B.C.E.) and after besieging Jerusalem finally retreated after King Hezekiah agreed to pay a heavy tax (see 2 Kings 18–19 and Isaiah 37).

Septuagint This Greek translation of the Hebrew Bible was said to have been commissioned by Ptolemy II (285–246 B.C.E.), but most scholars think that it was developed over a long period of time and is far more recent than that time. It contains several works that were not accepted as canon by the rabbis at Jamnia and are considered "apocrypha" by many Christians.

Sermon on the Mount This is a set of sayings attributed to Jesus found in Matthew 5:3–10. These sayings emphasize the spiritual rather than the physical and bless those who are "poor in spirit" and "hunger for righteousness." These blessings are not followed by a list of woes.

Sermon on the Plain This is a set of sayings attributed to Jesus found in Luke 6:20–31. They show a concern for physical well-being and bless the poor and those who are hungry. The blessing sayings are followed by a list of woes on those who are rich and not hungry.

Seth Seth was the son of Adam and Eve after their expulsion from the Garden of Eden (Genesis 4:25–26) and the progenitor of all humanity thereafter (Genesis 5—note that Noah is descended from Seth) since he was created in Adam's image and Adam in the image of God.

Shem The eldest of Noah's sons and the forbearer of the Semites (Genesis 9:21–28). He is considered specially blessed by his father.

Sheol This is the name given in the Hebrew Bible to the "underworld" to which the dead are assigned. Job 7:9 proclaims that "those who go down to Sheol do not come up." The Septuagint uses the word "Hades" to translate Sheol.

Shepherd of Hermas Part of the Christian Apocrypha, this work is found in Codex Sinaiticus as part of its canon. It reflects on Christian history and the imminent apocalyptic ending of time.

Shulamit This name is given to the bride in Song of Songs 6:13. It may be related to the designation of "Shunammite woman" given in 2 Kings 4:8–37.

Silas This name, probably Aramaic, was given to a disciple who accompanied Barnabas and Paul (Acts

15–17) He has been identified with Silvanus in 1 and 2 Thessalonians.

Simon son of Onias Ecclesiasticus (The Wsdom of Ben Sirah) 50 describes this high priest and the glory he brought to Jerusalem. He was high priest from 219–196 B.C.E. and conducted a pro-Egyptian policy.

Simon the Hasmonean This Simon was the brother of Judas the Maccabee and was recognized as both king and high priest by the Seleucids, Rome, and Sparta. 1 Maccabees 14 describes his reign (142–135 B.C.E.) in messianic terms as one in which peace prevailed and "every man sat under his vine and fig tree and none would make them afraid" (14:12).

Sinai This mountain is associated with the giving of the Torah at Mount Sinai and where Moses received God's commission (Exodus 6; 19–24) Other sources call the mountain Horeb (Exodus 3:1; Deuteronomy 2:6).

Sodom One of the cities said to have been destroyed by God's punishment (Genesis 19). Sodom came to be seen as a symbol of inhospitality (Matthew 10:15) or sexual offences (Jude 7).

Sol In ancient Rome the worship of the God of the Sun, Sol, was nearly identical to the worship of Mithra. Both cults celebrated the 25th of December as a major festival. In 307 C.E. the emperor Domitian made the worship of Sol the official religion of the Roman Empire.

Solomon The son of King David and Bathsheba, Solomon succeeded to his father's throne after a civil war (1 Kings 1:9–2:25). His long reign (961–922 B.C.E.) was marked by many international successes but also by divisions within the country. Upon his death Israel split into two countries—Israel in the north and Judah in the south.

Son of God This term, sometimes applied to Jesus (see John 1:18). It sometimes entails being adopted by God (Mark 1:1, 11) and sometimes seems an inherent identity (Luke 22:66; 27:54).

Son of Man This term, used often in the Gospels by Jesus to refer to himself (Matthew 8:20, 9:6; 26:64 and parallel passages in Luke and Mark). In the Hebrew Bible it refers to humaqn beings (see Psalm 8:4, 80:17; Ezekiel 2:1). In Daniel 7:1–14 uses the term for a particular, but undefined, visionary being.

Soter This Greek word means "savior." Only the Gospel of Luke uses it to describe Jesus. Its usage suggests a Hellenistic rather than Jewish understanding of what it means to be a Messiah.

Stephen This martyr or "witness" to the truth of Jesus is described in Acts 6:8–60. His review of Jewish history testifies that all of it anticipated the career of Jesus of Nazareth.

Stoicism This Greek philosophical school became popular in Hellenistic times.

Synoptic Gospels This name is given the Gospels of Matthew, Mark, and Luke since that "see with one eye" and share a common structure and chronology and several specific anecdotes and stories. Luke and Matthew share a large number of sayings attributed to Jesus that are not found in Mark, although they often occur in different places in each of the two Gospels. The so-called "synoptic problem" seeks to determine whether Mark is a condensation of Matthew and Luke or, as most scholars claim, Matthew and Luke built their narratives out of a combination of Mark, a common group of sayings attributed to Jesus, and their own special material.

Syria Known in biblical times as Aram, this land stretching from the Euphrates river down to Israel was thought to be intimately connected with the history of the Israelites. From there Abraham and his family had migrated to Canaan; interaction with that nation was always a danger and an attraction for the kings of both northern Israel and Judah.

Talmud This Hebrew word means "learning" or "study" and refers to a compilation of rabbinic teachings about various subjects according to their content (it is divided into six "orders" – agriculture, holidays, women, commerce, holy things, and purities). There are two versions of the Talmud, one compiled about 450 C.E. coming from the land of Israel and one compiled about 500 coming from Babylonia (usually called "Bavli" and considered the "standard" Talmud). The Talmud is composed on the Mishnah (finalized in 210 C.E.) and the Gemarah (the word means "completion" that comments on the Mishnah).

Tamar Two women bear the name Tamar in the Hebrew Bible. One was the widow of Er, the son of Judah, who tricked her father-in-law, Judah, into begetting children with her when he delayed in marrying her to her former husband's younger brother (Genesis 38). The other was the daughter of King David, sister of Absalom and half brother to Amnon. When she was raped by Amnon, Absalom began a civil war in revenge (2 Samuel 13).

Temple of Onias This Temple may have been built by Onias IV when he fled Judea for Egypt after the Seleucids gained control. Ruins of the Temple from about 145 B.C.E., show the assimilation of Jews to Hellenistic culture.

Testament The Latin word "testament" translates the Hebrew word "brith" or "covenant." It refers to an agreement between two parties, often between the divine and the human.

Theodicy This word, literally meaning "God's justice" denotes the attempt to reconcile the idea of divine power and goodness with the evil in the world. The book of Job in the Hebrew Bible addresses this issue.

Third Isaiah This label is given to Isaiah 56–66. These chapters seem not only different from Isaiah 1–39 but also from Isaiah 40–55. Unlike Second Isaiah these chapters do not include the servant motif, seem more concerned with ritual matters, and have vivid eschatological visions. Many people date this collection to somewhere between 530–510 B.C.E. when those who settled in Israel after the time of Zerubabbel realized that they would not achieve immediate success.

Tishre Leviticus 16:29–34 declares the tenth of the seventh month a holiday of atonement for the Israelites. Numbers 29 describes a "holy convocation" on the first day of the seventh month at which the ram's horn will be blown, the atonement festival on the tenth day of that month, and a festival of booths to be held from the 15th through the 22nd of the month. Nehemiah 8 describes the celebration of this festival by the Jews who had come from Babylonia to the land of Israel. The name is not mentioned in the Bible but is known from rabbinic writings.

Tithes Literally meaning a tenth, the term refers to the taxes due the priestly class in biblical Israel, to aliens, and to widows and orphans since these groups held no land or property (see Leviticus 27:30–33; Deuteronomy 26:12–13). Among the Hellenistic groups the Pharisees were the strictest concerning tithing. Jesus criticizes them for this in Luke 11:42 and 18:9.

Torah Literally meaning "Instruction" this term is used generally to mean "teaching" as in "The Torah of the Holocaust offering," "The Torah of the Meal offering," "The Torah of the Sin offering" (Leviticus 6). More specifically the term refers to the "Torah of Moses" (Joshua 23:6) in which case it consists of the first five books of the Bible, the first section of the Jewish canon often called the Pentateuch. In Jewish usage the term takes on the wider meaning of all learning and instruction.

Trajan This emperor of Rome (98–117 C.E.) persecuted Christians but also counseled Pliny the Younger not to denounce them as a group but only as individuals.

Universalism This concept entails an inclusive perspective in which God's concern extends to all human beings, not merely those of a specific group. It emphasizes responsibility to humanity as a whole and a common human morality.

Uriah the Hittite This mercenary in David's army had a beautiful wife, Bathsheba, who caught the interest of King David. After Bathsheba became pregnant from her affair with David, the king instructed his general Joab to manipulate the battle against the Ammonites so that Uriah would be on the frontlines and be killed. Nathan the Prophet confronted David with his sin (2 Samuel 11–12).

Utnapishtim The Babylonian epic of Gilgamesh includes his encounter with this survivor of an ancient flood. Many elements in the story of Utnapishtim parallel those in the biblical flood story.

Widow's Mite This refers to an anecdote found in the Gospels of Mark and Luke (Mark 12:41–44; Luke 21:1–4) in which Jesus praises a widow who gives only a penny's worth of charity since it is a greater sacrifice for her than the larger offerings of the rich are to them.

Wisdom This term (Hochma in Hebrew, Sophia in Greek) refers to a rational principle thought to permeate and govern reality. In Hellenistic Jewish thought it was identified with the Stoic idea of the logos and the Jewish concept of Torah (Wisdom of Solomon 9). In the New Testament it is identified with Jesus (John 1:1–18)

Wisdom Literature This refers to biblical books devoted to pragmatic expositions of human behavior. These books focus on the possibility of learning the divine law through observing the natural order. Examples of such writings are Proverbs, Ecclesiastes, Ecclesiasticus, and Wisdom of Solomon.

YHWH These four letters stand for the "tetragrammaton" or sacred letters of God's personal name. The Hebrew Bible relates that this name was entrusted to Moses when he was commissioned to lead the Jews from Egypt (Exodus 3:13–15; 6:2–6). In post-exilic times it was recited audibly only by the high priest on the Day of Atonement. Rabbinic Jews substitute the name with the Hebrew word for "My Lord," "Adonai." The English word "Jehovah" comes from an error that combined the consonants of YHWH with the vowels for Adonai.

Zealots Josephus calls these a "fourth philosophy" in addition to the three major groups of Jews—the Pharisees, Sadducees, and Essenes. They were characterized by a militant demand for an independent Jewish state and instigated the great war against the Romans.

Zerubbabel Appointed governor of the restored Jewish community under the Persians, this descendant of the Davidic kingship in Judah (his name means "born of Babylonia") is associated with the high priest Joshua in both Haggai and Zechariah. His failed attempts at becoming a messianic leader of an independent Jewish commonwealth led to his disappearance from the political scene (both Zechariah 3:1–10 and 6:9–14 have an enigmatic reference to "the branch" who will be brought to Joshua and serve either with or under him; this seems to be some anonymous messianic ruler rather than Zerubabbel).

Ziggurat This ramp-like structure was the characteristic religious building in Babylonia which, with a shrine at its top, joined the heavenly and earthly realms. The major ziggurat in Babylon was called "Bab-El" or "gateway to God;" the Tower of Babel in Genesis 11 is probably a polemic against this type of religious shrine.

Zillah A wife of Lamech who bore Tubal-Cain, the first metallurgist and tool maker, and Naama, whose profession is not mentioned (Genesis 4:22).

Index

This index notes the biblical passages and themes interpreted at length. The entries are organized by biblical book or theme and indexed by page number.

A

Aaron, 59, 89,175, 195, 276
Abel, 74, 76, 276
Abimelech, 89
Abraham, 24, 35, 59–62, 64–65, 114, 118, 150, 154, 175, 194, 196, 213, 248, 251–252, 272, 276
Achior, 164, 186
Acts (Book of), 41, 239–251
    1–2, 249
    9, 245–249
    10, 241, 251
    15, 250–251
    17, 250
    19, 250
    22, 249
    26, 249–250
Acts of Paul, 44
Adah, 74
Adam, 15, 73–75, 176, 183, 244, 251
Agag, 93, 152
Ahab, 112, 118–119, 303, 306, 307
Ahashuerus, 142, 151–152, 155
Ahaz, 113, 120–121
Ahijah, 90, 111–112
Akhenaton, 57, 71, 148
Akkadian, 57, 71
Alexander the Great, 8, 28, 141, 162, 166–167, 177
Alexandria, 28–30, 170–176
Alma, 120
Amalekites, 26, 93, 152

Amarna Letters, 68
Amaziah, king of Judah, 284
Amaziah, priest of Beth El, 115, 126
Amenemope, 144
Ammonites, 61, 88
Amos, 115, 119, 122, 123–124, 126, 286
Ananais, 246, 149
Angel, 186–187, 264, 270, 276, 288, 294–295, 300
AntiChrist, 268, 294
Antiochus III, 166, 167
Antiochus IV (Epiphanes), 169, 170, 177–178, 181
Apiru, 15, 61
Apocalypse, 44, 162, 281–295
Apocalypse of Peter, 44, 283
Apocrypha, 8, 41–42, 159–188
Aramaic, 37, 141
Aristobulus II, 170
Armageddon, 284, 294
Augur ben Jakeh, 144
Asclepius, 174, 187,
Asmodeus, 186
Assyria, 62
Athanasius, 44, 46

B

Baal, 67, 306
Babel, 67, 72, 76
Babylon, 24, 62, 293, 294
Babylonian Exile, 3, 24, 91, 96–99
Balaam, 274, 291

337

Index

Baptism, 195, 205–206, 213–215, 233, 240, 245, 252, 273, 275
Bar Kokhba, 172
Barak, 89
Barnabas, 262–263
Bathsheba, 117–118
Beatitudes, 228–229
Beloved Disciple, 217
Belshazzar, 141, 153
Beth El, 126
Ben Sirah (The Wisdom of, Ecclesiasticus), 7–11, 164–165, 173–177
Bildad, 146
Bishop, 262
Bithynia, 262
Boaz, 140, 151
Booths, 26–28, 150

C

Cain, 74, 76, 183, 272
Calendar, 27
Canaan, 59–61, 67, 284, 293, 300
Canonization,
 Jewish, 11–216, 20–28
 Protestant, 38–42
 Roman Catholic, 13, 38–42
Catholic Letters, 266–267, 273–278
Chaldean, 153
Christ, 35, 194
Christian Apocrypha, 44
1,2 Chronicles, 140–141, 149–150
1 Chronicles, 99, 101, 104–105
2 Chronicles, 101–104
 20, 154
Circumcision, 64–65, 177, 179, 186, 240, 255, 271
Claudius, 242
Clement of Rome, 262
Codex Sinaiticus, 44, 262
Colossians, 245, 253
Constantine, 44, 242, 283
Cornelius, 251
1–2 Corinthians, 244, 255–256
 1 Corinthians 11, 239–240, 255
 2 Corinthians 12, 252
Covenant, 34–36, 47–49, 63–64, 67–70, 87–88, 90, 93, 123–124, 137, 150, 154, 175–177, 185, 277
Crucifixion, 199, 252
Cyrus the Great, 83, 97, 140, 150

D

Damascus, 241, 248, 250
Daniel, 140–141, 152–153, 156–157, 163, 284, 287–9, 290, 292, 293, 310, 311
David, 35, 83, 90, 93–94, 99, 102. 112, 116–118, 140, 149–50, 176, 194, 248, 286, 291, 300
Day of Atonement, 26–27, 127–128, 267, 277
Day of the Lord, 284, 285, 286
Deacon, 262
Dead Sea Scrolls, 28, 120, 166, 176

Deborah, 89
Deuteronomy, 55–56, 82
 15, 69
 19:16–21, 69
 26, 62–64, 309, 310
Deuteronomic History, 81–97, 105, 111–112, 114–119
Devil (see Satan),
Diaspora, 10, 141–142
Didache, 44, 239, 262–263
Dietary Laws, 25, 140, 153, 181, 255, 271
Dionysius, 174, 183, 241
Documentary Hypothesis, 55
Domitian, 242, 262, 266, 291
Donatism, 272
Dura–Europos, 172

E

Ecclesiastes, 135, 138, 148
Edom, 169
Egypt, 11, 29–30, 59–62, 71, 148, 167, 172, 182
Elder, 262
Elephantine, 172
Eli, 82
Elihu, 146
Elijah, 111–112, 118–119, 217, 275, 303, 304, 306, 307, 308
Eliphaz, 146
Elisha, 111–112, 118–119
Enki, 66–67
Enoch, 175–176, 272, 288
Enuma Elish, 57, 71–72
Ephesians, 265–267
Epicureanism, 174
Eschatology, 115, 243-244, 253–254, 276, 291
2 Esdras 288
Essenes, 192, 195–196
Esther, 142, 151–152, 163, 185
Ethnarch, 168, 170
Eucharist, 36, 47–48, 233, 239, 244, 255–256
Eve, 15, 73–75
Exilarch, 97
Exodus from Egypt, 15, 27, 87, 93, 150, 183, 272, 300
Exodus (biblical book)
 21:22–25, 69–70
Ezekiel, 114, 122, 141, 284, 287, 289, 290, 292, 295, 300, 310, 311
Ezra, 24–25, 101, 140, 149–151, 176

F

Festival Scrolls, 27, 134
Former Prophets, 12, 111–112, 114–119, 194

G

Gad, 111–112. 117
Galilee, 201
Galatians, 244, 245–248, 252, 254–255, 282
Gamaliel, 248
Genesis (biblical book),

1:1–4.1, 72–76
  2:4–4:1, 301, 302
  4:1–16, 74–76
  9–11, 75–76
Gentiles, 178
Gentile Christians, 248, 250–251, 252, 269
Gerizim, 169
Gibeonites, 86
Gideon, 89
Gilgamesh, 57, 66–67
Glossolalia, 249
Gnosticism, 206
Gog, 284, 287, 192, 294
Gomorrah, 272
Gospels (canonical), 35, 43–46, 190–207, 210–235
Gospel of Thomas, 44, 227
Griesbach, Johann, 202

H

Habakkuk, 164
Habiru, 15, 61
Hagar, 59, 252
Haggai , 110, 117, 125
Ham, 75
Haman, 142, 151–152, 155
Hammurabi, 57, 68–70
Hanukkah, 164, 170, 178–179
Hasideans, 177
Hasmoneans, 166, 169–170, 177–182
Hebrews (Letter to the), 267, 275–278
Heliodorus, 190
Hellenism, 9, 28–30, 165, 166, 169–184
Heresy, 261–262, 292
Herod Agripipa, 169,
Herod Agrippa II, 249
Herod the Great, 167, 170–172, 213
Hesed, 117, 119, 151
Hezekiah, 83, 95–96, 112, 121–122, 176, 180
High Priest, 11, 125, 277
Historical Criticism, 3–4
Holofernes, 164, 186
Holy Ark, 85, 90, 99
Holy Spirit, 49, 204–207, 149–151, 255–256, 275, 294–295, 304, 305
Hosea, 116, 123–125
Hulda, 112
Hyksos, 61

I

Idumea, 166, 169–170
Incarnation, 252, 270
Inanna, 67
Isaac, 59114, 118, 150, 175, 252
Ishmael, 59, 252
Ishtar, 67
Isaiah, 110, 111, 113, 119–122, 284, 285, 286–287
  6, 121
  7, 120–121, 213, 300
  24, 303, 304
  37, 121–122
  40–55. 127
  44, 123–124
  58, 127–128
Isis, 175, 184, 285, 293
Israel, 8, 61–62
Israelite, 8, 61–62

J

Jacob, 59, 89, 114, 118, 150, 175, 183, 252
Jaddua, 162
Jafet, 75
James (Letter of), 266, 275
Jamnia, 11
Jehoiakim, 153
Jehoshaphat, 154
Jepthah, 88
Jeremiah, 113–114, 126–127, 139, 163, 180, 181, 185
  17, 126–127
  31, 122
Jericho, 88
Jerusalem, 8, 25, 121, 125, 127, 147, 178, 291, 303, 304
Jerusalem Temple, 8, 121, 125, 128, 147, 178, 277, 287, 289, 290, 294
Jesus of Nazareth, 35–37, 46, 167, 175, 197–201, 201–207, 210–235, 249, 170, 277, 286, 303–305, 306, 307
Jew, 15, 98
Jewish Christians, 239
Jezebel, 118–119, 291
Job, 145–147, 301, 302
John (Gospel of), 204, 206–7, 213–215, 219, 225–226, 233–234
  1, 214–216
  3, 233. 309, 310
  11, 233
  20, 304, 305–306
  24, 216–217
John (Letters of), 265–266, 272–273
John the Baptist, 205, 250
John Hyrcanus I, 162, 166, 169, 179, 186
John Hyrcanus II, 170
Jonah, 112, 115, 128
Jonathan the Hasmonean, 169
Joseph (biblical hero), 182, 248, 276
Joseph the Tobiad, 167
Josephus, Flavius, 162–163. 165, 192
Joshua, 22–23, 85–88
Joshua the High Priest, 125
Josiah, 9, 23–24, 81, 83, 96, 112, 175
Judah (biblical nation), 15, 121
Judas Iscariot, 199
Judas Maccabeus, 164, 166, 169, 170, 177–181
Judea, 8, 98
Jude, 265, 268, 273, 275, 300
Judges, 23, 82–86, 88–89
Judith, 164, 186

Justin Martyr, 42–43, 262

K

Ketuvim, 11–12, 27–28, 132–157
Kingdom of God, 194, 206, 233, 241
King Lemeuel, 138
1, 2 Kings, 113
1 Kings 17–21, 118–119, 303, 304, 306, 307, 308
2 Kings 22–23, 23
Kingship (in Israel), 89–97, 147
Koine Greek, 42–43
Korah, 272

L

Lamech, 74
Lamentations, 139
Latter Prophets, 12, 111, 113–114, 122–128
Lazarus, 206, 233
Leah, 59
Levite, 63, 154, 309, 310
Leviticus (biblical book)
   24:18–22, 69–70
Liturgy 14
Logos, 182, 206, 223
Lord's Prayer, 230–1, 309, 310
Lot, 59–61
Luke, 203, 205, 207, 218–222, 225–226, 228
   3, 217–218
   6, 229
   8, 218
   0, 230
   11, 231
   21, 289–91, 303–305
   24, 216–217

M

Maccabees (books of), 13, 25–26, 141, 162, 164, 177–182
Magog, 284, 287, 292
Major Prophets, 12, 111
Marcion, 35–36, 43
Marduk, 67, 72
Mark, 203, 205, 207, 219–222, 224–225, 231–233
   1, 212–213
   2, 222–223
   5, 222
   12, 232
   13, 289–291
   16, 215–216
Matthew, 203, 205, 207, 219–222. 224–225
   1–3, 213, 300, 301
   5, 227–229
   6, 230, 309, 310
   9, 223
   10, 227, 306, 307
   19, 228
   24, 289–291
   28, 215–216
Martyr, 181, 248

Mary Magdalene, 215–217
Mary and Martha of Bethany, 223
Mashal, 71, 229
Mattathias the Hasmonean, 177
Melchizedek, 195, 276
Merneptah, 11, 61–62, 126
Mesha, 57, 61, 97
Mesopotamia, 59
Messiah, 9, 46, 93, 99, 148, 177, 193–196, 199–201, 205–207, 241, 277, 288
Midrash, 133, 134, 142
Minor Prophets, 114–116
Miracle Stories, 217–227, 250
Mithras, 175, 178
Moab, 57, 61, 140, 150, 151
Mordecai, 142, 151–152
Mortal Sin, 273
Moses, 11, 22, 35, 56, 59, 68, 89, 180, 183, 196, 215, 248, 272
Muratorian Canon, 44, 283
Myth, 53–54, 58, 66–67, 70–76, 271, 291

N

Nabonidus, 141, 156
Naboth, 119, 309, 310
Nag Hammadi, 44
Naomi, 140, 151, 155
Nathan, 112, 117–118
Nazirite, 88–89
Nebuchadnezzar, 26, 96–97, 112, 141, 156, 164, 186–187, 310, 311
Necho, 11, 26, 96
Nehemiah, 101, 140, 164, 175, 179
Nero, 242, 293
Nevi'im, 11–12
Nicanor, 179, 180, 181
Nicodemus, 233, 309, 310
Noah, 34, 65–66, 75–76, 175, 183, 276, 290

O

Obadiah, 115, 118, 304, 306
Omri, 81, 83
Onias, 164, 172, 181
Orpah, 151

P

Parable, 225–226, 229–230, 232
Parable of the Talents, 289
Paraclete, 207
Parallelism, 134, 136
Parousia, 46, 253–254, 272, 289–291, 302, 303
Particularism, 119, 122, 125
Passover, 26–29, 36, 65, 99–103, 196–197, 201, 205–207, 240
Pastoral Letters, 264–272
Paul of Tarsus, 35. 167, 202, 236–257, 302–303, 306, 307, 308
Pentateuch, 11–15, 22–25, 52–78
Pentecost, 26–27, 249

Peter (Apostle), 217, 218–9, 248, 250–251
1, 2 Peter 266–267, 273–275
2 Peter,
   3:15–16, 47
Pharisees, 167, 192, 196–197, 201, 231
Philemon, 245
Philistines, 88–89, 300
Philippians, 245, 252–253
Philo Judeas of Alexandria, 167, 172–173, 174, 182–183, 206
Plato, 37, 174, 183
Pliny the Younger, 262
Pompey, 170, 172
Proverbs, 131, 137–138, 143–144, 149
Pseudepigrapha, 42, 162, 165
Pseudonimity, 260
Psalms, 134, 136–137, 142–143, 147–148
   2, 147
   19, 143, 304, 305
   23, 148
   73, 147
   78, 300, 301
   82, 143
   104, 148, 307
   139, 10
Ptolemies, 11, 28–29, 166
Purim, 142, 151–152, 154–155
Pythagorus, 73

Q

Q Source, 202
Qumran, 28, 166, 176

R

Rabbi, 11
Rachel, 59
Ras Shamra Tablets, 57–58
Rebecca, 59
Resurrection, 6, 46–47, 181, 199, 223, 232, 252, 288, 294
Revelation of John, 41, 284, 291–295, 310, 311
Romans (Letter to the), 244, 255
Ruth, 140, 142, 151–152, 154–5

S

Sabbath, 75–76, 126–128, 177, 231, 233, 262, 277, 289
Sadducees, 192, 194–195, 232
Samaria, 81
Samaritans, 91, 96, 150, 167
Samson, 88–89
Samuel, 26, 82, 83, 89–93, 309, 310
Samuel (biblical book)
   1 Samuel 15, 26, 309, 310
   2 Samuel 7, 93–94
   2 Samuel 23, 93
   2 Samuel 24, 102–105
Sarah, 59, 252, 276
Sargon the Great, 94

Satan, 99–105, 145–147, 183–8, 213–214, 232, 253, 263–264, 267–269, 276, 288, 292, 293–295, 302–303
Saul (King of Israel), 26, 83, 89, 152, 309, 310
Second Isaiah, 110, 111, 122, 123–124, 127
Seleucids, 166–167
Semites, 75
Sennacherib, 95–96
Septuagint, 8, 27–30, 120. 163
Sermon on the Mount, 228–229
Sermon on the Plain, 228–229
Seth, 75
Shem, 75
Sheol, 149
Shepherd of Hermas, 44
Shulamit, 138–139, 149
Silas, 250
Simon son of Onias, 164, 169–170, 173, 174
Simon the Hasmonean, 164, 166, 177–179
Sinai, 35, 68
Sodom, 59, 64, 300
Sol, 175, 178
Solomon, 83, 89, 248
Son of God, 199, 223
Son of Man, 199, 288, 289, 292
Song of Songs (Solomon), 27–28, 138–139, 149, 197, 293
Soter, 214
Stephen, 248
Stoicism, 174, 182–183, 206, 241, 250
Synoptic Gospels, 191, 202–205
Syria, 59–61, 167

T

Talmud, 150
Tamar, 55, 59
Temple of Onias, 170
Testament, 33–34, 36–37, 47–48
Theodicy, 117, 140, 145–147, 185
1, 2 Thessalonians, 244, 245, 253–254, 264, 302–303, 306, 307, 308
1,2 Timothy, 265, 269–270
Tishre, 150
Tithes, 117, 194, 196
Tobit, 163–164, 186–187
Torah (see Pentateuch)
Trajan, 262, 266

U

Universalism, 119, 122, 123
Uriah the Hittite, 93–94, 117
Utnapishtim, 67

W

Wellhausen, Julius, 55, 62
Widow's Mite, 290
Wisdom, 134–135, 137–138, 145–7, 154–155, 165, 182–183, 304, 305
Wisdom Literature, 14, 133–135, 147–149, 173, 291

Women, 47, 63, 73, 75, 88–89, 112, 148–149, 151, 215–218, 254, 269, 271

Y

YHWH, 65, 118–119, 128, 154, 306

Z

Zealots, 192, 194, 199–201, 241
Zechariah, 116, 284
Zerubbabel, 125, 141, 175
Ziggurat, 67
Zillah, 74
Zophar, 141
Zoroasterianism, 263, 285, 293

Photo Credits

Page 45: The head of Constantine. Photo Credit: Herve Champollion / akg-images; **Page 61**: The Stele of Merneptah. Photo Credit: Egyptian Museum / PhotoEdit; **Page 66**: Victory Stele of Mesha, King of Moab. Louvre, Paris, France. Photo Credit: Erich Lessing / Art Resource, NY; **Page 68**: Upper section of the stele of the Law Code of Hammurabi. Photo: Hervé Lewandowski. Louvre, Paris, France. Photo Credit: Réunion des Musées Nationaux / Art Resource, NY; **Page 120**: Fragment from the Dead Sea Scrolls containing Aramaic texts from the Book of Isaiah. Photo Credit: PhotoEdit; **Page 144**: The Wisdom of Amenemope papyrus (c. 1200 B.C.E.). Photo Credit: The British Museum; **Page 169**: Coin bearing the likeness of Antiochus IV. Photo Credit: Hirmer Fotoarchiv, Munich, Germany; **Page 173**: Arch of Titus, Rome, Italy. Photo Credit: Scala / Art Resource, NY; **Page 178**: *Left*: Coin of Antigonus, 40–37 B.C.E., last Hasmonaean King of Israel, shows a menorah. *Right*: inscription in the wreath: Period of John Hyrcanus II (High Priest, 67–40 B.C.E.). Reifenberg Collection. Israel Museum (IDAM), Jerusalem, Israel. Photo Credit: Erich Lessing / Art Resource, NY; **Page 184**: Greek statue: Isis (Farnese Collection). Museo Archeologico Nazionale, Naples, Italy. Photo Credit: Alinari / Art Resource, NY; **Page 200**: Ravenna mosaic of Jesus as the Good Shepherd. Photo Credit: Erich Lessing / PhotoEdit; **Page 218**: Rembrandt Harmensz. Van Rijn,(Leiden 1606–1669 Amsterdam) *The Hundred Guilder Print*.The Metropolitan Museum of Art, H. O. Havemeyer Collection, Bequest of Mrs. H. O. Havemeyer, 1929 (29.107.35) Image © The Metropolitan Museum of Art.; **Page 242**: Nero coin. Photo Credit: akg-images; **Page 243**: Rembrandt, van Rijn, *The Apostle Paul*. Widener Collection, Image © 2006 Board of Trustees, National Gallery of Art; **Page 290**: The Ravenna mosaic of *Christ Separating Sheep from Goats*. Photo Credit: Hirmer Fotoarchiv, Munich, Germany.